GREEK AND ROMAN AUTHORS

A Checklist of Criticism

SECOND EDITION

by
THOMAS GWINUP and
FIDELIA DICKINSON

The Scarecrow Press, Inc.
Metuchen, N.J., & London
MCMLXXXII

Library of Congress Cataloging in Publication Data

Gwinup, Thomas.
　Greek and Roman authors.

　1. Classical literature--History and criticism--
Bibliography.　I. Dickinson, Fidelia.　II. Title.
Z7016.C9　1981　[PA3001]　016.88'009　　82-690
ISBN 0-8108-1528-1　　　　　　　　　　AACR2

Copyright © 1982 by Thomas Gwinup and Fidelia Dickinson
Manufactured in the United States of America

CONTENTS

Introduction ... iv
Abbreviations of Periodicals ... vii

General Works ... 1
  Greece and Rome ... 1
  Greece ... 2
  Rome ... 9

Aeschylus	12	Menippus	152
Aesop	20	Moschus	152
Anacreon	21	Naevius	152
Apollonius Rhodius	22	Ovid	153
Apuleius	23	Pausanius	159
Aristophanes	26	Persius	160
Aristotle	30	Petronius	160
Augustine	46	Phaedrus	163
Bion	53	Pindar	163
Caesar	53	Plato	167
Callimachus	54	Plautus	197
Catullus	56	Pliny the Elder	201
Cicero	65	Pliny the Younger	202
Claudian	74	Plotinus	204
Demosthenes	75	Plutarch	207
Ennius	77	Propertius	210
Euripides	78	Quintilian	218
Gellius	90	Sallust	218
Heliodorus	90	Sappho	220
Herodotus	91	Seneca	221
Hesiod	95	Sophocles	226
Homer	98	Statius	234
Horace	115	Stesichorus	236
Isocrates	128	Strabo	236
Jerome	130	Suetonius	237
Juvenal	132	Tacitus	238
Livy	136	Terence	241
Longinus	139	Tertullian	243
Longus	140	Theocritus	245
Lucan	140	Thucydides	248
Lucian	142	Tibullus	255
Lucilius	143	Varro	257
Lucretius	143	Virgil	258
Martial	148	Xenophanes	277
Menander	149	Xenophon	278

INTRODUCTION TO THE FIRST EDITION

The purpose of this bibliography is to provide a comprehensive list of recent criticism of the authors of belles-lettres of ancient Greece and Rome. The items in it have not previously been brought together in a single, inclusive work. Although the only comprehensive annual bibliography of literature, the International Bibliography of the Modern Language Association, does include some ancient literature, such as Egyptian and Sanskrit, and includes Medieval and Neo-Latin, it excludes all of classical Greek and Latin literature as such. Greek and Roman Authors, therefore, may be expected to provide a useful supplement to it.

Inasmuch as ours is primarily a literary bibliography, there has in general been an exclusion of items of a character abstrusely philosophical, narrowly philological, or clearly doctrinal (the latter in the case of Augustine, Jerome, and Tertullian). There is, moreover, a definite emphasis on the inclusion of newer items, not only because these are more readily available in most libraries, but also because of the contemporary tendency toward the use of more recent criticism. For the greater portion of the some seventy classical authors contained herein, there is general criticism of the author as well as particular criticism of his individual works. Included at the beginning is a selective section consisting, with a few exceptions, of recently published or reprinted books on the civilization of Greece and of Rome. The items of criticism, numbering nearly four thousand, have been acquired both through the use of diverse bibliographical works and through original research.

Although the bibliography may prove quite advantageous for students of the classics, it has been designed principally for the use of students in the increasingly popular courses in comparative and world literature as well as other courses in the humanities. It may also be a useful guide to those students concerned with the history of ideas. The intention is that it will make criticism of the classical authors much more accessible to all these students. Formerly, to do research on a single classical author, they may well have had to search through catalogs, general indexes, and classical journals year by year, and to try to find the often elusive particular bibliographies of the classical period. Because of the use for which this work is intended, it has seemed appropriate to include only items written in English.

The authors wish to express their appreciation to the following persons at California State University, San Diego: to Louis Kenney, Director of the Library, for his invaluable cooperation; to Douglas Bush, Associate Director, for his encouragement of intellectual endeavors; to Muriel Ingham, Professor of English and Classical Languages, for her advice; and to Dale Kreiter, student, for his interest and dedication.

             Thomas Gwinup, M. A. , M. A. L. S.
             Fidelia Dickinson, Ph. D. , M. L. S.

San Diego State University

INTRODUCTION TO THE SECOND EDITION

In undertaking this new edition, the authors have had two main purposes. Almost a decade having passed since the gathering of the materials for the first edition, they have felt the need to make accessible a very large aggregate of new research. At the same time, they have profited from the experience of the long use of the first edition in academic libraries as well as from the suggestions of students, faculty, and colleagues. This time and experience have enabled them to make many useful revisions and additions in the original body of material. They wish to express their appreciation and indebtedness to all those who have helped them in this way.

Thomas Gwinup, M.A., M.A.L.S.
Fidelia Dickinson, Ph.D., M.L.S.

San Diego State University

ABBREVIATIONS OF PERIODICALS

AARJ	American Academy of Religion Journal
AClass	Acta Classica
ACR	American Classical Review
AHR	American Historical Review
AJA	American Journal of Archaeology
AJAH	American Journal of Ancient History
AJP	American Journal of Philology
AJPH	American Journal of Politics and History
AL	American Literature
APQ	American Philosophical Quarterly
AR	Antioch Review
AS	Annals of Science
AUMLA	Australian University Language and Literature Association
Agon	Agon
Akroterion	Akroterion
Ambix	Ambix
AmS	American Scholar
Analysis	Analysis
Antichthon	Antichthon
Antiq	Antiquity
Apeiron	Apeiron
Archaeol News	Archaeology News
Areth	Arethusa
Arion	Arion
Aug Stud	Augustinian Studies
BASP	Bulletin of the American Society of Papyrologists
BC	Book Collector
BHS	Bulletin of Hispanic Studies
BICS	Bulletin of the Institute of Classical Studies
BJA	British Journal of Aesthetics
BJHS	British Journal of the History of Science
BLR	Bodleian Library Record
BR	Bucknell Review
BSAP	Bibliographical Society of America. Papers
BUJ	Boston University Journal
Bl	Blackfriars
Britannia	Britannia
CB	The Classical Bulletin
CBST	Cambridge Bibliographical Society Transactions

CC	Cross Currents
CD	Criticism Drama
CF	Classical Folia
CHR	Catholic Historical Review
CJ	Classical Journal
CJP	Canadian Journal of Philosophy
CL	Comparative Literature
CLAJ	College Language Association Journal
CLS	Comparative Literature Studies
CM	Cornhill Magazine
CN & V	Classical News & Views
CP	Classical Philology
CQ	Classical Quarterly
CQR	Church Quarterly Review
CR	Classical Review
CSCA	California Studies in Classical Antiquity
CT	Criticism Theatre
CW	Classical Weekly
C World	Classical World
Camb Q	Cambridge Quarterly
Ch H	Church History
Chaucer R	Chaucer Review
Chris	Christendom
Cithara	Cithara
CoSHVB	Computer Studies in the Humanities and Verbal Behavior
Comm Q	Communication Quarterly
Commentary	Commentary
Comp D	Comparative Drama
Contemp R	Contemporary Review
Criticism	Criticism
DR	Downside Review
DS	Dance Scope
DT	Daily Telegraph
DUJ	Durham University Journal
Daedalus	Daedalus
Dialogue	Dialogue
Diogenes	Diogenes
Dram R	Drama Review
Dram S	Drama Survey
Drama	Drama
Dub R	Dublin Review
ECS	Eighteenth Century Studies
EIC	Essays in Criticism
ELH	English Literary History
ELN	English Language Notes
ES	English Studies
ET	Expository Times
ETJ	Educational Theatre Journal
Encounter	Encounter
Expedition	Expedition

Explicator	Explicator
FS	French Studies
Folklore	Folklore
Foundations	Foundations
GRBS	Greek, Roman and Byzantine Studies
G & R	Greece and Rome
Ga R	Georgia Review
Germ R	Germanic Review
HJ	Hibbert Journal
HOR	Horizon
HR	Hispanic Review
HSCP	Harvard Studies in Classical Philology
HT	History Today
HTR	Harvard Theological Review
H & T	History and Theory
Ha	Hermathena
Helios	Helios
Hermes	Hermes
Hesperia	Hesperia
History	History
Ho R	History of Religions
Hud R	Hudson Review
I	Isis
ICS	Illinois Classical Studies
IJ	Irish Jurist
IJAL	International Journal of American Linguistics
IJPR	International Journal for Philosophy of Religion
IPQ	International Philosophical Quarterly
Interp	Interpretation
JA	Journal of Antiquaries
JAAC	Journal of Aesthetics and Art Criticism
JAAR	Journal of the American Academy of Religion
JAF	Journal of American Folklore
JAH	Journal of Asian History
JARCE	Journal of the American Research Center in Egypt
JBL	Journal of Biblical Literature
JCS	Journal of Classical Studies
JDU	Journal of Durham University
JEGP	Journal of English and German Philology
JEH	Journal of Ecclesiastical History
JGP	Journal of General Psychology
JHBS	Journal of the History of the Behavioral Sciences
JHI	Journal of the History of Ideas
JHM	Journal of the History of Medicine
JHP	Journal of the History of Philosophy
JHS	Journal of Historical Studies
J Hel S	Journal of Hellenic Studies
JIES	Journal of Indo-European Studies
JIH	Journal of Interdisciplinary History
JML	Journal of Modern Literature

JNES	Journal of Near East Studies
JP	Journal of Philosophy
J Pol	Journal of Politics
J Psy	Journal of Psychology
JR	Journal of Religion
JRH	Journal of Religion and Health
JRLB	John Rylands Library, Bulletin
JRS	Journal of Roman Studies
JSS	Journal of Semitic Studies
JTS	Journal of Theological Studies
JVI	Journal of Value Inquiry
JWCI	Journal of the Warburg and Courtauld Institutes
L Ch Q	Lutheran Church Quarterly
LN	Library Notes
LQR	London Quarterly Review
LR	Long Room
Language	Language
List	Listener
MA	Medium Aevum
MFS	Modern Fiction Studies
MLN	Modern Language Notes
MLQ	Modern Language Quarterly
MLR	Modern Language Review
MM	Mariner's Mirror
MOS	Monastic Studies
MP	Modern Philology
MQ	Musical Quarterly
MQR	Michigan Quarterly Review
MR	Music Review
MS	Medieval Studies
M & Wo	Man & World
Mass R	Massachusetts Review
Midwest Q	Midwest Quarterly
Mind	Mind
Mnemosyne	Mnemosyne
Monist	Monist
Month	Month
Mus Afr	Museum Africum
NFS	Nottingham French Studies
NLH	New Literary History
NS	New Statesman
NYRB	New York Review of Books
N & C	Nigeria and the Classics
N & Q	Notes and Queries
New Soc	New Society
OR	Oxford Review
PACA	Proceedings of the African Classical Association
PACPA	Proceedings of the American Catholic Philosophical Association
PAPS	Proceedings of the American Philosophical Society
PAS	Proceedings of the Aristotelian Society

PBA	Proceedings of the British Academy
PCA	Proceedings of the Classical Association, London
PCP	Pacific Coast Philology
PCPS	Proceedings of the Cambridge Philological Society
PE & W	Philosophy East & West
PLL	Papers on Language and Literature
PLPLS	Proceedings of the Leeds Philosophical and Literary Society
PMLA	Publications of the Modern Language Association
PQ	Philological Quarterly
PR	Partisan Review
PS	Philosophy of Science
PSQ	Political Science Quarterly
PVS	Proceedings of the Vergil Society
P & P	Past & Present
P & PA	Philosophy and Public Affairs
P & Ph R	Philosophy and Phenomenological Research
P & R	Philosophy and Rhetoric
Pegasus	Pegasus
Person	Personalist
Ph Q	Philosophical Quarterly
Ph R	Philosophical Review
Ph S	Philosophical Studies
Philos	Philosophy
Phoenix	Phoenix
Phronesis	Phronesis; A Journal for Ancient Philosophy
Pl & Pl	Plays and Players
Pol Stud	Political Studies
Prudentia	Prudentia
Psychiatry	Psychiatry
QJS	Quarterly Journal of Speech
RAL	Research in African Literature
RES	Review of English Studies
RIL	Religion in Life
RIP	Rice Institute, Pamphlets
RM	Review of Metaphysics
RP	Romance Philology
R Pol	Review of Politics
RQ	Renaissance Quarterly
RR	Review of Religion
RS	Religious Studies
Ramus	Ramus
Ratio	Ratio
Roman R	Romanic Review
Roy Soc Can Trans	Royal Society of Canada, Transactions
SAQ	South Atlantic Quarterly
SCR	Studies in Comparative Religion
SEL	Studies in English Literature
SFQ	Southern Folklore Quarterly
SHPC	Studies in History and the Philosophy of Science

SJT	Scottish Journal of Theology
SM	Speech Monographs
SN	Studies in the Novel
SP	Studies in Philology
SR	Sewanee Review
S Romantic	Studies in Romanticism
SSF	Studies in Short Fiction
SWR	Southwest Review
S & EEJ	Slavic and East-European Journal
S & EER	Slavic and East European Review
Scand S	Scandinavian Studies
Shakespeare S	Shakespeare Survey
Sh Q	Shakespeare Quarterly
Sociol Soc Res	Sociology and Social Research
Southern R	Southern Review
Spec	Spectator
Speculum	Speculum
Symposium	Symposium; A Quarterly Journal in Modern Foreign Literature
TAPA	Transactions and Proceedings of the American Philological Association
THT	Theology Today
TLS	Times Literary Supplement
TPS	Transactions of the Philological Society
TQ	Theatre Quarterly
TRI	Theatre Research International
TSLL	Texas Studies in Language and Literature
Thomist	Thomist
Thought	Thought
Traditio	Traditio
UTQ	University of Toronto Quarterly
VP	Victorian Poetry
VQR	Virginia Quarterly Review
Vergilius	Vergilius
WACPA	Washington American Catholic Philosophical Association
W & MQ	William and Mary Quarterly
Wash Univ St Lang & Lit	Washington University Studies, Language and Literature
YCS	Yale Classical Studies
YFS	Yale French Studies
YLG	Yale University Library Gazette
YR	Yale Review
YT	Yale Theatre

GENERAL WORKS

Greece and Rome

Atkins, J. W. H. Literary Criticism in Antiquity; A Sketch of Its Development. Toronto: Macmillan, 1934, 2 Vols.
Bates, A. Greek and Roman Drama. New York: AMS, 1970.
Ferguson, J. Moral Values in the Ancient World. New York: Arno, 1979.
Finley, M. I. The Use and Abuse of History. London: Chatto and Windus, 1975.
Firebaugh, W. C. The Inns of Greece and Rome, and a History of Hospitality from the Dawn of Time to the Middle Ages. New York: Blom, 1972.
Grube, G. M. A. The Greek and Roman Critics. Toronto: University of Toronto, 1965.
Halliday, W. R. The Growth of the City State; Lectures on Greek and Roman History. Chicago: Argonaut, 1967.
Highet, G. Classical Literature; Greek and Roman Influences on Western Literature. New York: Knopf, 1957.
Kerényi, K. The Religion of the Greeks and Romans, tr. by C. Holme. Westport, Conn.: Greenwood, 1973.
Musarillo, H. Symbol and Myth in Ancient Poetry. New York: Fordham University Press, 1961.
Nash, P., A. M. Kazamias, and H. J. Perkinson, eds. The Educated Man; Studies in the History of Educational Thought. New York: Wiley, 1965.
Reece, D. W. "The Technological Weakness of the Ancient World," G & R 16 (April, 1969), 32-47.
Richter, G. M. A. Perspective in Greek and Roman Art. London: Phaidon, 1970.
Ruskin, A. Greek and Roman Art. New York: McGraw-Hill, 1968.
Sarton, G. Introduction to the History of Science. Baltimore: Williams and Wilkins, 1927-1948, Vol. 1.
Toutain, J. F. The Economic Life of the Ancient World. London: Routledge and K. Paul, 1969.
Van Rooy, C. A. Studies in Classical Satire and Related Theory. New York: Humanities, 1965.
Votaw, C. W. The Gospels and Contemporary Biographies in the Greco-Roman World. Philadelphia: Fortress, 1970.
White, M. V. The Greco-Roman Tradition. New York: Harper and Row, 1973.
Willoughby, W. W. Political Theories of the Ancient World. Freeport, N.Y.: Books for Libraries, 1969.

2 : Greek and Roman Authors

Greece

Abbott, E. Hellenica; A Collection of Essays on Greek Poetry, Philosophy, History, and Religion. Port Washington, N.Y.: Kennikat, 1971.
Adam, J. The Religious Teachers of Greece. Freeport, N.Y.: Books for Libraries, 1972.
Akurgal, E. The Birth of Greek Art: The Mediterranean and the Near East. London: Methuen, 1968.
Amantos, C. Prolegomena to the History of the Byzantine Empire, tr. by K. Johnstone. Amsterdam: Hakkert, 1969.
Angus, S. The Environment of Early Christianity. Freeport, N.Y.: Books for Libraries, 1971.
Arnold, E. The Poets of Greece. Freeport, N.Y.: Books for Libraries, 1972.
Avi-Yonah, M. Hellenism and the East: Contacts and Interrelations from Alexander to the Roman Conquest. Jerusalem: Hebrew University, University Microfilms International, 1978.
Aylen, L. Greece for Everyone. London: Sidgwick and Jackson, 1975.
Baldry, H. C. Ancient Greek Literature in Its Living Context. London: Thames and Hudson, 1968.
Barret, A. Greece Observed, tr. by S. Hardman. New York: Oxford University Press, 1974.
Bates, A. Greek Drama. New York: AMS Press, 1970.
Beazley, J. D., and B. Ashmole. Greek Sculpture and Painting. Cambridge: Cambridge University Press, 1966.
Bevan, E. R. Later Greek Religion. New York: AMS, 1973.
Beye, C. R. Ancient Greek Literature and Society. New York: Anchor, 1975.
Bianchi, U. The Greek Mysteries. Leiden: Brill, 1976.
Bilezikian, G. G. The Liberated Gospel: A Comparison of the Gospel of Mark and Greek Tragedy. Grand Rapids, Mich.: Baker Book House, 1977.
Birchall, A. Greek Gods and Heroes. London: British Museum Publications, 1974.
Boardman, J. Greek Art. New York: Praeger, 1973.
Boedeker, D. D. Aphrodite's Entry into Greek Epic. Lugduni Batavorum: Brill, 1974.
Bonnard, A. Greek Civilization. New York: Macmillan, 1957-61, 3 Vols.
Bowra, C. M. The Greek Experience. New York: Praeger, 1969.
Brandt, P. Sexual Life in Ancient Greece, tr. by J. H. Freese. Westport, Conn.: Greenwood, 1975.
Bremer, J. M. Hamartia: Tragic Error in the Poetics of Aristotle and in Greek Tragedy. Amsterdam: Hakkert, 1969.
Brilliant, R. Arts of the Ancient Greeks. New York: McGraw-Hill, 1973.
Brooke-Cunningham, C. A. Anglo-Saxon Unity, and Other Essays. Port Washington, N.Y.: Kennikat, 1971.
Burn, A. R. The Pelican History of Greece. Harmondsworth: Penguin, 1966.

Burns, C. D. Greek Ideals. New York: Haskell House, 1974.
Burrows, R. M. The Discoveries in Crete and Their Bearing on the History of Ancient Civilization. Port Washington, N.Y.: Kennikat, 1969.
Bury, J. B. The Hellenistic Age. New York: Norton, 1970.
Butcher, S. H. Harvard Lectures on Greek Subjects. Port Washington, N.Y.: Kennikat, 1969.
_____. Some Aspects of the Greek Genius. Port Washington, N.Y.: Kennikat, 1969.
Caldwell, W. E. Hellenic Conceptions of Peace. New York: AMS, 1967.
Campbell, L. Religion in Greek Literature, a Sketch in Outline. Freeport, N.Y.: Books for Libraries, 1971.
Chambers, M. Ancient Greece. Washington, D.C.: American Historical Association, 1973.
Charbonneaux, J., R. Martin, and F. Villard. Classical Greek Art (480-330 B.C.). New York: Braziller, 1972.
Clader, L. L. Helen: The Evolution from Divine to Heroic in Greek Epic Tradition. Lugduni Batavorum: Brill, 1976.
Coldstream, J. N. Geometric Greece. New York: St. Martin's, 1977.
Cook, A. S. Enactment: Greek Tragedy. Chicago: Swallow, 1971.
Cook, R. M. Greek Art: Its Development, Character, and Influence. New York: Farrar, Straus, 1973.
Cornford, F. M. Greek Religious Thought from Homer to the Age of Alexander. New York: AMS, 1969.
Couch, H. N. Classical Civilization. Westport, Conn.: Greenwood, 1973.
Croiset, A. An Abridged History of Greek Literature, tr. by G. F. Heffelbower. New York: AMS, 1970.
Crow, J. A. Greece: The Magic Spring. New York: Harper and Row, 1970.
Dale, A. M. Metrical Analysis of Tragic Choruses. London: Institute of Classical Studies, 1971.
Daniélou, J. Gospel Message and Hellenistic Culture, tr. by J. A. Baker. Philadelphia: Westminster, 1973.
Davidson, T. The Education of the Greek People and its Influence on Civilization. New York: AMS, 1971.
Dawe, H. A. Ancient Greece and Rome. Columbus, Ohio: Merrill, 1970.
Demargne, P. The Birth of Greek Art, tr. by S. Gilbert and J. Emmons. New York: Golden, 1964.
De Romilly, J. Time in Greek Tragedy. Ithaca, N.Y.: Cornell University Press, 1968.
Devereux, G. Dreams in Greek Tragedy: An Ethno-Psycho-Analytical Study. Berkeley: University of California Press, 1976.
Dicks, D. Early Greek Astronomy to Aristotle. London: Thames and Hudson, 1970.
Dietrich, B. C. The Origins of Greek Religion. Berlin: de Gruyter, 1974.
Dover, K. J. Greek Popular Morality in the Time of Plato and Aristotle. Berkeley: University of California Press, 1974.

4 : Greek and Roman Authors

Duruy, V. The World of the Greeks, tr. by J. Rosenthal. London: Gifford, 1971.
Earp, F. R. The Way of the Greeks. New York: AMS, 1971.
Ehrenberg, V. From Solon to Socrates. New York: Barnes and Noble, 1973.
Ellis, J. R. Philip II and Macedonian Imperialism. London: Thames and Hudson, 1976.
Else, G. F. The Origin and Early Form of Greek Tragedy. New York: Norton, 1972.
Epps, P. H. Thoughts from the Greeks. Columbia: University of Missouri Press, 1969.
Farnell, L. R. Outline-History of Greek Religion. Chicago: Ares, 1974.
Farrington, B. Head and Hand in Ancient Greece: Four Studies in the Social Relations of Thought. Folcroft, Pa.: Folcroft Library Editions, 1977.
Ferguson, J. A Companion to Greek Tragedy. Austin: University of Texas Press, 1972.
_____. The Heritage of Hellenism. New York: Science History, 1973.
_____. The Wit of the Greeks and Romans. London: Frewin, 1968.
Finley, M. I. The Ancient Economy. Berkeley: University of California Press, 1973.
_____. The Ancient Greeks. Harmondsworth: Penguin, 1975.
_____. Ancient Slavery and Modern Ideology. New York: Viking, 1980.
_____, ed. Atlas of Classical Archaeology. London: Chatto and Windus, 1977.
_____. Early Greece. New York: Norton, 1970.
_____. The Education of the Greek People and Its Influence on Civilization. St. Clair Shores, Mich.: Scholarly, 1969.
_____, and H. W. Pleket. The Olympic Games: The First Thousand Years. London: Chatto and Windus, 1976.
_____. Slavery in Classical Antiquity; Views and Controversies. Cambridge, Eng.: Heffer, 1960.
_____. Studies in Land and Credit in Ancient Athens, 500-200 B.C.; the Horoscriptions. New York: Arno, 1973.
Flaceliere, R. Daily Life in Greece at the Time of Pericles. New York: Macmillan, 1965.
Forrest, W. G. C. The Emergence of Greek Democracy: The Character of Greek Politics, 800-400 B.C. London: Weidenfeld and Nicolson, 1966.
Fowler, H. N. A Handbook of Greek Archaeology. New York: AMS, 1969.
Frankel, H. F. Early Greek Poetry and Philosophy, tr. by M. Hadas and J. Willis. New York: Harcourt, Brace, 1975.
Frisch, H. Might and Right in Antiquity. New York: Arno, 1976.
Frost, F. J. Greek Society. Lexington, Mass.: Heath, 1971.
Gardner, E. A. The Art of Greece. New York: Cooper Square, 1975.
_____. Religion and Art in Ancient Greece. Port Washington, N.Y.: Kennikat, 1969.

Gardner, P. New Chapters in Greek Art. New York: AMS, 1971.
Geddes, J. An Essay on the Composition and Manner of Writing of the Ancients, Particularly Plato. New York: Garland, 1970.
Glover, T. R. The Challenge of the Greek, and Other Essays. Freeport, N. Y.: Books for Libraries, 1972.
Gomme, A. W. Essays in Greek History and Literature. Freeport, N. Y.: Books for Libraries, 1967.
———. Greek Attitude to Poetry and History. Berkeley: University of California Press, 1954.
Goodell, T. D. Athenian Tragedy; A Study in Popular Art. Port Washington, N. Y.: Kennikat, 1969.
Gould, T. F., and C. J. Herington. Greek Tragedy. Cambridge: University Press, 1977.
Gouldner, A. W. The Hellenic World: A Sociological Analysis. New York: Harper and Row, 1969.
Grant, A. J. Greece in the Age of Pericles. New York: Cooper Square, 1973.
Graves, R. Greek Myths. 4th edition. London: Gassel, 1965.
Green, P. Ancient Greece. New York: Viking, 1973.
———. A Concise History of Ancient Greece to the Close of the Classical Era. London: Thames and Hudson, 1973.
———. The Shadow of the Parthenon. Berkeley: University of California Press, 1972.
Greene, W. C. Moira: Fate, Good, and Evil in Greek Thought. Gloucester, Mass.: Smith, 1968.
Gulick, C. B. The Life of the Ancient Greeks, with Special Reference to Athens. New York: Cooper Square, 1973.
Guthrie, W. K. C. A History of Greek Philosophy. Cambridge: Cambridge University Press, 1962-78, 5 vols.
Hack, R. K. God in Greek Philosophy to the Time of Socrates. New York: Franklin, 1970.
Hadas, M. Hellenistic Culture: Fusion and Diffusion. New York: Norton, 1972.
Hafner, G. Art of Crete, Mycenae and Greece. New York: Abrams, 1968.
Haigh, A. R. The Attic Theatre; A Description of the Stage and Theatre of the Athenians, and of the Dramatic Performances at Athens. New York: Haskell House, 1968.
Hale, W. H. Ancient Greece. New York: Heritage, 1970.
Hall, H. R. H. The Civilization of Greece in the Bronze Age. New York: Cooper Square, 1970.
Hammond, N. G. L. The Classical Age of Greece. New York: Barnes and Noble, 1976.
Havelock, C. M. Hellenistic Art; The Art of the Classical World from the Death of Alexander the Great to the Battle of Actium. Greenwich, Conn.: New York Graphic Society, 1970.
Henderson, J. The Maculate Muse: Obscene Language in Attic Comedy. New Haven: Yale University Press, 1975.
Hengel, M. Judaism and Hellenism: Studies in Their Encounter in Palestine During the Early Hellenistic Period, tr. by J. Bowden. Philadelphia: Fortress, 1974.
Hoffman, H. Collecting Greek Antiquities. Introduced by John D. Cooney; A Chapter on Coins by Herbert A. Cahn. New York: Potter, 1971.

6 : Greek and Roman Authors

Hogarth, D. G. Ionia and the East. New York: Haskell House, 1969.
Holloway, R. A View of Greek Art. Providence, R.I.: Brown University Press, 1973.
Hutton, M. The Greek Point of View. Port Washington, N.Y.: Kennikat, 1971.
Huxley, G. L. Greek Epic Poetry from Eumelos to Panyassis. London: Faber, 1969.
Irwin, E. Colour Terms in Greek Poetry. Toronto: Hakkert, 1974.
Jaeger, W. W. Paideia: The Ideals of Greek Culture, tr. by Gilbert Highet. Oxford: B. Blackwell, 1944-47. 3 vols.
Jepsen, L. Ethical Aspects of Tragedy. New York: AMS, 1971.
Johnston, A. W. The Emergence of Greece. Oxford: Elsevier-Phaidon, 1976.
Kirkwood, G. M. Early Greek Monody. Ithaca, N.Y.: Cornell University Press, 1974.
Kott, J. The Eating of the Gods, tr. by B. Toborski. New York: Vintage, 1974.
L'Orange, H. P. Likeness and Icon; Selected Studies in Classical and Early Mediaeval Art. Odense: Odense University Press, 1973.
Legrand, P. E. The New Greek Comedy, tr. by J. Loeb. Westport, Conn.: Greenwood, 1970.
Lesky, A. Greek Tragedy, tr. by H. A. Frankfort. 3rd edition. New York: Barnes and Noble, 1979.
_____. A History of Greek Literature, tr. by J. Willis and C. de Heer. New York: Crowell, 1966.
Lever, K. The Art of Greek Comedy. London: Methuen, 1956.
Levi, M. A. Alessandro Magno. Milano: Rusconi, 1977.
Liberman, A. Greek Gods and Art. Introduction by Robert Graves; Texts and Commentaries on the Photographs by Iris C. Love. London: Collins, 1968.
Lindsay, J. Helen of Troy: Woman and Goddess. London: Constable, 1974.
Little, A. M. G. Myth and Society in Attic Drama. New York: Octagon, 1966.
Livingstone, R. W. The Legacy of Greece. London: Oxford University Press, 1969.
Lloyd, A. Marathon: The Story of Civilizations on Collision Course. London: Souvenir, 1974.
Lloyd-Jones, H. The Greeks. Freeport, N.Y.: Books for Libraries, 1975.
_____. The Justice of Zeus. Berkeley: University of California Press, 1971.
Lofberg, J. O., and I. Barkan. Sycophancy in Athens and Capital Punishment in Ancient Athens. New York: Arno, 1979.
MacKendrick, P. The Greek Stones Speak. New York: St. Martin's, 1962.
McLeish, K. Greek Art and Architecture. London: Longman, 1975.
Mahaffy, J. P. Greek Life and Thought from the Age of Alexander to the Roman Conquest. New York: Arno, 1976.
_____. Rambles and Studies in Greece. Washington, D.C.: McGrath, 1973.

Marcade, J. Eroskalos: Essay on Erotic Elements in Greek Art. New York: Nagel, 1962.
Markman, S. D. The Horse in Greek Art. New York: Biblo and Tannen, 1969.
Momigliano, A. Alien Wisdom: The Limits of Hellenization. Cambridge: Cambridge University Press, 1975.
―――. The Development of Greek Biography. Cambridge: Harvard University Press, 1971.
―――. Second Thoughts on Greek Biography. Amsterdam: North-Holland, 1971.
Muller, K. O. A History of the Literature of Ancient Greece. Port Washington, N. Y. : Kennikat, 1971.
Murray, G. Five Stages of Greek Religion. New York: AMS, 1978.
―――. A History of Ancient Greek Literature. New York: Ungar, 1966.
Nilsson, M. P. A History of Greek Religion. 2nd edition. London: Oxford University Press, 1952.
Otto, W. F. The Homeric Gods: The Spiritual Significance of Greek Religion, tr. by M. Hadas. New York: Octagon, 1978.
Parke, H. W. Festivals of the Athenians. Ithaca, N. Y.: Cornell University Press, 1977.
Pater, W. H. Greek Studies; A Series of Essays. New York: Johnson Reprint, 1973.
Perowne, S. The Archaeology of Greece and the Aegean. New York: Viking, 1974.
Pickard-Cambridge, A. W. Demosthenes and the Last Days of Greek Freedom, 384-322 B. C. New York: AMS, 1978.
Pohlenz, M. Freedom in Greek Life and Thought; The History of an Ideal. New York: Humanities, 1966.
Pollitt, J. J. Art and Experience in Classical Greece. Cambridge: Cambridge University Press, 1972.
Pope, M. The Ancient Greeks: How They Lived and Worked. Chester Springs, Pa. : Dufour, 1976.
Ramsay, W. M. Asianic Elements in Greek Civilization. New York: AMS, 1969.
Richardson, B. E. Old Age Among the Ancient Greeks; The Greek Portrayal of Old Age in Literature, Art, and Inscriptions, with a Study of the Duration of Life Among the Ancient Greeks on the Basis of Inscriptional Evidence. New York: Greenwood, 1969.
Richmond, J. Chapters on Greek Fish-lore. Wiesbaden: Steiner, 1973.
Richter, G. M. A. A Handbook of Greek Art. London: Phaidon, 1969.
Robertson, M. A History of Greek Art. London: Cambridge University Press, 1975. 2 vols.
Rohde, E. Psyche; The Cult of Souls and Belief in Immortality Among the Greeks. Freeport, N. Y. : Books for Libraries, 1972.
Romilly, J. de. Time in Greek Tragedy. Ithaca: Cornell University Press, 1968.
Rosenmeyer, T. G. The Masks of Tragedy. New York: Gordian, 1971.
St. John, J. A. The History of the Manners and Customs of Ancient Greece. Port Washington, N. Y. : Kennikat, 1971.

8 : Greek and Roman Authors

Scarborough, J. Facets of Hellenic Life. Boston: Houghton Mifflin, 1976.
Schoder, R. V. Masterpieces of Greek Art. Chicago: Ares, 1975.
Schuchhardt, W. H. Greek Art. New York: Universe, 1972.
Schweitzer, B. Greek Geometric Art, tr. by P. and C. Usborne. New York: Phaidon, 1971.
Sheppard, J. T. Greek Tragedy. Norwood, Pa.: Norwood, 1977.
Sifakis, G. M. Parabasis and Animal Choruses: A Contribution to the History of Attic Comedy. London: Athlone, 1971.
Sikes, E. E. The Greek View of Poetry. New York: Barnes and Noble, 1969.
Silk, M. S. Interaction in Poetic Imagery: With Special Reference to Early Greek Poetry. New York: Cambridge University Press, 1974.
Sinclair, T. A. A History of Classical Greek Literature, from Homer to Aristotle. New York: Haskell House, 1973.
Snell, B. The Discovery of the Mind. Cambridge, Mass.: Harvard University Press, 1953.
———. Poetry and Society. Freeport, N. Y.: Books for Libraries, 1971.
Snodgrass, A. M. Archaeology and the Rise of the Greek State: An Inaugural Lecture. Cambridge: Cambridge University Press, 1977.
Soutar, G. Nature in Greek Poetry, Studies Partly Comparative. New York: Johnson Reprint, 1971.
Starr, C. G. The Ancient Greeks. New York: Oxford University Press, 1971.
Stobart, J. C. The Glory that was Greece; a Survey of Hellenic Culture and Civilization. New York: Praeger, 1971.
Strain, J. The Contribution of Ancient Greece. New York: Holt, Rinehart and Winston, 1971.
Symonds, J. A. A Problem in Greek Ethics. New York: Haskell House, 1971.
———. Studies in Sexual Inversion: Embodying a Study in Greek Ethics and a Study in Modern Ethics. New York: AMS, 1975.
Taplin, O. P. The Stagecraft of Aeschylus: The Dramatic Use of Exits and Entrances in Greek Tragedy. New York: Clarendon, 1977.
Tarbell, F. B. A History of Greek Art, with an Introductory Chapter on Art in Egypt and Mesopotamia. Westport, Conn.: Greenwood, 1971.
Thomson, J. A. K. The Greek Tradition. Freeport, N. Y.: Books for Libraries, 1971.
Toynbee, A. J. Some Problems of Greek History. London: Oxford University Press, 1969.
Trypanes, K. A. The Homeric Epics, tr. by W. Phelps. Warminster, Eng.: Aris and Phillips, 1977.
Van Duyn, J. H. The Greeks: Their Legacy. New York: McGraw-Hill, 1972.
Versenyi, L. Man's Measure. Albany: State University of New York Press, 1974.
Vickers, B. Towards Greek Tragedy: Drama, Myth, Society. London: Longmans, 1973.

Walters, H. B. The Art of the Greeks. Freeport, N. Y. : Books for Libraries, 1972.
Warner, R. Eternal Greece. London: Thames and Hudson, 1971.
Webster, T. B. L. Athenian Culture and Society. Berkeley: University of California Press, 1973.
_____. Studies in Later Greek Comedy. New York: Barnes and Noble, 1970.
_____. Tradition in Greek Dramatic Lyric. Christ-church, New Zealand: University of Canterbury Press, 1969.
Weil, S. Intimations of Christianity Among the Ancient Greeks, tr. by E. C. Geissbuhler. London: Routledge and K. Paul, 1976.
Welles, C. B. Alexander and the Hellenistic World. Toronto: Hakkert, 1970.
Wickersham, J. The Fourth Century B. C. Toronto: Hakkert, 1973.
Wright, F. A. Feminism in Greek Literature from Homer to Aristotle. Port Washington, N. Y. : Kennikat, 1969.
_____. Greek Social Life. New York: AMS, 1973.
Zielinski, T. The Religion of Ancient Greece, tr. by G. R. Noyes. Freeport, N. Y. : Books for Libraries, 1970.
Zuntz, G. Persephone: Three Essays on Religion and Thought in Magna Graecia. Oxford: Clarendon, 1971.

Rome

Balsdon, J. P. V. D. Life and Leisure in Ancient Rome. New York: McGraw-Hill, 1969.
Bertman, S. Art and the Romans: A Study of Roman Art as a Dynamic Expression of Roman Character. Lawrence, Kan. : Coronado, 1975.
Brilliant, R. Roman Art from the Republic to Constantine. New York: Praeger, 1974.
Carcopino, J. Daily Life in Ancient Rome: The People and the City at the Height of the Empire, tr. by E. O. Lorimer. London: Routledge and K. Paul, 1973.
Casson, L. The Horizon Book of Daily Life in Ancient Rome. New York: American Heritage, 1975.
Charles-Picard, G. The Ancient Civilization of Rome. New York: Cowles, 1969.
_____. Roman Painting. Greenwich, Conn. : New York Graphic Society, 1970.
Clark, E. Rome and a Villa. New York: Pantheon, 1975.
Copley, F. O. Latin Literature from the Beginnings to the Close of Second Century A. D. Ann Arbor: University of Michigan Press, 1969.
Daube, D. Roman Law: Linguistic, Social and Philosophical Aspects. Chicago: Aldine, 1969.
Day, A. A. The Origins of Latin Love-Elegy. Oxford: Blackwell, 1933.
Dorey, T. A., and D. R. Dudley, eds. Roman Drama. New York: Basic, 1965.
Duckworth, G. E. The Nature of Roman Comedy; A Study in Popular Entertainment. Princeton: Princeton University Press, 1952.

10 : Greek and Roman Authors

Earl, D. C. The Moral and Political Tradition of Rome. Ithaca, N. Y. : Cornell University Press, 1967.
Ferguson, J. The Religions of the Roman Empire. Ithaca, N. Y. : Cornell University Press, 1970.
Finley, M. I., ed. Studies in Roman Property. Cambridge: Cambridge University Press, 1976.
Fowler, W. W. The Roman Festivals of the Period of the Republic; An Introduction to the Study of the Religion of the Romans. Port Washington, N. Y. : Kennikat, 1969.
_____. Rome. 3rd edition. New York: Oxford University Press, 1967.
Frank, T. Aspects of Social Behavior in Ancient Rome. New York: Cooper Square, 1969.
Friedlander, L. Roman Life and Manners under the Early Empire. New York: Barnes and Noble, 1965.
Greenidge, A. H. J. Roman Public Life. New York: Cooper Square, 1970.
Grenier, A. The Roman Spirit in Religion, Thought, and Art. New York: Cooper Square, 1970.
Grimel, P. Love in Ancient Rome. New York: Crown, 1967.
Gruen, E. S. Imperialism in the Roman Republic. New York: Holt, Rinehart and Winston, 1970.
Hadas, M. History of Latin Literature. New York: Columbia University Press, 1952.
Hagendahl, H. Latin Fathers and the Classics. Stockholm: Almqvist and Wiksell, 1958.
Hanfmann, G. M. A. Roman Art: A Modern Survey of the Art of Imperial Rome. New York: Norton, 1975.
Heintze, H. Roman Art. New York: Universe, 1971.
Liversidge, J. Everyday Life in the Roman Empire. New York: Putnam, 1976.
L'Orange, H. P. Likeness and Icon: Selected Studies in Classical and Early Mediaeval Art. Odense: Odense University Press, 1973.
Louis, P. Ancient Rome at Work; An Economic History of Rome from the Origins to the Empire. New York: Barnes and Noble, 1965.
MacKendrick, P. The Mute Stones Speak. New York: St. Martin's, 1960.
Martin, G. "The Roman Hymn," CJ 34 (November, 1938), 86-97.
Mead, R. D. Hellas and Rome. New York: New American Library, 1972.
Mendell, C. W. Latin Poetry: The New Poets and the Augustans. London: Yale University Press, 1965.
Moore, R. W. The Roman Commonwealth. Port Washington, N. Y. : Kennikat, 1969.
Nicols, R., and K. McLeish. Roman Civilization in the Words of Roman Writers. Cambridge: Cambridge University Press, 1976.
Richmond, I. A. Roman Archaeology and Art. London: Faber, 1969.
Rose, J. H. The Roman Questions of Plutarch. New York: Arno, 1975.

General Works : 11

Rostovtzeff, M. Social and Economic History of the Roman Empire. 2nd edition, revised by P. M. Fraser. Oxford: Clarendon, 1957.
Rutland, J. See Inside a Roman Town. New York: Warwick, 1978.
Smith, P. A Desk in Rome. London: Collins, 1974.
Sticca, S. The Latin Passion Play: Its Origins and Development. Albany: State University of New York Press, 1970.
Storoni Mazzolani, L. The Idea of the City in Roman Thought: From Walled City to Spiritual Commonwealth. Bloomington: Indiana University Press, 1970.
Strong, E. Apotheosis and After Life. Freeport, N. Y. : Books for Libraries, 1969.
──────. Art in Ancient Rome. Westport, Conn. : Greenwood, 1970.
──────. Roman Art. Baltimore: Penguin, 1976.
Sullivan, J. P. , ed. Critical Essays on Roman Literature: Elegy and Lyric. Cambridge, Mass. : Harvard University Press, 1962.
Vogt, J. The Decline of Rome: The Metamorphosis of Ancient Civilization. London: Weidenfeld and Nicolson, 1967.
Williams, G. W. The Nature of Roman Poetry. London: Oxford University Press, 1970.
Wills, G. Roman Culture; Weapons and the Man. New York: Braziller, 1966.

GREEK AND ROMAN AUTHORS

AESCHYLUS

General Criticism

Ahrens, R. H. The Plays of Aeschylus. New York: Monarch, 1966.

Bacon, H. H. "Aeschylus," in his Barbarians in Greek Tragedy. New Haven, Conn.: Yale University Press, 1961, pp. 15-63.

———. "The Shield of Eteocles," Arion 3 (Autumn, 1964), 27-38.

Beck, R. H. Aeschylus: Playwright Educator. The Hague: Nijhoff, 1975.

Bond, G. W. "Euripides' Parody of Aeschylus," Ha 118 (Winter, 1974), 1-14.

Bonner, C. "Notes on Aeschylus," CP 37 (July, 1942), 263-274.

Broadhead, H. D. "Aeschylea," CQ 42 (January, 1948), 1-6.

Caldwell, R. S. "The Pattern of Aeschylean Tragedy," TAPA 101 (1970), 77-94.

Campbell, L. Tragic Drama in Aeschylus, Sophocles and Shakespeare. New York: Russell and Russell, 1965.

Costa, C. D. N. "Plots and Politics in Aeschylus," G & R 9 (March, 1962), 22-34.

Dawe, R. D. Repertory of Conjectures on Aeschylus. Leiden: Brill, 1965.

Dinsmore, C. A. "Aeschylus: His Genius and Spiritual Insights," in his Great Poets and the Meaning of Life. Boston: Houghton Mifflin, 1937, pp. 64-86.

Downs, R. B. "Father of Tragedy: Aeschylus," in his Famous Books, Ancient and Medieval. New York: Barnes and Noble, 1964, p. 43-48.

Earp, F. R. "Some Features in the Style of Aeschylus," J Hel S 65 (1945), 10-15.

———. The Style of Aeschylus. New York: Russell and Russell, 1970.

Easterling, P. E. "Presentation of Character in Aeschylus," G & R 20 (April, 1973), 3-19.

Else, G. F. "Ritual and Drama in Aeschyleian Tragedy," ICS 2 (1977), 70-87.

Finley, J. H. Pindar and Aeschylus. Cambridge, Mass.: Harvard University Press, 1955.

Flickinger, R. C. "The Theatre of Aeschylus," TAPA 61 (1930), 80-110.

Fraenkel, E. Aeschylus: New Texts and Old Problems. New York: Oxford University Press, 1943.

Gagarin, M. Aeschylean Drama. Berkeley: University of California Press, 1976.
Gassner, J. "Aeschylus--'The Father of Tragedy,'" in his Masters of the Drama. New York: Dover, 1954, p. 17-39.
Golden, L. Aeschylus and Ares: A Study in the Use of Military Imagery by Aeschylus. Chicago: University of Chicago Press, 1958.
Gomme, A. W. "Herodotus and Aeschylus," in his Greek Attitude to Poetry and History. Berkeley: University of California Press, 1954, pp. 95-115.
Green, P. "Some Versions of Aeschylus," in his Essays in Antiquity. New York: World, 1960, pp. 185-215.
Grube, G. M. A. "Zeus in Aeschylus," AJP 91 (January, 1970), 43-51.
Haldane, J. A. "Musical Themes and Imagery in Aeschylus," J Hel S 85 (1965), 33-41.
Hamilton, E. "Aeschylus, the First Dramatist," in his Great Age of Greek Literature. New York: Norton, 1942, pp. 239-257.
Hammond, N. G. L., and W. G. Moon. "Illustrations of Early Tragedy at Athens," AJA 82 (Summer, 1978), 371-383.
Harsh, P. W. "Aeschylus," in his Handbook of Classical Drama. Stanford: Stanford University Press, 1944, pp. 36-87.
Herington, C. J. "Aeschylus in Sicily," J Hel S 87 (1967), 74-85.
_____. "Aeschylus: The Last Phase," Arion 4 (Autumn, 1965), 387-403.
_____. "The Influence of Old Comedy on Aeschylus' Later Trilogies," TAPA 94 (1963), 113-125.
Howe, T. P. "The Style of Aeschylus as Satyr-playwright," G & R 6 (October, 1959), 150-164.
Jaeger, W. W. Paideia: The Ideals of Greek Culture. Oxford: B. Blackwell, 1944-47. Vol. 1, pp. 237-267.
Kerr, W. "Man--As Monster, or God," in E. T. Kirby, ed., Total Theatre; A Critical Anthology. New York: Dutton, 1969, pp. 78-83.
Kieffer, J. S. "Philoctetes and Arete; Comparison of the Plays of Aeschylus and Euripides with That of Sophocles," CP 37 (January, 1942), 38-50.
Kitto, H. D. F. "Aeschylus," in his Poiesis: Structure and Thought. Berkeley: University of California Press, 1966, pp. 33-115.
Berkeley: University of California Press, 1966, pp. 33-115.
_____. "The Idea of God in Aeschylus and Sophocles," in H. J. Rose, ed., La Notion du Divin. Berne: Vandoeuvres-Geneve, 1955, pp. 169-189.
Knight, W. J. F. "The Aeschylean Universe," J Hel S 63 (1943), 15-20.
_____. "The Tragic Vision of Aeschylus," G & R 5 (October, 1935), 29-40.
Kramer, F. R. "The Altar of Right: Reality and Power in Aeschylus," CJ 56 (October, 1960), 33-38.
Lasselle, M. "Improvising Aeschylus," YT 5 (Spring, 1974), 120-127.

Lesky, A. "Decision and Responsibility in the Tragedy of Aeschylus," J Hel S 86 (1966), 78-85.
Lloyd-Jones, H. "Zeus in Aeschylus," J Hel S 76 (1956), 55-67.
Lucas, D. W. "Aeschylus," in his Greek Tragic Poets; Their Contribution to Western Life and Thought. Boston: Beacon, 1952, pp. 49-105.
McCall, M. H., Jr. Aeschylus: A Collection of Critical Essays. Englewood Cliffs, N. J.: Prentice-Hall, 1972.
Murray, G. Aeschylus: The Creator of Tragedy. Oxford: Clarendon, 1962.
Musurillo, H. "Tragic Wisdom: Aeschylus and Sophocles," in his Symbol and Myth in Ancient Poetry. New York: Fordham University Press, 1961, pp. 61-70.
Myres, J. L. "Blood-feud and Justice in Homer and Aeschylus," CR 59 (May, 1945), 10.
Nicoll, A. "First Dramatist: Aeschylus," in his World Drama, from Aeschylus to Anouilh. New York: Harcourt, Brace, 1953, pp. 25-50.
Owen, E. T. Harmony of Aeschylus. Toronto: Clark, Irwin, 1952.
Piggott, S. "Iron, Cimmerians and Aeschylus," Antiq 38 (December, 1964), 300-303.
Pollard, J. R. J. "Birds in Aeschylus," G & R 17 (October, 1958), 116-126.
Post, L. A. "Social Consciousness of Aeschylus," in his From Homer to Menander; Forces in Greek Poetic Fiction. Berkeley: University of California Press, 1951, pp. 56-87.
Robertson, H. G. "Legal Expressions and Ideas of Justice in Aeschylus," CP 34 (July, 1939), 209-219.
Rose, H. J. A Commentary on the Surviving Plays of Aeschylus. Amsterdam: North-Holland, 1958.
_____. "Ghost Ritual in Aeschylus," HTR 43 (October, 1950), 257-280.
_____. "Theology and Mythology in Aeschylus," HTR 39 (January, 1946), 1-24.
Sansone, D. Aeschylean Metaphors for Intellectual Activity. Wiesbaden: Steiner, 1975.
Sheppart, J. T. Aeschylus: The Prophet of Greek Freedom. New York: Haskell House, 1974.
Smertenko, C. M. "The Political Sympathies of Aeschylus," J Hel S 53 (1933), 233-235.
Smyth, H. W. Aeschylean Tragedy. New York: AMS, 1972.
Solmsen, F. Hesiod and Aeschylus. New York: Johnson Reprint, 1949.
_____. "Strata of Greek Religion in Aeschylus," HTR 40 (October, 1947), 211-226.
Stanford, W. B. Aeschylus in His Style: A Study in Language and Personality. New York: Johnson Reprint, 1972.
Stoessl, F. "Aeschylus as a Political Thinker," AJP 73 (April, 1952), 113-139.
Taplin, O. P. "Aeschylean Silences and Silences in Aeschylus," HSCP 76 (1972), 57-98.
_____. The Stagecraft of Aeschylus: The Dramatic Use of Exits and Entrances in Greek Tragedy. New York: Clarendon, 1977.

Thomson, G. D. Aeschylus and Athens; Study in the Social Origins of Drama. New York: International, 1950.
Turyn, A. The Manuscript Tradition of the Tragedies of Aeschylus. Hildesheim: Olms, 1967.
Werre de Haas, M. Aeschylus. Leiden: Brill, 1961.
Wilson, P. C. "Notes of Freedom Sounded by Aeschylus," CP 42 (April, 1947), 383-390.

Individual Works

Agamemnon

Anderson, F. M. "Character of Clytemnestra," TAPA 60 (1929), 136-154.
Baldry, H. C. "House of the Atriade (in the Agamemnon)," CR (New Series) 5 (March, 1955), 16-17.
Booth, N. B. "Merciful Heavens? A Question in Aeschylus' Agamemnon," CQ (New Series) 26 (1976), 220-228.
Clinton, K. "Apollo, Pan, and Zeus: Avengers of Vultures. Agamemnon, 55-59," AJP 94 (Fall, 1973), 282-288.
Conacher, D. J. "Comments on an Interpretation of Aeschylus, Agamemnon 182-183," Phoenix 30 (Winter, 1976), 328-336.
Diggle, J. "Notes on the Agamemnon and Persae of Aeschylus," CR (New Series) 18 (March, 1968), 1-4.
Dover, K. J. "Some Neglected Aspects of Agamemnon's Dilemma," J Hel S 93 (1973), 58-69.
Duke, T. T. "Murder in the Bath," CJ (April, 1954), 325-330.
Earp, F. R. "Studies in Character: Agamemnon," G & R 19 (June, 1950), 49-61.
Ewans, M. "Agamemnon at Aulis: A Study in the Oresteia," Ramus 4 (January, 1975), 17-32.
Fitton-Brown, A. D. "Some Notes on the Agamemnon," CP 47 (July, 1952), 150-156.
Fletcher, F. Notes to the Agamemnon of Aeschylus. Oxford: Blackwell, 1949.
Heirman, L. J. "Kassandra's Glossolalia," Mnemosyne 28 (1975), 257-267.
Hooker, J. T. "The Sacrifice of Iphigeneia in the Agamemnon," Agon 2 (1968), 59-65.
Knox, B. M. W. "The Lion in the House (Agamemnon 717-736)," CP 47 (January, 1952), 17-25.
Lanahan, W. F. "Levels of Symbolism in the Red Carpet Scene of Agamemnon," CB 51 (December, 1974), 24-27.
Lawrence, S. E. "Artemis in the Agamemnon," AJP 97 (Summer, 1976), 97-110.
Lawson, J. C. "The Agamemnon of Aeschylus," J Hel S 53 (1933), 112.
Leahy, D. M. "The Authority of the Elders: A Note," CP 68 (July, 1973), 202-203.
_____. "The Representation of the Trojan War in Aeschylus' Agamemnon," AJP 95 (Spring, 1974), 1-23.

Lebeck, A. Image and Idea of the Agamemnon of Aeschylus. New York: Columbia University Press, 1964.
Lloyd-Jones, H. "The Guilt of Agamemnon," CQ (New Series) 12 (1962), 187-199.
⎯⎯⎯⎯. "Robes of Iphigeneia; Aeschylus, Agamemnon 228 ff.," CR (New Series) 2 (December, 1952), 132-135.
Marino, P. A. "A Lion Among the Flock," CB 51 (March, 1975), 77-78.
⎯⎯⎯⎯. The Cry of the Hoopoe," CB 51 (December, 1974), 30-31.
Olson, E. "The Agamemnon," in his Tragedy and the Theory of Drama. Detroit: Wayne State University Press, 1966, pp. 171-194.
Pope, M. "Merciful Heavens? A Question in Aeschylus' Agamemnon," J Hel S 94 (1974), 100-113.
Quincey, J. H. "The Beacon-sites in the Agamemnon," J Hel S 83 (1963), 118-132.
Smethurst, M. J. "The Authority of the Elders: The Agamemnon of Aeschylus," CP 67 (April, 1972), 89-93.
Sommerstein, A. H. "Aeschylus, Agamemnon 126-130," CR (New Series) 21 (March, 1971), 1-3.
Stanford, W. B. "Looking-glass of Society in Aeschylus, Agamemnon 838-840," CR (New Series) 4 (June, 1954), 82-85.
Thomson, G. "Bad Bronze; Aesch. Ag. 390-393," CR 58 (December, 1944), 35-37.
Thomson, J. A. K. "Mirror of the Saronic Gulf; Aeschylus, Agamemnon 305-308," CQ 40 (January, 1946), 56-59.
Tracy, H. L. "Dramatic Art in Aeschylus' Agamemnon," CJ 47 (December, 1951), 215-218, 251.
Vaughn, J. W. "The Watchman of the Agamemnon," CJ 71 (April-May, 1976), 335-338.
Wasserman, F. M. "Agamemnon in the Iphigeneia at Aulis: A Man in an Age of Crisis," TAPA 80 (1949), 174-186.
Whallon, W. "Why Is Artemis Angry?" AJP 82 (January, 1961), 78-88.
Young, D. C. C. "Gentler Medicines in the Agamemnon," CQ (New Series) 14 (1964), 1-23.

Choephoroe, or Libation-Bearers

Garvie, A. F. "The Opening of the Choephori," BICS 17 (1970), 79-91.
Hansen, P. A. "Robe Episode of the Choephori," CQ 28 (1978), 239-240.
Kenna, J. E. G. "The Return of Orestes," JHS 81 (1961), 99-104.
Lebeck, A. "First Stasimon of Aeschylus' Choephori: Myth and Mirror Image," CP 62 (July, 1967), 182-185.
Maxwell-Stuart, P. G. "The Appearance of Aeschylus' Erinyes," G & R 20 (April, 1973), 81-84.
Young, D. C. C. "Readings in Aeschylus' Choephori and Eumenides," GRBS 12 (Autumn, 1971), 303-330.

Danaid Tetralogy

Diamantopoulos, A. "The Danaid Tetralogy of Aeschylus," J Hel S 77, pt. 2 (1957), 220-229.
Mackinnon, J. K. "Reason for the Danaids' Flight," CQ 28 (1978), 74-82.
Sutton, D. F. "Aeschylus' Amymone," GRBS 15 (Summer, 1974), 193-202.
Winnington-Ingram, R. P. "The Danaid Trilogy of Aeschylus," J Hel S 81 (1961), 141-152.
Wolff, E. A. Aeschylus' Danaid Tetralogy, A Study. Ann Arbor: University Microfilms, 1957.

Eumenides

Bodkin, M. Quest for Salvation in an Ancient and Modern Play. New York: Oxford University Press, 1941.
Dover, K. J. "The Political Aspect of Aeschylus' Eumenides," J Hel S 77, pt. 2 (1957), 230-237.
Herington, C. J. "Athena in Athenian Literature and Cult," G & R 10 (1963) (Supplement), 61-73.
Maxwell-Stuart, P. G. "The Appearance of Aeschylus' Erinyes," G & R 20 (April, 1973), 81-84.
Moritz, H. E. "Hesiodic 'Personality' and Echoes of Hesiod in Aeschylus' Eumenides," CB 54 (1977-78), 52-56.
Young, D. C. C. "Readings in Aeschylus' Choephori and Eumenides," GRBS 12 (Autumn, 1971), 303-330.

Oresteia (trilogy of Agamemnon, Choephori, and Eumenides)

Amerasinghe, C. W. "A Note of Form and Meaning in the Oresteia," G & R 11 (October, 1964), 179-184.
Cole, J. R. "The Oresteia and Cimon," HSCP 81 (1977), 99-111.
Conacher, D. J. "Interaction Between Chorus and Characters in the Oresteia," AJP 95 (Winter, 1974), 323-343.
Cummingham, M. P. "Didactic Purpose in the Oresteia," CP 45 (July, 1950), 183-185.
Fleming, T. J. "The Musical Nomos in Aeschylus' Oresteia," CJ 72 (February-March, 1977), 222-233.
Fontenrose, J. "Gods and Men in the Oresteia," TAPA 102 (1971), 71-10⁰
Gagarin, M. "The Vote of Athena," AJP 96 (Summer, 1975), 121-127.
Gantz, T. N. "Fires of the Oresteia," J Hel S 97 (1977), 28-38.
Gassner, J. "Oresteia: Dramatic Form and Vision," in his Dramatic Soundings.... New York: Crown, 1968, pp. 3-20.
Hammond, N. G. L. "Personal Freedom and Its Limitations in the Oresteia," J Hel S 85 (1965), 42-55.
Higgins, W. E. "Double-Dealing Ares in the Oresteia," CP 73 (January, 1978), 24-35.

18 : Greek and Roman Authors

Knox, B. M. W. "Aeschylus and the Third Actor," AJP 93 (1972), 104-124.
Kuhns, R. The House, the City, and the Judge: The Growth of Moral Awareness in the Oresteia. Indianapolis: Bobbs-Merrill, 1962.
Lebeck, A. The Oresteia: A Study in Language and Structure. Washington, D. C.: Center for Hellenic Studies, 1971.
Oates, W. J., J. Barzun, and M. Van Doren. "Aeschylus: The Oresteia," in M. Van Doren, ed., New Invitation to Learning. New York: Random House, 1942, pp. 16-29.
Pugsley, J. W. "Fate Motive and Its Echoes in the Oresteia," TAPA 60 (1929), 38-47.
Rexroth, K. "Aeschylus: The Oresteia," in his Classics Revisited. Chicago: Quadrangle, 1968, pp. 46-50.
Rousseau, G. S. "Dream and Vision in Aeschylus' Oresteia," Arion 2 (Autumn, 1963), 101-136.
Scott, W. C. "Wind Imagery in the Oresteia," TAPA 97 (1966), 459-472.
Sider, D. "Stagecraft in the Oresteia," AJP 99 (Spring, 1978), 12-27.
Thomson, G. "Mystical Allusions in the Oresteia," J Hel S 53 (1933), 228-230.
──────. "Mystical Allusions in the Oresteia," J Hel S 55 (1935), 20-34.
Tierney, M. "The Mysteries and the Oresteia," J Hel S 57 (1937), 11-21.
Vellacott, P. "Has Good Prevailed? A Further Study of the Oresteia," HSCP 81 (1977), 113-122.
Zeitlin, F. I. "The Motif of the Corrupted Sacrifice in Aeschylus' Oresteia," TAPA 96 (1965), 463-508.
──────. "Postscript to Sacrificial Imagery in the Oresteia," TAPA 97 (1966), 645-653.

Persians, or Persae

Anderson, M. "The Imagery of the Persians," G & R 19 (October, 1972), 166-174.
Bernhardt, W. W. "Note on the Structure and Rhetoric in Aeschylus' Persae," EIC 16 (April, 1966), 207-211.
Broadhead, H. D. Persae of Aeschylus. London: Cambridge University Press, 1960.
Clifton, G. "The Mood of the Persai of Aeschylus," G & R 10 (October, 1963), 111-116.
Diggle, J. "Notes on the Agamemnon and Persae of Aeschylus," CR (New Series) 18 (March, 1968), 1-4.
Harmon, A. M. "The Scene of the Persians of Aeschylus," TAPA 63 (1932), 7-19.
Ireland, S. "Dramatic Structure in the Persae, and Prometheus of Aeschylus," G & R 20 (October, 1973), 162-168.
Winnington-Ingram, R. P. "Zeus in the Persae," J Hel S 93 (1973), 210-219.

Promethean Trilogy

Ballard, E. G. "The Unbinding of Prometheus," CJ 50 (1955), 217-220.
Conacher, D. J. "Prometheus as Founder of the Arts," GRBS 18 (Autumn, 1977), 189-206.
Donovan, B. E. "Prometheus Bound 114-117 Reconsidered," HSCP 77 (1973), 125-129.
Ewans, M. "Prometheus Bound," Ramus 6 (1977), 1-14.
Farnell, L. R. "The Paradox of the Prometheus Vinctus," J Hel S 53 (1933), 40-50.
Fitton-Brown, A. D. "Prometheia," J Hel S 79 (1959), 52-61.
Golden, L. In Praise of Prometheus. Chapel Hill: University of North Carolina Press, 1966.
Griffith, M. The Authenticity of "Prometheus Bound." Cambridge: Cambridge University Press, 1977.
Herington, C. J. The Author of the Prometheus Bound. Austin: University of Texas Press, 1970.
_____. "Introduction to Prometheus Bound," Arion (New Series) 1 (1973-74), 640-667.
_____. The Older Scholia on the Prometheus Bound. Leiden: Brill, 1972.
_____. "A Study in the Prometheia: Part I: The Elements in the Trilogy," Phoenix 17 (1963), 180-199.
_____. "A Study in the Prometheia: Part II: Birds and Prometheia," Phoenix 17 (1963), 236-243.
Inoue, E. "Prometheus as Teacher and the Chorus' Descent, P. V. 278 ff.," CQ (New Series) 27 (1977), 256-260.
Ireland, S. "Dramatic Structure in the Persae and Prometheus of Aeschylus," G & R 20 (October, 1973), 162-168.
_____. "Noun Participle in Aeschylus," CR (New Series) 24 (March, 1974), 2-3.
Konstan, D. "Ocean Episode in the Prometheus Bound," HR 17 (August, 1977), 61-72.
Podlecki, A. J. "The Spectacle of Prometheus," CF 27 (1973), 267-287.
Robertson, D. S. "Prometheus and Chiron," J Hel S 71 (1951), 150-155.
Taplin, O. "The Title of the Prometheus Desmotes," J Hel S 95 (1975), 184-186.
Tracy, S. V. "Prometheus Bound 114-117," HSCP 75 (1971), 59-62.
Vandvik, E. Prometheus of Hesiod and Aeschylus. Oslo: Dybwad, 1943.
Yu, A. C. "New Gods and Old: Tragic Theology in the Prometheus Bound," JAAR 39 (1971), 19-42.

Seven Against Thebes, or Septem

Brown, A. L. "The End of the Seven Against Thebes," CQ (New Series) 26 (1976), 206-219.
_____. "Eteocles and the Chorus in the Seven Against Thebes," Phoenix 31 (Winter, 1977), 300-318.

Burnett, A. P. "Curse and Dream in Aeschylus' Septem," GRBS 14 (Winter, 1973), 343-368.
Caldwell, R. S. "The Misogyny of Eteocles," Areth 6 (Fall, 1973), 197-231.
Cameron, H. D. "The Debt to Earth in the Seven Against Thebes," TAPA 95 (1964), 1-8.
──────. Studies on the Seven Against Thebes of Aeschylus. The Hague: Mouton, 1971.
Dawe, R. D. "The End of Seven Against Thebes," CQ (New Series) 17 (1967), 16-28.
Lloyd-Jones, H. "The End of the Seven Against Thebes," CQ (New Series) 9 (1959), 80-115.
Poldecki, A. J. "The Character of Eteocles in Aeschylus' Septem," TAPA 95 (1964), 283-299.
Rosenmeyer, T. "Seven Against Thebes: The Tragedy of War," Arion 1 (Spring, 1962), 48-78.
Solmsen, F. "The Erinyes in Aeschylus' Septem," TAPA 68 (1937), 197-220.
Winnington-Ingram, R. P. "Septem Contra Thebas," YCS 25 (1977), 1-45.

Suppliants, or Supplices

Caldwell, R. S. "The Psychology of Aeschylus' Supplices," Areth 7 (Spring, 1974), 45-70.
Edinger, H. G. Aeschylus' Suppliants 673," CP 67 (January, 1972), 46.
Garvie, A. F. Aeschylus' Supplices; Play and Trilogy. London: Cambridge University Press, 1969.
Lembke, J. "Aeschylus' Suppliants: Design in a Beholder's Eye," Arion (New Series) 1 (1973-1974), 627-639.
McCall, M. "The Secondary Choruses in Aeschylus' Supplices," CSCA 9 (1976), 117-131.
Murray, R. D. Motif of Io in Aeschylus' Suppliants. Princeton, N.J.: Princeton University Press, 1958.
Podlecki, A. J. "Politics in Aeschylus' Supplices," CF 26 (1972), 64-71.
Sommerstein, A. H. "Notes on Aeschylus' Suppliants," BICS 24 (1977), 67-84.
Spier, H. "The Motive for the Suppliants Flight," CJ 57 (April, 1962), 315-317.

AESOP

General Criticism

Baker, H. "Portrait of Aesop," SR 77 (Autumn, 1969), 557-590.
Birch, C. M. Traditions of the Life of Aesop. Ann Arbor, Mich.: University Microfilms, 1956.

Blunt, A. F. "Poussin and Aesop," JWCI 29 (1966), 436-437.
Chesterton, G. K. "Aesop," in his G. K. C. as M. C.; Being a Collection of Thirty-seven Introductions. Agincourt: Methuen, 1929, pp. 83-89.
Daube, D. "Counting," Mnemosyne 30 (February, 1977), 176-178.
Downs, R. B. "Famed Fabulist; Aesop," in his Famous Books, Ancient and Medieval. New York: Barnes and Noble, 1964, pp. 31-35.
Leonard, W. E. Aesop and Hyssop. LaSalle, Ill.: Open Court, 1912.
Perry, B. E. Aesopica. Urbana: University of Illinois Press, 1952.
_____. "Demetrius of Phalerum and the Aesopic Fables," TAPA 93 (1962), 287-346.
_____. "The Text Tradition of the Greek Life of Aesop," TAPA 64 (1933), 198-244.
Waddell, W. G. "A Plea for Aesop in the Greek Classroom," CJ 32 (December, 1936), 162-170.

Individual Works

Fables

Chesterton, G. K. "Aesop's Fables," in his The Spice of Life, and Other Essays. Chester Springs, Pa.: Dufour, 1966, pp. 61-65.
Clement, P. A. "Moralia 614 E: The Problem of the Lacuna at the Beginning of Plutarch's Version of Aesop's Fable of the Fox and the Crane," AJP 66 (April, 1945), 192-196.
Doberstein, J. W. "Luther and the Fables of Aesop," L Ch Q 13 (January, 1940), 69-74.
Keller, J. E., and J. H. Johnson. "Motif-index Classification of Fables and Tales of Ysopete Ystoriado," SFQ 18 (June, 1954), 85-117.
Kovacs, R. C. D. (Stafford) The Aesopic Fable in Ancient Rhetorical Theory and Practice. Urbana: University of Illinois Press, 1950.
Kubler, G. The Shape of Time. New Haven, Conn.: Yale University Press, 1962.
Megas, G. A. "Some Oral Greek Parallels to Aesop's Fables," in W. D. Hand and G. O. Arit, eds., Humaniora. Locust Valley, N. Y.: Augustin, 1960, pp. 195-207.

ANACREON

General Criticism

Davison, J. A. "Anacreon, Fr. 5 Diehl," TAPA 90 (1959), 40-47.
Thoreau, H. D. "Anacreon," in The Dial: A Magazine for Literature, Philosophy and Religion. New York: Russell and Russell, Vol. 3, 1961, pp. 483-485.

Wigodsky, M. "Anacreon and the Girl from Lesbos," CP 57 (April, 1962), 109.

Individual Works

Verse

Fucilla, J. G. "Cupid and the Bee: Addenda," PMLA 58 (June, 1943), 575-579.
Hutton, J. "Cupid and the Bee," PMLA 56 (December, 1941), 1036-1058.
Trypanis, C. A. "The Epigrams of Anacreon on Hermae," CQ (New Series) 1 (1951), 31-34.

APOLLONIUS RHODIUS

General Criticism

Anderson, W. D. "Notes on the Simile in Homer and His Successors: I. Homer, Apollonius Rhodius, and Vergil," CJ 53 (November, 1957), 81-87.
Bonnard, A. "Back to Poetry: Callimachus, Apollonius," in his Greek Civilization: From Euripides to Alexandria. New York: Macmillan, 1961, pp. 209-228.
Bulloch, A. W. "Callimachus' Erysichthon, Homer and Apollonius Rhodius," AJP 98 (Summer, 1979), 97-123.
Campbell, M. "Critical Notes on Apollonius Rhodius," CQ (New Series) 19 (November, 1969), 269-284.
Carspecken, J. F. "Apollonius Rhodius and the Homeric Epic," HSCP 60 (1955), 294-296.
———. "Apollonius Rhodius and the Homeric Epic," YCS 13 (1957), 33-143.
Edwards, W. M. "The Callimachus Prologue and Apollonius Rhodius," CQ 24 (April, 1930), 109-112.
Gow, A. S. F. "Apollonius Rhodius IV. 1486 ff.," CR 52 (December, 1938), 215.
Pearson, L. "Apollonius of Rhodes and the Old Geographers," AJP 59 (October, 1938), 443-459.
Phinney, E. "Hellenistic Painting and the Poetic Style of Apollonius," CJ 62 (January, 1967), 145-149.
West, M. L. "Critical Notes on Apollonius Rhodius," CR (New Series) 13 (March, 1963), 9-12.

Individual Works

Argonautica

Fraenkel, H. "Apollonius Rhodius as a Narrator in Argonautica 2. 1-140," TAPA 83 (1952), 144-155.

_____. "Problems of Text and Interpretation in Apollonius' Argonautica," AJP 71 (April, 1950), 113-133.
Garson, R. W. "Homeric Echoes in Apollonius Rhodius' Argonautica," CP 67 (January, 1972), 1-9.
George, E. V. "Poet and Characters in Apollonius Rhodius' Lemnian Episode," Hermes 100 (1972), 47-63.
Levin, D. N. Apollonius' Argonautica Re-examined, I: The Neglected First and Second Books. Leiden: Brill, 1971.
_____. "Apollonius' Heracles," CJ 67 (October-November, 1971), 22-28.
Phinney, E. "Narrative Unity in the Argonautica, the Medea-Jason Romance," TAPA 98 (1967), 327-342.

Verse

Duckworth, G. E. Foreshadowing and Suspense in the Epics of Homer, Apollonius and Vergil. Princeton, N. J.: Princeton University Press, 1933.
Stanford, W. B. "Two Homeric Echoes," CP 33 (July, 1938), 306-307.

APULEIUS

General Criticism

Berley, A. "Apuleius: Roman Provincial Life," HT 18 (September, 1968), 629-636.
Dietrich, B. C. "The Golden Art of Apuleius," G & R 13 (October, 1966), 189-206.
Ebel, H. "Apuleius and the Present Time," Areth 3 (Fall, 1970), 155-176.
Ferguson, J. "Apuleius," G & R 8 (March, 1961), 61-74.
Golann, C. P. The Life of Apuleius and His Connection with Magic. Ann Arbor, Mich.: University Microfilms, 1952.
Hadas, M. "Age of Hadrian," in his History of Latin Literature. New York: Columbia University Press, 1952, pp. 334-352.
Haight, E. H. "Apuleius and Boccaccio," in his More Essays on Greek Romances. New York: Longmans, Green, 1945, pp. 113-141.
_____. Apuleius and His Influence. New York: Cooper Square, 1963.
Hawes, A. B. "Light Reading from the Roman Empire (Apuleius)," in his Citizens of Long Ago; Essays on Life and Letters in the Roman Empire. Freeport, N. Y.: Books for Libraries, 1967, pp. 79-90.
Mackay, P. A. "Klephtika; The Tradition of the Tales of Banditry in Apuleius," G & R 10 (October, 1963), 147-152.
Pack, R. A. "Adventures of a Dilettante in a Provincial Family," CJ 35 (November, 1939), 67-80.

Rascoe, B. "Apuleius," in his Prometheans: Ancient and Modern. New York: Putnam's, 1933, pp. 175-190.
Schlam, C. C. "The Scholarship on Apuleius Since 1938," CW 64 (May, 1971), 285-309.
Scobie, A. Aspects of the Ancient Romance and Its Heritage; Essays on Apuleius, Petronius, and the Greek Romances. Meisenheim a. Glan: Hain, 1969.
Stephenson, W. E. "The Comedy of Evil in Apuleius," Arion 3 (Autumn, 1964), 87-93.

Individual Works

Amor and Psyche

Katz, P. B. "The Myth of Psyche: A Definition of the Nature of the Feminine?," Areth 9 (Spring, 1976), 111-118.
Neumann, E. Amor and Psyche; The Psychic Development of the Feminine; A Commentary on the Tale by Apuleius. New York: Pantheon, 1956.
Wright, J. R. G. "Folk Tale and Literary Technique in Cupid and Psyche," CQ 21 (1971), 273-284.

Apologia

Mortley, R. "Apuleius and Platonic Theology," AJP 93 (October, 1972), 584-590.
Winter, T. N. "The Publication of Apuleius' Apology," TAPA 100 (1969), 607-612.

Metamorphoses, or The Golden Ass

Cherpack, C. "Ideas and Prose Fiction in Antiquity," CLS 11 (September, 1974), 185-203.
Drake, G. C. "Candidus: A Unifying Theme in Apuleius' Metamorphoses," CJ 64 (December, 1968), 102-109.
_____. "Ghost Story in The Golden Ass by Apuleius," PLL 13 (Winter, 1977), 3-15.
Englert, J., and T. Long. "Functions of Hair in Apuleius' Metamorphoses," CJ 68 (February-March, 1972-1973), 236-239.
Ginsburg, G. N. "Rhetoric and Representation in the Metamorphoses of Apuleius," Areth 10 (Spring, 1977), 49-61.
Haight, E. H. "Apuleius' Art of Story Telling," in his Essays on Ancient Fiction. New York: Longmans, Green, 1936, pp. 151-194.
_____. "Comparison of the Greek Romance and Apuleius' Metamorphoses," in his Essays on the Greek Romances. New York: Longmans, Green, 1943, pp. 186-201.
_____. "Satire and the Latin Novel," in his Essays on Ancient Fiction. New York: Longmans, Green, 1936, pp. 86-120.

Kenny, B. "The Reader's Role in The Golden Ass," Areth 7 (Fall, 1974), 187-209.
Mackay, L. A. "The Sin of the Golden Ass," Arion 4 (Autumn, 1965), 474-480.
Mason, H. J. "Lucius at Corinth," Phoenix 25 (Summer, 1971), 160-165.
Mayrhofer, C. M. "On Two Stories in Apuleius," Antichthon 9 (1975), 68-80.
Nethercut, W. R. "Apuleius' Literary Art: Resonance and Depth in the Metamorphoses," CJ 64 (December, 1968), 110-119.
_____. "Apuleius' Metamorphoses: The Journey," Agon 3 (1969).
Penwill, J. L. "Slavish Pleasures and Profitless Curiosity: Fall and Redemption in Apuleius' Metamorphoses," Ramus 4 (1975), 49-82.
Rexroth, K. "Apuleius: The Golden Ass," in his Classics Revisited. Chicago: Quadrangle, 1968, pp. 116-120.
Sandy, G. N. "Foreshadowing and Suspense in Apuleius' Metamorphoses," CJ 68 (February-March, 1972-1973), 232-235.
_____. "Serviles Voluptates in Apuleius' Metamorphoses," Phoenix 28 (Summer, 1974), 234-244.
Schlam, C. C. "The Curiosity of the Golden Ass," CJ 64 (December, 1968), 120-125.
_____. "Platonica in the Metamorphoses of Apuleius," TAPA 101 (1970), 477-487.
Scobie, A. "Ancient Greek Drakos-Tale in Apuleius' Metamorphoses VIII, 19-21," JAF 90 (July, 1977), 339-343.
Smith, W. S. The Narrative Voice in Apuleius' Metamorphoses," TAPA 103 (1972), 513-534.
Summers, R. J. "Roman Justice and Apuleius' Metamorphoses," TAPA 101 (1970), 511-531.
Tatum, J. "Apuleius and Metamorphoses," AJP 93 (April, 1972), 306-313.
_____. "The Tales in Apuleius' Metamorphoses," TAPA 100 (1969), 487-527.
Todd, F. A. "Golden Ass," in his Some Ancient Novels. New York: Oxford University Press, 1940, pp. 102-140.
Walsh, P. G. The Roman Novel: The Satyricon of Petronius and the Metamorphoses of Apuleius. London: Cambridge University Press, 1970.
Wright, C. S. "No Art at All: A Note on the Prooemium of Apuleius' Metamorphoses," CP 68 (July, 1973), 217-219.

On the God of Socrates

Lewis, C. S. "Selected Materials: The Classical Period," in his The Discarded Image, an Introduction to Medieval and Renaissance Literature. London: Cambridge University Press, 1964, pp. 40-42.

Peri Hermeneias

Sullivan, M. W. Apuleian Logic: The Nature, Sources and Influence of Apuleius' Peri Hermeneias. New York: Humanities, 1967.

ARISTOPHANES

General Criticism

Atkins, J. W. H. "Beginnings: Aristophanes," in his Literary Criticism in Antiquity; A Sketch of Its Development. Toronto: Macmillan, 1934, Vol. 1, pp. 11-32.
Beare, W. "The Costume of the Actors in Aristophanic Comedy," CQ (New Series) 4 (1954), 64-75.
Bowra, C. M. "Love-duet," AJP 79 (October, 1958), 379-391.
Dearden, C. W. The Stage of Aristophanes. London: Athlone, 1976.
Dover, K. J. "Aristophanes' Speech in Plato's Symposium," J Hel S 86 (1966), 41-50.
_____. Aristophanic Comedy. Berkeley: University of California Press, 1972.
Downs, R. B. "Greek Comic Genius: Aristophanes," in his Famous Books, Ancient and Medieval. New York: Barnes and Noble, 1964, 76-81.
Ehrenberg, V. The People of Aristophanes: A Sociology of Old Attic Comedy. New York: Barnes and Noble, 1974.
Gassner, J. "Aristophanes, the Poet of Laughter," in his Masters of the Drama. New York: Dover, 1954, pp. 79-91.
Gomme, A. W. "Aristophanes and Politics," CR 52 (July, 1938), 97-109.
Grube, G. M. A. "Comedy: Aristophanes," in his The Greek and Roman Critics. Toronto: University of Toronto Press, 1965, pp. 22-32.
Hamilton, E. "Aristophanes and the Old Comedy," in his Great Age of Greek Literature. New York: Norton, 1942, pp. 126-158.
Harsh, P. W. "Aristophanes," in his Handbook of Classical Drama. Stanford, Calif.: Stanford University Press, 1944, pp. 264-312.
_____. "The Position of Parabasis in the Plays of Aristophanes," TAPA 65 (1934), 178-197.
Henderson, J. "Note on Aristophanes Acharnians 834-835," CP 68 (October, 1973), 289-290.
Hose, H. F. "Personalities in Aristophanes," G & R 9 (February, 1940), 88-95.
Jaeger, W. W. Paideia: The Ideals of Greek Culture. Oxford: B. Blackwell, 1944-47. Vol. 1, pp. 358-381.
Jernigan, C. C. Incongruity in Aristophanes. Greensboro: University of North Carolina, 1939.
Long, T. "Persuasion and the Aristophanic Agon," TAPA 103 (1972), 285-299.
_____. "Understanding Comic Action in Aristophanes," CWorld 70 (September, 1976), 1-8.
Lord, L. E. Aristophanes; His Plays and His Influence. New York: Cooper Square, 1963.

McEvilley, T. "Development in the Lyrics of Aristophanes," AJP 91 (July, 1970), 257-276.
McLeish, K. "Phusis: A Bawdy Joke in Aristophanes?," CQ (New Series) 27 (1977), 76-79.
Miller, D. L. "Salvation and the Image of Comedy: Pirandello and Aristophanes," RIL 33 (Summer, 1964), 451-464.
Miller, H. W. "Aristophanes and Medical Language," TAPA 76 (1945), 74-84.
———. "Repetition of Lines in Aristophanes," AJP 65 (January, 1944), 26-36.
Murphy, C. T. "Aristophanes and the Art of Rhetoric," HSCP 49 (1938), 69-113.
———. "Aristophanes, Athens and Attica," CJ 59 (April, 1964), 306-323.
———. "Popular Comedy in Aristophanes," AJP 93 (January, 1972), 169-189.
Murray, G. Aristophanes: A Study. New York: Oxford University Press, 1933.
Nicoll, A. "Aristophanes and the Old Comedy," in his World Drama, from Aeschylus to Anouilh. New York: Harcourt, 1953, pp. 90-106.
Perry, H. T. "First Literary Comedy: Aristophanes and Menander," in his Masters of Dramatic Comedy and Their Social Themes. Cambridge, Mass.: Harvard University Press, 1939, pp. 3-48.
Platnauer, M. "Aristophanes," AJP 67 (July, 1946), 262-265.
Reckford, K. "Desire with Hope: Aristophanes and the Comic Catharsis," Ramus 3 (January, 1974), 41-69.
Ruck, C. "Euripides Mother: Vegetables and the Phallos in Aristophanes," Arion (New Series) 2 (1975), 13-57.
Schlesinger, A. C. "Indication of Parody in Aristophanes," TAPA 67 (1936), 296-314.
Solomos, A. The Living Aristophanes. Ann Arbor: University of Michigan Press, 1974.
Somerstein, A. H. "Aristophanes and the Events of 411," J Hel S 97 (1977), 112-126.
Stewart, D. J. "Aristophanes and the Pleasures of Anarchy," AR 25 (Spring, 1965), 189-208.
———. "Definition in Pursuit of a Hero," Arion 5 (Spring, 1966), 99-119.
———. "The Poet as Bird in Aristophanes and Horace," CJ 62 (May, 1967), 357-361.
Stow, H. L. "Aristophanes' Influence upon Public Opinion," CJ (October, 1942), 83-92.
Ussher, R. G. "Old Comedy and Character: Some Comments," G & R 24 (April, 1977), 71-79.
Walcot, P. "Aristophanic and Other Audiences," G & R 18 (April, 1971), 35-50.
Whitman, C. "Aristophanes," Arion 7 (Autumn, 1968), 422-426.
Whitman, C. H. Aristophanes and the Comic Hero. Cambridge, Mass.: Harvard University Press, 1964.
Wycherley, R. E. "Aristophanes and Euripides," G & R 15 (October, 1946), 98-107.
Youman, A. E. "Aristophanes: Country Man or City Man?," CB 50 (March, 1974), 73-77.

Individual Works

Birds

Arrowsmith, W. "Aristophanes' Birds: The Fantasy Politics of Eros," Arion (New Series) 1 (1973), 119-167.
Blake, W. E. "The Aristophanic Bird Chorus--A Riddle," AJP 64 (January, 1943), 87-91.
Borthwick, E. K. "Two Notes on the Birds of Aristophanes," CR (New Series) 17 (December, 1967), 248-250.
Dale, A. M. "Hoopoe's Song (Aristophanes, Birds 227 ff), CR (New Series) 19 (December, 1969), 199-200.
Gelzer, T. "Some Aspects of Aristophanes' Dramatic Art in the Birds," BICS 23 (1976), 1-14.
Lawler, L. B. "Four Dances in the Birds of Aristophanes," TAPA 73 (1942), 58-63.
Pollard, J. R. T. "Birds of Aristophanes--A Source Book for Old Beliefs," AJP 69 (October, 1948), 353-376.
Quain, E. A. "Aristophanes: Lysistrata, Birds, Clouds," in H. C. Gardiner, Ed., Great Books: A Christian Appraisal; A Symposium on the First Year's Program of the Great Books Foundation. Old Greenwich, Conn.: Devin-Adair, 1949, pp. 19-24.
Wycherley, R. E. "Birds," CQ 31 (January, 1937), 22-31.

Clouds

Adkins, J. W. H. "Clouds, Mysteries, Socrates and Plato," Antichthon 4 (1970), 13-24.
Anselment, R. A. "Socrates and The Clouds: Shaftesbury and a Socratic Tradition," JHI 39 (April, 1978), 171-182.
Brumbaugh, R. S. "Scientific Apparatus on Stage in 423 B.C.," YCS 22 (1972), 215-221.
Haslam, M. W. "Attribution and Action in Aristophanes' Clouds 723-796," HSCP 80 (1976), 45-47.
Havelock, E. A. "The Socratic Self as It Is Parodied in Aristophanes' Clouds," YCS 22 (1972), 1-18.
Karavites, P. "Socrates in the Clouds," CB 50 (March, 1974), 65-69.
Quain, E. A. "Aristophanes: Lysistrata, Birds, Clouds," in H. C. Gardiner, ed., Great Books: A Christian Appraisal; A Symposium on the First Years's Program of the Great Books Foundation. Old Greenwich, Conn.: Devin-Adair, 1949, pp. 19-24.
Segal, C. "Aristophanes' Cloud Chorus," Areth 2 (Fall, 1969), 143-161.

Ecclesiazusae

Barry, E. Ecclesiazusae as a Political Satire. Chicago: University of Chicago Press, 1942.

Frogs

Borthwick, E. K. "Seeing Weasels: The Superstitious Background of the Empusa Scene in the Frogs," CQ (New Series), 18 (1968), 200-206.

Campbell, A. Y. "Aristophanes' Frogs," CR (New Series) 3 (December, 1953), 137-138.

Cary, A. L. M. "Appearance of Charon in the Frogs," CR 51 (May, 1937), 52-53.

Demand, N. "Identity of the Frogs," CP 65 (April, 1970), 83-87.

Denniston, J. D. "Technical Terms in the Frogs of Aristophanes," CQ 21 (July, 1927), 113-121.

Henderson, J. "The Lekythos and Frogs 1200-1248," HSCP 76 (1972), 133-144.

Higgins, W. E. "A Passage to Hades: The Frogs of Aristophanes," Ramus 6 (1977), 60-81.

Hooker, G. T. W. "The Topography of the Frogs," J Hel S 80 (1960), 112-117.

Hurst, A. "Aeschylus or Euripides," Hermes 99 (1971), 227-240.

Littlefield, D. J., ed. Twentieth Century Interpretations of the Frogs; A Collection of Critical Essays. Englewood Cliffs, N. J.: Prentice-Hall, 1968.

MacDowell, D. M. "The Frogs' Chorus," CR (New Series) 22 (March, 1972), 3-5.

Russo, C. F. "The Revision of Aristophanes' Frogs," G & R 13 (April, 1966), 1-13.

Sommerstein, A. H. "Aristophanes, Frogs 1463-1465," CQ (New Series) 24 (May, 1974), 24-27.

Wilson, A. M. "Eupolidean Precedent for the Rowing Scene in Aristophanes' Frogs?," CQ (New Series) 24 (December, 1974), 250-252.

Young, A. M. "The Frogs of Aristophanes as a Type of Play," CJ 29 (October, 1933), 23-32.

Zimbardo, R. A. "Comic Mockery of the Sacred: The Frogs and The Second Shepherds' Play," ETJ 30 (October, 1978), 398-406.

Knights

Littlefield, D. J. "Metaphor and Myth: The Unity of Aristophanes' Knights," SP 65 (January, 1968), 1-22.

Lysistrata

Elderkin, G. W. "Aphrodite and Athena in the Lysistrata of Aristophanes," CP 35 (October, 1940), 387-396.

Hulton, A. O. "The Women on the Acropolis: A Note on the Structure of the Lysistrata," G & R 19 (April, 1972), 32-36.

Quain, E. A. "Aristophanes: Lysistrata, Birds, Clouds," in H. C. Gardiner, ed. Great Books: A Christian Appraisal; A Symposium of the First Year's Program of the Great Books Foundation. Old Greenwich, Conn.: Devin-Adair, 1949, pp. 10-24.

Vaio, J. "The Manipulation of Theme and Action in Aristophanes' Lysistrata," GRBS 14 (Winter, 1973), 369-380.

Peace

Borthwick, E. K. "Beetle, Bell, Goldfinch, and Weasel in Aristophanes' Peace," CR (New Series) 18 (June, 1968), 134-139.

Thesmophoriazusae

Miller, H. W. "Euripides Telephus and the Thesmophoriazusae of Aristophanes," CP 43 (July, 1948), 174-183.
_____. "On the Parabasis of the Thesmophoriazusae," CP 42 (July, 1947), 180-181.
_____. "Some Tragic Influences in the Thesmophoriazusae of Aristophanes," TAPA 77 (1946), 171-182.
Sommerstein, A. H. "Aristophanes and the Events of 411," JHS 97 (1977), 112-126.

Wasps

Borthwick, E. K. "The Dances of Philocleon and the Sons of Carcinus in Aristophanes' Wasps," CQ (New Series) 18 (1968), 44-51.
Dale, A. M. "An Interpretation of AR Vesp. 130-210 and Its Consequences for the Stage of Aristophanes," J Hel S 77, pt. 2, (1957), 205-211.
Platnauer, M. "Three Notes on Aristophanes' Wasps," CR 63 (May, 1949), 6-7.
Post, L. A. "Catana the Cheese-Grater in Aristophanes' Wasps," AJP 53 (July, 1932), 265.
Reckford, K. J. "Catharsis and Dream--Interpretation in Aristophanes' Wasps," TAPA 107 (1977), 283-312.
Ruck, C. "Euripides' Mother: Vegetables and the Phallos in Aristophanes," Arion (New Series) 2 (1975), 13-57.
Sommerstein, A. H. "Notes on Aristophanes' Wasps," CQ (New Series) 27 (1977), 261-277.
Vaio, J. "Aristophanes' Wasps: The Relevance of the Final Scenes," GRBS 12 (Autumn, 1971), 335-351.

ARISTOTLE

General Criticism

Adkins, J. W. H. "Friendship and Self-sufficiency in Homer and Aristotle," CQ 13 (May, 1963), 101-104.
Adler, M. J. Aristotle for Everybody: Difficult Thought Made Easy. New York: Macmillan, 1978.

Agonito, R. "Paradox of Pleasure and Pain: A Study of the Concept of Pain in Aristotle," Person 57 (Spring, 1976), 105-112.
Allan, D. J. The Philosophy of Aristotle, 2nd edition. London: Oxford University Press, 1970.
Alpern, H. "Aristotle," in his March of Philosophy. New York: Dial, 1933, pp. 43-63.
Ando, T. Aristotle's Theory of Practical Cognition. The Hague: Nijhoff, 1971.
Annas, J. "Plato and Aristotle on Friendship and Altruism," Mind 86 (October, 1977), 532-554.
Bambrough, R., ed. New Essays on Plato and Aristotle. New York: Humanities, 1965.
Barnes, J., M. Schofield, and R. Sorabji, eds. Articles on Aristotle. London: Duckworth, 1975-, 4 vols.
Bertman, M. A. "The Function of the Rational Principle in Aristotle," Thomist 37 (October, 1973), 686-700.
Bhandari, D. R., and R. R. Sethi. Studies in Plato and Aristotle. Delhi: Chand, 1950.
Boas, G. Some Assumptions of Aristotle. Philadelphia: American Philosophical Society, 1959.
Bos, A. Providentia Divina: The Theme of Divine Pronoia in Plato and Aristotle. Assen: Van Gorcum, 1976.
Bremer, J. Hamartia: Tragic Error in the Poetics of Aristotle and in Greek Tragedy. Amsterdam: Hakkert, 1969.
Brentano, F. C. Aristotle and His World View. Berkeley: University of California Press, 1978.
Brink, K. O. "Callimachus and Aristotle," CQ 40 (January, 1946), 11-26.
Bywater, I. Contributions to the Textual Criticism of Aristotle's Nicomachean Ethics. New York: Arno, 1973.
Catlin, G. E. G. "Aristotle," in his Story of the Political Philosophers. New York: McGraw, 1939, pp. 72-104.
Charlesworth, M. J. Aristotle on Art and Nature. Auckland: Auckland University College Press, 1957.
Chen, C. H. Sophia: The Science Aristotle Sought. New York: Olms, 1976.
Chroust, A. H. Aristotle: New Light on His Life and on Some of His Lost Works. Notre Dame, Ind.: University of Notre Dame, 1973, Vol. 2.
_____. "Athens Bestows the Decree of Proxenia on Aristotle," Hermes 101 (1973), 187-194.
Clark, S. R. Aristotle's Man: Speculations upon Aristotelian Anthropology. Oxford: Clarendon, 1975.
Cooper, J. M. "Aristotle on the Forms of Friendship," RM 30 (June, 1977), 619-648.
_____. "Friendship and the Good in Aristotle," PR 86 (July, 1977), 290-315.
_____. Reason and Human Good in Aristotle. Cambridge, Mass.: Harvard University Press, 1975.
Corish, D. "Aristotle on Temporal Order: Now, Before, and After," I 69 (March, 1978), 68-74.
Davidson, T. Aristotle and Ancient Educational Ideals. New York: Franklin, 1969.

32 : Greek and Roman Authors

Engmann, J. "Aristotelian Universals," CP 73 (January, 1978), 17-23.
_____. "Imagination and Truth in Aristotle," JHP 14 (July, 1976), 259-265.
Evans, J. D. G. Aristotle's Concept of Dialectic. New York: Cambridge University Press, 1977.
_____. "The Codification of False Refutations in Aristotle's De Sophisticis Elenchis," PCPS (New Series) 21 (1975), 42-51.
Finley, M. I. "Aristotle and Economic Analysis," P & P 47 (May, 1970), 3-25.
Fortenbaugh, W. W. "Aristotle: Animals, Emotion, and Moral Virtue," Areth 4 (Fall, 1971), 137-165.
_____. Aristotle on Emotion: A Contribution to Philosophical Psychology, Rhetoric, Poetics, Politics, and Ethics. New York: Barnes and Noble, 1975.
_____. "On the Antecedents of Aristotle's Bipartite Psychology," GRBS 11 (Autumn, 1970), 233-250.
_____. "Recent Scholarship on the Psychology of Aristotle," CW 60 (April, 1967), 316-327.
Frank, E. "Fundamental Opposition of Plato and Aristotle," AJP 61 (January, 1940), 34-53.
_____. "Fundamental Opposition of Plato and Aristotle," AJP 61 (April, 1940), 166-185.
Golden, L. "Aristotle, Frye, and the Theory of Tragedy," CL 27 (Winter, 1975), 47-58.
_____. "Epic, Tragedy, and Catharsis," CP 71 (January, 1976), 77-85.
_____. "Katharsis as Clarification: An Objection Answered," CQ (New Series) 23 (May, 1973), 45-46.
_____. "The Purgation Theory of Catharsis," JAAC 31 (Summer, 1973), 473-479.
Gottschalk, H. B. "Notes on the Wills of the Peripatetic Scholarchs," Hermes 100 (1972), 314-342.
Gould, T. "Aristotle and the Irrational," Arion 2 (Summer, 1963), 55-74.
_____. "Plato and Aristotle," Arion 7 (Autumn, 1968), 426-434.
Grayeff, P. Aristotle and His School. New York: Barnes and Noble, 1974.
Grene, M. Portrait of Aristotle. Chicago: University of Chicago Press, 1963.
Grote, G. Aristotle. New York: Arno, 1973.
Hampshire, S. Two Theories of Morality. Oxford: Oxford University Press, 1977.
Hintikka, K. J. J. Time and Necessity: Studies in Aristotle's Theory of Modality. Oxford: Clarendon, 1973.
Huksar, V. "Aristotle and the Punishment of Psychopaths," Philos 39 (October, 1964), 323-340.
Huxley, G. L. "Aristotle as Antiquary," GRBS 14 (Autumn, 1973), 271-286.
_____. "On Aristotle's Historical Methods," GRBS 13 (Summer, 1972), 157-170.
_____. "Proverbs and Antiquarian Lore in Aristotle's Historical Thought," PCA 70 (April, 1973), 37.

Irwin, T. H. "Aristotle on Reason, Desire, and Virtue," JP 72 (October, 1975), 567-580.
Jaeger, W. W. Aristotle. Oxford: Clarendon, 1948.
Jancar, B. W. The Philosophy of Aristotle. New York: Simon and Schuster, 1966.
Keaney, J. J. "Two Notes on the Tradition of Aristotle's Writings," AJP 84 (January, 1963), 52-63.
King, H. R. "Aristotle and the Paradoxes of Zeno," JP 46 (October 13, 1949), 657-670.
Kirwan, C. "Logic and the Good in Aristotle," Ph Q 17 (April, 1967), 97-114.
Larkin, M. T. Language in the Philosophy of Aristotle. The Hague: Mouton, 1971.
Leclerc, I. "Platonism, Aristotelianism, and Modern Science," IPQ 16 (June, 1976), 135-149.
Leszl, W. Logic and Metaphysics in Aristotle. Padua: Antenore, 1970.
Lloyd, G. E. R. Aristotle: The Growth and Structure of His Thought. Cambridge: Cambridge University Press, 1968.
Lycos, K. "Aristotle and Plato on 'Appearing,'" Mind 73 (October, 1964), 496-514.
Lynch, J. P. Aristotle's School: A Study of a Greek Educational Institution. Berkeley: University of California Press, 1972.
McKeon, R. Introduction to Aristotle; With a General Introduction and Introductions to the Particular Works. New York: Modern Library, 1947.
Maniou-Vakali, M. "Some Aristotelian Views on Learning and Memory," JHBS 10 (January, 1974), 47-55.
Mathewson, R. "Aristotle and Anaxagoras: An Examination of F. M. Cornford's Interpretation," CQ 8 (1958), 67-81.
Merlan, P. Studies in Epicurus and Aristotle. Wiesbaden: Harrassowitz, 1960.
Moravcsik, J. M. E., ed. Aristotle: A Collection of Critical Essays. New York: Anchor, 1969.
Morrall, J. B. Aristotle. Boston: Allen and Unwin, 1977.
Mulgan, R. G. "Aristotle's Doctrine That Man Is a Political Animal," Hermes 102 (1974), 438-445.
Mure, G. R. G. Aristotle. Westport, Conn.: Greenwood, 1975.
Oehler, K. "Aristotle on Self-knowledge," PAPS 118 (December, 1974), 493-506.
Patch, H. R. "Last Line of the Commedia," Speculum 14 (January, 1939), 56-65.
Pavlovskis, Z. "Aristotle, Horace, and the Ironic Man," CP 63 (January, 1968), 22-41.
Phillips, E. D. The Greek Endeavor in Biological Science: An Inaugural Lecture Delivered Before The Queen's University of Belfast on 20 November, 1974. Belfast: Queen's University, 1975.
Plochmann, G. K. "Nature and Living Thing in Aristotle's Biology," JHI 14 (April, 1953), 167-190.
Post, L. A. "Aristotle and Menander," TAPA 69 (1938), 1-42.
Preus, A. Science and Philosophy in Aristotle's Biological Works. New York: Olms, 1975.

Randall, J. H. Aristotle. New York: Columbia University Press, 1960.
Reinhold, M. A Simplified Approach to Plato and Aristotle. Woodbury, N. Y.: Barron, 1964.
Rist, J. M. "One of Plotinus and the God of Aristotle," RM 27 (September, 1973), 75-87.
_____. "Some Aspects of Aristotelian Teleology," TAPA 96 (1965), 337-350.
Ross, W. D. Aristotle. New York: Barnes and Noble, 1966.
Rowe, C. The Eudemian and Nicomachean Ethics: A Study in the Development of Aristotle's Thought. Cambridge, Eng.: Cambridge Philological Society, 1971.
Schmitt, C. B. A Critical Survey and Bibliography of Studies on Renaissance Aristotelianism. Padua: Antenore, 1971.
Sellers, W. "Substance and Form in Aristotle," JP 54 (October 24, 1957), 688-699.
Shute, R. On the History of the Process by Which the Aristotelian Writings Arrived at Their Present Form. New York: Arno, 1976.
Sinnige, T. G. "Cosmic Religion in Aristotle," GRBS 14 (Spring, 1973), 15-34.
Sokolowski, R. "Scientific and Hermeneutic Questions in Aristotle," P & R 4 (Fall, 1971), 242-261.
Solmsen, F. Aristotle's System of the Physical World. New York: Johnson Reprint, 1970.
_____. "Platonic Values in Aristotle's Science," JHI 39 (January, 1978), 3-23.
Sorabji, R. "Aristotle on Demarcating the Five Senses," Ph R 80 (January, 1971), 55-79.
_____. "Aristotle, Mathematics, and Colour," CQ (New Series) 22 (November, 1972), 293-308.
Spangler, G. A. "Aristotle on Saying Something," Apeiron 10 (November, 1976), 38-46.
Sprague, R. K. "Aristotle and the Metaphysics of Sleep," RM 31 (December, 1977), 230-241.
Starr, D. E. Entity and Existence: An Ontological Investigation of Aristotle and Heidegger. New York: Franklin, 1975.
Stemmer, N. "Towards an Aristotelian Theory of Scientific Explanation," PC 40 (September, 1973), 393-396.
Stevenson, J. G. "Aristotle as Historian of Philosophy," J Hel S 94 (1974), 138-143.
_____. "Being qua Being," Apeiron 9 (February, 1975), 42-50.
Stewart, D. "Aristotle's Doctrine of the Unmoved Mover," Thomist 37 (July, 1973), 522-547.
Stigen, A. The Structure of Aristotle's Thought: An Introduction to the Study of Aristotle's Writings. Oslo: Universitetsforlaget, 1966.
Stinton, T. C. W. "Hamartia in Aristotle and Greek Tragedy," CQ 25 (December, 1975), 221-254.
Stroh, G. W. Plato and Aristotle. San Francisco: Boyd and Fraser, 1970.
Thayer, H. S. "Aristotle on Nature: A Study in the Relativity of Concepts and Procedures of Analysis, RM 28 (June, 1975), 725-744.

Thompson, W. N. Aristotle's Deduction and Induction: Introductory Analysis and Synthesis. Amsterdam: Rodopi, 1975.
Tracy, T. J. Physiological Theory and the Doctrine of the Mean in Plato and Aristotle. Chicago: Loyola University Press, 1969.
Veatch, H. B. Aristotle: A Contemporary Appreciation. Bloomington: Indiana University Press, 1974.
Wallace, E. Outlines of the Philosophy of Aristotle. New York: Arno, 1976.
Warry, J. G. Greek Aesthetic Theory; A Study of Callistic and Aesthetic Concepts in the Works of Plato and Aristotle. New York: Barnes and Noble, 1962.
Whitehead, D. "Aristotle the Metic," PCPS (New Series) 21 (1975), 94-99.
Wimsatt, W. K., and C. Brooks. "Verbal Medium: Plato and Aristotle," in their Literary Criticism. New York: Knopf, 1957, pp. 57-76.

Individual Works

Athenian Constitution, or Athenaion Politeia

Andrews, A. "Androtion and the Four Hundred," PCPS (New Series) 22 (1976), 14-25.
Chambers, M. "Aristotle on Solon's Reform of Coinage and Weights," CSCA 6 (1973), 1-16.
———. "Aristotle's 'Forms of Democracy,'" TAPA 92 (1961), 20-36.
———. "More Notes on the Text of the Ath. Pol.," TAPA 102 (1971), 41-47.
Day, J. "Accidents in Aristotle, Ath. Pol. 26.1," TAPA 92 (1961), 52-61.
———. and M. Chambers. Aristotle's History of Athenian Democracy. Berkeley: University of California Press, 1962.
Dorjahn, A. P. "On Aristotle, Ath. Pol., XXXVIII, 3," PQ 23 (October, 1944), 289-296.
Fornara, C. W. "The Diapsephismos of Ath. Pol. 13.5," CP 65 (October, 1970), 243-246.
McCoy, W. J. "Aristotle's Athenaion Politeia and the Establishment of the Thirty Tyrants," YCS 24 (1975), 131-145.
Ruebel, J. R. "The Tyrannies of Persistratos," GRBS 14 (Summer, 1973), 125-136.
Scott, R. D. "Aristotle Ath. Pol. 26.1 on Cimon," CP 69 (April, 1974), 117-118.
Vlastos, G. "Constitution of the Five Thousand [in the Athenaion Politeia]," AJP 73 (April, 1952), 189-198.
Von Fritz, K. "The Composition of Aristotle's Constitution of Athens and the So-called Dracontian Constitution," CP 49 (April, 1954), 73-93.

Metaphysics

Amaral, P., and J. Allison. "Aristotle Metaphysics 13.10. 1086b32-37,"

CP 70 (April, 1975), 121-123.
Annas, J. "Aristotle, Number and Time," Ph Q 25 (April, 1975), 97-113.
Calvert, B. "Aristotle and the Megarians on the Potentiality-Actuality Conflict," Apeiron 10 (January, 1976), 34-41.
Chroust, A. H. "Origin of 'Metaphysics,'" RM 14 (June, 1961), 601-616.
Doig, J. C. Aquinas on Metaphysics. The Hague: Nijhoff, 1972.
Evans, J. D. G. "Aristotle on Relativism," Ph Q 24 (July, 1974), 193-203.
Grayeff, P. Aristotle and His School. London: Duckworth, 1974.
Irwin, T. H. "Aristotle's Discovery of Metaphysics," RM 31 (December, 1977), 210-229.
Kenny, A. "The Argument from Illusion in Aristotle's Metaphysics (T 1009-10)," Mind 76 (April, 1967), 184-197.
Kirk, G. S. "Problem of Cratylus," AJP 72 (July, 1951), 225-253.
Leszl, W. Aristotle's Conception of Ontology. Padua: Antenore, 1975.
Mamo, P. S. "Energia and Kinesis in Metaphysics 0.6," Apeiron 4 (August, 1970), 24-34.
Merlan, P. From Platonism to Neoplatonism. The Hague: Nijhoff, 1969.
Miller, F. D. jr. "Aristotle on Sameness and Oneness," Ph R 82 (October, 1973), 483-490.
Miller, P. "What Aristotle Should Have Said: An Experiment in Metaphysics," APQ 9 (April, 1972), 207-212.
Mitcham, C. "Non-Aristotelian Simile in Metaphysics 2.1," CP 65 (January, 1970), 44-46.
Moore, F. C. T. "Aristotle on Relativism," Ph Q 25 (January, 1975), 58-59.
Romano, J. J. "Aristotle's Assumption of an Intelligible World," Apeiron 7 (May, 1973), 1-16.
Russell, B. R. "Aristotle's Metaphysics," in his History of Western Philosophy. New York: Simon and Schuster, 1954, pp. 159-172.
Scholar, M. "Aristotle, Metaphysics T 1010b1-3," Mind 80 (April, 1971), 266-268.
Sokolowski, R. "Matter, Elements and Substance in Aristotle," JHP 8 (July, 1970), 263-288.
Sprague, R. K. "Aristotle and the Metaphysics of Sleep," RM 31 (December, 1977), 230-241.
Tanner, R. G. "Aristotle as a Structural Linguist," TPS (1969), 99-164.
Taran, L. "Aristotle's Classification of Number in Metaphysics M6, 1080a15-37," GRBS 18 (Spring, 1978), 83-90.
Thayer, H. S. "Aristotle on Nature: A Study in the Relativity of Concepts and Procedures of Analysis," RM 28 (June, 1975), 725-744.
Van Steenberghen, F. Aristotle in the West, tr. by L. Johnston. Louvain: Nauwelaerts, 1970.
_____. "Problem of the Existence of God in Saint Thomas' Commentary on the Metaphysics of Aristotle," RM 27 (March, 1974), 554-568.

Nichomachean Ethics

Ackrill, J. L. "Aristotle on Action," Mind 87 (October, 1978), 595-601.
_____. "Aristotle on Eudaimonia," PBA 60 (October, 1974), 339-359.
Adkins, J. W. H. "Paralysis and Akrasia in Eth. Nic. 1102b 16ff.," AJP 97 (Spring, 1976), 62-64.
_____. "Theoria Versus Praxis in the Nicomachean Ethics and the Republic," CP 73 (October, 1978), 297-313.
Adler, M. J. "Aristotle," in his Poetry and Politics. Pittsburgh: Duquesne University Press, 1956, pp. 19-51.
Barnes, J., M. Schofield, and R. Sorabji, eds. Articles on Aristotle. London: Duckworth, 1977, 3 vols.
Bertman, M. A. "Pleasure and the Two Happinesses in Aristotle," Apeiron 6 (September, 1972), 30-36.
Bowra, C. M. "Aristotle's Hymn to Virtue in Nicomachean Ethics," CQ 32 (July, 1938), 182-189.
Cairns, H., et al. "Aristotle; Ethics," in their Invitation to Learning. New York: Random House, 1941, pp. 51-65.
Cashdollar, S. "Aristotle's Politics of Morals," JHP 11 (April, 1973), 145-160.
Clapp, J. G. "On Freedom; In the Light of Aristotle's Conception of the Conditions of a Moral Act," JP 40 (February 18, 1943), 85-100.
Cooper, J. M. The Magna Moralia and Aristotle's Moral Philosophy," AJP 94 (Winter, 1973), 327-349.
Crossett, J. "Aristotle as a Poet: The Hymn to Hermeias," PQ 46 (April, 1967), 145-155.
Eby, L. S. "Aristotle's Nichomachean Ethics," in his Quest for Moral Law. New York: Columbia University Press, 1944, pp. 63-72.
Fortenbaugh, W. W. "Aristotle's Conception of Moral Virtue and Its Perceptive Role," TAPA 95 (1964), 77-87.
Hardie, W. F. R. "Aristotle and the Free Will Problem," Philos 43 (July, 1968), 274-278.
_____. "Aristotle's Ethical Theory. Oxford: Clarendon, 1968.
Jackson, R. "Rationalism and Intellectualism in the Ethics of Aristotle," Mind 51 (October, 1942), 343-360.
Joachim, H. H. Aristotle: The Nichomachean Ethics; A Commentary. Oxford: Clarendon, 1951.
Johnson, V. "Aristotle on Nomos," CJ 33 (March, 1938), 351-356.
Joseph, H. W. B. "Purposive Action," in his Essays in Ancient and Modern Philosophy. Oxford: Clarendon, 1935, pp. 178-208.
Jost, L. J. "Is Aristotle an Ethical Intuitionist?," Apeiron 10 (January, 1976), 15-19.
Kenny, A. Aristotle's Theory of the Will. New Haven, Conn.: Yale University Press, 1979.
Lee, H. D. P. "Legal Background of Two Passages in the Nichomachean Ethics," CQ 31 (July, 1937), 129-140.
Lind, L. R. "The Modernity of Aristotle's Ethics," CJ 30 (April, 1935), 418-423.

McConnell, T. "Is Aristotle's Account of Incontinence Inconsistent?," CJP 4 (June, 1975), 635-651.
Miller, F. D., Jr. "Actions and Results," Ph Q 25 (October, 1975), 350-354.
Monan, J. D. Moral Knowledge and Its Methodology in Aristotle. Oxford: Clarendon, 1968.
Morrall, J. B. Aristotle. Boston: Allen and Unwin, 1977.
Mulhern, J. J. "Aristotle and the Socratic Paradoxes," JHI 35 (April, 1974), 293-299.
Rist, J. M. "The Value of Man and the Origin of Morality," CJP 4 (September, 1974), 1-21.
Rorty, A. O. "Place of Contemplation in Aristotle's Nicomachean Ethics," Mind 87 (July, 1978), 343-358.
_____. "The Place of Pleasure in Aristotle's Ethics," Mind 83 (October, 1974), 481-497.
Rowe, C. The Eudemian and Nicomachean Ethics: A Study in the Development of Aristotle's Thought. Cambridge, Eng.: Cambridge Philological Society, 1971.
Russell, B. R. "Aristotle's Ethics," in his History of Western Philosophy. New York: Simon and Schuster, 1945, pp. 172-184.
Schofield, M. "Aristotelian Mistakes," PCPS (New Series) 19 (1973), 66-70.
Sharpe, R. A. "Actions and Results," Ph Q 26 (July, 1976), 258-260.
Sifakis, G. M. Aristotle, E.N., Iv, 2, 1123a19-24, and the Comic Chorus in the Fourth Century," AJP 92 (July, 1971), 410-432.
Solmsen, F. "Aristotle EN 10.7, 1177b6-15," CP 72 (January, 1977), 42-43.
Solomon, R. C. "Is There Happiness After Death?," Philos 51 (April, 1976), 189-193.
Stack, G. J. "Aristotle and Kierkegaard's Existential Ethics," JHP 12 (January, 1974), 1-19.
Stahl, G. "The Function of Analytic Premises in Aristotle's Ethics," IPQ 10 (March, 1970), 63-74.
Stewart, J. A. Notes on the Nicomachean Ethics of Aristotle. New York: Arno, 1973.
Sullivan, R. J. Kantian Critique of Aristotle's Moral Philosophy," RM 28 (September, 1974), 24-53.
_____. Morality and the Good Life: A Commentary on Aristotle's Nicomachean Ethics. Memphis, Tenn.: Memphis State University Press, 1977.
Tracy, T. J. Physiological Theory and the Doctrine of the Mean in Plato and Aristotle. Chicago: Loyola University Press, 1969.
Urmson, J. O. "Aristotle's Doctrine of the Mean," APQ 10 (July, 1973), 223-230.
Walsh, J. J. Aristotle's Ethics: Issues and Interpretations. Belmont, Calif.: Wadsworth, 1967.
Wilkes, K. V. "Good Man and the Good for Man in Aristotle's Ethics," Mind 87 (October, 1978), 553-571.
Williams, B. "Aristotle on the Good: A Formal Sketch," Ph Q 12 (October, 1962), 289-296.
Zeigler, G. M. "Aristotle's Analysis of Akrasia," Person 58 (October, 1977), 321-332.

On the Heavens, or De Caelo

Bolzan, J. E. "Aristotles: De Caelo, 310b11-14," JHP 11 (1973), 443-451.
Sinnige, T. G. "Cosmic Religion in Aristotle," GRBS 14 (Spring, 1973), 15-34.
Williams, C. J. F. "Aristotle and Corruptibility: A Discussion of Aristotle De Caelo 1, xii," RS 1 (October, 1965).
─────. "Aristotle and Corruptibility: A Discussion of Aristotle De Caelo 1, xii," RS 1 (April, 1966), 203-215.

On the Soul, or De Anima

Baumrin, J. M. "Active Power and Causal Flow in Aristotle's Theory of Vision," JHBS 12 (July, 1976), 254-259.
Bernardete, S. "Aristotle, De Anima III, 3-5," RM 28 (June, 1975), 611-622.
Blumental, H. J. "Neoplatonic Interpretations of Aristotle on Phantasia," RM 31 (December, 1977), 242-257.
Hamlyn, D. W. "Aristotle's Account of Aesthesis in the De Anima," CQ 9 (1959), 6-16.
Hardie, W. F. R. "Concepts of Consciousness in Aristotle," Mind 85 (July, 1976), 388-411.
Harvey, P. "Aristotle on Truth and Falsity in De Anima 3.6," JHP 16 (April, 1978), 219-220.
Matson, W. "Why Isn't the Mind-Body Problem Ancient?," in P. K. Feyerabend, and G. Maxwell, eds. Mind, Matter, and Method: Essays in Philosophy and Science in Honor of Herbert Feigl. Minneapolis: University of Minnesota, 1976, pp. 92-102.
Olshewsky, T. M. "On the Relations of Soul to Body in Plato and Aristotle," JHP 14 (October, 1976), 391-404.
Owens, J. "A Note on Aristotle, De Anima 3.4, 429b9," Phoenix 30 (Summer, 1976), 107-118.
Rist, J. M. "Notes on Aristotle, De Anima 3-5," CP 61 (January, 1966), 8-20.
─────. "One of Plotinus and the God of Aristotle," RM 27 (September, 1973), 75-89.
Robinson, H. M. "Mind and Body in Aristotle," CQ (New Series) 28 (1978), 105-124.
Robinson, T. M. "Soul and Definitional Priority: De An. 414a4-14," Apeiron 4 (January, 1970), 4-12.
Schiller, J. "Aristotle and the Concept of Awareness in Sense Perception," JHP 13 (July, 1973), 283-296.
Shiner, R. A. "More on Aristotle De Anima 414a4-14," Phoenix 24 (Spring, 1970), 29-38.
Sorabji, R. "Aristotle on Demarcating the Five Senses," Ph R 80 (January, 1971), 55-79.
─────. "Body and Soul in Aristotle," Philos 49 (January, 1974), 63-89.
Wijsenbeek-Wijler, H. Aristotle's Concept of Soul, Sleep and Dreams. Amsterdam: Hakkert, 1978.

Poetics, or Poetica

Abercrombie, L. "Aristotle's Poetics," in his Principles of Literary Criticism. New York: Barnes and Noble, 1960, pp. 63-117.
Adler, M. J. "Aristotle," in his Poetry and Politics. Pittsburgh: Duquesne University Press, 1965, pp. 19-51.
Allan, D. J. "Some Passages in Aristotle's Poetics," CQ (New Series) 21 (May, 1971), 81-92.
Armstrong, A. "Aristotle's Theory of Poetry," G & R 10 (May, 1941), 120-125.
Baldry, H. C. "Aristotle and the Dramatization of Legend," CQ 4 (1954), 151-157.
Bates, W. N. "Notes on the Text of Aristotle's Poetics," TAPA 68 (1937), 84-87.
Boggess, W. F. "Aristotle's Poetics in the Fourteenth Century," SP 67 (July, 1970), 278-294.
Brereton, G. "The Legacy of Aristotle," in his Principles of Tragedy. Coral Gables, Fla.: University of Miami Press, 1968, pp. 21-47.
Brunius, T. Inspiration and Katharsis. Uppsala: Uppsala University Press, 1966.
Burke, K. "Rhetoric and Poetics," in his Language as Symbolic Action. Berkeley: University of California Press, 1966, pp. 295-307.
Butcher, S. H. Aristotle's Theory of Poetry and Fine Art. New York: Dover, 1951.
Cairns, H., et al. "Aristotle; Poetics," in their Invitation to Learning. New York: Random House, 1941, pp. 215-227.
Coggin, P. A. "Aristotle," in his Uses of Drama. New York: Braziller, 1956, pp. 16-21.
Cooper, L. Aristotelian Theory of Comedy. Ithaca, N. Y.: Cornell University Press, 1923.
_____. Poetics of Aristotle, Its Meaning and Influence. Westport, Conn.: Greenwood, 1972.
_____. "Verbal 'Ornament' in Aristotle's Art of Poetry," in L. W. Jones, ed., Classical and Medieval Studies in Honor of Edward Kennard Rand. New York: Published by the Editor, 1938, pp. 61-77.
Daiches, D. "Aristotelian Solution," in his Critical Approaches to Literature. Englewood Cliffs, N. J.: Prentice-Hall, 1956, pp. 23-49.
Dickson, K. A. "Lessing's Creative Misinterpretation of Aristotle," G & R 14 (April, 1967), 53-60.
Dyer, R. R. "Hamartia in the Poetics and Aristotle's Model of Failure," Arion 4 (Winter, 1965), 658-664.
Else, G. F. "Aristotle and Satyr-play, I.," TAPA 70 (1939), 139-157.
_____. "Aristotle on the Beauty of Tragedy," HSCP 49 (1938), 179-204.
_____. Aristotle's Poetics: The Argument. Cambridge, Mass.: Harvard University Press, 1958.
Flickinger, R. C. "Aristotle's Poetics 1460 b 15-26," PQ 19 (October, 1940), 321-327.

Gassner, J. "Aristotelian Literary Criticism," in his Dramatic Soundings. New York: Crown, 1968, 133-152.
Gearhart, S. M. Aristotle and Modern Theorists on the Elements of Tragedy. Ann Arbor, Mich.: University Microfilms, 1957.
Gilbert, A. H. "Aristotle's Four Species of Tragedy (Poetics 18) and Their Importance for Dramatic Criticism," AJP 68 (October, 1947), 363-381.
_____, and H. L. Snuggs. "On the Relation of Horace to Aristotle in Literary Criticism," JEGP 46 (July, 1947), 233-247.
Golden, L. "Aristotle and the Audience for Tragedy," Mnemosyne 29 (1976), 351-359.
_____. "Mimesis and Katharsis," CJ 64 (July, 1969), 145-153.
_____, and O. Hardison. Aristotle's Poetics. Englewood Cliffs, N. J.: Prentice-Hall, 1967.
Gomme, A. W. "Some Problems in Aristotle's Poetics," in his Greek Attitude to Poetry and History. Berkeley: University of California Press, 1954, pp. 49-72.
Goodman, P. "Analysis of the 'Deus ex Machina' in Philoctetes," in his Structure of Literature. Chicago: University of Chicago Press, 1954, pp. 49-57.
_____. "Oedipus Rex: A Complex Tragic Plot," in his Structure of Literature. Chicago: University of Chicago Press, 1954, pp. 27-49.
Gresseth, G. K. "The System of Aristotle's Poetics," TAPA 89 (1958), 312-335.
Gulley, N. Aristotle on the Purposes of Literature: An Inaugural Lecture Delivered at Saint David's University College, Lampeter, on St. David's Day, 1971. Cardiff: University of Wales Press, 1971.
Hardison, O. B. Aristotle's Poetics: A Translation and Commentary for Students of Literature. Englewood Cliffs, N. J.: Prentice-Hall, 1968.
Hassan, R. Practical Criticism and Some Aspects of Aristotle's Poetics. Lahore: Imperial Book Depot, 1967.
Henn, T. R. "Aristotelian Induction: And Some Related Problems," in his Harvest of Tragedy. London: Methuen, 1956, pp. 1-7.
Hogan, J. C. "Aristotle's Criticisms of Homer in the Poetics," CP 68 (April, 1973), 95-108.
House, A. H. Aristotle's Poetics. London: Hart-Davis, 1956.
Householder, R. W. "First Chapter of the Poetics," AJP 66 (July, 1945), 266-278.
Huxley, G. "Aristotle's Interest in Biography," GRBS 15 (Summer, 1974), 203-213.
Jepsen, J. "Ethos in Tragedy," in his Ethical Aspects of Tragedy. Gainesville: University of Florida Press, 1953, pp. 1-7.
Jones, H. J. F. "Aristotle's Poetics," in his On Aristotle and Greek Tragedy. Oxford: Clarendon, 1962, pp. 11-62.
_____. "Sophocles and the Poetics," in his On Aristotle and Greek Tragedy. Oxford: Clarendon, 1962, pp. 159-166.
Kaufmann, W. A. "The Riddle of Oedipus: Tragedy and Philosophy," in The Isenberg Memorial Lecture Series, 1965-1966. East Lansing: Michigan State University Press, 1969, pp. 193-222.

Kitto, H. D. F. "Criticism and Chaos," in his Poiesis: Structure and Thought. Berkeley: University of California Press, 1966, pp. 1-32.
Lord, C. "Aristotle's History of Poetry," TAPA 104 (1974), 195-229.
Lucas, D. W. Poetics. Oxford: Clarendon, 1968.
Lucas, F. L. Tragedy: Serious Drama in Relation to Aristotle's Poetics. New York: Macmillan, 1958.
MacKay, L. A. "Aristotle, Poetics, 1455 b 7-8, 1456 a 7-9," AJP 75 (July, 1954), 300-302.
McKeon, R. P. "Aristotle's Conception of Language and the Arts of Language," in R. S. Crane, ed., Critics and Criticism, Ancient and Modern. Chicago: University of Chicago Press, 1952, pp. 176-231.
Marcotte, P. J. Notes Towards an Understanding of Aristotle's Poetics. Ottawa: Runge, 1963.
Mills, J. L. "Spenser's Letter to Raleigh and the Averroistic Poetics," ELN 14 (June, 1977), 246-249.
Mulroy, D. "Pity and Fear," CB 50 (February, 1974), 53-55.
Myers, H. A. "Aristotle's Study of Tragedy," in his Tragedy: A View of Life. Ithaca, N.Y.: Cornell University Press, 1956, pp. 28-53.
Newman, J. H. Cardinal. "Poetry with Reference to Aristotle's Poetics," in his Essays and Sketches. New York: Longmans, 1949, Vol. 1, pp. 55-81.
Olson, E., ed. Aristotle's Poetics and English Literature. Chicago: University of Chicago Press, 1965.
Papanoutsos, E. P. "The Aristotelian Katharsis," BJA 17 (Autumn, 1977), 361-364.
Pearson, L. "Characterization in Drama and Oratory--Poetics 1450 '20,'" CQ 18 (May, 1968), 76-83.
Peltz, R. "Classification and Evolution in Aesthetics: Weitz and Aristotle," JAAC 30 (Fall, 1971), 69-78.
Pitcher, S. M. "Aristotle's Good and Just Heroes," PQ 24 (January, 1945), 1-11; 25 (April, 1945), 190-191.
_____. "'Epic as I Here Define It,' Poetics, I, 1447 a 28-69," AJP 65 (October, 1944), 340-353.
Post, L. A. "Aristotle and the Philosophy of Fiction," in his From Homer to Menander. Berkeley: University of California Press, 1951, pp. 245-269.
Pritchard, J. P. "Poetics and the Ars Poetica," in his Return to the Fountains. Durham, N.C.: Duke University Press, 1942, pp. 6-12.
Ransom, J. C. "Cathartic Principle," in his World's Body. New York: Scribner's, 1938, pp. 173-192.
_____. "Literary Criticism of Aristotle," in R. P. Blackmur, et al., Lectures in Criticism. New York: Pantheon, 1949.
_____. "Mimetic Principle," in his World's Body. New York: Scribner's, 1938, pp. 193-211.
Rapin, R. "Reflections of Aristotle's Book of Poesy in Particular," in S. Elledge and D. S. Schier, eds., The Continental Model. Minneapolis: University of Minnesota Press, 1960, pp. 293-302.

_____. "Reflections of Aristotle's Treatise of Poesy in General," in S. Elledge and D. S. Schier, eds., The Continental Model. Minneapolis: University of Minnesota Press, 1960, pp. 275-302.
Rees, B. R. "Pathos in the Poetics of Aristotle," G & R 19 (April, 1972), 1-11.
Reeves, C. H. "Aristotelian Concept of the Tragic Hero," AJP 73 (April, 1952), 172-188.
Sanborn, H. "A Side-light on the Katharsis," CJ 33 (March, 1938), 322-335.
Sastri, P. S. Aristotle's Theory of Poetry and Drama, with Chapters on Plato and Longinus. Allahabad: Kitab Mahal, 1963.
Schauroth, E. G. "Some Observations on Aristotle's View of Tragedy," CJ 27 (February, 1932), 352-368.
Schendler, A. E. An Aristotelian Theory of Comedy. Ann Arbor, Mich.: University Microfilms, 1955.
Schoder, R. V. "Literary Sources Cited by Aristotle in the Poetics, II," CJ 65 (May, 1970), 359.
Sengupta, S. Some Problems of Aristotle's Poetics. Calcutta: Pustakam, 1966.
Shell, M. "Golden Fleece and the Voice of the Shuttle: Economy in Literary Theory," Ga R 30 (Summer, 1976), 406-429.
Skulsky, H. "Aristotle's Poetics Revisited," JHI 19 (April, 1958), 147-160.
Srivastava, K. G. "How Does Tragedy Achieve Katharsis According to Aristotle?," BJA 15 (Spring, 1975), 132-143.
Stevens, E. B. "Envy and Pity in Greek Philosophy," AJP 69 (April, 1948), 171-189.
Todd, O. J. "One Circuit of the Sun: A Dilemma; Aristotle's De Arte Poetica v. 4 (1449b 12-14)," Roy Soc Can Trans (Series 3) 36, Sec. 2 (1942), 119-132.
Urban, R. T. "All or Nothing at All: Another Look at the Unity of Time in Aristotle," CJ 61 (March, 1966), 262-264.
Weinberg, B. "Robortello on the Poetics," in R. S. Crane, ed., Critics and Criticism, Ancient and Modern. Chicago: University of Chicago Press, 1952, pp. 319-348.
Welch, L. M. "Catharsis, Structural Purification and Else's Aristotle," BR 19 (Winter, 1971), 31-50.
Wheelwright, P. E. "Mimesis and Katharsis: An Archetypal Consideration," in English Institute Essays, 1946-1952. New York: Columbia University Press, 1951, pp. 3-30.
Will, F. "Aristotle and the Question of Character in Literature," in his Literature Inside Out. Cleveland: Western Reserve University Press, 1966, pp. 85-93.
_____. "Aristotle and the Source of the Art Work," in his Literature Inside Out. Cleveland: Western Reserve University Press, 1966, pp. 118-136.
Wimsatt, W. K., and C. Brooks. "Aristotle: Tragedy and Comedy," in their Literary Criticism. New York: Knopf, 1957, pp. 35-56.
_____. "Aristotle's Answer: Poetry as Structure," in their Literary Criticism. New York: Knopf, 1957, pp. 21-34.

Politics

Adler, M. J. "Aristotle," in his Poetry and Politics. Pittsburgh: Duquesne University Press, 1965, pp. 19-51.
Barnes, J., M. Schofield, and R. Sorabji, eds. Articles on Aristotle. London: Duckworth, 1977, Vol. 2.
Cairns, H., et al. "Aristotle; Politics," in their Invitation to Learning. New York: Random House, 1941, pp. 3-18.
Chambers, M. "Aristotle's 'Forms of Democracy,'" TAPA 92 (1961), 20-36.
De Laix, R. A. "Aristotle's Conception of the Spartan Constitution," JHP 12 (January, 1974), 21-30.
Golden, L. "Aristotle and the Audience for Tragedy," Mnemosyne 29 (1976), 351-359.
Huxley, G. "Crete in Aristotle's Politics," GRBS 12 (Winter, 1971), 505-515.
Lord, C. "Politics and Philosophy in Aristotle's Politics," Hermes 106 (1978), 336-357.
Lowry, S. T. "Aristotle's Natural Limit and the Economics of Price Regulation," GRBS 15 (April, 1974), 57-63.
Morrall, J. B. Aristotle. Boston: Allen and Unwin, 1977.
Mulgan, R. "Aristotle and Absolute Power," Antichthon 8 (1974), 21-28.
_____. Aristotle's Political Theory: An Introduction for Students of Political Theory. New York: Clarendon, 1977.
Oppenehimer, J. M. "When Sense and Life Begin: Background for a Remark in Aristotle's Politics," Areth 8 (Fall, 1975), 331-343.
Rowe, C. J. "Aims and Methods in Aristotle's Politics," CQ (New Series) 27 (1977), 159-172.
Russell, B. A. W. R., 3rd Earl. "Aristotle's Politics," in his History of Western Philosophy. New York: Simon and Schuster, 1945, pp. 184-195.
Saunders, T. J. "A Note on Aristotle, Politics I, 1," CQ (New Series) 26 (1976), 316-317.
Todd, O. J. "Aristotle's Politics, IV, xii, 11-13," AJP 62 (October, 1941), 416-425.
Welch, L. M. "Catharsis, Structural Purification, and Else's Aristotle," BR 19 (Winter, 1971), 31-50.

Rhetoric

Cope, E. M. An Introduction to Aristotle's Rhetoric. Hildesheim: Olms, 1970.
Douglass, R. B. "An Aristotelian Orientation to Rhetorical Communication," P & R 7 (Spring, 1974), 80-88.
Erickson, K. Aristotle: The Classical Heritage of Rhetoric. Metuchen, N.J.: Scarecrow, 1974.
Grimaldi, W. M. Studies in the Philosophy of Aristotle's Rhetoric. Wiesbaden: Steiner, 1972.
Harris, H. A. "Simile in Aristotle's Rhetoric," CR (New Series) 24 (November, 1974), 178-179.

MacKay, L. A. "Aristotle, Rhetoric, III, 16, 11 (1417 b 12-20)," AJP 74 (July, 1953), 281-286.
Oravec, C. " 'Observation' in Aristotle's Theory of Epideictic," P & R 9 (Summer, 1976), 162-173.
Rosenfield, L. W. Aristotle and Information Theory: A Comparison of the Influence of Casual Assumptions on Two Theories of Communication. The Hague: Mouton, 1971.
Ryan, E. E. "Aristotle's Rhetoric and Ethics and the Ethos of Society," GRBS 13 (Autumn, 1972), 291-308.
Solmsen, F. "Aristotle and Cicero on the Orator's Playing upon the Feelings," CP 33 (October, 1938), 390-404.
Taran, S. L. "Aristotle, Rhetoric 3.2-7, An Analysis," GRBS 15 (Spring, 1974), 65-72.
Thompson, W. N. "Stasis in Aristotle's Rhetoric," QJS 58 (April, 1972), 134-141.

Miscellaneous

Baumrin, J. M. "Active Power and Causal Flow in Aristotle's Theory of Vision," JHBS 12 (July, 1976), 254-259.
Burstein, S. M. "Alexander, Callisthenes and the Sources of the Nile," GRBS 17 (Summer, 1976), 135-146.
Chroust, A. H. "Some Reflections on the Aeternitas Mundi in Aristotle's On Philosophy," AClass 16 (1973), 25-32.
Cole, J. W. "Peisistratus on the Strymon," G & R 22 (April, 1975), 42-44.
Crossett, J. "Aristotle as a Poet: The Hymn to Hermeias," PQ 46 (April, 1967), 145-155.
Dickason, A. "Aristotle, the Sea Fight, and the Cloud," JHP 14 (January, 1976), 11-22.
Gyekye, K. "Aristotle on Language and Meaning," IPQ 14 (March, 1974), 71-77.
Hardie, I. "The Aristotelian Motif in Filmer's Patriarcha: A Second Look," Pol Stud 22 (December, 1974), 479-484.
Owen, G. E. L. "Aristotelian Pleasures," PAS (New Series) 72 (1972), 135-152.
Rowe, C. J. "A Reply to John Cooper on the Magna Moralia," AJP 96 (Summer, 1975), 160-172.
Ryan, W. F. "Old Russian Version of the Pseudo-Aristotelian Secreta Secretorum," S & EER 56 (April, 1978), 242-260.
Sorabji, R. "Aristotle, Mathematics, and Colour," CQ (New Series) 22 (November, 1972), 293-308.
_____. Aristotle on Memory. Providence, R. I.: Brown University Press, 1972.
Stern, S. M. Aristotle on the World-State. Columbia: University of South Carolina Press, 1970.
Todd, R. B. "The Four Causes: Aristotle's Exposition and the Ancients," JHI 37 (April/June, 1976), 319-322.
Wijsenbeek-Wijler, H. Aristotle's Concept of Soul, Sleep and Dreams. Amsterdam: Hakkert, 1978.
Wolfson, H. A. Crescas' Critique of Aristotle's Physics in Jewish and Arabic Philosophy. Cambridge, Mass.: Harvard University Press, 1972.

46 : Greek and Roman Authors

AUGUSTINE

General Criticism

Abbo, J. A. "Christ and Christianity: St. Augustine," in his Political Thought: Men and Ideas. Paramus, N. J.: Newman, 1960, pp. 70-81.

Adams, J. D. The Populus of Augustine and Jerome: A Study in the Patristic Sense of Community. New Haven, Conn.: Yale University Press, 1971.

Alexander, W. A. "Sex and Philosophy in Augustine," Aug. Stud. 5 (1974), 197-208.

Augustine Studies; Papers Read at Recent Augustinian Educational Conferences. Freeport, N. Y.: Books for Libraries, 1967.

Ayers, R. H. "Language Theory and Analysis in Augustine," SJT 29 (February, 1976), 1-12.

Battenhouse, R. E., ed. Companion to the Study of St. Augustine. New York: Oxford University Press, 1955.

Beach, W., and H. R. Niebuhr, eds. "St. Augustine," in their Christian Ethics; Sources of the Living Traditions. New York: Ronald, 1955, pp. 100-139.

Beyenka, B. "The Names of St. Ambrose in the Works of St. Augustine," Aug. Stud. 5 (1974), 19-28.

Bourke, V. J. "Augustine and the Roots of Moral Virtues," Aug. Stud. 6 (1975), 65-74.

──────. Augustine's View of Reality. Villanova, Pa.: Villanova University Press, 1964.

Boyer, C. E. "St. Augustine," in J. Walsh, ed., Spiritually through the Centuries; Ascetics and Mystics of the Western Church. New York: Kenedy, 1964, pp. 15-24.

Breckenridge, J. "Augustine and the Donatists," Foundations 19 (January, 1976), 69-77.

Brown, L. F., and G. B. Carson. "World of St. Augustine," in their Men and Centuries of European Civilization. New York: Knopf, 1948, pp. 17-25.

Brown, P. R. L. Augustine of Hippo. Berkeley: University of California Press, 1967.

──────. Religion and Society in the Age of Saint Augustine. London: Faber and Faber, 1972.

──────. "St. Augustine's Attitude to Religious Coercion," JRS 54 (1964), 107-116.

Bubacz, B. S. "Augustine's Account of Factual Memory," Aug. Stud. 6 (1975), 181-192.

Burkill, T. A. "St. Augustine's Notion of Nothingness in the Light of Some Recent Cosmological Speculation," Aug. Stud. 5 (1974), 15-17.

Burns, J. H. "Political and Social Thought in St. Augustine," Month 30 (November, 1963), 304-305.

Callahan, J. F. "Augustine: Time, a Distention of Man's Soul," in his Four Views of Time in Ancient Philosophy. Cambridge, Mass.: Harvard University Press, 1948, pp. 149-187.

Chambliss, R. "Augustine," in his Social Thought; From Hannibal to Comte. New York: Dryden, 1954, pp. 233-259.

Chapman, E. Saint Augustine's Philosophy of Beauty. New York: Sheed and Ward, 1939.
Christian, W. A. "Augustine on the Creation of the World," HTR 46 (January, 1953), 1-25.
Chroust, A. H. "Philosophy of Law of St. Augustine," Ph R 53 (March, 1944), 195-202.
Costas, O. "Influential Factors in the Rhetoric of Augustine," Foundations 16 (July, 1973), 208-221.
Coulton, G. G. "Augustine," in his Studies in Medieval Thought. London: Nelson, 1940, pp. 24-35.
Cranz, F. E. "Development of Augustine's Ideas on Society Before the Donatist Controversy," HTR 47 (October, 1954), 255-316.
Currie, H. M. "Saint Augustine and Virgil," PVS 14 (1974-1975), 6-16.
Cushman, R. E. "Faith and Reason in the Thought of St. Augustine," Ch H 19 (December, 1950), 271-294.
Deane, H. A. The Political and Social Ideas of St. Augustine. New York: Columbia University Press, 1963.
Downs, R. B. "Chief Architect of the Middle Ages: St. Augustine," in his Famous Books, Ancient and Medieval. New York: Barnes and Noble, 1964, pp. 253-259.
Dunham, J. H. "Augustine," in his Religion of Philosophers. Pittsburgh: University of Pennsylvania Press, 1947, pp. 120-150.
Duvall, T. G. "What Augustine Did to the Philosophy of Jesus," in his Great Thinkers; The Quest of Life for Its Meaning. London: Oxford University Press, 1937, pp. 159-181.
Ebenstein, W. "St. Augustine," in his Great Political Thinkers, Plato to the Present. New York: Rinehart, 1952, pp. 167-172.
Ferguson, M. W. "Saint Augustine's Region of Unlikeness: The Crossing of Exile and Language," Ga R 29 (Winter, 1975), 842-864.
Ferran, L. C. "The Boyhood Beatings of St. Augustine," Aug. Stud. 5 (1974), 1-14.
Flood, J. M. The Mind and Heart of Augustine. Sausalito, Calif.: Academy Guild, 1961.
Fortin, E. L. Political Idealism and Christianity in the Thought of St. Augustine. Villanova, Pa.: Villanova University Press, 1972.
Fremantle, A. J. "St. Augustine," in her Age of Belief; The Medieval Philosophers. Boston: Houghton Mifflin, 1955, pp. 23-53.
Gilmore, A. A. "Augustine and the Critical Method," HTR 39 (April, 1946), 141-163.
Greenwood, D. Saint Augustine. New York: Vantage, 1957.
Hamilton, R. "St. Augustine and the Problem of the Self," Dub R 214 (April, 1944), 108-115.
Hare, B. W. "The Educational Apostulate of St. Augustine," Prudentia 2 (1970), 71-77 and 3 (1971), 15-23.
Hartigan, R. S. "Saint Augustine on War and Killing: The Problem of the Innocent," JHI 27 (April, 1966), 195-204.
Hausheer, H. "St. Augustine's Conception of Time," Ph R 46 (September, 1937), 503-512.
Henry, P. Saint Augustine on Personality. New York: Macmillan, 1960.

Hill, E. "Augustine Semper Vivus," B1 43 (October, 1962), 428-438.
Hodgson, L. "Christian Citizenship; Some Reflections on St. Augustine," CQR 145 (October, 1947), 1-11.
Howie, G. Educational Theory and Practice in St. Augustine. London: Routledge and K. Paul, 1969.
Hugo, J. J. St. Augustine on Nature, Sex and Marriage. Chicago: Scepter, 1969.
Jaspers, K. "Augustine," in his The Great Philosophers. New York: Harcourt, Brace, 1962, pp. 175-229.
Johnson, W. R. "Isocrates Flowering: The Rhetoric of Augustine," P & R 9 (Fall, 1976), 217-231.
Jordan, R. "Time and Contingency in St. Augustine," RM 8 (March, 1955), 394-417.
Keenan, M. E. "Terminology of Witchcraft in the Works of Augustine," CP 35 (July, 1940), 294-297.
Keyes, G. L. Christian Faith and the Interpretation of History; A Study of St. Augustine's Philosophy of History. Lincoln: University of Nebraska Press, 1966.
Kibre, P. "The Christian: Augustine," in P. Nash, A. M. Kazanias, and H. J. Perkinson, eds., The Educated Man; Studies in the History of Educational Thought. New York: Wiley, 1965, pp. 97-112.
Lacey, H. M. "Empiricism and Augustine's Problems About Time," RM 22 (December, 1968), 219-245.
Leff, M. C. "St. Augustine and Martianus Capella: Continuity and Change in the Fifth-Century Latin Rhetorical Theory," Comm Q 24 (Fall, 1976), 2-9.
McGiffert, A. C. "Augustine," in his History of Christian Thought. New York: Scribner's, 1932-1933, Vol. 2, pp. 71-124.
Markus, R. A. Augustine; A Collection of Critical Essays. New York: Anchor, 1972.
_____. "Marius Victorinus and Augustine," in A. H. Armstrong, ed., The Cambridge History of Later Greek and Early Medieval Philosophy. London: Cambridge University Press, 1967, pp. 327-419.
_____. Saeculum: History and Society in the Theology of St. Augustine. London: Cambridge University Press, 1970.
Martin, R. "The Two Cities in Augustine's Political Philosophy," JHI 33 (April-June, 1972), 195-216.
Mazzeo, J. A. "St. Augustine's Rhetoric of Silence: Truth vs. Eloquence and Things vs. Signs," in his Renaissance and Seventeenth-Century Studies. New York: Columbia University Press, 1964, pp. 1-28.
Moore, K. G. "Aurelius Augustine on Imagination," J Psy (April, 1947), 161-168.
Mourant, J. A. Augustine on Immorality. Villanova, Pa.: Villanova University Press, 1969.
Mundle, C. W. K. "Augustine's Pervasive Error Concerning Time," Philos 41 (April, 1966), 165-168.
Nash, R. H. The Light of the Mind: St. Augustine's Theory of Knowledge. Lexington: University Press of Kentucky, 1969.

O'Connell, R. J. St. Augustine's Early Theory of Man. Cambridge, Mass.: Harvard University Press, 1968.
O'Meara, J. J. "St. Augustine's Attitude to Love in the Context of His Influence on Christian Ethics," Areth 2 (Spring, 1969), 46-60.
_____. The Young Augustine; The Growth of Augustine's Mind up to His Conversion. London: Longman, 1954.
O'Toole, C. J. Philosophy of Creation in the Writings of St. Augustine. Washington, D. C.: Catholic University of America Press, 1944.
Perl, C. J. "Augustine and Music," MQ 41 (October, 1955), 496-510.
Portalie, E. A Guide to the Thought of Saint Augustine. Westport, Conn.: Greenwood, 1975.
Reuther, R. R. "Augustine and Christian Political Theology," Interpretation 29 (July, 1975), 252-265.
Roberts, D. E. "Augustine's Earliest Writings," JR 33 (July, 1953), 161-181.
Schevill, F. "St. Augustine: Destroyer and Preserver," in his Six Historians. Chicago: University of Chicago Press, 1956, pp. 33-60.
Schnittkind, H. T., and D. A. Schnittkind. "Pilgrimage of Augustine --From Sinner to Saint," in their Living Adventures in Philosophy. Garden City, N. Y.: Hanover House, 1954, pp. 95-103.
Sullivan, J. E. Image of God: The Doctrine of St. Augustine and Its Influence. Chicago: Priory, 1963.
Swift, L. J. "Augustine on War and Killing: Another View," HTR 66 (July, 1973), 369-383.
Taylor, H. O. "Augustine," in his Prophets, Philosophers and Other Poets of the Ancient World. New York: Ungar, 1964; pp. 238-275.
TeSelle, E. Augustine the Theologian. New York: Herder and Herder, 1970.
_____. "Porphyry and Augustine," Aug. Stud. 5 (1974), 113-147.
Thomas, G. F. "Christian Philosophy: Augustine," in his Religious Philosophies of the West. New York: Scribner's, 1965, pp. 70-96.
Van Antwerp, E. I. St. Augustine: The Divination of Demons and Care for the Dead. Washington, D. C.: Catholic University of America Press, 1955.
Van Fleteren, F. E. "Authority and Reason, Faith and Understanding in the Thought of St. Augustine," Aug. Stud. 4 (1973), 33-72.
Van Jess, W. G. "Divine Eternity in the Doctrine of St. Augustine," Aug. Stud. 6 (1975), 75-96.
_____. "Reason as Propaedeutic to Faith in Augustine," IJPR 5 (Winter, 1974), 225-233.
Vernon, A. W. "Saints and Women in the Fourth Century," Chris 10, No. 2, (1945), 163-175.
Versfeld, M. "St. Augustine as Psychotherapist," Bl 45 (March, 1964), 98-110.
Warfield, B. B. Studies in Tertullian and Augustine. Westport, Conn.: Greenwood, 1970.
Wassmer, T. A. "Trinitarian Theology of Augustine and His Debt to Plotinus," HTR 53 (October, 1960), 261-268.

Watson, R. I. "Plotinus and Augustine: The Patristic Period," in his The Great Psychologists: From Aristotle to Freud. New York: Lippincott, 1963, pp. 82-96.
Williams, C. "Augustine and Athanasius," in his Image of the City, and Other Essays. London: Oxford University Press, 1958, pp. 89-91.
Wills, G. "Radical Creativity," MLN 89 (December, 1974), 1019-1028.
Wilson-Kastner, P. "Grace as Participation in the Divine Life in the Theology of Augustine," Aug Stud. 7 (1976), 135-152.
Windaas, S. "Saint Augustine and the Just War," Bl 43 (November, 1962), 460-468.

Individual Works

City of God, or De Civitate Dei

Barker, E. "St. Augustine's Theory of Society," in his Essays on Government. New York: Oxford University Press, 1951, pp. 234-269.
Baynes, N. H. "Political Ideas of St. Augustine's De Civitate Dei," in his Byzantine Studies and Other Essays. London: Athlone, 1955, pp. 288-306.
Brookes, E. H. The City of God and the Politics of Crisis. London: Oxford University Press, 1960.
Burleigh, J. H. The City of God; A Study of St. Augustine's Philosophy. London: Nisbet, 1949.
Cranz, F. E. "De Civitate Dei, XV, 2, and Augustine's Idea of the Christian Society," Speculum 25 (April, 1950), 215-225.
Ferrari, L. C. "Background to Augustine's City of God," CJ 67 (February-March, 1972), 198-208.
Figgis, J. N. The Political Aspects of St. Augustine's City of God. London: Peter Smith, 1963.
Hearnshaw, F. J. C. "St. Augustine and the City of God," in his Some Great Political Idealists of the Christian Era. London: Harrap, 1937, pp. 9-21.
Henry, M. "Tradition and Rebellion," Southern R (New Series) 12 (January, 1976), 32-53.
Horton, J. T. "The De Civitate Dei as Religious Satire," CJ 60 (February, 1965), 193-203.
Kiszely-Payzs, K. "St. Augustine on Peace," in various authors, Essays in Modern Scholasticism in Honor of John F. McCormick. Paramus, N.J.: Newman, 1944, pp. 67-89.
Lowith, K. "Augustine," in his Meaning in History: The Theological Implications of the Philosophy of History. Chicago: University of Chicago Press, 1949, pp. 160-173.
Markus, R. A. "Two Conceptions of Political Authority: Augustine, De Civitate Dei, 19, 14-15, and Some Thirteenth-Century Interpretations," JTS 16 (April, 1965), 68-100.
Marshall, R. T. Studies in the Political and Socio-Religious Terminology of the De Civitate Dei. Washington, D.C.: Catholic University of America Press, 1952.

Augustine : 51

Mommsen, T. E. "Orosius and Augustine," in his Medieval and Renaissance Studies. Ithaca, N.Y.: Cornell University Press, 1959, pp. 325-348.

_____. "St. Augustine and the Christian Idea of Progress: The Background of the City of God," in his Medieval and Renaissance Studies. Ithaca, N.Y.: Cornell University Press, 1959, pp. 265-298.

Niebuhr, R. "Augustine's Political Realism," in his Christian Realism and Political Problems. New York: Scribner's, 1953, pp. 119-146.

O'Meara, J. J. Charter of Christendom. New York: Macmillan, 1961.

Russell, B. R. "Saint Augustine's Philosophy and Theology," in his History of Western Philosophy. New York: Simon and Schuster, 1945, pp. 352-366.

Versfeld, M. Guide to the City of God. New York: Sheed and Ward, 1958.

Confessions

Burke, K. The Rhetoric of Religion: Studies in Logology. Berkeley: University of California Press, 1970.

Burrell, D. "Reading the Confessions of Augustine: An Exercise in Theological Understanding," JR 50 (October, 1970), 327-351.

Cooper, J. C. "Why Did Augustine Write Books XI-XIII of the Confessions?," Aug Stud. 2 (1971), 37-46.

Cress, D. A. "Hierius and St. Augustine's Account of the Lost De Pulchro et Apto. Confessions IV, 13-15," Aug Stud. 7 (1976), 153-163.

Ferrari, L. C. "Christus' via in Augustine's Confessions," Aug Stud 7 (1976), 47-58.

_____. "Symbols of Sinfulness in Book II of Augustine's Confessions," Aug Stud 2 (1971), 93-104.

Findlay, J. N. "Time: A Treatment of Some Puzzles," in A. G. N. Flew, ed., Essays on Logic and Language. Oxford: Blackwell, 1960 (First Series), pp. 37-54.

Flores, R. "Reading and Speech in St. Augustine's Confessions," Aug Stud 6 (1975), 1-13.

Harvey, J. F. Moral Theology of the Confessions of Saint Augustine. Washington, D. C.: Catholic University of America Press, 1951.

Miller, F. L. "The Fundamental Option in the Thought of St. Augustine," DR 95 (October, 1977), 271-283.

O'Brien, W. J. "Toward Understanding Original Sin in Augustine's Confessions," Thought 49 (December, 1974), 436-446.

O'Connell, R. J. St. Augustine's Confessions; The Odyssey of Soul. Cambridge, Mass.: Harvard University Press, 1969.

Pincherle, A. "The Confessions of St. Augustine," Aug Stud 7 (1976), 119-133.

Starnes, C. "Saint Augustine and the Vision of Truth," Dionysius 1 (1977), 85-126.

_____. "Saint Augustine on Infancy and Childhood: Commentary of the First Book of Augustine's Confessions," Aug Stud 6 (1975), 15-43.

Taylor, J. H. "Augustine, Conf. IX, 10, 24," AJP 79 (January, 1958), 66-70.
———. "St. Augustine and the Hortensius of Cicero," SP 60 (July, 1963), 487-498.
Vance, E. "Augustine's Confessions and the Poetics of the Law," MLN 93 (May, 1978), 618-634.
Wagner, M. M. "Plan in the Confessions of St. Augustine," PQ 23 (January, 1944), 1-23.

On Free Will

Hopkins, J. "Augustine on Foreknowledge and Free Will," IJPR 8 (1977), 111-126.
MacQueen, D. J. "Augustine on Free Will and Predestination: A Critique of J. H. Rist," Mus Afr 3 (1974), 17-28.
Rist, J. M. "Augustine on Free Will and Predestination," JTS 20 (October, 1969), 420-447.
Rowe, W. L. "Augustine on Foreknowledge and Free Will," RM 18 (December, 1964), 356-363.
Sontag, F. "Augustine's Metaphysics and Free Will," HTR 60 (July, 1967), 297-306.

On the Christian Life, or De Vita Christiana

Evans, R. F. "Pelagius, Fastidius, and the Pseudo-Augustinian De Vita Christiana," JTS 13 (April, 1962), 72-98.
Huppe, B. F. Doctrine and Poetry; Augustine's Influence on Old English Poetry. Albany: State University of New York Press, 1959.
Young, A. M. "Some Aspects of St. Augustine's Literary Aesthetics, Studied Chiefly in De Doctrina Christiana," HTR 62 (July, 1969), 289-299.

Miscellaneous

Blackmur, R. P. "St. Augustine's De Musica, A Synopsis," in his Language as Gesture; Essays in Poetry. New York: Harcourt, 1952, pp. 365-371.
Buckenmeyer, R. E. "Augustine and the Life of Man's Body in the Early Dialogues," Aug. Stud. 2 (1971), 197-211, and 3 (1972), 131-146.
Fortin, E. L. "Augustine and the Problem of Christian Rhetoric," Aug Stud. 5 (1974), 85-100.
Heil, J. "Augustine's Attack on Skepticism, the Contra Academicos," HTR 65 (January, 1972), 99-116.
Keenan, M. E. "Classical Writers in the Letters of Augustine," CJ 32 (October, 1936), 35-37.
McDonnell, M. F., Sister. An Analysis of the Notion of Order in St. Augustine's De Ordine. Washington, D. C.: Georgetown University, 1948.

Newman, F. X. "St. Augustine's Three Visions and the Structure of the Commedia," MLN 82 (January, 1967).
Treloar, A. "St. Augustine's Views on Marriage," Prudentia 8 (May, 1976), 41-50.

BION

General Criticism

Allen, D. C. "Three Poems on Eros," CL 8 (Summer, 1956), 177-193.

CAESAR

General Criticism

Adcock, F. E. Caesar as Man of Letters. Hamden, Conn.: Archon, 1969.
Alexander, W. H. "Julius Caesar in the Pages of Seneca the Philosopher," Roy Soc Can Trans (Series 3) 35, Sec. 2 (1941), 15-28.
Balsdon, J. P. V. D. Julius Caesar; A Political Biography. New York: Atheneum, 1967.
Collins, J. H. Propaganda, Ethics, and Psychological Assumptions in Caesar's Writings. Frankfurt am Main, [n. p.], 1952.
DeWitt, N. J. "The Non-Political Nature of Caesar's Commentaries," TAPA 73 (1942), 341-352.
Frederikson, M. W. "Caesar, Cicero and the Problem of Debt," JRS 56 (1966), 128-141.
Gelzer, M. Caesar: Politician and Statesman. Cambridge, Mass.: Harvard University Press, 1968.
Hadas, M. "Caesar, Sallust, and Others," in his History of Latin Literature. New York: Columbia University Press, 1952, pp. 88-107.
Lofstedt, E. "Roman Publicist and Historian," in his Roman Literary Portraits. Oxford: Clarendon, 1958, pp. 93-117.
Spaeth, J. W. "Caesar's Friends and Enemies Among the Poets," CJ 32 (June, 1937), 541-556.
Usher, S. "Julius Caesar and His Commentaries," HT 15 (Spring, 1965), 651-658.

Individual Works

Civil War, or De Bello Civili

Goldhurst, R. "Style in De Bello Civili," CJ 49 (April, 1954), 299-303.

Rowe, G. O. "Dramatic Structures in Caesar's Bellum Civile," TAPA 98 (1967), 399-414.

Gallic War

Coolidge, O. E. Caesar's Gallic War. Boston: Houghton Mifflin, 1961.
Downs, R. B. "Military Genius: Caius Julius Caesar," in his Famous Books, Ancient and Medieval. New York: Barnes and Noble, 1964, pp. 166-169.
Martin, H. "The Image of Caesar in Bellum Gallicum 1," CJ 61 (November, 1965), 63-67.
Murphy, C. T. "The Use of Speeches in Caesar's Gallic War," CJ 45 (December, 1949), 120-127.
Murphy, P. R. "Themes of Caesar's Gallic War," CJ 72 (February-March, 1977), 234-243.
Rexroth, K. "Julius Caesar: The War in Gaul," in his Classics Revisited. Chicago: Quadrangle, 1968, pp. 94-98.
Russell, A. G. "Caesar: De Bello Gallico, Book 1 cc. 1-41," G & R 5 (October, 1935), 12-21.
Van der Veer, J. A. G. "Caesar's Campaign Against the Maritime States (De Bello Gallico, iii. 7-17)," G & R 8 (February, 1939), 65-74.
Wuras, H. Helps to the Study of Caesar's Gallic War. London: Hortors, 1938.

CALLIMACHUS

General Criticism

Atkins, J. W. H. "New Poetics: Neoptolemus of Parium, Callimachus, and Aristarchus," in his Literary Criticism in Antiquity; A Sketch of Its Development. Toronto: Macmillan, 1934, Vol. 1, pp. 164-194.
Barber, E. A. "Callimachea Varia," CR (New Series) 5 (December 1955), 241-242.
──────. "Lock of Berenice: Callimachus and Catullus," in Greek Poetry and Life; Essays Presented to Gilbert Murray. Oxford: Clarendon, 1936, pp. 343-363.
Bonnard, A. "Back to Poetry: Callimachus, Apollonius," in his Greek Civilization: From Euripides to Alexandria. New York: Macmillan, 1961, pp. 209-228.
Daly, L. W. "Callimachus and Catullus," CP 47 (April, 1952), 97-99.
Edwards, W. M. "The Callimachus Prologue and Apollonius Rhodius," CQ (April, 1930), 109-112.
Giangrande, G. "Emendations to Callimachus," CQ 12 (November, 1962), 212-222.

Snell, B. "Art and Play in Callimachus," in his Discovery of the Mind; The Greek Origins of European Thought. Cambridge, Mass.: Harvard University Press, 1953, pp. 264-280.

Individual Works

Causes, or Aetia

Bulloch, A. W. "A New Interpretation of a Fragment of Callimachus' Aetia: Antinoopolis Papyrus 113 fr. I (b)," CQ 20 (November, 1970), 269-276.

Epigrams

Ferguson, J. "The Epigrams of Callimachus," G & R 17 (April, 1970), 64-80.

McKay, K. J. "An Experiment in Hellenistic Epigram," AUMLA No. 22 (November, 1964), 191-199.

Expositions, or Diegeseis

Barber, E. A. "Notes on the Diegeseis of Callimachus," CQ 33 (April, 1939), 65-68.

Hymns

Bulloch, A. W. "Callimachus' Erysichthon, Homer and Apollonius Rhodius," AJP 98 (Summer, 1977), 97-123.

Bundy, E. L. "The Quarrel Between Kallimachos and Apollonius, I: The Epilogue of Kallimachos' Hymn to Apollo," CSCA 5 (1972), 39-94.

Huxley, G. "Kallimachos, the Assyrian River and the Bees of Demeter," GRBS 12 (Summer, 1971), 211-215.

McKay, K. J. "Crime and Punishment in Kallimachos' Hymn to Delos," Antichthon 3 (1969), 27-28.

Iambic Poems, or Iambi

Dawson, C. M. "Alexandrian Prototype of Marathus? The Fragments Known as the Iambi of Callimachus," AJP 67 (January, 1946), 1-15.

CATULLUS

General Criticism

Atkinson, J. E. "Catullus: The Historical Background," Akroterion 20 (February-March, 1975), 38-53.

Barber, E. A. "Lock of Berenice: Callimachus and Catullus," in Greek Poetry and Life; Essays Presented to Gilbert Murray. Oxford: Clarendon, 1936, pp. 343-363.

Barnds, W. P. "Poems of Lament in Catullus," CJ 33 (November, 1937), 88-98.

Barsby, J. A. "Rhythmical Factors in Catullus 72, 75 and 85," Phoenix 29 (Spring, 1975), 83-88.

Collins, J. H. "Cicero and Catullus," CJ 48 (October, 1952), 11-17.

Copley, F. O. "Emotional Conflict and Its Significance in the Lesbia-poems of Catullus," AJP 70 (January, 1949), 22-40.

Crowther, N. B. "Catullus and the Traditions of Latin Poetry," CP 66 (October, 1971), 246-249.

———. "Horace, Catullus, and Alexandrianism," Mnemosyne 31 (1978), 33-44.

Dale, F. R. "The Attis of Catullus," G & R 11 (March, 1964), 43-47.

Debatin, F. M. "Catullus--A Pivotal Personality," CJ 26 (December, 1930), 207-222.

Downs, R. B. "Rome's Supreme Lyric Poet: Gaius Valerius Catullus," in his Famous Books, Ancient and Medieval. New York: Barnes and Noble, 1964, pp. 177-179.

Duhigg, J. "The Elegiac Metre of Catullus," Antichthon 5 (1971), 57-67.

Elder, J. P. "Catullus' Attis," AJP 68 (October, 1947), 394-403.

Ferguson, J. "Catullus and Horace," AJP 77 (January, 1956), 1-18.

———. "A Note on Catullus' Hendecasyllabics," CP 65 (July, 1970), 173-177.

———. "The Renunciation Poems of Catullus," G & R 3 (March, 1956), 52-57.

Forsyth, P. Y. "The Gellius Cycle of Catullus," CJ 68 (December, 1972), 175-177.

Frank, T. Catullus and Horace; Two Poets in Their Environment. New York: Russell and Russell, 1965, pp. 3-114.

Goold, G. Interpreting Catullus. London: Lewis, 1974.

Hadas, M. "Lucretius and Catullus," in his History of Latin Literature. New York: Columbia University Press, 1952, pp. 69-87.

Hardie, C. G. "Three Roman Poets," in J. P. V. D. Balsdon, ed., The Romans. New York: Basic, 1966, pp. 226-248.

Harrington, K. P. Catullus and His Influence. New York: Cooper Square, 1963.

Havelock, E. A. Lyric Genius of Catullus. Oxford: Blackwell, 1939.

Highet, G. "Catullus: Life and Love," in his Poets in a Landscape. New York: Knopf, 1957, pp. 3-44.

Johnson, S. "A Fresh Solution of a Famous Crux in Catullus," CJ 40 (October, 1944), 10-18.

Konstan, D. "Two Kinds of Love in Catullus," CJ 68 (December, 1972), 102-106.
Lateiner, D. "Obscenity in Catullus," Ramus 6 (1977), 15-32.
Loomis, J. W. Studies in Catullan Verse: An Analysis of Word Types and Patterns in the Polymetra (Mnemosyne Supplement 24). Leiden: Brill, 1972.
McCarren, V. A Critical Concordance to Catullus. Leiden: Brill, 1977.
McGushin, P. "Catullus' Sanctae Foedus Amicitiae," CP 62 (April, 1967), 85-93.
McKay, A. G., and D. M. Shepherd. Roman Lyric Poetry by Catullus and Horace. New York: St. Martin's, 1969.
Macleod, C. W. "Parochy and Personalities in Catullus," CQ (New Series) 23 (November, 1973), 294-303.
McPeek, J. A. S. Catullus in Strange and Distant Britain. New York: Russell and Russell, 1972.
O'Gorman, G. J. "Codex Vat. Lat. 1608: A Source for Catullus," TAPA 100 (1969), 321-329.
Onetti, S. "The Technique of Counterbalancing in Catullus," AClass 19 (1976), 59-74.
Quinn, K. Approaches to Catullus. New York: Barnes and Noble, 1972.
_____. The Catullan Revolution. London: Cambridge University Press, 1959.
_____. Catullus: An Interpretation. New York: Barnes and Noble, 1973.
_____. "Docte Catulle," in J. P. Sullivan, ed., Critical Essays on Roman Literature: Elegy and Lyric. Cambridge, Mass.: Harvard University Press, 1962, pp. 31-63.
Reynolds, T. "Catullus," Arion 7 (Autumn, 1968), 453-465.
Ross, D. O. Style and Tradition in Catullus. Cambridge, Mass.: Harvard University Press, 1969.
Scott, W. C. "Catullus and Ceasar (c. 29)," CP 66 (January, 1971), 17-25.
_____. "Catullus and Cato (c. 56)," CP 64 (January, 1969), 24-29.
Soles, M. Studies in Colloquial Language in the Poems of Catullus. Ann Arbor, Mich.: University Microfilms, 1954.
Thomson, D. F. S. "Catullus and Cicero: Poetry and the Criticism of Poetry," C World 60 (February, 1967), 225-230.
_____. "A New Look at the Manuscript Tradition of Catullus," YCS 23 (1973), 113-129.
Tracy, H. L. "The Lyric Poet's Repertoire," CJ 61 (October, 1965), 22-26.
Wheeler, A. L. Catullus and the Traditions of Ancient Poetry. Berkeley: University of California Press, 1964.
Wiseman, T. P. Catullan Questions. Leicester: Leicester University Press, 1969.
Woolam, J. F. "Catullus and the Gods: A Study in Treatment and Symbolism," Pegasus 14 (February, 1972), 12-20.
Wright, F. A. Three Roman Poets: Plautus, Catullus, Ovid. New York: Dutton, 1938.

Zarker, J. W. "Lesbia's Charms," CJ 68 (December, 1972), 107-115.
Zetzel, J. E. G. "Homeric Reminiscence in Catullus," AJP 99 (Fall, 1978), 332-333.

Individual Works (Carmina)

One

Copley, F. O. "Catullus, c. 1," TAPA 82 (1951), 200-206.
Levine, P. "Catullus, c. 1: A Prayerful Dedication," CSCA 2 (1969), 209-216.
Singleton, D. "A Note on Catullus' First Poem," CP 67 (July, 1972), 192-196.

Two

Bishop, J. D. "Catullus 2 and Its Hellenistic Antecedents," CP 61 (July, 1966), 158-167.

Four

Copley, F. O. "Catullus c. 4: The World of the Poem," TAPA 89 (1958), 9-13.
Khan, H. A. "Humor of Catullus Carm. 4, and the Theme of Virgil, Catalepton 10," AJP 88 (April, 1967), 163-172.
Putnam, M. C. J. "Catullus' Journey (Carm. 4)," CP 57 (January, 1962), 10-19.
Richardson, L. "Catullus 4 and Catalepton 10 Again," AJP 93 (January, 1972), 215-222.

Five

Commager, S. "The Structure of Catullus 5," CJ 59 (May, 1964), 361-363.
Fredricksmeyer, E. A. "Observations on Catullus 5," AJP 91 (October, 1970), 431-445.
Grimm, R. E. "Catullus 5 Again," CJ 59 (October, 1963), 15-22.
Segal, C. "Catullus 5 and 7: A Study in Complementaries," AJP 89 (July, 1968), 284-301.

Six

Morgan, M. G. "Nescio Quid Febriculosi Scorti; A Note on Catullus 6," CQ (New Series) 27 (1977), 338-341.

Seven

Segal, C. "Catullus 5 and 7: A Study in Complementaries," AJP 89 (July, 1968), 284-301.

──────. "More Alexandrianism in Catullus VII?," Mnemosyne 27 (1974), 139-143.

Eight

Connor, P. J. "Catullus 8: The Lover's Conflict," Antichthon 8 (1974), 93-96.

Dyson, M. "Catullus 8 and 76," CQ (New Series) 23 (May, 1973), 127-143.

Fraenkel, E. "Two Poems of Catullus," JRS 51 (1961), 46-53.

Rowland, R. L. "Miser Catulle: An Interpretation of the Eighth Poem of Catullus," G & R 13 (April, 1966), 15-21.

Skinner, M. B. "Catullus 8: The Comic Amator as Eiron," CJ 66 (April-May, 1971), 298-305.

Ten

Sedgwick, W. B. "Catullus X: A Rambling Commentary," G & R 16 (October, 1947), 108-114.

Eleven

Allen, A. "Catullus' English Channel," CW 66 (November, 1972), 146-147.

Mulroy, D. "An Interpretation of Catullus 11," CW 61 (December-January, 1977-1978), 237-247.

Putnam, M. C. J. "Catullus 11: The Ironies of Integrity," Ramus 3 (1974), 70-86.

Sixteen

Sandy, G. N. "Catullus 16," Phoenix 25 (Spring, 1971), 51-57.

Winter, T. "Catullus Purified: A Brief History of Carmen 16," Areth 6 (Fall, 1973), 257-265.

Seventeen

Glenn, J. "Fossa in Catullus' Simile of the Cut Tree (17.18-19)," CP 65 (October, 1970), 256-257.

Khan, H. A. "Image and Symbol in Catullus 17," CP 64 (April, 1969), 88-97.

Quinn, K. "Practical Criticism: A Reading of Propertius i. 21 and Catullus 17," G & R 16 (April, 1969), 19-29.

Eighteen

Zarker, J. W. "Catullus 18-20," TAPA 93 (1962), 502-522.

Nineteen

Zarker, J. W. "Catullus 18-20," TAPA 93 (1962), 502-522.

Twenty

Zarker, J. W. "Catullus 18-20," TAPA 93 (1962), 502-522.

Twenty-five

Allen, A. "Goddess in Catullus," CP 69 (July, 1974), 212.

Twenty-seven

Cairns, F. "Catullus 27," Mnemosyne 28 (1975), 24-29.

Twenty-nine

Allen, A. "An Adjective for Caesar and Pompey," CJ 68 (December, 1972), 177-178.
Badian, E. "Mamura's Fourth Fortune," CP 72 (October, 1977), 320-322.
Cameron, A. "Catullus 29," Hermes 104 (1976), 155-162.
DeAngeli, E. S. "The Unity of Catullus 29," CJ 65 (November, 1969), 81-83.
Minyard, J. D. "Critical Notes on Catullus 29," CP 66 (July, 1971), 174-181.
Young, P. R. "Catullus 29," CJ 64 (April, 1969), 327-328.

Thirty-one

McCaughey, J. "The Mind Lays by Its Troubles: Catullus 31," Arion 9 (Winter, 1970), 362-365.
Witke, C. "Verbal Art in Catullus 31," AJP 93 (January, 1972), 239-251.

Thirty-five

Copley, F. O. "Catullus, 35," AJP 74 (April, 1953), 149-160.
Fisher, J. M. "Catullus 35," CP 66 (January, 1971), 1-5.
Khan, H. A. "Catullus 35--and the Things Poetry Can Do to You!," Hermes 102 (1974), 475-490.

Thirty-six

Østerud, S. "Sacrifice and Bookburning in Catullus' Poem 36," Hermes 106 (1978), 138-155.

Forty-two

Fraenkel, E. "Two Poems of Catullus," JRS 51 (1961), 46-53.

Forty-four

DeAngeli, E. S. "A Literary Chill: Catullus 44," C World 62 (May, 1969), 354-356.

Forty-five

Baker, S. "Irony of Catullus' Septimius and Acme," CP 53 (April, 1958), 110-112.
Ross, D. O. Jr. "Style and Content in Catullus 45," CP 60 (October, 1965), 256-259.
Singleton, D. "Form and Irony in Catullus 45," G & R 18 (October, 1971), 180-187.

Forty-nine

Fredricksmeyer, E. A. "Catullus 49, Cicero, and Caesar," CP 68 (October, 1973), 268-278.
Laughton, E. "Catullus 49: An Acknowledgement," CP 66 (January, 1971), 36-37.

Fifty

Scott, W. C. "Catullus and Calvus (Cat. 50)," CP 64 (July, 1969), 169-173.
Segal, C. P. "Catullan Otiosi: The Lover and the Poet," G & R 17 (April, 1970), 25-31.

Fifty-one

Frank, R. I. "Catullus 51: Otium Versus Virtus," TAPA 99 (1968), 233-240.
Fredricksmeyer, E. A. "On the Unity of Catullus 51," TAPA 96 (1965), 153-164.
Kidd, D. A. "The Unity of Catullus 51," AUMLA No. 20 (November, 1963), 298-308.
Lattimore, R. "Sappho 2 and Catullus 51," CP 39 (July, 1944), 184-187.

62 : Greek and Roman Authors

Segal, C. P. "Catullan Otiosi: The Lover and the Poet," G & R 17 (April, 1970), 25-31.
Wilkinson, L. P. "Ancient and Modern: Catullus LI Again," G & R 21 (April, 1974), 82-85.

Fifty-two

Barrett, A. A. "Catullus 52 and the Consulship of Vatinius," TAPA 103 (1972), 23-38.

Fifty-five

Foster, J. "Catullus, 55.9-12," CQ (New Series) 21 (May, 1971), 186-187.
Peachy, F. "Catullus 55," Phoenix 26 (Autumn, 1972), 258-267.

Sixty-three

Cohen, S. W. "Catullus 63: Attis the Dreamer," CB 54 (1977-1978), 49-52.
Forsyth, P. Y. "The Marriage Theme in Catullus 63," CJ 66 (October-November, 1970), 66-69.
Glenn, J. "The Yoke of Attis," CP 68 (January, 1973), 59-61.
Harkins, P. W. "Autoallegory in Catullus 63 and 64," TAPA 90 (1959), 102-116.
Knobles, C. "A Significant Elision (Cat. 63.37)," CP 66 (January, 1971), 35-36.
Mulroy, D. "Hephaestion and Catullus 63," Phoenix 30 (Spring, 1976), 61-72.
Rubino, C. A. "Myth and Mediation in the Attis Poem of Catullus," Ramus 3 (1974), 152-175.
Sandy, G. N. "Catullus 63 and the Theme of Marriage," AJP 92 (April, 1971), 185-195.
_____. "The Imagery of Catullus 63," TAPA 99 (1968), 389-400.
Scott, R. D. "Catullus 63.9," CP 68 (July, 1973), 214-215.

Sixty-four

Bramble, J. C. "Structure and Ambiguity in Catullus LXIV," PCPS 16 (1970), 22-41.
Clausen, W. "Ariadne's Leave-taking: Catullus 64. 116-120," ICS 2 (1977), 219-223.
Crabbe, A. M. "Ignoscenda Quidem; Catullus 64 and the Fourth Georgic," CQ (New Series) 27 (1977), 342-351.
Daniels, M. L. "Personal Revelation in Catullus 64," CJ 62 (May, 1962), 351-356.
_____. "The Song of the Fates in Catullus 64: Epithalamium or Dirge?," CJ 68 (December, 1972), 97-101.

Forsyth, P. Y. "Catullus 64: The Descent of Man," Antichthon 9 (1975), 41-51.
Harkins, P. W. "Autoallegory in Catullus 63 and 64," TAPA 90 (1959), 102-116.
Knopp, S. E. "Catullus 64 and the Conflict Between Amores and Virtues," CP 71 (July, 1976), 207-213.
Murley, C. "The Structure and Proportion of Catullus LXIV," TAPA 68 (1937), 305-317.
Skinner, M. B. "Iphigenia and Polyxena: A Lucretian Allusion in Catullus," PCP 11 (October, 1976), 52-61.
Thomson, D. F. S. "Aspects of Unity in Catullus 64," CJ 57 (November, 1961), 49-57.
Tracy, H. L. "A Note on Catullus 64.346," CJ 66 (October-November, 1970), 64-66.
Wolf, R. J. "Imagery in Catullus 64," C World 62 (April, 1969), 297-300.

Sixty-five

Van Sickle, J. B. "About Form and Feeling in Catullus 65," TAPA 99 (1968), 487-508.

Sixty-six

Clausen, W. "Catullus and Callimachus," HSCP 74 (1970), 85-94.
Forsyth, P. Y. "Catullus 66.54: A Note," CJ 68 (December, 1972), 174-175.
Kidd, D. A. "Some Problems in Catullus 66," Antichthon 4 (1970), 38-49.

Sixty-seven

Copley, F. O. "The Riddle of Catullus 67," TAPA 80 (1949), 245-253.
Richardson, L. "Catullus 67: Interpretation and Form," AJP 88 (October, 1967), 423-433.

Sixty-eight

Levine, P. "Catullus c. 68: A New Perspective," CSCA 9 (1976), 61-88.
McClure, R. "The Structure of Catullus 68," CSCA 7 (1974), 215-229.
Phillips, J. E. "The Pattern of Images in Catullus 68.51-62," AJP 97 (Winter, 1976), 340-343.
Prescott, H. W. "The Unity of Catullus LXVIII," TAPA 71 (1940), 473-500.
Robson, A. G. "Catullus 68.53: The Coherence and Force of Tradition," TAPA 103 (1972), 433-439.

Skinner, M. B. "The Unity of Catullus 68: The Structure of 68a," TAPA 103 (1972), 495-512.
Wilkinson, L. P. "Domina in Catullus 68," CR (New Series) 20 (December, 1970), 290.
Wiseman, T. P. "Catullus 68. 157.," CR (New Series) 24 (March, 1974), 6-7.

Seventy-two

Davis, J. T. "Poetic Counterpoint: Catullus, 72," AJP 92 (April, 1971), 196-201.
Harmon, D. P. "Catullus 72. 3-4," CJ 65 (April, 1970), 321-322.

Seventy-six

Bishop, J. D. "Catullus 76: Elegy or Epigram?," CP 67 (October, 1972), 293-294.
Dyson, M. "Catullus 8 and 76," CQ (New Series) 23 (May, 1973), 127-143.
Freis, R. "Form and Thought in Catullus 76," Agon 2 (1968), 39-58.
Rubino, C. A. "The Erotic World of Catullus," CW 68 (February, 1975), 289-298.

Eighty

Curran, L. C. "Gellius and the Lover's Pallor: A Note on Catullus 80," Arion 5 (Spring, 1966), 24-27.

Eighty-two

Forsyth, P. Y. "Catullus 82," CJ 70 (March, 1975), 33-35.

Eighty-four

Baker, R. J. and B. A. Marshall. "Avunculus Liber (Catullus 84,5)," Mnemosyne 30 (1977), 292-293.
———. "Commoda and Insidiae: Catullus 84. 1-4," CP 73 (January, 1978), 49-50.
Holoka, J. P. "Self-Delusion in Catullus 83 and 92," CW 69 (September, 1975), 119-120.

Ninety-six

Davis, J. T. "Quo Desiderio: The Structure of Catullus 96," Hermes 99 (1971), 297-302.

Ninety-nine

Marshall, J. C. D. "Catullus 99," CW 65 (October, 1971), 57-58.

One hundred

Forsyth, P. Y. "The Irony of Catullus 100," CW 70 (February, 1977), 313-317.

One hundred one

Howe, N. P. "The Terce Muse of Catullus 101," CP 69 (October, 1974), 274-276.

One hundred three

De Grummond, W. W. "A Note on Catullus 103," CP 66 (July, 1971), 188-189.

One hundred eleven

Bush, A. C. "A Further Note on Catullus 111," CW 65 (January, 1972), 148-151.
De Grummond, W. W. "A Note on Catullus 111," CW 64 (September, 1970), 120-121.

One hundred sixteen

Macleod, C. W. "Catullus 116," CQ (New Series) 23 (November, 1973), 304-309.
Forsyth, P. Y. "Comments on Catullus 116," CQ (New Series) 27 (1977), 352-353.

CICERO

General Criticism

Abbo, J. A. "Ancient Greece and Rome: Cicero," in his Political Thought: Men and Ideas. Westminster, Md.: Newman, 1960, pp. 50-60.
Allen, W. "Cicero's Conceit," TAPA 85 (1954), 121-144.
⸺⸺. "On the Importance of Young Men in Ciceronian Politics," CJ 33 (March, 1938), 357-359.
Atkins, J. W. H. "Critical Beginnings at Rome and the Classical

Reaction: Terence, Lucilius, and Cicero," in his Literary Criticism in Antiquity; A Sketch of Its Development. Toronto: Macmillan, 1934, Vol. 2, pp. 1-46.

Badian, E. "Cicero: Words and Illusions," HT 9 (January, 1959), 13-21.

Baley, M. T. "Ciceronian Metrics and Clausulae," CJ 33 (March, 1938), 336-350.

Barbary, J. Young Cicero. New York: Roy, 1965.

Baron, H. "Cicero and the Roman Civic Spirit in the Middle Ages and the Early Renaissance," JRLB 22 (1938), 72-97.

Bennett, H. "The Wit's Progress--A Study in the Life of Cicero," CJ 30 (January, 1935), 193-202.

Clarke, M. L. "Cicero at School," G & R 15 (April, 1968), 18-22.
──────. Roman Mind; Studies in the History of Thought from Cicero to Marcus Aurelius. Cambridge, Mass.: Harvard University Press, 1956, pp. 8-18; 42-65.

Coleman-Norton, P. R. "Cicero and the Music of the Spheres," CJ 45 (February, 1950), 237-241.

Collins, J. H. "Cicero and Catullus," CJ 48 (October, 1952), 11-17.

Conway, R. S. "Originality of Cicero," JRLB 14 (1930), 361-385.

Cowell, F. R. Cicero and the Roman Republic. New York: Chanticleer, 1948.

Davies, J. C. "Was Cicero Aware of Natural Beauty?," G & R 18 (October, 1971), 152-165.

DeGraff, T. B. "Plato in Cicero," CP 35 (April, 1940), 143-153.

Delayen, G. Cicero, tr. by F. Symons. London: Dent, 1931.

Dorey, T. A., ed. Cicero. New York: Basic, 1965.

Douglas, A. E. Cicero (Greece and Rome: New Surveys in the Classics no. 2). Oxford: Clarendon, 1968.

Downs, R. B. "Greatest Roman Orator: Marcus Tullius Cicero," in his Famous Books, Ancient and Medieval. New York: Barnes and Noble, 1964, pp. 158-165.

Dutton, A. R. "What Ministers Men Must, for Practice, Use: Ben Jonson's Cicero," ES 59 (August, 1978), 324-335.

Emilie, S. G. "Cicero and the Roman Pietas," CJ 39 (June, 1944), 536-542.

Fantham, E. "Aequabilitas in Cicero's Political Theory and the Greek Tradition of Proportional Justice," CQ (New Series) 23 (November, 1973), 285-290.

Feibleman, J. K. "Some Classical Theories of Comedy," in his In Praise of Comedy; A Study in Its Theory and Practice. New York: Macmillan, 1939, pp. 74-122.

Forbat, S. Tremulous Hero. London: Pallas, 1939.

Frederiksen, M. W. "Caesar, Cicero and the Problem of Debt," JRS 56 (1966), 128-141.

Fulford-Jones, P. W. "Calvus Ex Nanneianis," CQ (New Series) 21 (May, 1971), 183-185.

Geweke, L. K. "Notes on the Political Relationship of Cicero and Atticus from 56 to 43 B.C.," CJ 32 (May, 1937), 467-481.

Grant, W. L. "Cicero on the Moral Character of the Orator," CJ 38 (May, 1943), 472-478.

Guite, H. "Cicero's Attitude to the Greeks," G & R 9 (October, 1962), 142-159.
Hadas, M. "Cicero," in his History of Latin Literature. New York: Columbia University Press, 1952, pp. 108-139.
Hamilton, J. R. "Pen or Dagger?," CR (New Series) 14 (March, 1964), 10-12.
Haskell, H. J. This Was Cicero; Modern Politics in a Roman Toga. London: Secker and Warburg, 1943.
Hayes, G. P. "Cicero's Humanism Today," CJ 34 (February, 1939), 283-290.
Hough, L. H. Great Humanists. Nashville, Tenn.: Abingdon, 1952.
Howe, H. M. "Amatinius, Lucretius and Cicero," AJP 72 (January, 1951), 57-62.
Hunt, H. A. K. Humanism of Cicero. Carlton, Australia: Melbourne University Press, 1954.
Johnson, W. R. Luxuriance and Economy: Cicero and the Alien Style. Berkeley: University of California Press, 1971.
Lacey, W. K. Cicero and the end of the Roman Republic. New York: Barnes and Noble, 1978.
Laughton, E. "Cicero and the Greek Orators," AJP 82 (January, 1961), 27-49.
Levine, P. "Cicero and the Literary Dialogue," CJ 53 (January, 1958), 146-151.
Lintott, A. W. "Reflections on Cicero by a Ciceronian," CW 63 (January, 1970), 145-153.
Loefstedt, E. "Cicero's Life and Work," in his Roman Literary Portraits. Oxford: Clarendon, 1958, pp. 67-92.
McDermott, W. C. "Reflections on Cicero by a Ciceronian," C World 63 (January, 1970), 145-153.
Martyn, J. R. C. Cicero and Virgil. Amsterdam: Hakkert, 1972.
Meinecke, B. "The Medical Conceptions of a Roman Layman," CJ 41 (December, 1945), 113-118.
Murray, R. J. "Cicero and the Gracchi," TAPA 97 (1966), 91-299.
Newman, J. H. "Personal and Literary Character of Cicero," in his Essays and Sketches. New York: Longmans, Green, 1948, Vol. 1, pp. 1-53.
Petersson, T. Cicero: A Biography. New York: Biblo and Tannen, 1963.
Petrarch, F. "On His Own Ignorance and That of Many Others," in E. Cassirer, P. O. Kristeller, and J. H. Randall, eds., Renaissance Philosophy of Man. Chicago: University of Chicago Press, 1948, pp. 47-133.
Poteat, H. M. "One Who Loved His Country Well," CJ 29 (December, 1933), 169-188.
Ramage, E. S. "Urbanitas: Cicero and Quintilian, a Contrast in Attitudes," AJP 84 (October, 1963), 390-414.
Rawson, E. "Cicero the Historian and Cicero the Antiquarian," JRS 62 (1972), 33-45.
──────. Cicero: A Portrait. London: Lane, 1975.
──────. "Lucius Crassus and Cicero," PCPS 17 (1971), 79-88.
Richards, G. C. Cicero; A Study. Westport, Conn.: Greenwood, 1970.

68 : Greek and Roman Authors

Rolfe, J. C. Cicero and His Influence. New York: Cooper Square, 1963.
Rowland, R. J. "Cicero and the Greek World," TAPA 103 (1972), 451-461.
_____. "A Survey of Selected Ciceronian Bibliography, 1953-1965, I.," C World 60 (October, 1966), 51-65.
_____. "A Survey of Selected Ciceronian Bibliography, 1953-1965, II.," C World 60 (November, 1966), 101-115.
Savage, J. J. "Catiline in Vergil and in Cicero," CJ 36 (January, 1941), 225-226.
Shackleton Bailey, D. R. Cicero. New York: Scribner's, 1971.
Shaull, D. "Cicero and Modern Problems," CJ 26 (January, 1931), 266-272.
Sihler, E. G. Cicero of Arpinum. New York: Cooper Square, 1969.
Silk, E. T. "Notes on Cicero and the Odes of Horace," YCS 13 (1952), 145-158.
Sinkovitch, K. A. "Roman History According to Cicero," CN & V 17 (October, 1973), 102-106.
Smethurst, S. E. "Cicero and Isocrates," TAPA 84 (1953), 262-320.
Smith, R. E. Cicero the Statesman. London: Cambridge University Press, 1966.
Solmsen, F. "Aristotle and Cicero on the Orator's Playing upon the Feelings," CP 33 (October, 1938), 390-404.
Sprott, S. E. "Cicero's Theory of Prose Style," PQ 34 (January, 1955), 1-17.
Steiner, G. "Cicero as a Mythologist," CJ 63 (February, 1968), 193-199.
Stockton, D. Cicero: A Political Biography. London: Oxford University Press, 1971.
Strachan-Davidson, J. L. Cicero and the Fall of the Roman Republic. Freeport, N. Y.: Books for Libraries, 1972.
Sullivan, F. A. "Intimations of Immorality Among the Ancient Romans," CJ 39 (October, 1943), 15-24.
Taylor, L. R. "Cicero's Aedileship," AJP 60 (April, 1939), 194-202.
Treggiari, S. "The Freedmen of Cicero," G & R 16 (October, 1969), 195-204.
Ullman, B. L. "Cicero and Modern Politics," CJ 30 (April, 1935), 385-402.
Wagener, A. P. "Reflections of Personal Experience in Cicero's Ethical Doctrine," CJ 31 (March, 1936), 359-370.
Wilkin, R. N. "Cicero: Oracle of Natural Law," CJ 44 (May, 1949), 453-456.
_____. Eternal Lawyer: A Legal Biography of Cicero. New York: Macmillan, 1947.

Individual Works (Letters)

General

Austin, L. "The Caerellia of Cicero's Correspondence," CJ 41 (April, 1946), 305-309.

Carcopino, J. Cicero, the Secrets of His Correspondence, tr. by
　　E. O. Lorimer. New Haven, Conn.: Yale University Press,
　　1951.
Colaclides, P. "Ennius and Cicero, Philosophiae Fontes Aperiemus,"
　　CSCA 4 (1971), 111-113.
Fernandes, J. J. "Public Letters of Cicero," Comm Q 26 (Winter,
　　1978), 21-26.
Finch, C. E. "Codices Vat. Lat. 1701, 2110, and 8591 as Sources
　　for Cicero's Topica," CP 67 (April, 1972), 112-117.
Fredricksmeyer, E. A. "Catullus 49, Cicero and Caesar," CP 68
　　(October, 1973), 268-278.
Gonin, H. L. "Potentia by Cicero. 'N Woordondersoek," AClass
　　17 (1974), 49-57.
Holliday, V. L. "Pompey in Cicero's Correspondence and Lucan's
　　Civil War," Studies in Classical Literature III. The Hague: Mou-
　　ton, 1969.
Imboltz, A. A. "Gladiatorial Metaphors in Cicero's Pro Sex. Roscio
　　Amerino," CW 65 (March, 1972), 228-230.
McDermott, W. C. "Cicero: The Human Side," CB 49 (December,
　　1972), 17-25.
MacLaren, M. "The Dating of Cicero's Letters by Consular Names,"
　　CJ 65 (January, 1970), 168-172.
_____. "Wordplays Involving Bovillae in Cicero's Letters," AJP
　　87 (April, 1966), 192-202.
Wiseman, T. P. "Two Friends of Clodius in Cicero's Letters,"
　　CQ (New Series) 18 (1968), 297-302.

Ad Atticum

Bailey, D. R. S. "Expectatio Corfiniensis [relevant letters in Ci-
　　cero's correspondence]," JRS 46 (1956), 57-64.
Brunt, P. A. "Cicero, Ad Atticum xiv. 5. 1.," CR (New Series)
　　11 (December, 1961), 199-200.
Hathorn, R. Y. The Political Implications of the Trial of P. Clo-
　　dius, 61 B. C. Ann Arbor, Mich.: University Microfilms, 1950.
Innes, D. C. "Cicero, Ad Atticum i. 14. 4.," CR (New Series) 16
　　(June, 1966), 145-146.
Jocelyn, H. D. "Cicero, Ad Atticum i. 18. 1.," CR (New Series)
　　16 (June, 1966), 149-150.
Watt, W. S. "Cicero. Ad Atticum 4.3," CQ 43 (1949), 9-21.
_____. "Cicero. Ad Atticum v. 12.2," CR (New Series) 13
　　(June, 1963), 129-131.
_____. "Notes on Cicero, Ad Atticum 1 and 2," CQ (New Series)
　　12 (1962), 252-262.

Ad Familiares

Grant, W. L. "Cicero, Ad fam. viii, 8,9.," CR 61 (May, 1947),
　　10-11.
Mitchell, T. N. "Cicero Before Luca (September 57-April 56 B.C.),"
　　TAPA 100 (1969), 295-320.

Stroux, J. "Cicero an Volumnius (Ad fam. VII 33)," Philologus 93 No. 3 (1939), 408-411.

Ad Quintum fratrem

Baldson, J. P. V. D. "The Commentariolum Petitionis," CQ (New Series) 13 (1963), 242-250.
Marshall, A. J. "Cicero, Ad Quintum fratrem ii, 10, 1," CR (New Series) 18 (March, 1968), 16-17.

Orations

General

Clarke, M. L. "Ciceronian Oratory," G & R 14 (June, 1945), 72-82.
Matthews, V. J. "Some Puns on Roman Cognomina," G & R 20 (April, 1973), 20-24.
McDermott, W. C. "In Ligarianam," TAPA 101 (1970), 317-347.
Nisbet, R. G. M. "The Speeches," in T. A. Dorey, ed., Cicero. New York: Basic, 1965, pp. 47-79.
Solmsen, F. "Cicero's First Speeches: A Rhetorical Analysis," TAPA 69 (1938), 542-556.
Usher, S. "Occultatio in Cicero's Speeches," AJP 86 (April, 1965), 175-192.

De Haruspicum Responso

Lenaghan, J. O. A Commentary on Cicero's Oration De Haruspicum Responso. The Hague: Mouton, 1969.

De Imperio Cn. Pompei

Jonkers, E. J. Social and Economic Commentary on Cicero's De Imperio Cn. Pompei. Leiden: Brill, 1959.

In Catilinam

Crane, T. "Times of the Night in Cicero's First Catilinarian," CJ 61 (March, 1961), 264-267.
Matier, K. O. "Cicero the Orator," Akroterion 22 (April, 1977), 1-10.

In Pisonem

Marshall, B. A. "The Date of Delivery of Cicero's In Pisonem," CQ (New Series) 25 (1975), 88-93.

Pearce, T. E. V. "Notes on Cicero, In Pisonem," CQ (New Series) 20 (November, 1970), 309-320.

In Vatinium

Pocock, L. G. A Commentary on Cicero in Vatinium. Amsterdam: Hakkert, 1967, pp. 1-28.

Philippicae

Dorey, T. A. "Cicero Philippic 14. 18, De Contentione Principatus," CP 65 (April, 1970), 98-99.
Frisch, H. Cicero's Fight for the Republic. Copenhagen: Gyldendal, 1946.
Plumpe, J. C. "Roman Elements in Cicero's Panegyric on the Legio Martia," CJ 36 (February, 1941), 275-289.

Pro Archia

Taylor, J. H. "Political Motives in Cicero's Defense of Archias," AJP 73 (January, 1952), 62-70.

Pro Caelio

Dorey, T. A. "Cicero, Clodia and the Pro Caelio," G & R 5 (1958), 175-180.
Geffcken, K. A. Comedy in the Pro Caelio, with an Appendix on the In Clodium et Curionem. Leiden: Brill, 1973.
Volpe, M. "The Persuasive Force of Humor: Cicero's Defense of Caelius," QJS 63 (October, 1977), 311-312.

Pro Cluentio

Hoenigswald, G. S. "The Murder Charges in Cicero's Pro Cluentio," TAPA 93 (1962), 109-123.
May, E. C. A Rhetorical Commentary on Cicero's Pro Cluentio. Ann Arbor, Mich.: University Microfilms, 1952.
Woodley, E. C. "Cicero's Pro Cluentio: An Ancient Cause Célèbre," CJ 42 (April, 1947), 415-418.

Pro Lege Manilia

Claassen, J. M. "An Introduction to Cicero's Pro Lege Manilia," Akroterion 20 (January, 1975), 14-21.

Pro Sestio

Lacey, W. K. "Cicero, Pro Sestio 96-143," CQ (New Series) 12 (1962), 67-71.
Tucker, G. M. "Cicero, Pro Sestio, 72," CR 56 (July, 1942), 68-69.

Philosophy

General

Buckley, M. J. "Philosophic Method in Cicero," JHP 8 (April, 1970), 143-154.
Cairns, G. "Cicero," in his Legal Philosophy from Plato to Hegel. Baltimore: Johns Hopkins Press, 1949, pp. 127-162.
Coleman-Norton, P. R. "The Fragmentary Philosophical Treatises of Cicero," CJ 34 (January, 1939), 213-228.
Douglas, A. E. "Cicero the Philosopher," in T. A. Dorey, ed., Cicero. New York: Basic, 1965, pp. 135-170.
McNamee, M. B. "Cicero's Magnanimous Man," in his Honor and the Epic Hero; A Study of the Shifting Concept of Magnanimity in Philosophy and Epic Poetry. New York: Holt, Rinehart and Winston, 1960, pp. 40-50.
Zetzel, J. E. G. "Cicero and the Scipionic Circle," HSCP 76 (1972), 173-180.

De Fato

Luck, G. "On Cicero, De Fato 5 and Related Passages," AJP 99 (Summer, 1978), 155-158.

De Natura Deorum

Ardley, G. W. R. "Cotta and the Theologians," Prudentia 5 (May, 1973), 33-50.
Solmsen, F. "Cicero De natura deorum iii. 53ff.," CP 39 (January, 1944), 44-47.
_____. Cleanthes or Posidonius? The Basis of Stoic Physics. Amsterdam: North-Holland, 1961.

De Officiis

Higgenbotham, J. "Introduction," On Moral Obligation. Berkeley: University of California Press, 1967, pp. 11-30.
Holden, H. A., ed., M. Tulli Ciceronis De Officiis libri tres. Amsterdam: Hakkert, 1966, pp. xiii-xxxiii.
Korfmacher, W. C. "Cicero and the Bellum Lustum," CB 48 (February, 1972), 49-52.

McMullin, B. J. "Immaculate Cicero: The Foulis Press De Officiis (1757)," BSAP 72 (April, 1978), 161-168.
Walcot, P. "Cicero on Private Property Theory and Practice," G & R 22 (October, 1975), 120-128.
Wellman, R. R. "An Argument in De Officiis," CJ 60 (March, 1965), 271-272.

De Oratore

Dyck, A. R. "Cicero De Oratore 2. 100.," CP 73 (July, 1978), 232-233.
Fantham, E. "Imitation and Evolution: The Discussion of Rhetorical Imitation in Cicero De Oratore 2, 87-97 and Some Related Problems of Ciceronian Theory," CP 73 (January, 1978), 1-16.

De Republica

Behr, C. A. "New Fragment of Cicero's De Republica," AJP 95 (Summer, 1974), 141-149.
Hathaway, R. F. "Cicero, De Republica II, and His Socratic Views of History," JHI 29 (January, 1968), 3-12.
Nicholls, J. J. "Cicero De Republica 2. 39-40 and the Centuriate Assembly," CP 59 (April, 1964), 102-105.
Sumner, G. V. "Cicero on the Comitia Centuriate: De Republica, II, 22, 39-40," AJP 81 (April, 1960), 136-156.

De Senectute, or Cato Major

Blaiklock, E. M. Cicero on Old Age (Classics Series, 7). Auckland: University of Auckland, 1966.

Somnium Scipionis

Macrobius, A. A. T. Commentary on the Dream of Scipio. New York: Columbia University Press, 1952, pp. 3-65.
Sier, A. A. C. Cicero's Somnium Scipionis. [n. p.]: Nijmegen, 1945.

Poetry

General

Jocelyn, H. D. "Greek Poetry in Cicero's Prose Writings," YCS 23 (1973), 61-111.
Morford, M. P. O. "Ancient and Modern in Cicero's Poetry," CP 62 (April, 1967), 112-116.
Spaeth, J. W. "Cicero the Poet," CJ 26 (April, 1931), 500-512.

Thomson, D. F. S. "Catullus and Cicero: Poetry and the Criticism of Poetry," C World 60 (February, 1967), 225-230.
Townend, G. B. "The Poems," in T. A. Dorey, ed., Cicero. New York: Basic, 1965, pp. 109-134.

Rhetoric

General

Grube, G. M. A. "Cicero: The Education of the Orator," in his The Greek and Roman Critics. Toronto: University of Toronto Press, 1965, pp. 168-192.
MacKendrick, P. "Cicero's Ideal Orator--Truth and Propaganda," CJ 43 (March, 1948), 339-347.
Meador, P. H. "Rhetoric and Humanism in Cicero," P & R 3 (Winter, 1970), 1-12.

Brutus, or De Claris Oratoribus

Douglas, A. E. "Oratorum Aetates," AJP 87 (July, 1966), 290-306.
Fantham, E. "Cicero, Varro, and M. Claudius Marcellus," Phoenix 31 (Autumn, 1977), 208-213.
Sumner, G. V. The Orators in Cicero's Brutus: Prosopography and Chronology. Toronto: University of Toronto Press, 1973.

De Oratore

Fantham, E. "Ciceronian Conciliare and Aristotelian Ethos," Phoenix 27 (Autumn, 1973), 262-275.
Kinsey, T. E. "Cicero, De Oratore II 124," Mnemosyne 30 (1977), 74-75.

CLAUDIAN

General Criticism

Bruere, R. T. "Lucan and Claudian: The Invectives," CP 59 (October, 1964), 223-256.
Cameron, A. Claudian: Poetry and Propaganda at the Court of Honorius. Oxford: Clarendon, 1970.
_____. "Notes on Claudian's Invectives," CQ (New Series) 18 (November, 1968), 387-411.
Christiansen, P. G. "Claudian Versus the Opposition," TAPA 97 (1966), 45-54.
_____. The Use of Images by Claudius Claudianus. The Hague: Mouton, 1969.

Dilke, O. A. W. Claudian: Poet of Declining Empire and Morals. Leeds: Leeds University Press, 1969.
Eaton, A. H. Influence of Ovid on Claudian. Washington, D. C.: Catholic University of America Press, 1943.
Hadas, M. "Humanist Survival in Poetry," in his History of Latin Literature. New York: Columbia University Press, 1952, pp. 381-413.
Levy, H. L. "Claudian's Neglect of Magic as Motif," TAPA 79 (1948), 87-91.
──────. "Themes of Encomium and Invective in Claudian," TAPA 89 (1958), 336-347.
Semple, W. H. "Notes on Some Astronomical Passages of Claudian," CQ 31 (July, 1937), 161-169.
──────. "Notes on Some Astronomical Passages of Claudian," CQ 33 (January, 1939), 1-8.

Individual Works

Against Rufinus, or In Rufinum

Levy, H. L. Claudian's In Rufinum. Cleveland: Case Western Reserve, 1971.
──────. "Claudian's In Rufinum and an Epistle of St. Jerome," AJP 69 (January, 1948), 62-68.
──────. "Two Notes on Claudian's In Rufinum; Punitive Metempsychosis in II, 480-490; Tisiphone and Dualism," AJP 68 (January, 1947), 64-73.

DEMOSTHENES

General Criticism

Adams, C. D. Demosthenes and His Influence. New York: Cooper Square, 1963.
Bonnard, A. "Demosthenes and the End of the World of City-states," in his Greek Civilization: From Euripides to Alexandria. New York: Macmillan, 1961, 64-74.
Cawkwell, G. L. "The Crowning of Demosthenes," CQ (New Series) 19 (May, 1969), 163-180.
Davies, J. K. "Demosthenes on Liturgies: A Note," J Hel S 87 (1967), 33-40.
Downs, R. B. "Supreme Orator: Demosthenes," in his Famous Books, Ancient and Medieval. New York: Barnes and Noble, 1964, pp. 104-107.
Dunkel, H. B. "Was Demosthenes a Panhellenist?" CP 33 (July, 1938), 291-305.
Ellis, J. R., and R. D. Milns. The Spectre of Philip. Sydney: Sydney University Press, 1970.

Goldstein, J. A. The Letters of Demosthenes. New York: Columbia University Press, 1968.
Jaeger, W. W. "Demosthenes: The Death-struggle and Transfiguration of the City-state," in his Paideia: The Ideals of Greek Culture. Oxford: B. Blackwell, 1944-1947. Vol. 3, pp. 263-289.
_____. Demosthenes, the Origin and Growth of His Policy. Berkeley: University of California Press, 1938.
Jebb, R. C. "The Matured Civil Eloquence," in his The Attic Orators; From Antiphon to Isaeos. New York: Russell and Russell, 1962, Vol. 2, pp. 369-418.
Jones, A. H. M. The Athens of Demosthenes. London: Cambridge University Press, 1952.
Pearson, L. The Art of Demosthenes. Meisenheim a. Glan: Hain, 1976.
_____. "The Virtuoso Passages in Demosthenes' Speeches," Phoenix 29 (Autumn, 1975), 214-230.
Pickard-Cambridge, A. W. Demosthenes and the Last Days of Greek Freedom, 384-322 B.C. New York: AMS, 1978.
Ryder, B. "Demosthenes and Philip's Peace of 338/7 B.C.," CQ (New Series) 26 (1976), 85-87.
Usher, S. "Demosthenes, Statesman and Patriot," HT 26 (March, 1976), 164-171.
Vince, J. H. Demosthenes. Cambridge, Mass.: Harvard University, 1937.

Individual Works

Chersonese, or De Chersoneso

Daitz, S. G. "Relationship of the De Chersoneso and the Philippica Quarta of Demosthenes," CP 52 (July, 1957), 145-162.

On the Crown, or De Corona

Donnelly, F. P. "Argument Used Seventy-two Times in the Crown Speech of Demosthenes," in his Literature, the Leading Educator. New York: Longmans, 1938, pp. 73-87.
Murphy, J. J., ed. Demosthenes' On the Crown. New York: Random House, 1967.
Rowe, G. O. "The Portrait of Aeschines in the Oration on the Crown," TAPA 97 (1966), 397-406.

Phillipics

Calhoun, G. M. "Demosthenes' Second Phillipic," TAPA 64 (1933), 1-17.
Daitz, S. G. "Relationship of the De Chersoneso and the Philppica Quarta of Demosthenes," CP 52 (July, 1957), 145-162.

Wooten, C. W. "A Few Observations on Form and Content in Demosthenes," Phoenix 31 (Autumn, 1977), 258-261.

ENNIUS

General Criticism

Hadas, M. "The Beginnings," in his History of Latin Literature. New York: Columbia University Press, 1952, pp. 15-32.
Lefkowitz, M. R. "Metaphor and Simile in Ennius," CJ 55 (December, 1963), 123-125.
MacKay, L. A. "In Defense of Ennius," CR (New Series) 13 (December, 1963), 264-265.
Newman, J. K. "Ennius the Mystic. 1. The Terms of the Debate," G & R 10 (October, 1963), 132-139.
_____. "Ennius the Mystic. 2. The Technical Revolution," G & R 12 (April, 1965), 42-49.
_____. "Ennius the Mystic. 3. Man Becomes God," G & R 14 (April, 1967), 44-51.
Poesch, J. "Ennius and Basinio of Parma," JWCI 25 (January/June, 1962), 116-118.
Scullard, H. H. "Ennius, Cato, and 'Surus,'" CR (New Series) 3 (December, 1953), 140-142.
Skutsch, O. "Notes on Metempsychosis (Peacock in the Ancestry of Pythagoras and of Ennius)," CP 54 (April, 1959), 114-116.

Individual Works

Annales

Fraenkel, E. "Enniana V," CQ (New Series) 13 (May, 1963), 89-100.
Korfmacher, W. C. "Epic Quality in Ennius," CJ 50 (November, 1954), 79-84.
Lembke, J. "Questions and Answers," Arion 7 (Winter, 1968), 608-614.
Skutsch, O. The Annals of Quintus Ennius. London: Published for the University by H. K. Lewis, 1953.
_____. "Enniana I," CQ 38 (July, 1944), 79-86.
_____. "Enniana II," CQ 42 (July, 1948), 94-101.
_____. "Enniana III," CQ (New Series) 10 (November, 1960), 188-198.
_____. "Enniana IV," CQ (New Series) 11 (November, 1961), 252-267.
_____. "Enniana VI," CQ (New Series) 14 (May, 1964), 85-93.
_____. "Notes on Ennius, III," BICS 24 (1977), 1-6.
_____. Studia Enniana. London: Athlone, 1968.

78 : Greek and Roman Authors

Tragedies

Brooks, R. A. "Ennius and Roman Tragedy," HSCP 60, 291-294.
Jocelyn, H. D. "The Tragedies of Ennius: The Fragments," in his Ennius. London: Cambridge University Press, 1967, pp. 3-63.

EURIPIDES

General Criticism

Abel, D. H. "Euripides' 'Deus ex Machina,'" CJ 50 (December, 1954), 127-130.
Appleton, R. B. Euripides the Idealist. Freeport, N.Y.: Books for Libraries, 1972.
Arnott, G. "Euripides and the Unexpected," G & R 20 (April, 1973), 49-64.
Bacon, H. H. "Euripides," in his Barbarians in Greek Tragedy. New Haven, Conn.: Yale University Press, 1961, pp. 115-188.
Barlow, S. A. The Imagery of Euripides: A Study in the Dramatic Use of Pictorial Language. London: Methuen, 1970.
Bates, W. N. Euripides. Cranbury, Conn.: Barnes, 1961.
Blaiklock, E. M. Male Characters of Euripides. Wellington: New Zealand University Press, 1952.
Bogardus, E. S. "Social Distance in Greek Drama," Sociol Soc Res 33 (March, 1949), 291-295.
Brown, S. G. "Metrical Innovations in Euripides' Later Plays," AJP 95 (Fall, 1974), 207-234.
Burian, P. "Euripides the Contortionist," Arion (New Series) 3 (1976), 96-113.
Burnett, A. P. Catastrophe Survived: Euripides' Plays of Mixed Reversal. Oxford: Clarendon, 1971.
Buttrey, T. V. "Tragedy as Form in Euripides," MQR 15 (Spring, 1976), 155-172.
Collard, C. "Formal Debates in Euripides' Drama," G & R 22 (April, 1975), 58-71.
Conacher, D. J. Euripidean Drama: Myth, Theme and Structure. Toronto: University of Toronto Press, 1967.
Decharme, P. Euripides and the Spirit of His Dramas. Port Washington, N.Y.: Kennikat, 1968.
Downs, R. B. "First Modern Playwright: Euripides," in his Famous Books, Ancient and Medieval. New York: Barnes and Noble, 1964, pp. 60-68.
Finley, J. H. "Euripides and Thucydides," HSCP 49 (1938), 23-68.
Gassner, J. W. "Euripides, the Modern," in his Masters of the Drama. New York: Random House, 1940, pp. 56-78.
Gehrke, R. D. A Study of the Prayers in Euripidean Drama. Chicago Library, 1959.
Gredley, B. "Choruses in Euripides," BICS 20 (May, 1973), 164-165.

Greenwood, L. H. G. Aspects of Euripidean Tragedy. New York: Russell and Russell, 1972.
Grube, G. M. A. The Drama of Euripides. New York: Barnes and Noble, 1973.
Hamilton, E. "Euripides, the Modern Mind," in her Great Age of Greek Literature. New York: Norton, 1942, pp. 271-283.
Hamilton, R. "Prologue Prophecy and Plot in Four Plays of Euripides," AJP 99 (Fall, 1978), 277-302.
Harsh, P. W. "Euripides," in his Handbook of Classical Drama. Stanford, Calif. : Stanford University Press, 1944, pp. 156-253.
Jaeger, W. W. Paideia: The Ideals of Greek Culture. Oxford: B. Blackwell, 1944-47. Vol. 1, pp. 332-357.
Kieffer, J. S. "Philoctetes and Arete; Comparison of the Plays of Aeschylus and Euripides with That of Sophocles," CP 37 (January, 1942), 38-50.
Koniaris, G. L. "Alexander, Palomedes, Troades, Sisyphus: A Connected Tetralogy? A Connected Trilogy?" HSCP 77 (1973), 85-124.
Lucas, D. W. "Euripides," in his Greek Tragic Poets; Their Contribution to Western Life and Thought. Boston: Beacon, 1952, pp. 155-224.
Lucas, F. L. Euripides and His Influence. New York: Cooper Square, 1963.
Melchinger, S. Euripides. New York: Ungar, 1973.
_____. Euripides, tr. by S. R. Rosenbaum. New York: Ungar, 1973.
Mierow, H. E. "The Amazing Modernity of Euripides," CJ 48 (March, 1953), 247-252.
Moore, G. S. The Theme of Family Disaster in the Tragedies of Euripides and Shakespeare. Ann Arbor, Mich. : University Microfilms, 1960.
Muller, H. J. "Euripides, the Rebel," in his Spirit of Tragedy. New York: Knopf, 1956, pp. 103-136.
Murray, G. Euripides and His Age. London: Oxford University Press, 1965.
_____. "Ritual Elements in the New Comedy," CQ 37 (January, 1943), 36-54.
Nicoll, A. "Dawn of Realism: Euripides," in his World Drama, from Aeschylus to Anouilh. New York: Harcourt, Brace, 1953, pp. 69-89.
Norwood, G. Essays on Euripidean Drama. Berkeley: University of California Press, 1954.
Post, L. A. "Euripidean Tragedy," in his From Homer to Menander; Forces in Greek Poetic Fiction. Berkeley: University of California Press, 1951, pp. 122-155.
Pratt, N. T. "Tragedy and Moralism, Euripides and Seneca," in N. P. Stallknecht and H. Franz, eds. , Comparative Literature: Method and Perspective. Carbondale: Southern Illinois University Press, 1961, pp. 189-203.
Pucci, P. "Euripides Heautontimoroumenos," TAPA 98 (1967), 365-372.
Rexroth, K. "Euripides," in his Classics Revisited. Chicago: Quadrangle, 1968, pp. 56-60.

Russell, A. G. "Euripides and the New Comedy," G & R 6 (February, 1937), 103-110.
Salter, W. H. Essays on Two Moderns: Euripides and Samuel Butler. Port Washington, N. Y.: Kennikat, 1970.
Segal, E., ed. Euripides: A Collection of Critical Essays. Englewood Cliffs, N. J.: Prentice-Hall, 1968.
Sri, Pathmanathan, R. "A Playwright Relaxed or Overworked?" G & R 10 (October, 1963), 123-130.
Stahl, H. P. "On 'Extra-Dramatic' Communication of Characters in Euripides," YCS 25 (1977), 159-176.
Stanley-Porter, D. P. "Mute Actors in the Tragedies of Euripides," BICS 20 (1973), 68-93.
Sutton, D. F. "The Relation Between Tragedies and Fourth Place Plays in Three Instances," Areth 4 (Spring, 1971), 55-72.
Todd, O. J. "Euripides and Aristophanes; Ancient and Modern Criticism of the Greek Dramatists," Roy Soc Can Trans (Series 3) 41 Sec. 2 (1947), 115-135.
Vellacott, P. Ironic Drama: A Study of Euripides' Method and Meaning. London: Cambridge University Press, 1975.
Verral, A. W. Euripides the Rationalist: A Study in the History of Art and Religion. New York: Russell and Russell, 1967.
Webster, T. B. L. The Tragedies of Euripides. London: Methuen, 1967.
Whitman, C. H. Euripides and the Full Circle of Myth. Cambridge, Mass.: Harvard University Press, 1974.
Wycherley, R. E. "Aristophanes and Euripides," G & R 15 (October, 1946), 98-107.
Zuntz, G. The Political Plays of Euripides. Manchester: Manchester University Press, 1955.

Individual Works

Alcestis

Blumenthal, H. J. "Euripides: Alcestis 282ff and the Authenticity of Antigone 905ff," CR (New Series) 24 (November, 1974), 174-175.
Burnett, A. P. "Virtues of Admetus," CP 60 (October, 1965), 240-255.
Driver, T. F. Sense of History in Greek and Shakespearean Drama. New York: Columbia University Press, 1960, pp. 168-198.
Golden, L. "Euripides' Alcestis: Structure and Theme," CJ 66 (January, 1971), 116-125.
Gross, N. P. "Alcestis and the Rhetoric of Departure," QJS 60 (October, 1974), 296-305.
Jones, D. M. "Euripides' Alcestis; Certain Features of Dramatic Importance in the Composition of the Play," CR 62 (September, 1948), 50-55.
Nielsen, R. M. "Alcestis: A Paradox in Dying," Ramus 5 (1976), 92-102.
Pandin, T. A. "Alcestis 1052 and the Yielding of Admetus," CJ 70 (February, 1974), 50-52.

Rosenmeyer, T. G. The Masks of Tragedy: Essays on Six Greek
 Dramas. Austin: University of Texas Press, 1963, pp. 199-248.
Thomson, J. A. K. "Alcestis and Her Hero; Excerpt from 'The
 Greek Tradition,'" in Q. Anderson and J. A. Mazzeo, eds.,
 The Proper Study; Essays on Western Classics. New York: St.
 Martin's, 1962, pp. 102-120.

Alexander

Coles, R. A. A New Oxyrhynchus Papyrus: The Hypothesis of
 Euripides' Alexandros. London: Institute of Classical Studies,
 1974.

Andromache

Borthwick, E. K. "Two Scenes of Combat in Euripides," J Hel S
 90 (1970), 15-21.
Hangard, J. "Euripides, Andromache 356," Mnemosyne 31 (1978),
 70-71.
Kovacs, P. D. "Three Passages from the Andromache," HSCP 81
 (1977), 123-156.
Lee, K. H. "Euripides' Andromache: Observations on Form and
 Meaning," Antichthon 9 (1975), 4-16.

Andromeda

Sutton, D. F. "The Relation Between Tragedies and Fourth Place
 Plays in Three Instances," Areth 4 (Spring, 1971), 55-72.

Antiope

Snell, B. "Vita Activa and Vita Contemplativa in Euripides' Antiope,"
 in his Scenes from Greek Drama. Berkeley: University of California Press, 1964, pp. 70-98.

Bacchae

Arthur, M. "The Choral Odes of the Bacchae of Euripides," YCS
 22 (1972), 145-179.
Barnard, A. S. C. "The Problem of the Bacchae," G & R 2 (May,
 1933), 170-172.
Burnett, A. P. "Pentheus and Dionysus: Host Guest," CP 65 (January, 1970), 15-29.
Castellani, V. "That Troubled House of Pentheus in Euripides' Bacchae," TAPA 106 (1976), 61-83.
Deverux, G. "The Psycho-therapy Scene in Euripides' Bacchae,"
 J Hel S 90 (1970), 35-48.

Dodds, E. R. "Maenadism in the Bacchae," HTR 33 (July, 1940), 155-176.
Dyer, R. R. "Image and Symbol: The Link Between the Two Worlds of the Bacchae," AUMLA No. 21 (May, 1964), 15-26.
Grube, G. M. A. "Dionysus in the Bacchae," TAPA 66 (1935), 37-54.
Hamilton, R. "Bacchae 47-52: Dionysus' Plan," TAPA 104 (1974), 139-149.
Hathorn, R. Y. Tragedy, Myth, and Mystery. Bloomington: Indiana University Press, 1962, pp. 113-142.
Larue, J. A. "Prurience Uncovered: The Psychology of Euripides' Pentheus," CJ 63 (February, 1968), 209-214.
Lattimore, R. A. "Euripides: The Bacchae," in his Poetry of Greek Tragedy. Baltimore: Johns Hopkins Press, 1958, pp. 126-145.
Lynch, W. F. "Euripides' Bacchae: The Mind in Prison," CC 25 (Summer, 1975), 163-174.
Mead, L. M. "Euripides and the Puritan Movement. A Study of the Bacchae," G & R 10 (October, 1940), 22-28.
Musurillo, H. S. J. "Euripides and Dionysiac Piety (Bacchae 370-433)," TAPA 97 (1966), 299-310.
Norwood, G. Essays on Euripidean Drama. Berkeley: University of California Press, 1954, pp. 52-73.
Rosenmeyer, T. G. The Masks of Tragedy; Essays on Six Greek Dramas. Austin: University of Texas Press, 1963, pp. 103-152.
Scott, W. C. "Two Suns Over Thebes: Imagery and Stage Effects in the Bacchae," TAPA 105 (1975), 333-346.
Seidensticker, B. "Comic Elements in Euripides' Bacchae," AJP 99 (Fall, 1978), 70-71.
Sale, W. "The Psychoanalysis of Pentheus in the Bacchae of Euripides," YCS 22 (1972), 63-82.
Soyinka, W. The Bacchae of Euripides, A Communion Rite. New York: Norton, 1974.
Winnington-Ingram, R. P. Euripides and Dionysus, An Interpretation of the Bacchae. London: Cambridge University Press, 1948.

Cyclops

Arnott, P. D. "The Overworked Playwright: A Study in Euripides' Cyclops," G & R 8 (October, 1961), 164-169.
Diggle, J. "Notes on the Cyclops of Euripides," CQ (New Series) 21 (May, 1971), 42-50.
Seaford, R. "Euripides, Cyclops 393-402," CQ (New Series) 26 (1976), 316-316.
_____. "Some Notes on Euripides' Cyclops," CQ 25 (December, 1975), 193-208.
Sutton, D. F. The Date of Euripides' Cyclops. Ann Arbor, Mich.: Xerox University Microfilms, 1975.
_____. "The Relation Between Tragedies and Fourth Place Plays in Three Instances," Areth 4 (Spring, 1971), 55-72.
Ussher, R. G. "The Cyclops of Euripides," G & R 18 (October, 1971), 166-179.

Electra

Bain, D. "[Euripides], Electra 518-544," BICS 24 (1977), 104-116.
Bond, G. W. "Euripides' Parody of Aeschylus," Ha 118 (Winter, 1974), 1-14.
Burnshaw, S., ed. Varieties of Literary Experience; Eighteen Essays in World Literature. New York: New York University Press, 1962, pp. 259-282.
Haslam, M. W. "'O' Ancient Argos of the Land': Euripides, Electra 1," CQ (New Series) 26 (1976), 4-10.
O'Brien, M. J. "Orestes and the Gorgon: Euripides' Electra," AJP 85 (January, 1964), 13-39.
Polack, B. H. "Euripides, Electra 473-475," CQ (New Series) 26 (1976), 3.
Rosivach, V. J. "Golden Lamb Ode in Euripides' Electra," CP 73 (July, 1978), 189-199.
Sider, D. "Two Stage Directions for Euripides," AJP 98 (Spring, 1977), 16-19.
Zeitlin, F. I. "The Argive Festival of Hera and Euripides' Electra," TAPA 101 (1970), 645-669.

Hecuba

Abrahamson, E. L. "Euripides' Tragedy of Hecuba," TAPA 83 (1952), 120-129.
Adkins, A. W. H. "Basic Greek Values in Euripides' Hecuba and Hercules Furens," CQ (New Series) 16 (1966), 193-219.
Daitz, S. G. "Concepts of Freedom and Slavery in Euripides' Hecuba," Hermes 99 (1971), 217-226.
Luschnig, C. A. E. "Euripides' Hecuba: The Time Is Out of Joint," CJ 71 (February-March, 1976), 227-234.
Merridor, R. "Eur. Hec. 1035-1038," AJP 96 (Spring, 1975), 5-6.
———. "Hecuba's Revenge; Some Observations on Euripides' Hecuba," AJP 99 (Spring, 1978), 28-35.
Rosivach, V. J. "The First Stasimon of the Hecuba 444ff," AJP 96 (Winter, 1975), 349-362.
Sutton, D. F. "The Relation Between Tragedies and Fourth Place Plays in Three Instances," Areth 4 (Spring, 1971), 55-72.

Helena

Dimock, G. "God, or Not God, or Between the Two?"--Euripides' Helen. Northampton, Mass.: Smith College, 1977.
Garton, C. "Euripides, Helen 1564," CQ (New series) 27 (1977), 295-296.
Griffith, J. G. "Some Thoughts on the Helena of Euripides," J Hel S 73 (1953), 36-41.
Kessels, A. H. M. "Euripides, Helen 78-88," Mnemosyne 28 (1975), 63-65.
Lattimore, R. A. "Euripides: Medea, Helen," in his Poetry of

Greek Tragedy. Baltimore: Johns Hopkins Press, 1958, pp. 103-124.

Padel, R. "Imagery of the Elsewhere: Two Choral Odes of Euripides," CQ 24 (November, 1974), 227-241.

Pippin, A. N. "Euripides' Helen: A Comedy of Ideas," CP 55 (July, 1960), 151-163.

Podlecki, A. J. "The Basic Seriousness of Euripides' Helen," TAPA 101 (1970), 401-418.

Schmiel, R. "The Recognition Duo in Euripides' Helen," Hermes 100 (1972), 274-294.

Segal, C. "The Two Worlds of Euripides' Helen," TAPA 102 (1971), 553-614.

Stanley-Porter, D. P. "Who Opposes Theoclymenus?," CP 72 (January, 1977), 45-48.

Sutton, D. F. "The Relation Between Tragedies and Fourth Place Plays in Three Instances," Areth 4 (Spring, 1971), 55-72.

Wolff, C. "On Euripides' Helen," HSCP 77 (1973), 61-84.

Young, D. C. C. "The Text of the Recognition Duet in Euripides' Helena," GRBS 15 (Spring, 1974), 39-56.

Heracles

Adkins, A. W. H. "Basic Greek Values in Euripides' Hecuba and Hercules Furens," CQ (New Series) 16 (1966), 193-219.

Bremer, J. M. "Euripides' Heracles 581," CQ (New Series) 22 (November, 1972), 236-240.

Chalk, H. H. O. "Apeth and Bia in Euripides' Herakles," J Hel S 82 (1962), 7-18.

Diggle, J. "On the Heracles and Ion of Euripides," PCPS (New Series) 20 (1974), 3-36.

Ferguson, J. "Tetralogies, Divine Paternity, and the Plays of 414," TAPA 100 (1969), 109-117.

Gregory, J. W. "Euripides' Heracles," YCS 25 (1977), 259-275.

Ruck, C. A. P. "Duality and the Madness of Herakles," Areth 9 (1976), 53-75.

Heracleidae

Avery, H. C. "Euripides' Heracleidae," AJP 92 (October, 1971), 539-565.

Burian, P. "Euripides' Heracleidae: An Interpretation," CP 72 (January, 1977), 1-21.

Burnett, A. P. "Tribe and City, Custom and Decree in Children of Heracles," CP 71 (January, 1976), 4-26.

Diggle, J. "Euripides, Heraclidae 145-150," CQ (New Series) 27 (1977), 236.

———. "Notes on the Heraclidae," CQ (New Series) 22 (November, 1972), 241-245.

Lesky, A. "On the Heraclidae of Euripides," YCS 25 (1977), 227-238.

Hippolytus

Bremer, J. M. "Meadow of Love and Two Passages in Euripides' Hippolytus," Mnemosyne 28 (1975), 268-280.
Claus, D. "Phaedra and the Socratic Paradox," YCS 22 (1972), 223-238.
Conacher, D. J. "A Problem in Euripides' Hippolytus," TAPA 92 (1961), 37-44.
Crocker, L. G. "On Interpreting Hippolytus," P 101 (1957), 238-246.
Dimock, G. E. "Euripides' Hippolytus, or Virtue Rewarded," YCS 25 (1977), 239-258.
Fitzgerald, G. J. "Misconception, Hypocrisy, and the Structure of Euripides' Hippolytus," Ramus 2 (1973), 20-40.
Flygt, S. "Treatment of Character in Euripides and Seneca: The Hippolytus," CJ 29 (April, 1934), 507-516.
Frischer, B. D. "Concordia Discors and Characterization in Euripides' Hippolytos," GRBS 11 (Summer, 1970), 85-100.
Glenn, J. "The Phantasies of Phaedra: A Psychoanalytic Reading," C World 69 (April-May, 1976), 435-442.
Graham, H. F. "The 'Escape' Ode in Hippolytus, 735-775," CJ 42 (February, 1947), 275-276.
Grene, D. "Interpretation of the Hippolytus of Euripides," CP 34 (January, 1939), 45-58.
Hathorn, R. Y. "Rationalism and Irrationalism in Euripides' Hippolytus," CJ 52 (1957), 211-218.
Henry, A. S. "Euripides, Hippolytos 790-855," CQ (New Series) 26 (1976), 229-231.
Huxley, G. L. "Euripides, Hippolytus 1120-1130," GRBS 12 (Autumn, 1971), 331-333.
Lattimore, R. "Phaedra and Hippolytus," Arion 1 (Autumn, 1962), 5-18.
Levin, D. N. "Euripides, Hippolytus 88-89; Another Possibility," CB 47 (January, 1971), 44-45.
Meridor, R. "Euripides' Hippolytus 1120-1150," CQ (New Series) 22 (November, 1972), 231-235.
Moline, J. "Euripides, Socrates and Virtue," Hermes 103 (1975), 45-67.
Musurillo, H. "The Problem of Lying and Deceit and the Two Voices of Euripides' Hippolytus 925-931," TAPA 104 (1974), 231-238.
Padel, R. "Imagery of the Elsewhere: Two Choral Odes of Euripides," CQ 24 (November, 1974), 227-241.
Rankin, A. V. "Euripides' Hippolytus: A Psychopathological Hero," Areth 7 (Spring, 1974), 71-94.
Reckford, K. J. "Phaedra and Pasiphae: The Pull Backward," TAPA 104 (1974), 307-328.
———. "Phaethon, Hippolytus, and Aphrodite," TAPA 103 (1972), 405-432.
Segal, C. "Curse and Oath in Euripides' Hippolytus," Ramus 1 (1972), 165-180.
———. "The Order of Lines in Hippolytus 1452-1456," GRBS 11 (Summer, 1970), 101-107.

———. "Shame and Purity in Euripides' Hippolytus," Hermes 98 (1970), 278-299.
Sider, D. "Two Stage Directions for Euripides," AJP 98 (Spring, 1977), 16-19.
Smoot, J. J. "Hippolytus as Narcissus, An Amplification," Areth 9 (Spring, 1976), 37-51.
———. "Literary Criticism on a Vase-Painting: A Clearer Picture of Euripides' Hippolytus," CLS 13 (December, 1976), 292-303.
Snell, B. "Passion and Reason: Phaedra in Hippolytus I," in his Scenes from Greek Drama. Berkeley: University of California Press, 1964, pp. 23-46.
———. "Passion and Reason: Medea and Phaedra in Hippolytus II," in his Scenes from Greek Drama. Berkeley: University of California Press, 1964, pp. 47-69.
Solmsen, F. " 'Bad Shame' and Related Problems in Phaedra's Speech (Eur. Hipp. 380-388)," Hermes 101 (1973), 420-425.
Whittaker, J. "The Hypotheses of Euripides' Hippolytus," CR (New Series) 21 (March, 1971), 9.

Ion

Conacher, D. J. "The Paradox of Euripides' Ion," TAPA 90 (1959), 20-39.
Ferguson, J. "Tetrologies, Divine Paternity, and the Plays of 414," TAPA 100 (1969), 109-117.
Hanson, J. O. de G. "Euripides' Ion: Tragic Awakening and Disillusionment," Mus Afr 4 (1975), 27-42.
Mastronarde, D. J. "Iconography and Imagery in Euripides' Ion," CSCA 8 (1975), 163-176.
Rosenmeyer, T. G. The Masks of Tragedy; Essays on Six Greek Dramas. Austin: University of Texas Press, 1963, pp. 103-152.
Rosivach, J. "Earthborns and Olympians: The Parados of the Ion," CQ (New Series) 27 (1977), 284-294.
Walsh, G. B. "The Rhetoric of Birthright and Race in Euripides' Ion," Hermes 106 (1978), 301-315.
Wasserman, F. M. "Divine Violence and Providence in Euripides' Ion," TAPA 71 (1940), 587-604.
Willetts, R. F. "Action and Character in the Ion of Euripides," J Hel S 93 (1973), 201-209.

Iphigeneia at Aulis

Bain, D. "Prologues of Euripides' Iphigeneia in Aulis," CQ (New Series) 27 (1977), 10-26.
Ferguson, J. "Iphigeneia at Aulis," TAPA 99 (1968), 157-164.
Knox, B. M. W. "Euripides' Iphigenia in Aulide 1-163," YCS 22 (1972), 239-261.
O'Sullivan, J. N. "Euripides I. A. 1550 and Achilles Tatius 3. 14. 3," AJP 97 (Summer, 1976), 111-113.

Suriya, B. J. "Euripides, Iphigenia at Aulis 579-586," CR (New Series) 24 (November, 1974), 175.
Walsh, G. B. "Iphigenia in Aulis, Third Stasimon," CP 69 (October, 1974), 241-248.
Will, F. "Remarks on Counterpoint Characterization in Euripides," CJ 55 (1960), 328-344.
Willink, C. W. "The Prologue of Iphigenia at Aulis," CQ (New Series) 21 (November, 1971), 343-364.

Iphigenia in Taurus

Diggle, J. "Notes on the Iphigenia in Tauris of Euripides," PCPS (New Series) 22 (1976), 42-45.
Caldwell, R. "Tragedy Romanticized: The Iphigenia Taurica," CJ 70 (December-January, 1974), 23-40.
Sansone, D. "The Sacrifice-Motif in Euripides' IT," TAPA 105 (1975), 283-295.
Shafer, G. "Iphigeneia in Tauris: Criticism," ETJ 30 (March, 1978), 107.
Strachan, J. C. G. "Iphigenia and Human Sacrifice in Euripides' Iphigenia Taurica," CP 71 (April, 1976), 131-140.

Medea

Arthur, D. "Medea: Criticism," ETJ 29 (October, 1977), 414-415.
Blaiklock, E. M. "Nautical Imagery of Euripides' Medea," CP 50 (October, 1955), 233-237.
Blitzen, C. "The Senecan and Euripidean Medea: A Comparison," CB 52 (April, 1976), 86-90.
Bongie, E. B. "Heroic Elements in the Medea of Euripides," TAPA 107 (1977), 27-56.
Burnett, A. P. "Medea and the Tragedy of Revenge," CP 68 (January, 1973), 1-24.
Buttrey, T. V. "Accident and Design in Euripides' Medea," AJP 79 (January, 1958), 1-17.
Dunkle, J. R. "The Aegeus Episode and the Theme of Euripides' Medea," TAPA 100 (1969), 97-107.
Easterling, P. E. "The Infanticide in Euripides' Medea," YCS 25 (1977), 177-191.
Elliot, A. Medea. London: Oxford University Press, 1977, pp. vii-lxviii.
Golden, L. "Children in the Medea," CB 48 (November, 1971), 10-15.
Knox, B. M. W. "The Medea of Euripides," YCS 25 (1977), 193-225.
Lattimore, R. A. "Euripides: Medea, Helen," in his Poetry of Greek Tragedy. Baltimore: Johns Hopkins Press, 1958, pp. 103-124.
McDonald, W. P. "Blackness of Medea," CLAJ 19 (September, 1975), 20-37.

Mead, L. M. "A Study in the Medea," G & R 12 (January, 1943), 15-20.
Musurillo, H. "Euripides' Medea: A Reconsideration," AJP 87 (January, 1966), 52-74.
Palmer, R. B. "An Apology for Jason: A Study of Euripides' Medea," CJ 53 (1957), 49-55.
Pucci, P. "Euripides: The Monument and the Sacrifice," Areth 10 (Spring, 1977), 165-196.
Reckford, K. J. "Medea's First Exit," TAPA 99 (1968), 329-360.
Reeve, M. D. "Euripides, Medea 1021-1080," CQ (New Series) 22 (May, 1972), 51-61.
Shafer, G. "Medea: Criticism," ETJ 30 (March, 1978), 107.
Zuger, H. "The Aegeus Episode and the Poetic Structure of Euripides' Medea," CB 49 (December, 1972), 29-31.

Orestes

Feaver, D. D. "Diphonal Diphthong in the Orestes Papyrus," AJP 99 (Spring, 1978), 38-40.
Gassner, J. "Oresteia: Dramatic Form and Vision," in S. Burnshaw, ed., Varieties of Literary Experience: Eighteen Essays in World Literature. New York: New York University Press, 1962, pp. 259-282.
Greenberg, N. A. "Euripides' Orestes; An Interpretation," HSCP 66 (1962), 157-192.
Mullens, H. G. "Meaning, of Euripides' Orestes," CQ 34 (July, 1940), 153-158.
Parry, H. "Euripides' Orestes: The Quest for Salvation," TAPA 100 (1969), 337-353.
Rawson, E. "Aspects of Euripides' Orestes," Areth 5 (Fall, 1972), 155-167.
Solomon, J. "Orestes 344-345: Colometry and Music," GRBS 18 (Spring, 1977), 71-83.
Solomon, J. D. "A Diphonal Diphthong in the Orestes Papyrus," AJP 97 (Summer, 1976), 172-173.

Phaethon

Calder, W. M. "A Note on the Dating of Euripides' Phaethon," CP 67 (October, 1972), 291-293.
Reckford, K. J. "Phaethon, Hippolytus, and Aphrodite," TAPA 103 (1972), 405-432.

Phoenician Maidens, or Phoenissae

Arthur, M. B. "The Curse of Civilization: The Choral Odes of the Phoenissae," HSCP 81 (1977), 163-185.
Haslam, M. W. "The Authenticity of Euripides, Phoenissae 1-2 and Sophocles Electra 1," GRBS 16 (Summer, 1975), 149-174.

_____. "Interpolations in the Phoenissae: Papyrus Evidence," CQ (New Series) 26 (1976), 4-10.
Kitto, H. D. F. "Final Scenes of the Phoenissae," CR 53 (July, 1939), 104-111.
Meredith, H. O. "End of the Phoenissae," CR 53 (July, 1937), 97-103.
Podlecki, A. J. "Some Themes in Euripides' Phoenissae," TAPA 93 (1962), 355-373.

Rhesus

Kitto, H. D. F. "The Rhesus and Related Matters," YCS 25 (1977), 317-350.
Ritchie, W. The Authenticity of the Rhesus of Euripides. London: Cambridge University Press, 1964.
Rawson, E. "Family and Fatherland in Euripides' Phoenissae," GRBS 11 (Summer, 1970), 109-127.
Rosivach, V. J. "Hector in the Rhesus," Hermes 106 (1978), 54-73.

Suppliant Women

Gamble, R. B. "Euripides' 'Suppliant Women': Decision and Ambivalence," Hermes 98 (1970), 385-405.

Suppliants, or Supplices

Ackerman, R. "Verrall on Euripides Supplicants 939ff.," GRBS 14 (Spring, 1973), 103-108.
Burian, P. H. "Euripides' Supplices 694ff.," CR 24 (November, 1974), 175-176.
Collard, C. "The Funeral Oration in Euripides' Supplices," BICS 19 (1972), 39-53.
Conacher, D. J. "Religious and Ethical Attitudes in Euripides' Suppliants," TAPA 87 (1956), 8-26.
Smith, W. D. "Dramatic Structure and Technique in Euripides' Suppliants," HSCP 62 (1957), 152-154.

Telephus

Handley, E. W., and J. Rea. The Telephus of Euripides. London: University of London Institute of Classical Studies, 1957.

Theseus

Sutton, D. F. "Euripides' Theseus," Hermes 106 (1978), 49-53.

Trojan Women, or Troades

Fontenrose, J. "Poseidon in the Troades," Agon 1 (April, 1967), 135-141.
Gilmartin, K. "Talthybius in the Trojan Women," AJP 91 (April, 1970), 213-222.
Luschnig, C. A. E. "Euripides' Trojan Women; All Is Vanity," CW 65 (September, 1971), 8-12.
Mead, L. M. "The Troades of Euripides," G & R 8 (February, 1939), 102-109.
O'Neill, G. "The Prologue of the Troades of Euripides," TAPA 72 (1941), 288-320.
Poole, A. "Total Disaster: Euripides' The Trojan Women," Arion (New Series) 3 (1976), 257-287.
Simon, S. J. "Euripides' Defense of Women," CB 50 (January, 1974), 39-42.

GELLIUS

General Criticism

Baldwin, B. "Aulus Gellius and His Circle," AClass 16 (1973), 103-107.
_____. "Aulus Gellius on Vergil," Vergilius 19 (1973), 22-27.
_____. Studies in Aulus Gellius. Lawrence, Kan.: Coronado, 1975.
Levy, H. L. "Gnomonica in Aulus Gellius," AJP 60 (July, 1939), 301-306.
Yoder, E. "A Second-century Classical Scholar," CJ 33 (February, 1938), 280-294.

HELIODORUS

Individual Works

Aethiopica

Garson, R. W. "Notes on Some Homeric Echoes in Heliodorus' Aethiopica," AClass 18 (1975), 137-140.
Glava, Z. A. A Study of Heliodorus and His Romance, the Aethiopica, with a Critical Evaluation of His Work as a Serious Source of Information on Ancient Aethiopia. New York: New York University Press, 1937.
Haight, E. H. "Aethiopica of Heliodorus," in her Essays on the Greek Romances. New York: Longmans, 1943, pp. 61-94.

O'Sullivan, J. N. "On Heliodorus Aethiopica 7. 12. 6," CQ (New Series) 27 (1977), 239-240.

HERODOTUS

General Criticism

Baldwin, B. "How Credulous Was Herodotus?" G & R 11 (October, 1964), 167-177.
Barron, J. P. "The Sixth Century Tyranny at Samos," CQ (New Series) 14 (November, 1964), 210-229.
Biamire, A. "Herodotus and Histiaeus," CQ (New Series) 9 (1959), 142-154.
Brown, T. S. "Herodotus and His Profession," AHR 59 (July, 1954), 829-843.
──────. "Herodotus Speculates About Egypt," AJP 86 (January, 1965), 60-76.
Chrimes, K. M. T. "Herodotus and the Reconstruction of History," J Hel S 50 (1930), 89-98.
Cook, A. "Herodotus: The Act of Inquiry as a Liberation from Myth," Helios 3 (May, 1976), 23-66.
Croix, G. E. M. de Ste. "Herodotus," G & R 24 (October, 1977), 130-148.
DeQuincey, T. "The Philosophy of Herodotus," in his Historical and Critical Essays. Boston: Ticknor, Reed, and Fields, 1856, Vol. 1, pp. 113-167.
DeSelincourt, A. The World of Herodotus. London: Secker and Warburg, 1962.
Dionysius. "Dionysius of Halicarnassus on Herodotus, Thucydides and Theopompus," in A. J. Toynbee, Greek Historical Thought: From Homer to the Age of Heraclius. Boston: Beacon, 1950, pp. 223-229.
Downs, R. B. "Father of History: Herodotus," in his Famous Books, Ancient and Medieval. New York: Barnes and Noble, 1964, pp. 57-60.
Drews, R. The Greek Accounts of Eastern History. Cambridge, Mass.: Harvard University Press, 1973.
──────. "Herodotus' Other Logic," AJP 91 (April, 1970), 181-191.
Evans, J. A. S. "Father of History or Father of Lies; the Reputation of Herodotus," CJ 64 (October, 1968), 11-17.
Flory, S. "The Personality of Herodotus," Arion 8 (Spring, 1969), 99-109.
Fornara, C. W. Herodotus: An Interpretative Essay. Oxford: Clarendon, 1971.
Forster, E. S. "Trees and Plants in Herodotus," CR 56 (July, 1942), 57-63.
Fritz, K. V. "Herodotus and the Growth of Greek Historiography," TAPA 67 (1936), 315-340.

Glover, T. R. Herodotus. New York: AMS, 1969.
———. "Welding of Mankind," in his Springs of Hellas, and Other Essays. New York: Macmillan, 1946, 78-100.
Gomme, A. W. "Herodotus," in his Greek Attitude to Poetry and History. Berkeley: University of California Press, 1954, pp. 73-94.
———. "Herodotus and Aeschylus," in his Greek Attitude to Poetry and History. Berkeley: University of California Press, 1954, pp. 95-115.
Grene, D. "Herodotus: The Historian as Dramatist," JP 58 (August 31, 1961), 477-488.
Hamilton, E. "Herodotus, the First Sightseer," in her Great Age of Greek Literature. New York: Norton, 1942, pp. 159-182.
How, W. W., and J. Wells, eds. Commentary on Herodotus. Oxford: Clarendon, 1967.
Immerwahr, H. R. "Aspects of Historical Causation in Herodotus," TAPA 87 (1956), 241-280.
———. "Ergon: History as a Monument in Herodotus and Thucydides," AJP 81 (July, 1960), 261-290.
———. Form and Thought in Herodotus. Chapel Hill, N. C.: Press of Western Reserve University, 1966.
———. "Historical Action in Herodotus," TAPA 85 (1954), 16-45.
———. "The Samian Stories of Herodotus," CJ 52 (April, 1957), 312-322.
Jarjeon, E. The Wonders of Herodotus. London: Nelson, 1948.
Lattimore, R. "Wise Advisor in Herodotus," CP 34 (January, 1939), 24-35.
MacKendrick, P. "Herodotus, 1963-1969," C World 63 (October, 1969), 37-44.
Meiggs, R. "Herodotus," HT 7 (November, 1957), 729-738.
Murray, O. "Herodotus and Hellenistic Culture," CQ (New Series) 22 (November, 1972), 200-213.
Myres, J. L. Herodotus, Father of History. Chicago: Regnery, 1971.
Parry, A. "Herodotus and Thucydides," Arion 7 (Autumn, 1968), 409-416.
Pearson, L. "Credulity and Scepticism in Herodotus," TAPA 72 (1941), 335-356.
Plutarchus. "Is Herodotus Malicious?," in A. J. Toynbee, Greek Historical Thought; From Homer to the Age of Heraclius. Boston: Beacon, 1950, pp. 229-236.
Podlecki, A. J. "Creon and Herodotus," TAPA 97 (1966), 359-372.
Powell, J. E. The History of Herodotus. Cambridge: Cambridge University Press, 1939.
———. "Puns in Herodotus," CR 51 (July, 1937), 103-105.
Rose, H. J. "Some Herodotean Rationalisms," CQ 34 (January, 1940), 78-84.
Tillyard, E. M. W. "Greek Historians," in his English Epic and Its Background. London: Chatto and Windus, 1954, pp. 41-51.
Treves, P. "Herodotus, Gelon, and Pericles, and the Famous Phrase, 'The Spring Has Been Taken out of Athens' Year,'" CP 36 (October, 1941), 321-345.

Wardman, A. E. "Herodotus on the Cause of the Greco-Persian Wars," AJP 82 (April, 1961), 133-150.
Wells, J. Studies in Herodotus. Freeport, N. Y.: Books for Libraries, 1970.
Young, G. M. "Herodotus," in his Today and Yesterday; Collected Essays and Addresses. London: Hart-Davis, 1948, pp. 255-258.
Zabkar, L. V. "Herodotus and the Egyptian Idea of Immorality," JNES 22 (January, 1963), 57-63.

Individual Works

History of the Greek and Persian War

Alexander, J. W. "The Marriage of Megacles," CJ 56 (December, 1959), 129-134.
Avery, H. C. "Herodotus' Picture of Cyrus," AJP 93 (October, 1972), 529-546.
―――. "Herodotus VI, 112,2," TAPA 103 (1972), 15-22.
Balcer, J. M. "The Date of Herodotus IV, 1, Darius' Scythian Expedition," HSCP 76 (1972), 99-132.
Benardete, S. Herodotean Inquiries. The Hague: Nijhoff, 1969.
Bicknell, P. J. "Herodotus, Kallimachos and the Bean," AClass 14 (1971), 147-149.
Brown, T. S. "Aristodicus of Cyme and the Branchidae," AJP 99 (Spring, 1978), 64-78.
Buck, R. J. "Boeotarchs at Thermopylae," CP 69 (January, 1974), 47-48.
Cole, J. W. "Peisistratus on the Strymon," G & R 22 (April, 1975), 42-44.
Conradie, P. J. "Op Soek Na Pheidippides," Akroterion 18 (January, 1973), 19-21.
Di Scala, S. Review Notes and Study Guide to the Persian Wars by Herodotus. New York: Monarch, 1966.
Donlan, W., and J. Thompson. "The Charge at Marathon: Herodotus 6.112," CJ 71 (April-May, 1976), 339-343.
Enos, R. L. "Rhetorical Intent in Ancient Historiography: Herodotus and the Battle of Marathon," Comm Q 24 (Winter, 1976), 24-31.
Evans, J. A. S. "The Dream of Xerxes and the 'Nomoi' of the Persians," CJ 57 (December, 1961), 109-111.
―――. "The Settlement of Artaphrenes," CP 71 (October, 1976), 344-348.
Flory, S. "Laughter, Tears and Wisdom in Herodotus," AJP 99 (Summer, 1978), 145-153.
Fornara, C. W. "Evidence for the Date of Herodotus' Publication," J Hel S 91 (1971), 25-34.
―――. Herodotus: An Interpretative Essay. Oxford: Clarendon, 1971.
Guzie, T. W. "Poetic Element in Herodotus' Speeches," CJ 50 (April, 1955), 326-328.
Hohti, P. The Interrelation of Speech and Action in the Histories of Herodotus. Helsinki: Societas Scientiarum Fennica, 1976.

Holland, L. A. "Herodotus I, 94: A Phocaean Version of an Etruscan Tale," AJA 41 (July, 1937), 377-382.
How, W. W., and J. Wells. A Commentary on Herodotus. Oxford: Clarendon, 1967, 2 vols.
Immerwahr, H. R. Form and Thought in Herodotus. Cleveland: Press of Western Reserve University, 1967.
Jeffery, L. H. "Campaign Between Athens and Aegina in the Years Before Salamis (Herodotus, VI, 87-93)," AJP 83 (January, 1962), 44-54.
Jordan, B. "Herodotus V, 71, 2 and the Naukraroi of Athens," CSCA 3 (1970), 153-175.
Kopff, E. C. "Emmendation in Herodotus 7. 9.B. 2," AJP 96 (Summer, 1975), 117-120.
Lang, M. L. "War and the Rape-Motif, or Why Did Cambyses Invade Egypt?," PAPS 116 (October, 1972), 410-414.
Lloyd, A. B. Herodotus, Book II: Introduction. Leiden: Brill, 1975.
———. "Perseus and Chemmis (Herodotus II 91)," J Hel S (1969), 79-86.
Macan, R. W., ed. Herodotus: The Fourth, Fifth, and Sixth Books. New York: Arno, 1973.
———. "Herodotus: The Seventh, Eighth and Ninth Books. New York: Arno, 1973, 2 Vols.
Manville, P. B. "Aristagoras and Histiaios: The Leadership Struggle in the Ionian Revolt," CQ (New Series) 27 (1977), 80-91.
Mitchell, B. M. "Herodotus and Samos," J Hel S 95 (1975), 75-91.
Neville, J. W. "Herodotus on the Trojan War," G & R 24 (April, 1977), 3-12.
Nevins, A., et al. "Herodotus: History," in M. Van Doren, ed., New Invitation to Learning. New York: Random House, 1942, pp. 255-268.
O'Sullivan, J. N. "Herodotus 7.9 B2, A Polar Error?," AJP 97 (Summer, 1976), 168-169.
———. "On Herodotus 7. 183: Three Sound Ships for Salamis," CQ (New Series) 27 (1977), 92-94.
Ravn, O. E. Herodotus' Description of Babylon. Copenhagen: Busck, 1942.
Rexroth, K. "Herodotus: History," in his Classics Revisited. Chicago: Quadrangle, 1968, pp. 61-65.
Robertson, N. "Thessalian Expedition of 480 B.C.," J Hel S 96 (1976), 100-120.
Robinson, K. S. "Herodotus and the Scythians," Expedition 17 (April, 1975), 16-20.
Rowland, R. J. "The Biggest Island in the World," CW 68 (April-May, 1975), 438-439.
Sacks, K. S. "Herodotus and the Dating of the Battle of Thermopylae," CQ (New Series) 26 (1976), 232-248.
Sealey, R. "Causes of the Peloponnesian War," CP 70 (April, 1975), 89-109.
———. "The Pit and the Well: The Persian Heralds of 491 B.C.," CJ 72 (October-November, 1976), 13-20.
Solmsen, F. Two Crucial Decisions in Herodotus. Amsterdam: North-Holland, 1974.

Solmsen, L. "Speeches in Herodotus' Account of the Battle of Plataea," CP 39 (October, 1944), 241-253.
_____. "Speeches in Herodotus' Account of the Ionic Revolt," AJP 64 (April, 1943), 194-207.
Stahl, H. P. "Learning Through Suffering? Croesus' Conversations in the History of Herodotus," YCS 24 (1975), 1-36.
Vaggione, R. P. "Over All Asia? The Extent of the Scythian Domination in Herodotus," JBL 92 (December, 1973), 523-530.
Wainwright, G. A. "Herodotus II, 28 or the Sources of the Nile," J Hel S 73 (1953), 104-107.
Wallace, M. B. "Herodotus and Euboia," Phoenix 28 (Spring, 1974), 22-44.
Waters, K. H. "Herodotus and Politics," G & R 19 (October, 1972), 136-150.
_____. Herodotus on Tyrants and Despots; A Study in Objectivity. Wiesbaden: Steiner, 1971.
_____. "The Structure of Herodotus' Narrative," Antichthon 8 (1974), 1-10.
Wood, H. The Histories of Herodotus: An Analysis of the Formal Structure. The Hague: Mouton, 1972.

HESIOD

General Criticism

Burn, A. R. World of Hesiod: A Study of the Greek Middle Ages c. 900-700 B.C. 2nd edition, corrected. New York: Blom, 1966.
Dickie, M. W. "'Dike' as a Moral Term in Homer and Hesiod," CP 73 (April, 1978), 91-101.
Downs, R. B. "Farmer's Friend: Hesiod," in his Famous Books, Ancient and Medieval. New York: Barnes and Noble, 1964, pp. 24-27.
Edwards, G. P. The Language of Hesiod in Its Traditional Context. Oxford: Blackwell and Mott, 1971.
Fisher, R. "Astronomy and the Calendar in Hesiod," CN & V 21 (1977), 58-63.
Forbes, P. B. R. "Hesiod Versus Perses," CR 64 (December, 1950), 82-87.
Green, P. "Peasant on Helicon: A Study of Hesiod and His Society," HT 9 (November, 1959), 729-735.
Hadas, M. "Nature and Convention," in his The Living Tradition. New York: New American Library, 1967, pp. 25-39.
Hershbell, J. P. "Hesiod and Empedocles," CJ 65 (January, 1970), 145-161.
_____. "Idea of Strife in Early Greek Thought," Person 55 (Summer, 1974), 205-215.
Jaeger, W. W. Paideia: The Ideals of Greek Culture. Oxford: B. Blackwell, 1944-47. Vol. 1, pp. 57-76.

Lawton, W. C. The Successors of Homer. New York: Cooper Square, 1969.
Lloyd-Jones, H. "Females of the Species," Encounter 44 (May, 1975), 42-51.
Meritt, B. D. "Hollow Month at Athens," Mnemosyne 30 (1977), 217-242; see pp. 224-226.
Michaelson, S., A. Q. Morton, and J. B. Hainsworth. "The Authorship and Integrity of the Poems of Hesiod," Ph J 9 (January, 1972), 61-79.
Minton, W. W. "Invocation and Catalogue in Hesiod and Homer," TAPA 93 (1962), 188-212.
Pellikaan-Engel, M. E. Hesiod and Parmenides: A New View on Their Cosmologies and on Parmenides' Proem. Amsterdam: Hakkert, 1974.
Pucci, P. Hesiod and the Language of Poetry. Baltimore: Johns Hopkins Press, 1977.
Salama, A. Hesiod's Ethical Poetry. Cairo: [n. p.], 1946.
Sarton, G. "Dawn of Greek Culture: Homer and Hesiod," in his History of Science; Ancient Science through the Golden Age of Greece. Cambridge, Mass.: Harvard University Press, 1952, pp. 130-153.
Solmsen, F. "The Gift of Speech in Homer and Hesiod," TAPA 85 (1954), 1-15.
_____. Hesiod and Aeschylus. Ithaca, N. Y.: Cornell University Press, 1949.
Stewart, D. J. "Hesiod and the Birth of Reason," AR 26 (Summer, 1966), 213-231.
Suhr, E. G. "Winged Words," Folklore 85 (Autumn, 1974), 169-172.
Vandvik, E. Prometheus of Hesiod and Aeschylus. Oslo: Dybwad, 1943.
Walcot, P. Hesiod and the Near East. Cardiff: University of Wales Press, 1966.
Wallace, P. W. "Hesiod and the Valley of the Muses," GRBS 15 (Spring, 1974), 5-24.
Welch, L. C. "Prometheus: A Conjecture about the Origins of a Myth," CJ 55 (March, 1960), 269-273.
West, M. L. "The Contest of Homer and Hesiod," CQ (New Series) 17 (1967), 433-450.
Young, D. "Never Blotted a Line? Formula and Premeditation in Homer and Hesiod," Arion 6 (Autumn, 1967), 279-324.

Individual Works

Shield of Heracles

Cook, R. M. "Date of the Hesiodic Shield," CQ 31 (July, 1937), 204-214.
Myres, J. L. "Hesiod's Shield of Herakles: Its Structure and Workmanship," J Hel S 61 (1941), 17-38.

Theogony

Combellack, F. M. "Hesiod's Kings and Nicarchus' Nestor," CP 69 (April, 1974), 124.
Cornford, F. M. "Ritual Basis for Hesiod's Theogony," in his Unwritten Philosophy, and Other Essays. London: Cambridge University Press, 1950, pp. 95-116.
Meltzer, E. S. "Egyptian Parallels for an Incident in Hesiod's Theogony and an Episode in the Kumarbi Myth," JNES 33 (January, 1974), 154-157.
Minton, W. W. "The Frequency and Structuring of Traditional Formulas in Hesiod's Theogony," HSCP 79 (1975), 25-54.
──────. "The Proem-Hymn of Hesiod's Theogony," TAPA 101 (1970), 357-377.
Østerud, S. "The Individuality of Hesiod," Hermes 105 (1976), 13-29.
Prier, R. A. "On Theogony 118 and 119," CP 67 (January, 1972), 54-55.
Pucci, P. Hesiod and the Language of Poetry. Baltimore: Johns Hopkins Press, 1977.
Roth, C. P. "The Kings and the Muses in Hesiod's Theogony," TAPA 106 (1976), 331-338.
Sale, W. "Aphrodite in the Theogony," TAPA 92 (1961), 508-521.
──────. "The Dual Vision of the Theogony," Arion 4 (Winter, 1965), 668-699.
Steadman, J. M. "Sin, Echidna and the Viper's Brood," MLR 56 (January, 1961), 62-66.
Walcot, P. "The Text of Hesiod's Theogony and the Hittite Epic of Kumarbi," CQ (New Series) 6 (1956), 198-206.

Works and Days (or Erga for Works)

Baldry, G. C. "Who Invented the Golden Age?," CQ (New Series) 2 (1952), 83-92.
Benardete, S. "Hesiod's Works and Days: A First Reading," Agon 1 (April, 1967), 150-174.
Beye, C. R. "The Rhythm of Hesiod's Works and Days," HSCP 76 (1972), 23-44.
Claus, D. B. "Defining Moral Terms in Works and Days," TAPA 107 (1977), 73-84.
Daly, L. W. "Hesiod's Fable," TAPA 92 (1961), 45-51.
Dickie, M. W. "'Dike' as a Moral Term in Homer and Hesiod," CP 73 (April, 1978), 91-101.
Fontenrose, J. "Work, Justice, and Hesiod's Five Ages," CP 69 (January, 1974), 1-16.
Frazer, R. M. "Pandora's Diseases, Erga 102-4," GRBS 13 (Autumn, 1972), 235-238.
Gagarin, M. "Dike in the Works and Days," CP 68 (April, 1973), 81-94.
──────. "Hesiod's Dispute with Perses," TAPA 104 (1974), 103-111.

Griffiths, J. G. "Archeology and Hesiod's Five Ages," JHI 17 (January, 1956), 109-119.
_____. "Did Hesiod Invent the Golden Age?," JHI 19 (January, 1958), 91-93.
Herington, C. J. "Works and Days," G & R 13 (June, 1944), 86-89.
Latimer, J. F. "Perses Versus Hesiod," TAPA 61 (1930), 70-79.
McKay, K. J. "Hesiod's Rejuvenation," CQ (New Series) 9 (1959), 1-5.
Nussbaum, G. "Labour and Status in the Works and Days," CQ (New Series) 10 (1960), 213-220.
Østerud, S. "The Individuality of Hesiod," Hermes 104 (1976), 13-29.
Peabody, B. The Winged Word: A Study in the Technique of Ancient Greek Oral Composition as Seen Principally Through Hesiod's Works and Days. Albany: State University of New York Press, 1975.
Porter, H. N. "Hesiod and Aratus," TAPA 77 (1946), 158-170.
Pucci, P. Hesiod and the Language of Poetry. Baltimore: Johns Hopkins Press, 1977.
Samuel, A. E. "The Days of Hesiod's Month," TAPA 97 (1966), 421-430.
Sheehan, D. "Hesiod's Works and Days: An Introduction," Arion (New Series) 3 (1976), 452-482.
Solmsen, F. "The Days of the Works and Days," TAPA 94 (1963), 293-320.
Stewart, D. J. "Hesiod and History," BR 18 (Spring, 1970), 37-52.
Taggart, F. J. "Argument of Hesiod's Works and Days; the Myth of Prometheus and Pandora and the Legend of the Golden Race, Presenting Two Ancient and Opposing Conceptions of the Original Condition of Man," JHI 8 (January, 1947), 45-77.
Verdenius, W. J. "Three Notes on the Works and Days," Mnemosyne 28 (1975), 190-191.
Von Fritz, K. "Pandora, Prometheus, and the Myth of the Ages," RR 11 (March, 1947), 227-260.
West, M. L. Hesiod: Works and Days, ed. with Prolegomena and Commentary. Oxford: Clarendon, 1978.

HOMER

General Criticism

Adkins, A. W. H. "'Friendship' and 'Self-sufficiency' in Homer and Aristotle," CQ (New Series) 13 (May, 1963), 30-45.
_____. "Homeric Gods and the Values of Homeric Society," J Hel S 89 (1969), 7-21.
_____. "Homeric Values and Homeric Society," J Hel S 9 (1971), 1-14.
_____. "Threatening, Abusing and Feeling Angry in the Homeric Poems," J Hel S 89 (1969), 7-21.

Anderson, W. D. "Notes on the Simile in Homer and His Successors: I. Homer, Apollonius Rhodius, and Vergil," CJ 53 (November, 1957), 81-87.
Ashely, A. M. "Poetic Imagery in Homer and Virgil," G & R 2 (October, 1932), 21-28.
Austin, N. "One and the Many in the Homeric Cosmos," Arion (New Series) 1 (1973-1974), 219-274.
Autenrieth, G. G. P. Homeric Dictionary for Schools and Colleges. Norman: University of Oklahoma Press, 1958.
Bassett, S. E. Poetry of Homer. Berkeley: University of California Press, 1939.
Beye, C. R. "Male and Female in the Homeric Poems," Ramus 3 (1974), 87-101.
Blackwell, T. An Enquiry into the Life and Writings of Homer. New York: Garland, 1970.
Bowra, C. M. "Comparative Study of Homer," AJA 54 (July, 1950), 184-192.
_____. Homer. New York: Scribner's, 1972.
_____. "Recent Homeric Studies," SR 63 (Spring, 1955), 337-343.
_____. "Some Characteristics of Literary Epic," in his From Virgil to Milton. New York: Macmillan, 1945, pp. 1-32.
Calhoun, G. M. "Divine Entourage in Homer," AJP 61 (July, 1940), 257-277.
_____. "Higher Criticism on Olympus," AJP 58 (July 1937), 257-274.
_____. "Homer's Gods--Myth and Maerchen," AJP 60 (January, 1939), 1-28.
_____. "Homer's Gods--Prolegomena," TAPA 68 (1937), 11-25.
_____. "Poet and the Muses in Homer," CP 33 (April, 1938), 157-166.
_____. "Zeus the Father in Homer," TAPA 66 (1935), 1-17.
Campbell, J. M. "Homer and Chastity," PQ 28 (July, 1949), 333-359.
Carne-Ross, D. S. "Homer," Arion 7 (Autumn, 1968), 400-408.
_____. "Means and the Moment," Arion 7 (Winter, 1968), 549-556.
Carpenter, R. Folktale, Fiction and Saga in the Homeric Epics. Berkeley: University of California Press, 1946.
Carspecken, J. F. "Apollonius Rhodius and the Homeric Epic," YCS 13, 33-143.
Casey, G. "Shield of Achilles," SCR 10 (Spring, 1976), 93-98.
Chittenden, J. "Diaktoros Argeiphontes," AJA 52 (January, 1948), 24-33.
Clarke, H. W. "The Humor of Homer," CJ 64 (March, 1969), 246-252.
Clay, J. "The Planktai and Moly: Divine Naming and Knowing in Homer," Hermes 100 (1972), 127-131.
Coffey, M. "Function of the Homeric Simile," AJP 78 (April, 1957), 113-132.
Coldstream, J. N. "Hero-cults in the Age of Homer," J Hel S 96 (1976), 8-17.

Combellack, F. M. "Homer the Innovator," CP 71 (January, 1976), 44-55.
_____. "Homer's Savage Fish," CJ 48 (March, 1953), 257-261.
_____. "New Light on Homer's Profession," CJ 42 (January, 1947), 210.
_____. Omitted Speech Formulas in Homer. Berkeley: University of California Press, 1939.
_____. "Some Formulary Illogicalities in Homer," TAPA 96 (1965), 41-56.
_____. "Speakers and Scepters in Homer," CJ 43 (January, 1948), 209-217.
Cook, R. M. "Notes on the Homeric Epigram to the Potters," CR 62 (September, 1948), 55-57; (New Series) 1 (March, 1951), 9.
Couch, H. N. "Fishing in Homer," CJ 31 (February, 1936), 303-314.
_____. "A Prelude to Speech in Homer," TAPA 68 (1937), 129-140.
Crossett, J. "The Art of Homer's Catalogue of Ships," CJ 64 (March, 1969), 241-245.
Davis, S. "Argeiphontes in Homer--The Dragon-slayer," G & R 22 (February, 1953), 33-38.
Davison, J. A. "Peisistratus and Homer," TAPA 86 (1955), 1-21.
DeVries, G. J. "Phaeacian Manners," Mnemosyne 30 (1977), 113-121.
Dickie, M. W. " 'Dike' as a Moral Term in Homer and Hesiod," CP 73 (April, 1978), 91-101.
Dietrich, B. C. Death, Fate and the Gods: The Development of a Religious Idea in Greek Popular Belief in Homer. London: University of London, 1965.
Dinsmore, C. A. "Homer: What He Believed and What He Valued," in his Great Poets and the Meaning of Life. Boston: Houghton Mifflin, 1937, pp. 31-63.
Downs, R. B. "Epic Poet: Homer," in his Famous Books, Ancient and Medieval. New York: Barnes and Noble, 1964, pp. 17-24.
Duckworth, G. E. Foreshadowing and Suspense. Princeton, N. J.: Princeton University Press, 1933.
Duffy, J. "Homer's Conception of Fate," CJ 42 (May, 1947), 477-485.
Earp, F. R. "The Gods of Homer," G & R 6 (March, 1959), 42-44.
Edelstein, L. "Golden Chain of Homer," in Johns Hopkins University, History of Ideas Club, Studies in Intellectual History. Baltimore: Johns Hopkins Press, 1953, pp. 48-66.
Eddy, L. R. "Homer and Ancient Technology," CB 51 (April, 1975), 86-90.
Edwards, M. W. "Homeric Speech Introductions," HSCP 74 (1970), 1-36.
_____. "Some Features of Homeric Craftsmanship," TAPA 97 (1966), 115-180.
_____. "Type Scenes and Homeric Hospitality," TAPA 105 (1975), 51-72.
Elderkin, G. W. "Homeric Cave on Ithaca," CP 35 (January, 1940), 52-54.

Else, G. F. Homer and the Homeric Problem. Cincinnati: University of Cincinnati Press, 1965.
Ewlank, D. R. "Structure of the Ordeal of Richard Feverel," ES 57 (August, 1976), 348-352.
Feldman, A. B. "Homer and Democracy," CJ 47 (May, 1952), 337-343; 345.
Feldman, L. H. "Ascanius and Astyanax: A Comparative Study of Virgil and Homer," CJ 53 (May, 1958), 361-366.
Fenick, B. C. Homer, Tradition and Invention. Leiden: Brill, 1978.
Giangrande, L. "Pseudo-, 'International,' Olympian and Personal Place in Homeric Epic," CJ 68 (October-November, 1972), 1-10.
Gienapp, N. F. Paired Expressions in Homer. Ann Arbor, Mich.: University Microfilms, 1958.
Glenn, J. "Polyphemus Myth: Its Origin and Interpretation," G & R 25 (October, 1978), 141-155.
Glover, T. R. "Homer and His Readers," in his Challenge of the Greek, and Other Essays. New York: Macmillan, 1942, pp. 182-217.
Gomme, A. W. "Homer," in his Greek Attitude to Poetry and History. Berkeley: University of California Press, 1954, pp. 1-48.
Goold, G. P. "The Nature of Homeric Composition," ICS 2 (1977), 1-34.
Gordon, C. H. "Further Observations on Homer," in his Before the Bible; The Common Background of Greek and Hebrew Civilizations. New York: Harper, 1962, pp. 218-277.
_____. Homer and Bible; The Origin and Character of East Mediterranean Literature. Ventnor, N.J.: Ventnor, 1967.
Gordon, K. "Homer on Imagination," JGP 23 (October, 1940), 401-413.
Gould, G. P. "Homer and the Alphabet," TAPA 91 (1960), 272-291.
Gray, D. H. F. "Homeric Epithets for Things," CQ 41 (July, 1947), 109-121.
_____. "Metal-working in Homer," J Hel S 74 (1954), 1-15.
Griffin, J. "Epic Cycle and the Uniqueness of Homer," J Hel S 97 (1977), 39-53.
_____. "Homeric Pathos and Objectivity," CQ (New Series) 26 (1976), 161-187.
Grube, G. M. A. "The Beginnings of Criticism," in his The Greeks and Roman Critics. Toronto: University of Toronto Press, 1965, pp. 1-21.
Gunn, D. M. "Narrative Inconsistency and the Oral Dictated Text in the Homeric Epic," AJP 91 (April, 1970), 192-203.
_____. "Thematic Composition and Homeric Authorship," HSCP 75 (1971), 1-31.
Hainsworth, J. B. "The Criticism of an Oral Homer," J Hel S 90 (1970), 90-98.
_____. The Flexibility of the Homeric Formula. Oxford: Clarendon, 1968.
_____. Homer. Oxford: Clarendon, 1969.
_____. "Joining Battle in Homer," G & R 13 (October, 1966), 158-166.

Harrison, F. E. "Homer and the Poetry of War," G & R 7 (March, 1960), 9-19.
Hirvonen, K. Matriarchal Survival and Certain Trends in Homer's Female Characters. Helsinki: Suomalainen Tiedeakatemia, 1968.
Hoekstra, A. Homeric Modifications of Formulaic Prototypes; Studies in the Development of Greek Epic Diction. Amsterdam: North-Holland, 1965.
Hooker, J. T. "Homer and Late Minoan Crete," J Hel S 89 (1969), 60-71.
Jaeger, W. W. Paideia: The Ideals of Greek Culture. Oxford: B. Blackwell, 1944-47. Vol. 1, pp. 3-56.
Jebb, R. C. Homer; An Introduction to the Iliad and the Odyssey. Port Washington, N. Y.: Kennikat, 1969.
Johnson, E. M. "Who Homer Really Was," CLAJ 22 (September, 1978), 54-61.
Jones, F. P. and Gray, F. E. "Hexameter Patterns, Statistical Inference, and the Homeric Question: An Analysis of the La Roche Data," TAPA 103 (1972), 187-209.
Kakridis, J. T. Homer Revisited. Lund: Gleerup, 1971.
Kennedy, G. A. "Ancient Dispute over Rhetoric in Homer," AJP 78 (January, 1957), 23-35.
Kirk, G. S. "Homer and Modern Oral Poetry: Some Confusions," CQ (New Series) 10 (1960), 271-281.
_____. Homer and the Oral Tradition. New York: Cambridge University Press, 1976.
_____. The Homeric Poems as History. London: Cambridge University Press, 1964.
_____. The Language and Background of Homer; Some Recent Studies and Controversies. Cambridge, Eng.: Heffer, 1964.
_____. "The Search for the Real Homer," G & R 20 (October, 1973), 124-139.
Knight, W. F. J. Many-minded Homer. New York: Barnes and Noble, 1968.
_____. Vergil and Homer. Devon, Eng.: Virgil Society, 1950.
Knox, M. O. "House and Palace in Homer," J Hel S 90 (1970), 117-120.
Lang, A. Homer and His Age. New York: AMS, 1968.
_____. Homer and the Epic. New York: AMS, 1970.
_____. The World of Homer. New York: AMS, 1968.
Lang, M. L. "Reason and Purpose in Homeric Prayers," CW 68 (February, 1975), 309-314.
Lattimore, R. "Man and God in Homer," PAPS 114 (December, 1970), 411-422.
Lawler, L. B. "On Certain Homeric Epithets," PQ 27 (January, 1948), 80-84.
Le Comte, E. S. "Homer Transposed," CJ 45 (April, 1950), 315-321.
Leaf, W. Troy: A Study in Homeric Geography. Freeport, N. Y.: Books for Libraries, 1971.
Lessing, E. The Voyages of Ulysses: A Photographic Interpretation of Homer's Classic; With Commentaries. London: Macmillan, 1966.

Lewisohn, L. "Homer," in his Magic World: Studies in the Nature of Poetry. New York: Farrar, Straus, 1950, pp. 26-66.
Long, A. A. "Morals and Values in Homer," J Hel S 90 (1970), 121-139.
Lord, A. B. "Homer and Huso II: Narrative Inconsistencies in Homer and Oral Poetry," TAPA 69 (1938), 439-445.
_____. "Homer's Originality: Oral Dictated Texts," TAPA 84 (1953), 124-134.
_____. Singer of Tales. New York: Atheneum, 1965.
Lord, M. L. "Withdrawal and Return: An Epic Story Pattern in the Homeric Hymn to Demeter and in the Homeric Poems," CJ 62 (March, 1967), 241-248.
Lorimer, H. L. "Homer and the Art of Writing: A Sketch of Opinion Between 1713 and 1939," AJA 52 (January, 1948), 11-23.
_____. Homer and the Monuments. New York: Macmillan, 1951.
Luce, J. V. Homer and the Heroic Age. New York: Harper and Row, 1975.
Lyding, E. Homeric Enjambement. Ann Arbor, Mich.: University Microfilms, 1949.
Macdonell, P. J. "Who's Who in Homer," CR 55 (March, 1941), 13-22.
MacLeod, M. D. "Homeric Parody in Lucian," CR (New Series) 10 (June, 1960), 103.
Michalopoulos, A. Homer. New York: St. Martin's, 1975.
Miller, D. G. "Language Change and Poetic Options," Language 53 (March, 1977), 21-38.
Miller, H. W. "Homeric Commentator," CP 36 (April, 1941), 187-188.
Minton, W. W. "Invocation and Catalogue in Hesiod and Homer," TAPA 93 (1962), 188-212.
Mireaux, E. Daily Life in the Time of Homer, tr. by I. Sells. New York: Macmillan, 1959.
Moulton, C. Similes in the Homeric Poems. Göttingen: Vandenhoeck and Ruprecht, 1977.
Murray, G. Rise of the Greek Epic. New York: Oxford University Press, 1960.
Mylonas, G. B. "Homeric and Mycenaean Burial Customs," AJA 52 (January, 1948), 56-81.
Myres, J. L. "Blood-feud and Justice in Homer and Aeschylus," CR 59 (May, 1945), 10.
Nagler, M. N. Spontaneity and Tradition: A Study in the Oral Art of Homer. Berkeley: University of California Press, 1975.
Nehring, A. "Homer's Descriptions of Syncopes," CP 42 (April, 1947), 106-121.
Nilsson, M. P. Homer and Mycenae. New York: Cooper Square, 1968.
Notopoulos, J. A. "Homeric Hymns as Oral Poetry; A Study of the Post-Homeric Oral Tradition," AJP 83 (October, 1962), 337-368.
_____. "Homeric Similes in the Light of Oral Poetry," CJ 52 (April, 1957), 323-328.
_____. "Parataxis in Homer: A New Approach to Homeric Criticism," TAPA 80 (1949), 1-23.

Nye, I. "When Homer Smiles," CJ 33 (October, 1937), 25-37.
Otto, W. F. The Homeric Gods. New York: Pantheon, 1954.
Packard, D. W. A Bibliography of Homeric Scholarship; Preliminary Edition, 1930-1970. Malibu, Calif.: Undena, 1974.
———. "Sound-patterns in Homer," TAPA 104 (1974), 239-260.
Parry, A. "Language and Characterization in Homer," HSCP 76 (1972), 1-22.
Parry, M. The Making of Homeric Verse: The Collected Papers of Milman Parry. Oxford: Clarendon, 1971.
Pearson, L. I. C. "Homer," in his Popular Ethics in Ancient Greece. Stanford, Calif.: Stanford University Press, 1962, pp. 34-64.
Perry, W. C. The Women of Homer. New York: Dodd, Mead, 1898.
Plommer, H. "Shadowy Megara," J Hel S 97 (1977), 75-83.
Pollard, J. R. T. "Muses and Sirens," CR (New Series) 2 (June, 1952), 60-63.
Pope, M. W. M. "Athena's Development in Homeric Epic," AJP 81 (April, 1960), 113-135.
Post, L. A. From Homer to Menander; Forces in Greek Poetic Fiction. Berkeley: University of California Press, 1951.
———. "The Moral Pattern in Homer," TAPA 70 (1939), 158-190.
Powell, B. B. "Word Patterns in the Catalogue of Ships (B 494-709): A Structural Analysis of Homeric Language," Hermes 106 (1978), 255-264.
Prescot, K. Letters Concerning Homer, the Sleeper in Horace. New York: Garland, 1970.
Pye, D. W. "Wholly Spondaic Lines in Homer," G & R 11 (March, 1964), 2-6.
Rambo, E. F. "On Homer's Epithets," CJ 28 (November, 1932), 128-130.
———. "On Homer's Similes," CJ 28 (October, 1932), 22-31.
Rapp, A. "The Dawn of Humor," CJ 43 (February, 1948), 275-279.
Rexine, J. E. "The Nature and Meaning of Justice in Homer," CB 54 (1977), 1-6.
Rose, H. J. "Divine Disguisings [Question of the Shapes Assumed by the Greek Gods]," HTR 49 (January, 1956), 63-72.
Rouse, W. H. D. Homer. Folcroft, Pa.: Folcroft Library Editions, 1977.
Russo, J. A. "A Closer Look at Homeric Formulas," TAPA 94 (1963), 235-247.
———. "Homer Against His Tradition," Arion 7 (Summer, 1968), 275-295.
———. "How, and What, Does Homer Communicate? The Medium and Message of Homeric Verse," CJ 71 (April-May, 1976), 289-299.
Russo, J. A., and Simon, B. "Homeric Psychology and the Oral Epic Tradition," JHI 29 (October, 1968), 483-498.
Sarton, G. "Dawn of Greek Culture. Homer and Hesiod," in his History of Science; Ancient Science through the Golden Age of Greece. Cambridge, Mass.: Harvard University Press, 1952, pp. 130-153.

Sasson, J. M. "Some Literary Motifs in the Composition of the Gilgamesh Epic," SP 69 (July, 1972), 259-279.
Schlunk, R. R. The Homeric Scholia and the Aeneid: A Study of the Influence of Ancient Homeric Literary Criticism on Vergil. Ann Arbor: University of Michigan Press, 1974.
―――. "Vergil and the Homeric Scholia," AJP 88 (January, 1967), 33-44.
Scott, J. A. Homer and His Influence. New York: Cooper Square, 1963.
―――. Unity of Homer. New York: Biblo and Tannen, 1965.
Scott, W. C. The Oral Nature of the Homeric Simile. Leiden: Brill, 1974.
Severyns, A. "Homeric Formulas and Archaean History," BR 18 (Spring, 1970), 26-36.
Shewan, A. Homeric Essays. New York: Sallock, 1935.
Shipp, G. P. Studies in the Language of Homer. Cambridge: Cambridge University Press, 1972.
Sikes, E. E. "Humor of Homer," CR 54 (September, 1940), 121-127.
Simonsuuri, K. Homer's Original Genius: Eighteenth Century Notions of the Early Greek Epic (1688-1798). New York: Cambridge University Press, 1979.
Small, G. P. "On Allegory in Homer," CJ 44 (April, 1949), 423-430.
Smith, J. E. S. "Icarus' Astral Navigation," G & R 21 (April, 1974), 19-20.
Smith, J. R., ed. Homeric Studies. London: Grafton, 1938.
Snell, B. "Homer's View of Man," in his Discovery of the Mind; The Greek Origins of European Thought. Cambridge, Mass.: Harvard University Press, 1953, pp. 1-22.
Snodgrass, A. M. "An Historical Homeric Society?," J Hel S 94 (1974), 114-125.
Solmsen, F. "The Gift of Speech in Homer and Hesiod," TAPA 85 (1954), 1-15.
Stanford, W. B. "Remarks on the Collected Works of Milman Parry," Ha 112 (Autumn, 1971), 36-51.
Steiner, G., and R. Fagles, Eds. Homer: A Collection of Critical Essays. Englewood Cliffs, N. J.: Prentice-Hall, 1963.
Stephenson, R. T. "The Jacob's Ladder in Homer," CJ 30 (June, 1935), 515-530.
Suhr, E. G. "Winged Words," Folklore 85 (Autumn, 1974), 169-172.
Tashiro, T. T. "Three Passages in Homer, and the Homeric Legacy," AR 25 (Spring, 1965), 63-89.
Thomas, C. G. Homer's History: Mycenaean or Dark Age? New York: Holt, Rinehart and Winston, 1970.
Thorpe, M. Homer. London: Macmillan, 1973.
Trypanes, K. A. The Homeric Epics. Warminster, Eng.: Aris and Phillips, 1977.
Tsagarakis, O. Nature and Background of Major Concepts of Divine Power in Homer. Amsterdam: Gruner, 1977.
Verdenius, W. J. Homer, the Educator of the Greeks. Amsterdam: North-Holland, 1970.

Vivante, P. "Homer and the Aesthetic Moment," Arion 4 (Autumn, 1965), 415-438.
_____. The Homeric Imagination; A Study of Homer's Poetic Perception of Reality. Bloomington: Indiana University Press, 1970.
_____. "On Homer's Winged Words," CQ 25 (May, 1975), 1-12.
_____. "On Poetry and Language in Homer," Ramus 2 (1973), 143-162.
_____. "On the Representation of Nature and Reality in Homer," Arion 5 (Summer, 1966), 149-190.
Voegelin, E. "World of Homer," R Pol 15 (October, 1953), 491-523.
Wace, A. J. B., and F. H. Stubbings, eds. A Companion to Homer. London: Macmillan, 1962.
Watts, A. C. The Lyre and the Harp; A Comparative Reconsideration of Oral Tradition in Homer and Old English Epic Poetry. New Haven, Conn.: Yale University Press, 1969.
Webster, T. B. L. "Homer and His Immediate Predecessors," in his From Mycenae to Homer. New York: Praeger, 1958, pp. 208-283.
Wender, D. "Homer, Avdo Mededović and the Elephant's Child," AJP 98 (Winter, 1977), 327-347.
Whitman, C. H. Homer and the Heroic Tradition. Cambridge, Mass.: Harvard University Press, 1958.
Willcock, M. M. "Hysteron Proteron in the Homeric Style," AJP 96 (Summer, 1975), 107-109.
Wood, R. An Essay on the Original Genius and Writings of Homer. New York: Garland, 1971.
Young, D. "Never Blotted a Line? Formula and Premeditation in Homer and Hesiod," Arion 6 (Autumn, 1967), 279-324.

Individual Works

Hymns

Freed, G., and R. Bentman. "The Homeric Hymn to Aphrodite," CJ 50 (January, 1955), 153-159.
Greene, W. C. "Return to Persephone and the Hymn to Demeter," CP 41 (April, 1946), 105-107.
Hoekstra, A. The Sub-epic Stage of the Formulaic Tradition: Studies in the Homeric Hymns to Apollo, to Aphrodite and to Demeter. Amsterdam: North-Holland, 1969.
Knight, W. F. J. "Integration and the Hymn to Apollo," AJP 62 (July, 1941), 302-313.
Lawton, W. C. The Successors of Homer. New York: Cooper Square, 1969.
Mylonas, G. E. "Hymn to Demeter and Her Sanctuary at Bleusis," Wash Univ St Lang & Lit (New Series) 13 (1942), 99.
Porter, H. N. "Repetition in the Homeric Hymn to Aphrodite," AJP 70 (July, 1949), 249-272.
Richardson, N. J. The Homeric Hymn to Demeter. Oxford: Clarendon, 1974.

Walton, F. R. "Athens, Eleusis, and the Homeric Hymn to Demeter," HTR 45 (April, 1952), 105-114.

Iliad

Adkins, A. W. H. "Art, Beliefs, and Values in the Later Books of the Iliad," CP 70 (October, 1975), 239-254.
Anderson, W. D. "Achilles and the Dark Night of the Soul," CJ 51 (March, 1956), 265-268.
Armstrong, J. I. "Arming Motif in the Iliad," AJP 79 (October, 1958), 337-354.
Atchity, K. J. Homer's Iliad: The Shield of Memory. Carbondale: Southern Illinois University Press, 1977.
_____. "The Message of Idaios: Formulaic Departure?," CP 68 (October, 1973), 297.
Benardete, S. Achilles and Hector: The Homeric Hero. Chicago: Dept. of Photographic Reproduction, University of Chicago Library, 1955.
Bespaloff, R. On the Iliad, tr. by M. McCarthy. Princeton, N.J.: Princeton University Press, 1947.
Beye, C. R. The Iliad, the Odyssey, and the Epic Tradition. New York: Gordian, 1976.
Bolling, G. M. Athetized Lines of the Iliad. Baltimore: Linguistic Society of America, 1944.
Bonnard, A. "Iliad and Homer's Humanism," in his Greek Civilization; from the Iliad to the Parthenon. New York: Macmillan, 1957, pp. 30-58.
Bowra, C. M. "Homeric Epithets for Troy," J Hel S 80 (1960), 16-23.
_____. Tradition and Design in the Iliad. London: Oxford University Press, 1930.
Braswell, B. K. "Mythological Innovation in the Iliad," CQ (New Series) 21 (May, 1971), 16-26.
Brenk, F. E. "Aphrodite's Girdle: No Way to Treat a Lady (Iliad 14.214-223)," CB 54 (1977), 17-20.
Clark, F. L. A Study of the Iliad in Translation. Chicago: University of Chicago Press, 1927.
Clarke, W. M. "Achilles and Patroclus in Love," Hermes 106 (1978), 381-396.
Combellack, F. M. "Homer and Hector; A Discussion of J. A. Scott's Theory That Hector Was the Invention of the Poet," AJP 65 (July, 1944), 209-243; Reply, J. A. Scott, 66 (April, 1945), 187-189.
Cramer, O. C. "Speech and Silence in the Iliad," CJ 71 (April-May, 1976), 300-304.
Davenport, G. Pennant Key-Indexed Study Guide to Homer's Iliad. Philadelphia: Educational Research Associates, 1967.
Dodds, E. R. "Agamemnon's Apology," in his Greeks and the Irrational. Berkeley: University of California Press, 1951, pp. 1-27.
Donlan, W. "Homer's Agamemnon," CW 65 (December, 1971), 109-115.

Duethorn, G. A. Achilles' Shield and the Structure of the Iliad. Amherst, Mass.: Amherst College Press, 1962.

Entwistle, W. J. "New Light on the Epic-Ballad Problem [Ballad Origins of the Iliad and Odyssey]," JAF 62 (October, 1949), 375-381.

Fenik, B. Typical Battle Scenes in the Iliad: Studies in the Narrative Techniques of Homeric Battle Description. Wiesbaden: Steiner, 1968.

Finley, M. I. "Lost: The Trojan War," in his Aspects of Antiquity; Discoveries and Controversies. New York: Viking, 1968, pp. 24-37.

Friedrich, P. "Defilement and Honor in the Iliad," JIES 1 (Summer, 1973), 119-126.

Friedrich, P., and J. Redfield. "Speech as a Personality Symbol: The Case of Achilles," Language 54 (June, 1978), 263-288.

Friis, J. K. The Iliad in Early Greek Art. Copenhagen: Munksgaard, 1967.

Gaunt, D. M. "The Change of Plan in the Doloneia," G & R 18 (October, 1971), 191-198.

Graves, R. "Greek Myths and Pseudo Myths [in History or the Trojan War]," Hud R 8 (Summer, 1955), 212-230.

Greene, T. M. "The Iliad," in his The Descent from Heaven, a Study in Epic Continuity. New Haven, Conn.: Yale University Press, 1963, pp. 26-51.

Griffin, J. "Divine Audience and the Religion of the Iliad," CQ (New Series) 28 (1978), 1-22.

―――. "Epic Cycle and the Uniqueness of Homer," J Hel S 97 (1977), 39-53.

―――. "Homeric Pathos and Objectivity," CQ (New Series) 26 (1976), 161-187.

Groten, F. J. "Homer's Helen," G & R 15 (April, 1968), 33-39.

Hawley, R. C. "The Antiphonal Muse: Comic Sub-theme in the Iliad," C World 62 (November, 1968), 81-82.

Hope, S. R., and J. F. Lazenby. The Catalogue of the Ships in Homer's Iliad. London: Clarendon, 1970.

Hutson, A. E., and P. McCoy, eds. "Iliad and the Odyssey," in their Epics of the Western World. Philadelphia: Lippincott, 1954, pp. 19-171.

Huxley, G. "Homer's Perception of His Ionian Circumstances," Maynooth Review 3 (1977), 73-84.

Ingalls, J. "Structural Unity of the Iliad," CJ 42 (April, 1947), 399-406.

Kirk, G. S. "Homer's Iliad and Ours," PCPS (New Series) 16 (1970), 48-59.

Leadbeater, L. W. Homer's Iliad. New York: Barrister, 1966.

Leaf, W. Troy; A Study in Homeric Geography. Freeport, N. Y.: Books for Libraries, 1971.

Lee, D. N. J. The Similes of the Iliad and the Odyssey Compared. London: Cambridge University Press, 1965.

Leinieks, V. "A Structural Pattern in the Iliad," CJ 69 (December 1973), 102-107.

Levin, S. "Love and the Hero of the Iliad," TAPA 80 (1949), 37-49.

MacKay, L. A. Wrath of Homer. Toronto: University of Toronto Press, 1948.
McNamee, M. B. "Proud Achilles, the Noblest Achaean of Them All," in his Honor and the Epic Hero; A Study of the Shifting Concept of Magnanimity in Philosophy and Epic Poetry. New York: Holt, 1960, pp. 8-39.
Mason, H. A. "An Episode in the Sixth Book of Homer's Iliad," Camb Q 6 (1973), 143-150.
_____. "Introducing Homer's Iliad, Camb Q 4 (Winter, 1968-1969), 15-37.
Moulton, C. "Similes in the Iliad," Hermes 102 (1974), 381-397.
Mueller, M. "Knowledge and Delusion in the Iliad," Mosaic 3 (Winter, 1970), 86-103.
Murray, G. "The Background of the Iliad: The Birth of Homer," in his The Rise of the Greek Epic. London: Oxford University Press, 1960, pp. 218-237.
_____. "The Iliad as a Great Poem," in his The Rise of the Greek Epic. London: Oxford University Press, 1960, pp. 238-260.
Myres, J. L. "The Last Book of the Iliad," J Hel S 51 (1931), 264-296.
_____. "The Structure of the Iliad, Illustrated by the Speeches," J Hel S 74 (1954), 122-141.
Nagler, M. W. Spontaneity and Tradition: A Study in the Oral Art of Homer. Berkeley: University of California Press, 1974.
Nethercut, W. R. "The Epic Journey of Achilles," Ramus 5 (1976), 1-17.
_____. "Hector at the Abyss," CB 49 (November, 1972), 7-9.
Ogilvy, J. "Animals in the Iliad," CN & V 16 (April, 1972), 49-53.
Owen, E. T. Story of the Iliad. London: Oxford University Press, 1947.
Page, D. L. History and the Homeric Iliad. Berkeley: University of California Press, 1963.
Porter, D. H. "Violent Juxtaposition in the Similes of the Iliad," CJ 68 (October-November, 1972), 11-21.
Post, L. A. "Tragic Pattern of the Iliad," in his From Homer to Menander; Forces in Greek Poetic Fiction. Berkeley: University of California Press, 1951, pp. 27-55.
Prendergast, G. L. A Compete Concordance to the Iliad of Homer. Revised and enlarged by B. Marzullo. Hildesheim: Olms, 1971.
Redfield, J. M. Nature and Culture in the Iliad; The Tragedy of Hector. Chicago: University of Chicago Press, 1975.
Reeve, M. D. "The Language of Achilles," CQ (New Series) 23 (November, 1973), 193-195.
Reid, S. "The Iliad: Agamemnon's Dream," AI 30 (Spring, 1973), 33-56.
Rexroth, K. "Homer: The Iliad," in his Classics Revisited. Chicago: Quadrangle, 1968, pp. 7-11.
Rosner, J. A. "The Speech of Phoenix: Iliad 9. 434-605," Phoenix 30 (Winter, 1976), 314-327.
Rouman, J. C., and W. H. Held. "More Still on the Trojan Horse," CJ 67 (April-May, 1972), 327-330.
Ryan, G. J. "Helen in Homer," CJ 61 (December, 1965), 115-117.

Sale, W. "Achilles and Heroic Values," Arion 2 (Autumn, 1963), 86-100.
Schlunk, R. R. "The Theme of the Suppliant-Exile in the Iliad," AJP 97 (Fall, 1976), 199-209.
Segal, C. P. "Andromache's Anagnorisis: Formulaic Artistry in the Iliad 22. 437-476," HSCP 75 (1971), 33-57.
_____. " 'The Myth Was Saved': Reflections on Homer and the Mythology of Plato's Republic," Hermes 106 (1978), 315-336.
_____. The Theme of the Mutilation of the Corpse in the Iliad. Leiden: Brill, 1971.
Shannon, R. S. The Arms of Achilles and Homeric Compositional Technique. Leiden: Brill, 1975.
Sheppard, J. T. The Pattern of the Iliad. Barnes and Noble, 1969.
Simpson, R. H., and J. F. Lazenby. The Catalogue of the Ships in Homer's Iliad. Oxford: Clarendon, 1970.
Smith, L. F. "Chariot Fighting and a Crux in Homer," AJP 64 (January, 1943), 92-94.
Tait, M. "The Tragic Philosophy of the Iliad," TAPA 74 (1943), 49-59.
Trapp, R. L. "Ajax in the Iliad," CJ 56 (March, 1961), 271-275.
Tsagarakis, O. "The Achaean Embassy and the Wrath of Achilles," Hermes 99 (1971), 257-277.
Van Doren, M. "The Iliad," in his Noble Voice; A Study of Ten Great Poems. New York: Holt, 1946, pp. 1-44.
Wade-Gery, H. T. Poet of the Iliad. London: Cambridge University Press, 1952.
Walcot, P. "Judgement of Paris," G & R 24 (April, 1977), 31-39.
West, D. "Deaths of Hector and Turnus," G & R 21 (April, 1974), 21-31.
West, W. A. "Homer's Aias," Arion 4 (Summer, 1965), 291-294.
Whallon, W. "Formulas for Heros in the Iliad and in Beowulf," MP 63 (November, 1965), 95-104.
Willcock, M. M. "Ad Hoc Invention in the Iliad," HSCP 81 (1977), 41-53.
_____. A Commentary on Homer's Iliad, Books 1-6. New York: St. Martin's, 1970.
_____. A Companion to the Iliad, Based on the Translation by R. Lattimore. Chicago: University of Chicago Press, 1976.
_____. "The Funeral Games of Patroclus," BICS 20 (1973), 1-11.
_____. "The Funeral Games of Patroclus," PCA 70 (1973), 36.
_____. "Mythological Paradeigma in the Iliad," CQ (New Series) 14 (1964), 141-154.
_____. "Some Aspects of the Gods in the Iliad," BICS 17 (1970), 1-10.
Wilson, J. R. "The Wedding Gifts of Peleus," Phoenix 28 (Winter, 1974), 385-389.
Wilson, P. O. "Battle Scenes in the Iliad," CJ 47 (April, 1952), 269-274; 299-300.
Wright, J., ed. Essays on the Iliad: Selected Modern Criticism. Bloomington: Indiana University Press, 1978.
Youman, A. E. "Climactic Themes in the Iliad," CJ 61 (February, 1966), 222-228.

Zarker, J. W. "King Eetion and Thebe as Symbols in the Iliad," CJ 61 (December, 1965), 110-114.

Odyssey

Allen, W., Jr. "The Theme of the Suitors in the Odyssey," TAPA 70 (1939), 104-124.
Armstrong, J. I. "The Marriage Song--Odyssey 23," TAPA 89 (1958), 38-43.
Auerbach, E. "Scar of Ulysses [the Representation of Reality in Homer and the Old Testament], tr. by J. Meserve," PR 17 (May, 1950), 411-432.
Austin, N. Archery at the Dark of the Moon: Poetic Problems in Homer's Odyssey. Berkeley: University of California Press, 1975.
———. "Name Magic in the Odyssey," CSCA 5 (1972), 1-20.
———. "Telemachos Polymechanos," CSCA 2 (1969), 45-63.
Belmont, D. E. "Telemachus and Nausicaa: A Study of Youth," CJ 63 (October, 1967), 1-9.
———. "Twentieth-century Odysseus," CJ 62 (November, 1966), 49-56.
Bérard, V. Did Homer Live?, tr. by B. Rhys. New York: Dutton, 1931.
Beye, C. R. The Iliad, the Odyssey, and the Epic Tradition. New York: Gordian, 1976.
Bonnard, A. "Odysseus and the Sea," in his Greek Civilization; From the Iliad to the Parthenon. New York: Macmillan, 1957, pp. 59-71.
Bradford, E. D. S. Ulysses Found. New York: Harcourt, Brace, 1964.
Bradley, E. M. "The Greatness of His Nature; Fire and Justice in the Odyssey," Ramus 5 (1976), 137-148.
Brain, P., and D. D. Skinner. "Odysseus and the Axes: Homeric Ballistics Reconstructed," G & R 25 (April, 1978), 55-58.
Bright, D. F. "Homeric Ambiguity," Mnemosyne 30 (1977), 423-426.
Brown, C. S. "Odysseus and Polyphemus: The Name and the Curse," CL 18 (Summer, 1966), 193-202.
Bryce, T. R. "Pandaros, a Lycian at Troy," AJP 98 (Fall, 1977), 213-218.
Burrows, R. Z. "Deception as a Comic Device in the Odyssey," C World 59 (October, 1965), 33-36.
Butler, S. The Authoress of the Odyssey. Chicago: University of Chicago Press, 1967.
Clarke, H. W. Art of the Odyssey. Englewood Cliffs, N. J.: Prentice-Hall, 1967.
———. "Fire Imagery in the Odyssey," CJ 57 (May, 1962), 358-360.
———. "Telemachus and the Telemacheia," AJP 84 (April, 1963), 129-145.
Clay, J. S. "The Beginning of the Odyssey," AJP 97 (Winter, 1976), 313-326.

112 : Greek and Roman Authors

Clissold, P. "The Voyage of Odysseus," MM 62 (February, 1976), 52-54.
Combellack, F. M. "Odysseus and Anticleia," CP 69 (April, 1974), 121-123.
──────. "Three Odyssean Problems," CSCA 6 (1973), 17-46.
Couch, H. N. "Nausicaa and Dido," CJ 37 (May, 1942), 453-462.
Creed, R. P. "Singer Looks at His Sources," CL 14 (Winter, 1962), 44-52.
Damon, P. "Dilation and Displacement in the Odyssey," PCP 5 (April, 1970), 19-23.
Davenport, G. Pennant Key-Indexed Study Guide to Homer's Odyssey. Philadelphia: Educational Research Associates, 1967.
Dimock, G. "Crime and Punishment in the Odyssey," YR 60 (December, 1970), 199-214.
Dimock, G. E. "Name of Odysseus," Hud R 9 (Spring, 1956), 52-70.
Dunbar, H. A Complete Concordance to the Odyssey of Homer, revised by B. Marzullo. Hildesheim: Olms, 1962.
Dunmore, C. W. Homer's Odyssey. New York: Barrister, 1966.
Dyson, M. "The Second Assembly of the Gods in the Odyssey," Antichthon 4 (1970), 1-12.
Eckert, C. W. "Initiatory Motifs in the Story of Telemachus," CJ 59 (November, 1963), 49-57.
Entwistle, W. J. "New Light on the Epic-Ballad Problem [Ballad Origins of the Iliad and Odyssey]," JAF 62 (October, 1949), 375-381.
Fenik, B. Studies in the Odyssey. Wiesbaden: Steiner, 1974.
Finley, J. H. Homer's Odyssey. Cambridge, Mass.: Harvard University Press, 1978.
Finley, M. I. World of Odysseus. New York: Viking, 1954.
──────. "The World of Odysseus Revisited," PCA 71 (1974), 13-31.
Garrido-Bazic, I. M. "Mud and Smoke in the Odyssey," G & R 15 (October, 1946), 108-113.
Gaunt, D. M. Surge and Thunder: Critical Readings in Homer's Odyssey. New York: Oxford University Press, 1971.
Gran, P. "The Curse of the Cyclops," CB 50 (December, 1973), 31-32.
Gray, D. "Houses in the Odyssey," CQ (New Series) 5 (1955), 1-12.
Greene, T. M. "Form and Craft in the Odyssey," in his The Descent from Heaven, a Study in Epic Continuity. New Haven, Conn.: Yale University Press, 1963, pp. 52-73.
Gresseth, G. K. "The Homeric Sirens," TAPA 101 (1970), 203-218.
Gross, N. P. "Nausicaa: A Feminine Threat," CW 69 (February, 1976), 311-317.
Gwatkin, W. E. "Dodona, Odysseus, and Aeneas," CJ 57 (December, 1961), 97-102.
Hainsworth, J. B. "No Flames in the Odyssey," J Hel S 78 (1958), 49-56.
Hansen, W. F. The Conference Sequence: Patterned Narration and Narrative Inconsistency in the Odyssey. Berkeley: University of California Press, 1972.

Harsh, P. W. "Penelope and Odysseus in Odyssey XIX," AJP 71 (January, 1950), 1-21.
Hart, W. M. High Comedy in the Odyssey. Berkeley: University of California Press, 1943.
Heatherington, M. E. "Chaos, Order, and Cunning in the Odyssey," SP 73 (July, 1976), 225-228.
Hogan, J. C. "The Temptation of Odysseus," TAPA 106 (1976), 187-210.
Holtsmark, E. B. "Spiritual Rebirth of the Hero: Odyssey 5," CJ 61 (February, 1966), 206-210.
Jones, D. M. Ethical Themes in the Plot of the Odyssey. London: Westfield College, 1956.
Jones, F. W. "The Formulation of the Revenge Motif in the Odyssey," TAPA 72 (1941), 195-202.
Kitto, H. D. F. "The Odyssey," in his Poiesis; Structure and Thought. Berkeley: University of California Press, 1966, pp. 116-152.
Lee, D. J. N. The Similes of the Iliad and the Odyssey Compared. London: Cambridge University Press, 1965.
Lessing, E. The Adventures of Ulysses: Homer's Epic in Pictures. New York: Dodd, Mead, 1970.
Levy, H. L. "The Odyssean Suitors and the Host-Guest Relationship," TAPA 94 (1963), 145-153.
Macdonell, P. J. "The Tactics of Odysseus," G & R 5 (February, 1936), 103-120.
Millar, C. M. H., and J. W. S. Carmichael. "The Growth of Telemachus," G & R (New Series) 1 (June, 1954), 58-64.
Moulton, C. "The End of the Odyssey," GRBS 15 (Summer, 1974), 153-169.
Musial, T. J. "Two Heros, Two Bards, and Two Worlds of the Odyssey," SR 76 (Winter, 1968), 106-116.
Myres, J. L. "The Pattern of the Odyssey," J Hel S 72 (1952), 1-19.
Nagler, M. N. "Dread Goddess Endowed with Speech," Archaeol News 6 (1977), 77-85.
Nelson, C. E., ed. Homer's Odyssey; A Critical Handbook. Belmont, Calif.: Wadsworth, 1969.
O'Nolan, K. "Doublets in the Odyssey," CQ (New Series) 28 (1978), 23-37.
Page, D. Folktales in Homer's Odyssey. Cambridge, Mass.: Harvard University Press, 1973.
_____. The Homeric Odyssey. Westport, Conn.: Greenwood, 1976.
Parry, A. A. "Homer as Artist," CQ (New Series) 21 (May, 1971), 1-15.
Peradotto, J. "Odyssey 8. 564-571: Verisimilitude, Narrative Analysis, and Bricolage," TSLL 15 (Winter, 1974), 803-833.
Phillips, E. D. "The Comic Odysseus," G & R 6 (March, 1959), 58-66.
Pillot, G. The Secret Code of the Odyssey: Did the Greeks Sail the Atlantic?, tr. by F. E. Albert. London: Abelard-Schuman, 1972.

Pocock, L. G. Odyssean Essays. New York: Barnes and Noble, 1965.
Podlecki, A. J. "Omens in the Odyssey," G & R 14 (April, 1967), 12-23.
―――. "Some Odyssean Similes," G & R 18 (April, 1971), 81-90.
Porter, R. J. "Singer in the Song: Autobiography & Time in the Odyssey," Mass R 18 (Winter, 1977), 801-820.
Post, L. A. "Pattern of Success: Homer's Odyssey," in his, From Homer to Menander; Forces in Greek Poetic Fiction. Berkeley: University of California Press, 1951.
Powell, B. B. Composition By Theme in the Odyssey. Meisenheim a. Glan: Hain, 1977.
―――. "Narrative Pattern in the Homeric Tale of Menelaus," TAPA 101 (1970), 419-431.
Rexroth, K. "Homer: The Odyssey," in his Classics Revisited. Chicago: Quadrangle, 1968, pp. 12-16.
Rose, G. P. "Odyssey 15.143-82: A Narrative Inconsistency?," TAPA 102 (1971), 509-514.
―――. "The Quest of Telemachus," TAPA 98 (1967), 391-398.
―――. "The Unfriendly Phaeacians," TAPA 100 (1969), 387-406.
Russo, J. "Inner Man in Archilochus and the Odyssey," GRBS 15 (Summer, 1974), 139-152.
Schein, S. L. "Odysseus and Polyphemus in the Odyssey," GRBS 11 (Summer, 1970), 73-83.
Schmiel, R. "Telemachus in Sparta," TAPA 103 (1972), 463-472.
Scott, J. A. "The First Book of the Odyssey," TAPA 67 (1936), 1-6.
Scott, W. C. "A Repeated Episode at Odyssey 1.125-48," TAPA 102 (1971), 541-551.
Segal, C. P. "Circean Temptations: Homer, Vergil, Ovid," TAPA 99 (1968), 419-442.
―――. "The Phaeacians and the Symbolism of Odysseus' Return," Arion 1 (Winter, 1962), 17-64.
Seidensticker, B. "Archilochus and Odysseus," GRBS 19 (Spring, 1978), 5-22.
Shapiro, H. A. "Odyssey 2.40-79: Telemachus as Rhetorician," CB 48 (February, 1972), 57-58.
Sheppard, J. T. "Great-hearted Odysseus," J Hel S 56 (1936), 36-47.
Snyder, P. G. "Homer's Apocalypse," Arion (New Series) 1 (1973), 67-111.
Stanford, W. B. "The Ending of the Odyssey: An Ethical Approach," Ha 100 (Summer, 1965), 5-20.
―――. "New Name for Ulysses' Daughter?," CR (New Series) 23 (December, 1973), 126.
―――. The Ulysses Theme. Oxford: Blackwell, 1963. Steele, T. J. "The Oral Patterning of the Cyclops Episode, Odyssey IX," CB 48 (February, 1972), 54-56.
Stewart, D. J. The Disguised Guest: Rank, Role and Identity in the Odyssey. Lewisburg, Pa.: Bucknell University Press, 1976.

Taylor, C. H., ed. Essays on the Odyssey: Selected Modern Criticism. Bloomington: Indiana University Press, 1963.
Thomson, J. A. K. Studies in the Odyssey. New York: Haskell House, 1966.
Thornton, A. People and Themes in Homer's Odyssey. London: Methuen, 1970.
_____. "Why Do the Suitors Feast in the House of Odysseus?," AUMLA No. 20 (November, 1963), 341-345.
Timpe, E. F. "Ulysses and the Archetypal Feminine," in J. Strelka, ed., Perspectives in Literary Criticism. University Park: Pennsylvania State University Press, 1968, pp. 199-213.
Van Doren, M. "The Odyssey," in his Noble Voice; A Study of Ten Great Poems. New York: Holt, 1946, pp. 45-85.
West, M. L. "Achaean Wall," CR (New Series) 19 (December, 1969), 255-260.
Will, F. "Odysseus the Hero," in his Literature Inside Out; Ten Speculative Essays. Cleveland: Western Reserve University Press, 1966, pp. 71-82.
Williams, H. "Viewing the Stubble: A Note on the Odyssey," CJ 68 (October-November, 1972), 75-78.
Woolsey, R. B. "Repeated Narratives in the Odyssey," CP 36 (April, 1941), 167-181.
Wormhoudt, A. Muse at Length. Boston: Christopher, 1953.
Wyatt, W. F., Jr. "Penelope's Fat Hand," CP 73 (October, 1978), 343-344.
Ziolkowski, T. "The Odysseus Theme in Recent German Fiction," CL 14 (Summer, 1962), 225-246.

HORACE

General Criticism

Adams, F. P., I. Edman, and M. Van Doren. "Horace: Odes, Satires and Epistles," in M. Van Doren, ed., New Invitation to Learning. New York: Random House, 1942, pp. 30-43.
Andrews, M. "Aspects of Horatian Imagery," CR 62 (December, 1948), 111-112.
Avery, W. T. "Homeric Hospitality in Alcaeus and Horace," CP 59 (April, 1964), 107-109.
Baldwin, B. "Horace on Sex," AJP 91 (October, 1970), 460-465.
Bridge, J. "Horace: The Beginning of the Silver Age," in L. W. Jones, ed., Classical and Medieval Studies in Homer of Edward Kennard Rand, Presented upon the Completion of His Fortieth Year of Teaching. New York: Published by the Editor, 1938, pp. 21-32.
Bury, F. H. "Horace's Personality and Outlook on Life as Revealed in His Satires and Epistles," G & R 3 (February, 1934), 65-73.
Campbell, A. Y. Horace: A New Interpretation. Westport, Conn.: Greenwood, 1970.

Chapman, J. B. Horace and His Poetry. New York: AMS, 1972.
Cody, J. V. Horace and Callimachean Aesthetics. Brussels: Latomus, 1976.
Costa, C. D. N. Horace. London: Routledge and K. Paul, 1973.
Crowther, N. B. "Horace, Catullus, and Alexandrianism," Mnemosyne 31 (1978), 33-44.
D'Alton, J. F. Horace and His Age. New York: Russell and Russell, 1962.
Dearing, B. "Notes on Horace as a 'Metaphysical' Poet," CJ 47 (March, 1952), 230-231.
DeWitt, N. W. "Epicurean Doctrine in Horace," CP 34 (April, 1939), 127-134.
Downs, R. B. "Best-loved Latin Poet: Quintus Horatius Flaccus," in his Famous Books, Ancient and Medieval. New York: Barnes and Noble, 1964, pp. 183-187.
Dyer, R. R. "Diffugere Nives: Horace and the Augustan Spring," G & R 12 (April, 1965), 79-84.
Ferguson, J. "Catullus and Horace," AJP 77 (January, 1956), 1-18.
Fiske, G. C. Lucilius and Horace; A Study in the Classical Theory of Imitation. Westport, Conn.: Greenwood, 1971.
Flickinger, R. C. "Perpetually Imitated and Perpetually Inimitable," CJ 31 (December, 1935), 131-134.
Fraenkel, E. Horace. Oxford: Clarendon, 1957.
Frank, T. Catullus and Horace; Two Poets in Their Enviornment. New York: Russell and Russell, 1965.
Goad, C. M. Horace in the English Literature of the Eighteenth Century. New York: Haskell House, 1956.
Grube, G. M. A. "Horace," in his The Greek and Roman Critics. Toronto: University of Toronto Press, 1965, pp. 231-255.
Hadas, M. "Horace," in his History of Latin Literature. New York: Columbia University Press, 1952, pp. 164-183.
Haight, E. H. "Horace on Art: Ut Pictura Poesis," CJ 47 (February, 1952), 157-162.
Herrick, M. T. Fusion of Horatian and Aristotelian Literary Criticism, 1531-1555. Urbana: University of Illinois Press, 1946.
Hewitt, J. W. "The Gratitude of Horace to Maecenas," CJ 36 (May, 1941), 464-472.
Highet, G. "Horace: A Career Open to the Talents," in his Poets in a Landscape. New York: Knopf, 1957, pp. 106-155.
_____. "Libertino Patre Natus," AJP 94 (Fall, 1973), 268-281.
Hunt, N. A. B. Horace the Minstrel; A Practical and Aesthetic Study of His Aeolic Verse. Kineton, Eng.: Roundwood, 1969.
Huxley, H. H. "Horace and Heraldry," G & R 17 (January, 1948), 24-34.
Jaffee, H. Horace: An Essay in Poetic Therapy. Chicago: [n. p.], 1944.
Johnson, S. "Intimations of Immortality in the Major Lyric and Elegiac Poets of Rome; Horace," Roy Soc Can Trans (Series 3) 44 Sec. 2 (1950), 65-75.
Johnson, W. R. "The Boastful Bird: Notes on Horatian Modesty," CJ 61 (March, 1966), 272-275.
_____. "Queen, Great Queen? Cleopatra and the Politics of Misrepresentation," Arion 6 (Autumn, 1967), 387-402.

Kegel-Brinkgreve, E. "Byron and Horace," ES 57 (April, 1976), 128-138.
Kennedy, N. T. "Pindar and Horace," AClass 18 (1975), 9-24.
Levin, D. N. "Horace's Preoccupation with Death," CJ 63 (April, 1968), 315-320.
Lord, L. E. "Horace as an Occasional Poet," CJ 31 (December, 1935), 152-166.
McCrea, N. G. Literature and Liberalism, with Other Classical Papers. New York: Columbia University Press, 1936, pp. 43-71; 113-140.
McKay, A. G., and D. M. Shepperd, eds. Roman Lyric Poetry. New York: St. Martin's, 1969.
MacKay, L. A. "Notes on Horace," CP 37 (January, 1942), 79-81.
McKinlay, A. P. "The Wine Element in Horace," CJ 42 (December, 1946), 161-167; 42 (January, 1947), 229-235.
McNaughton, D. A. "Horace's Criticism of Life," G & R 7 (February, 1938), 101-113.
Musurillo, H. A. "Focal Symbols in Horace's Poetry," in his Symbol and Myth in Ancient Poetry. New York: Fordham University Press, 1961, pp. 127-148.
_____. "Horace and His Friends: Brundisium," in his Symbol and Myth in Ancient Poetry. New York: Fordham University Press, 1961, pp. 149-158.
Noyes, A. Horace: A Portrait. New York: Sheed and Ward, 1947.
Nybakken, O. E. Analytical Study of Horace's Ideas. Iowa City: University of Iowa Press, 1937.
Oates, W. J. The Influence of Simonides of Ceos upon Horace. New York: Haskell House, 1971.
Otis, B. "Horace and the Elegists," TAPA 76 (1945), 177-190.
_____. "The Relevance of Horace," Arion 9 (Summer-Autumn, 1970), 145-174.
Pavlovskis, Z. "Aristotle, Horace, and the Ironic Man," CP 63 (January, 1968), 22-41.
Perret, J. Horace, tr. by Bertha Humez. New York: New York University Press, 1964.
Phelps, W. G. Three Roman Poets and Their Messages. Shreveport, La.: Centenary College Press, 1938.
Prescot, K. Letters Concerning Homer, the Sleeper in Horace. New York: Garland, 1970.
Pritchard, J. P. "The Poetics and the Ars Poetica," in his Return to the Fountains; Some Classical Sources of American Criticism. New York: Octagon, 1966, pp. 6-12.
Rand, E. K. "Horace and the Spirit of Comedy," RIP 24 (April, 1937), 39-117.
Reckford, K. J. Horace. New York: Twayne, 1969.
Rudd, N. "Patterns in Horatian Lyric [Imagery]," AJP 81 (October, 1960), 373-392.
Sedgwick, H. D. Horace; A Biography. Cambridge, Mass.: Harvard University Press, 1947.
Sellar, W. Y. The Roman Poets of the Augustan Age; Horace and the Blegiac Poets. New York: Biblo and Tannen, 1965.
Showerman, G. Horace and His Influence. New York: Cooper Square, 1963.

Silk, E. T. "Fresh Approach to Horace," AJP 77 (July, 1956), 255-263.
Smiley, C. N. Horace; His Poetry and Philosophy. New York: King's Crown, 1945.
Smith, P. L. "Poetic Tensions in the Horatian Recusatio," AJP 89 (January, 1968), 56-65.
Soulbury, L. "An Address on Horace," CJ 44 (October, 1948), 7-14.
Stewart, D. J. "The Poet as Bird in Aristophanes and Horace," CJ 62 (May, 1967), 357-361.
Strodach, G. K. "Horace's Individualism Reconsidered," CJ 36 (October, 1940), 1-19.
Sullivan, F. A. "Horace and the Afterlife," CP 37 (July, 1942), 275-287.
Taylor, M. E. "Horace: Laudator Temporis Acti?," AJP 83 (January, 1962), 23-43.
Thayer, M. R. The Influence of Horace on the Chief English Poets of the Nineteenth Century. New York: Russell and Russell, 1968.
Tracy, H. L. "The Lyric Poet's Repertoire," CJ 61 (October, 1965), 22-26.
Ullman, B. L. "Horace and the Philologians," CJ 31 (April, 1936), 403-417.
West, D. A. Reading Horace. Edinburgh: Edinburgh University Press, 1967.
Wilkinson, L. P. Horace and His Lyric Poetry. 2nd edition. London: Cambridge University Press, 1968.
_____. "The Language of Virgil and Horace," CQ (New Series) 9 (1959), 181-192.
Williams, G. Horace. Oxford: Clarendon, 1972.
_____. "Poetry in the Moral Climate of Augustan Rome," JRS 52 (1962), 28-46.
Wimsatt, W. K. and C. Brooks. "Roman Classicism: Horace," in their Literary Criticism; A Short History. New York: Knopf, 1957, pp. 77-96.
Young, G. M. "Art of Horace," in his Today and Yesterday: Collected Essays and Addresses. Chester Springs, Pa.: Dufour, 1959, pp. 165-174.

Individual Works

Art of Poetry, or Ars Poetica (Epistle to the Pisos)

Alexander, W. H. "Spe Longus, Horace, Ars Poetica 172," CJ 33 (January, 1938), 226-228.
Brink, C. O. Horace on Poetry; 1. Prolegomena to the Literary Epistles. Cambridge: Cambridge University Press, 1963.
_____. Horace on Poetry; 2. London: Cambridge University Press, 1971.
Duckworth, G. E. "Horace's Hexameters and the Date of the Ars Poetica," TAPA 96 (1965), 73-96.
Frank, T. "Horace's Definition of Poetry," CJ 31 (December, 1935), 167-174.

Gilbert, A. H., and H. L. Snuggs. "On the Relation of Horace to Aristotle in Literary Criticism," JEGP 46 (July, 1947), 223-247.
Haight, E. H. "Horace on Art: Ut Pictura Poesis," CJ 47 (February, 1952), 157-162.
Kenny, M. "The Critic Looks at Horace," CJ 31 (December, 1935), 183-188.
LaDriere, C. "Horace and the Theory of Imitation," AJP 60 (July, 1939), 288-300.
Perret, J. "Glorius Epilogues," in his Horace, tr. by Bertha Humez. New York: New York University Press, 1969, pp. 148-167.
Tracy, H. L. "Horace's Ars Poetica: A Systematic Argument," G & R 17 (October, 1948), 104-115.
Trimpi, W. "The Meaning of Horace's 'Ut Pictura Poesis,'" JWCI 36 (1973), 1-34.
White, P. "Horace A. P. 128-130: The Intent of the Wording," CQ (New Series) 27 (1977), 191-201.
Zumwalt, N. K. "Horace, C. 1.22: Poetic and Political Integrity," TAPA 105 (1975), 417-431.

Carmen Saeculare

Alexander, W. H. Horace's Odes and Carmen Saeculare. Berkeley: University of California Press, 1947.
Hendrickson, G. L. "The So-called Prelude to the Carmen Saeculare," CP 48 (April, 1953), 73-79.

Epistles

Allen, W. "The Addresses in Horace's First Book of Epistles," SP 67 (July, 1970), 255-266.
―――――. "Horace's First Book of Epistles as Letters," CJ 68 (December, 1972), 119-133.
Bonner, S. F. "The Street Teacher: An Educational Scene in Horace," AJP 93 (October, 1972), 509-528.
Brink, C. O. Horace on Poetry; 1. Prolegomena to the Literary Epistles. Cambridge: Cambridge University Press, 1963.
Cameron, A. "Horace, Epistles ii. 2. 87ff," CR (New Series) 15 (March, 1965), 11-13.
Foster, J. "Horace, Epistles, 1. 16.35ff," CQ (New Series) 21 (May, 1971), 241.
Gilbert, C. D. "Horace, Epistles 1. 19. 37-40," CQ (New Series) 26 (1976), 110.
Haight, E. H. "Epistula Item Quaevis Non Magna Poema Est: A Fresh Approach to Horace's First Book of Epistles," SP 45 (October, 1948), 525-540.
―――――. "Lyre and Whetstone: Horatius Redivivus," CP 41 (July, 1946), 135-142.
Heller, J. L. "Horace, Epist. I, 1, 47-54," AJP 85 (July, 1964), 297-303.
Kenney, E. J. "A Question of Taste: Horace Epistles 1.14.6-9," ICS 2 (1977), 229-239.

Kilpatrick, D. "Horace on His Critics: Epist. 1. 19," Phoenix 29 (Summer, 1975), 117-127.
Kilpatrick, R. S. "Fact and Fable in Horace, Epistle I. 7," CP 68 (January, 1973), 47-53.
McGann, M. J. "Horace, Epistles II. 2. 87ff: Another View," CR (New Series) 16 (December, 1966), 266-267.
──────. "The Sixteenth Epistle of Horace," CQ (New Series) 10 (1960), 205-212.
Macleod, C. W. "Poet, the Critic, and the Moralist: Horace, Epistles 1. 19," CQ (New Series) 27 (1977), 359-376.
Musurillo, H. "A Formula for Happiness: Horace Epist. 1. 6 to Numicius," CW 67 (February, 1974), 193-204.
Nisbet, R. G. M. "Notes on Horace, Epistles 1," CQ (New Series) 9 (1959), 73-76.
Perret, J. "The Book of Epistles," in his Horace, tr. by Bertha Humez. New York: New York University Press, 1964, pp. 101-123.
Peterson, R. G. "The Unity of Horace Epistle 1.7," CJ 63 (April, 1968), 309-314.
Skalitzky, R. I. "Horace on Travel (Epist. I, 11)," CJ 68 (April-May, 1973), 316-321.

Epodes

Andrewes, M. "Horace's Use of Imagery in the Epodes and Odes," G & R 19 (October, 1950), 106-115.
Babcock, C. L. "Omne Militabitur Bellum: The Language of Commitment in Epode 1," CJ 70 (January, 1974), 14-31.
──────. Si Certus Intrarit Dolor; A Reconsideration of Horace's Fifteenth Epode," AJP 87 (October, 1966), 400-419.
Brophy, R. H. "Emancipatus Feminae: A Legal Metaphor in Horace and Plautus," TAPA 105 (1975), 1-11.
Bushalo, E. W. "Laboriosus Ulixes," CJ 64 (October, 1968), 7-10.
Carrubba, R. W. The Epodes of Horace: A Study in Poetic Arrangement. The Hague: Mouton, 1969.
Clayman, D. L. "Horace's Epodes VIII and XII: More than Clever Obscenity?," CW 69 (September, 1975), 55-61.
Hubbard, M. "Two Questions About the Sixteenth Epode," CQ (New Series) 27 (1977), 356-358.
Huxley, H. H. "An Introduction to the Epodes of Horace," PLPLS 11 (August, 1964), 61-79.
Kilpatrick, R. S. "An Interpretation of Horace, Epodes 13," CQ (New Series) 20 (May, 1970), 135-141.
Lindo, L. I. "Horace's Second Epode," CP 63 (July, 1968), 206-208.
──────. "Horace's Seventeenth Epode," CP 64 (July, 1969), 176-177.
Perret, J. "Epodes and Satires," in his Horace, tr. by Bertha Humez. New York: New York University Press, 1964, pp. 33-67.
Ruoff, A. L. "Walter Savage Landor's Criticism of Horace: The Odes and the Epodes," Arion 9 (Summer-Autumn, 1970), 189-204.

Wistrand, E. Horace's Ninth Epode and Its Historical Background. Stockholm: Almqvist and Wiksell, 1958.

Odes--General

Alexander, W. H. Horace's Odes and Carmen Saeculare. Berkeley: University of California Press, 1947.
Andrewes, M. "Horace's Use of Imagery in the Epodes and Odes," G & R 19 (October, 1950), 106-115.
Bonavia-Hunt, N. A. Horace the Minstrel: A Practical and Aesthetic Study of His Aeolic Verse. Kineton, Eng.: Roundwood, 1969.
──────. Horace the Minstrel: A Study of His Sapphic and Alcaic Lyrics. London: Musical Opinion, 1955.
Bowra, C. M. "Odes of Horace," in his Inspiration and Poetry. New York: St. Martin's, 1955, pp. 26-44.
Boyle, A. J. "The Edict of Venus: An Interpretive Essay on Horace's Amatory Odes," Ramus 2 (1973), 163-188.
Broege, V. "Divine Polarity in Horace's Lyric Poetry," CN & V 16 (January, 1972), 1-3.
Cairns, F. "Five Religious Odes of Horace," (I, 10; I, 21; and IV, 6; I, 30; I, 15.) AJP 92 (July, 1971), 433-452.
Carter, C. J. "God, King, Law--and Augustus?--in Horace's Odes I-III," PCA 70 (1973), 39-40.
Collinge, N. E. "Form and Content in the Horatian Lyric," CP 50 (July, 1955), 161-168.
──────. The Structure of Horace's Odes. New York: Oxford University Press, 1961.
Commager, S. "The Function of Wine in Horace's Odes," TAPA 88 (1957), 68-80.
──────. The Odes of Horace: A Critical Study. New Haven, Conn.: Yale University Press, 1962.
Corday, J. M. "The Structure of Horace's Odes: Some Typical Patterns," CJ 52 (December, 1956), 113-116.
Coulter, C. C. "Aeolian Strains on the Roman Lyre," CJ 31 (December, 1935), 175-182.
Frieman, R. L. "Wine and Politics in Horace," CN & V 16 (October, 1972), 84-91.
Henderson, W. J. The Imagery of Horace's Odes; A Study in Latin Poetic Imagination. Stellenbosch, South Africa: n.p., 1970.
──────. "The Paraklausithyron Motif in Horace's Odes," AClass 16 (1973), 51-67.
Lee, M. O. "Catullus in the Odes of Horace," Ramus 4 (1975), 33-48.
──────. Word, Sound and Image in the Odes of Horace. Ann Arbor: University of Michigan Press, 1969.
Lindo, L. I. "Tyrtaeus and Horace Odes 3.2," CP 66 (October, 1971), 258-260.
McDermott, E. A. "Horatius Callidus," AJP 98 (Winter, 1977), 363-380.
Mason, H. A. "Horace's Ode to Pyrrha," Camb Q 7 (1976), 27-62.
Moritz, L. A. "Some 'Central' Thoughts on Horace's Odes," CQ (New Series) 18 (1968), 116-131.

Nisbet, R. G. M. "Romanae Fidicen Lyrae: The Odes of Horace," in J. P. Sullivan, ed., Critical Essays of Roman Literature: Elegy and Lyric. Cambridge, Mass.: Harvard University Press, 1962, pp. 181-218.
Perret, J. "The Three Books of Odes," in his Horace, tr. by Bertha Humez. New York: New York University Press, 1964, pp. 68-100.
Reckford, K. J. "Some Studies in Horace's Odes on Love," CJ 55 (October, 1959), 25-33.
Ruoff, A. L. "Walter Savage Landor's Criticism of Horace: The Odes and the Epodes," Arion 9 (Summer-Autumn, 1970), 189-204.
Silk, E. T. "Notes on Cicero and the Odes of Horace," YCS 13 (1952), 145-158.
Verral, A. E. Studies, Literary and Historical, in the Odes of Horace. Port Washington, N. Y.: Kennikat, 1969.

Odes: Book 1

Alexander, W. H. "Nunc Tempus Erat: Horace, Odes I, 37, 4," CJ 39 (January, 1944), 231-233.
Anderson, W. S. "Horace Carm. 1.14: What Kind of Ship?," CP 61 (April, 1966), 84-98.
"The Archytas Ode. 'Patricius,'" G & R 12 (April, 1965), 51-53.
Babcock, C. L. "Horace Carm. 1. 32 and the Dedication of the Temple of Apollo Palatinus," CP 62 (July, 1967), 189-194.
_____. "The Role of Faunus in Horace, Carmina 1. 4," TAPA 92 (1961), 13-19.
Baker, R. J. "The Rustle of Spring in Horace (Carm., I, 23)," AJP 92 (January, 1971), 71-75.
Barr, W. "Horace, Odes 1.4," CR (New Series) 12 (March, 1962), 5-11.
Callahan, P. V., and H. Musurillo. "Handful of Dust: The Archytas Ode [Horace Corm. 1.28]," CP 59 (October, 1964), 262-266.
Campbell, A. Y. "Horace, Odes I. xxviii. 7-15 and 24," CR 60 (December, 1946), 103-106.
Catlow, L. W. "Fact, Imagination and Memory in Horace Odes 1.9," G & R 23 (April, 1976), 74-81.
Commager, S. "Horace, Carmina I, 2," AJP 80 (January, 1959), 37-55.
Cunningham, M. P. "Enarratio of Horace Odes 1. 9," CP 52 (April, 1957), 98-102.
Davis, A. T. "Cleopatra Rediviva," G & R 16 (April, 1969), 91-94.
Dunston, A. J. "Horace, Odes I, 12 Yet Again," Antichthon 7 (1973), 54-59.
Dyson, M. "Horace: Odes I, 16," AUMLA No. 30 (November, 1968), 169-179.
Edinger, H. G. "Horace, C. 1.17," CJ 66 (April-May, 1971), 306-311.
Elder, J. P. "Horace, C. I, 3," AJP 73 (April, 1952), 140-158.
_____. "Horace Carmen 1.7," CP 48 (January, 1963), 1-8.

Esler, C. C. "Horace's Socrate Ode: Imagery and Perspective," C World 62 (April, 1969), 300-305.

Fredericksmeyer, E. A. "Horace C. 1.34: The Conversion," TAPA 106 (1976), 155-176.

———. "Horace's Ode to Pyrrha [Carm. 1.5]," CP 60 (July, 1965), 180-185.

Fuqua, C. "Horace Carm. 1. 23-25," CP 63 (January, 1968), 44-46.

Goar, R. J. "Horace and the Betrayal of a Philosophy, Odes I. 29," CJ 68 (December, 1972), 116-118.

Goodrich, S. P. "Horace, Carmina 1.7," CJ 56 (May, 1961), 352-356.

Griffith, J. G. "Horace, Odes, I. 28.7-9," CR 59 (December, 1945), 44-45.

Hirst, M. E. "Portents in Horace, Odes I. 2.1-20," CQ 32 (January, 1938), 7-9.

Hulton, A. O. "Horace, Odes I. 2.6-7," CR (New Series) 8 (June, 1958), 106-107.

Jacobson, H. "Horace and Augustus: An Interpretation of Carm. 1.35," CP 63 (April, 1968), 106-113.

Jocelyn, H. D. "Horace, Odes I. 12.33-36: Some Final Remarks," Antichthon 7 (1973), 62-64.

Johnson, W. R. "Queen, Great Queen? Cleopatra and the Politics of Misrepresentation," Arion 6 (Autumn, 1967), 387-402.

Kilpatrick, S. "Archytas at the Styx (Horace Carm. 1.28)," CP 63 (July, 1968), 201-206.

Kimber, R. B. "The Structure of Horace, Odes 1.15," CJ 53 (November, 1957), 74-77.

Konet, R. I. "Semonides Iambographus and Horace, Odes 1.11," CW 68 (December-January, 1974-1975), 257-258.

Lee, M. O. "Horace Carm. 1.23: Simile and Metaphor," CP 60 (July, 1965), 185-186.

———. "Horace Odes 1.11: The Lady Whose Name Was Leu," Arion 3 (Winter, 1964), 117-124.

———. "Horace, Odes, I, 38: Thirst for Life," AJP 86 (July, 1965), 278-281.

Levin, D. N. "Thought-progression in Horace, Carmina 1.5," CJ 56 (May, 1961), 356-358.

Lockyer, C. W. "Horace Odes 1.9," CJ 63 (April, 1968), 304-308.

———. "Horace's Propempticon and Vergil's Voyage," C World 61 (October, 1967), 42-45.

Luce, J. V. "Cleopatra as Fatale Monstrum (Horace, Carm. I. 37,21)," CQ (New Series) 13 (1963), 251-257.

McCormick, J. "Horace's Integer Vitae," C World 67 (October, 1973), 28-33.

McDermott, E. "Horatius Callidus," AJP 98 (Winter, 1977), 363-380.

MacKay, L. A. "Horace, Augustus, and Ode, I, 2," AJP 83 (April, 1962), 168-177.

———. "Horatiana: Odes 1.9 and 1.28," CP 72 (October, 1977), 316-318.

———. "Odes, 1.16 and 17: Omatre Pulchra ... , Velox Amoenum ... ," AJP 83 (July, 1962), 298-300.

Marcellino, R. "Propertius and Horace," CJ 50 (April, 1955), 321-325.
Mayer, R. "A Note on Horace Carmina I. 32.1," Agon 3 (1969), 15-23.
Mendell, C. W. "Horace 1.14," CP 33 (April, 1938), 145-156.
Moritz, L. A. "Snow and Spring: Horace's Socratic Ode Once Again," G & R 23 (October, 1976), 169-176.
Moskovit, L. "Horace's Socrate Ode as a Poetic Representation of an Experience," SP 74 (April, 1977), 113-129.
Musurillo, H. "The Poet's Apotheosis: Horace, Odes 1.1," TAPA 93 (1962), 231-239.
Nisbet, R. G. M., and M. Hubbard. A Commentary on Horace: Odes, Book 1. Oxford: Clarendon, 1970.
Nussbaum, G. B. "A Study of Odes I. 37 and 38: The Psychology of Conflict and Horace's Humanities," Areth 4 (Spring, 1971), 91-97.
Pucci, P. "Horace's Banquet in Odes 1.17," TAPA 105 (1975), 259-281.
Putnam, M. C. J. "Horace Carm. 1.5: Love and Death," CP 65 (October, 1970), 251-254.
―――. "Horace c. 1.20," CJ 64 (January, 1969), 153-157.
Quinn, K. "Horace as a Love Poet: A Reading of Horace Odes 1.5," Arion 2 (Autumn, 1963), 59-77.
Reckford, K. J. "Horace, Odes 1.34: An Interpretation," SP 63 (July, 1966), 499-532.
Solmsen, F. "Horace's First Roman Ode," AJP 68 (October, 1947), 337-352.
St. John, J. "Horace, Odes I, 9," CN & V 16 (January, 1972), 4-11.
Sullivan, G. J. "Horace: Odes, 1.9," AJP 84 (July, 1963), 290-294.
Tillotson, K. "Yes: In the Sea of Life," RES 3 (October, 1952), 346-364.
Treloar, A. "Horace Odes I 12.35," Antichthon 3 (1969), 48-51.
―――. Horace Odes I, 12 Yet Again, a Rejoinder," Antichthon 7 (1973), 60-61.
Vaio, J. "Unity and Historical Occasion of Horace Carm. 1.7," CP 61 (July, 1966), 168-175.
Williams, G. "Horace Odes I, 12 and the Succession to Augustus," Ha 118 (Winter, 1974), 147-155.
―――. "Horace, Odes I. 32. 15-16," CR (New Series) 8 (December, 1958), 208-212.
Wilson, A. E. "The Path of Indirection: Horace's Odes 3.27 and 1.7," C World 63 (October, 1969), 44-46.
Witke, E. C. "Varro and Horace Carm. 1.9," CP 58 (April, 1963), 112-115.
Womble, H. "Horace, Carmina I, 2," AJP 91 (January, 1970), 1-30.
Wright, J. R. G. "Iccius' Change of Character: Horace, Odes I. 29," Mnemosyne 27 (1974), 44-52.
Wussbaum, G. "Postscript on Horace, Carm. I, 2," AJP 82 (October, 1961), 406-417.

Zumwalt, N. K. "Horace c. 1. 34: Poetic Change and Political Equivocation," TAPA 104 (1974), 435-467.

Odes: Book 2

Alexander, W. H. "Relicta Non Bene Parmula: Horace, Odes, 2. 7. 10," Roy Soc Can Trans (Series 3) 36 Sec. 2 (1942), 13-24.
Brink, C. O. "Horatian Notes, II: Despised Readings in the Manuscripts of the Odes, Book II," PCPS 17 (1971), 17-29.
Calder, W. M. "Irony in Horace Carm. 2. 2: Nullus Argento Color Est Avaris," CP 56 (July, 1961), 175-178.
Cody, J. V. "The Motif of Bucolic Repose in Horace, Carmina 2. 3 and 2. 11," CB 50 (February, 1974), 55-59.
Dahl, C. "Liquid Imagery in Eheu Fugaces," CP 48 (October, 1953), 240.
Edelstein, L. "Horace, Odes, II, 7. 9-10," AJP 62 (October, 1941), 441-451.
Henderson, W. J. "A Note on the Unity of Horace, Carm. II. 3," AClass 18 (1975), 144-146.
Kidd, D. A. "The Metamorphosis of Horace," AUMLA No. 35 (May, 1971), 5-16.
Mendell, C. W. "Horace, Odes II. 18," YCS 11 (1950), 279-292.
Morris, B. R., and R. D. Williams. "Identity of Licymnia: Horace Odes II, xii," PQ 42 (April, 1963), 145-150.
Murgatroyd, P. "Horace, Odes II 9," Mnemosyne 28 (1975), 69-71.
Nisbet, R. G. M. Commentary on Horace Odes, Book 2. Oxford: Clarendon, 1978.
Rudd, N. "Horace, Odes 2. 18 A Pedagogic Exercise," Ha 118 (Winter, 1974), 99-109.
Sullivan, F. A. "Horace's Ode to Quintius Hirpinus (2. 11)," CP 57 (July, 1962), 167-170.
Tatum, J. "Non Usitata Nec Tenui Ferar," AJP 94 (Spring, 1973), 4-25.
Witke, E. C. "Questions and Answers in Horace Odes 2. 3," CP 61 (October, 1966), 250-252.
Womble, H. "Horace, Carm. II, 16," AJP 88 (October, 1967), 385-409.
―――. "Repetition and Irony: Horace, Odes 2. 18," TAPA 92 (1961), 537-549.
Woodman, A. J. "Horace, Odes, II, 3," AJP 91 (April, 1970), 165-180.

Odes: Book 3

Bradshaw, A. "Horace and the Therapeutic Myth," Hermes 106 (1978), 156-176.
Cairns, F. "Splendide Mendax. Horace Odes III. 11," G & R 22 (October, 1975), 129-139.
Cameron, E. "An Analysis of Horace, Odes, III. 2," Akroterion 18 (February, 1973), 17-22.

Connor, P. J. "The Balance Sheet: Considerations of the Second Roman Ode," Hermes 100 (1972), 241-248.
_____. "Enthusiasm, Poetry, and Politics: A Consideration of Horace, Odes, III, 25," AJP 92 (April, 1977), 266-274.
Copley, F. O. "Horace, Odes, 3, 5, 13-18," AJP 62 (January, 1941), 87-89.
Dunston, A. J. "Horace: Odes 111.4 and the 'Virtues' of Augustus," AUMLA No. 31 (May, 1969), 9-19.
Dyson, M. "Horace, Odes III. 4," G & R 20 (October, 1973), 169-179.
Gornoll, J. F. G. "Horace, Odes III, 19: Does It Contain a Gap in Time?," G & R 18 (October, 1971), 188-190.
Holoka, J. P. "Horace, Carm. 3.4: The Place of the Poet," CB 52 (January, 1976), 41-46.
Malcolm, D. A. "Horace Odes III. 4," CR (New Series) 5 (December, 1955), 242-244.
Putnam, M. C. J. "Horace C. 3.30: The Lyricist as Hero," Ramus 2 (1973), 1-19.
_____. "Horace Odes III, 15: The Design of Decus," CP 71 (January, 1976), 90-96.
Schovanek, J. G. "Horace, Augustus and Odes 3.14," CN & V 17 (January, 1974), 1-7.
Sullivan, F. "Horace's Ode to Rustica Phidyle," CP 55 (April, 1960), 109-113.
Thornton, A. H. F. "Horace's Ode to Calliope (III,4)," AUMLA No. 23 (May, 1965), 96-102.
Tracy, H. L. "Two Footnotes on Horace, Odes, 3.3, 37-38," CN & V 16 (October, 1972), 92-93.
Wilson, A. E. "The Path of Indirection: Horace's Odes 3. 27 and 1.7," C World 63 (October, 1969), 44-46.
Wilson, J. R. "O Fons Bandusiae," CJ 63 (April, 1968), 289-296.

Odes: Book 4

Ambrose, J. W. "Horace on Foreign Policy: Odes 4.4," CJ 59 (October-November, 1973), 26-33.
_____. "The Ironic Meaning of the Lollius Ode," TAPA 96 (1965), 1-10.
Benario, J. M. "Book 4 of Horace's Odes: Augustan Propaganda," TAPA 91 (1960), 339-352.
Bradshaw, A. T. von S. "Horace, Odes 4.1," CQ (New Series) 20 (May, 1970), 142-153.
Minadeo, R. "Vergil in Horace's Odes 4.12," CJ 71 (January, 1976), 161-164.
Moritz, L. A. "Horace's Virgil," G & R 16 (October, 1969), 174-193.
Porter, D. H. "The Recurrent Motifs of Horace, Carmina IV," HSCP 79 (1975), 189-228.
Reckford, K. J. "The Eagle and the Tree (Horace, Odes 4.4)," CJ 56 (October, 1960), 23-28.

Satires, or Sermones

Anderson, W. S. "Horace, the Unwilling Warrior: Satire I,9," AJP 77 (April, 1956), 148-166.
_____. "Horace's Siren (Serm. 2.3.14)," CP 56 (April, 1961), 105-108.
_____. "Imagery in the Satires of Horace and Juvenal," AJP 81 (July, 1960), 225-260.
Brink, C. O. On Reading a Horatian Satire: An Interpretation of Sermones II.6. Sydney: Sydney University Press, 1965.
Bushala, E. W. "The Motif of Sexual Choice in Horace, Satire 1.2," CJ 66 (April-May, 1971), 312-315.
Campbell, A. Y. "On the Cruces of Horace, Satires 2.2," CQ (New Series) 1 (1951), 136-142.
Dessen, C. "Poetic Unity of Horace's Serm. I,4," AJP 88 (January, 1967), 78-81.
_____. "Sexual and Financial Mean in Horace's Serm. 1.2," AJP 89 (April, 1968), 200-208.
Glazewski, J. "Plenus Vitae Conviva: A Lucretian Concept in Horace's Satires," CB 47 (April, 1971), 85-88.
Haight, E. H. "Menander at the Sabine Farm, 'Exemplar Vitae,'" CP 42 (July, 1947), 147-155.
Horwood, W. P. "A Note on Horace, Satire I, 5, 1-24," CJ 32 (January, 1937), 225-228.
Kells, J. H. "Two Notes on the Satires of Horace," CR (New Series) 9 (December, 1959), 202-205.
Leon, E. F. "The Psychiatric Cases in Horace, Satires 2.3," CJ 47 (March, 1952), 211-214.
McGann, M. J. "Matter of Taste in Horace (Sat. ii. 7.95ff)," CR (New Series) 6 (June, 1956), 97-99.
MacKay, L. A. "Horace, Satires II, 3, 84-103," CJ 36 (December, 1940), 164-166.
Perret, J. "Epodes and Satires," in his Horace, tr. by Bertha Humez. New York: New York University Press, 1964, pp. 33-67.
Rooy, C. A. van. "Arrangement and Structure of Horace, Sermones, Book I, Satires 5 and 6," AClass 8 (1970), 45-59.
_____. "Arrangement and Structure of Satires in Horace, Sermones, Book I, Satires I,4 and I,10," AClass 8 (1970), 7-27.
_____. "Imitation of Vergil Eclogues in Horace, Satires, Book I," AClass 16 (1973), 69-88.
Rudd, N. "Had Horace Been Criticized? A Study of Serm. 1.4," AJP 76 (April, 1955), 165-175.
_____. "The Names in Horace's Satires," CQ (New Series) 10 (1960), 161-178.
_____. "The Poet's Defence (1)," CQ (New Series) 5 (1955), 142-148.
_____. "The Poet's Defence (2)," CQ (New Series) 5 (1955), 149-156.
_____. 'Satires' of Horace. Cambridge: Cambridge University Press, 1966.

Ullman, B. L. "Psychological Foreshadowing in the Satires of Horace and Juvenal," AJP 71 (October, 1950), 408-416.

ISOCRATES

General Criticism

Atkins, J. W. H. "Development of Rhetorical Theory: Isocrates, Aristotle, and Theophrastus," in his Literary Criticism in Antiquity; A Sketch of Its Development. Toronto: Macmillan, 1934, Vol. 1, pp. 120-163.
Baynes, N. H. "Isocrates," in his Byzantine Studies and Other Essays. London: Athlone, 1955, pp. 144-167.
Grube, G. M. A. "Thucydides, Socrates, Isocrates," in his The Greek and Roman Critics. Toronto: University of Toronto Press, 1965, pp. 33-45.
Harding, P. "The Purpose of Isokrates' Archidamos and On the Peace," CSCA 6 (1973), 137-149.
Heilbrunn, G. "Isocrates on Rhetoric and Power," Hermes 103 (1975), 154-178.
Howland, R. L. "Attack on Isocrates in the Phaedrus," CQ 31 (July, 1937), 151-159.
Hudson-Williams, H. L. "A Greek Humanist," G & R 9 (May, 1940), 166-173.
_____. "Isocrates and Recitations," CQ 43 (1949), 65-69.
_____. "Thucydides, Isocrates, and the Rhetorical Method of Composition," CQ 42 (July, 1948), 76-81.
Jaeger, W. W. "Isocrates Defends Hispaideia," in Paideia: The Ideals of Greek Culture. Oxford: B. Blackwell, 1944-47. Vol. 3, pp. 132-155.
_____. "Rhetoric of Isocrates and Its Cultural Ideal," in Paideia: The Ideals of Greek Culture. Oxford: B. Blackwell, 1944-47. Vol. 3, pp. 46-70.
Jebb, Sir R. C. "Isokrates: Life," in his Attic Orators: From Antiphon to Isaeos. New York: Russell and Russell, 1962, Vol. 2, pp. 1-35.
_____. "Isokrates: Style," in his Attic Orators: From Antiphon to Isaeos. New York: Russell and Russell, 1962, Vol. 2, pp. 54-79.
_____. "Isokrates: Works," in his Attic Orators: From Antiphon to Isaeos. New York: Russell and Russell, 1962, Vol. 2, pp. 80-149.
_____. "Isokrates: Works. Forensic Speeches," in his Attic Orators: From Antiphon to Isaeos. New York: Russell and Russell, 1962, Vol. 2, pp. 214-237.
_____. "Isokrates: Works; Letters; Fragments," in his Attic Orators: From Antiphon to Isaeos. New York: Russell and Russell, 1962, Vol. 2, pp. 238-260.

_____. "Isokrates: Works; Political Writings," in his Attic Orators: From Antiphon to Isaeos. New York: Russell and Russell, 1962, Vol. 2, pp. 158-213.

Laughton, E. "Cicero and the Greek Orators," AJP 82 (January, 1961), 27-49.

Marrou, H. I. "Masters of the Classical Tradition. II Isocrates," in his History of Education in Antiquity. New York: Sheed and Ward, 1956, pp. 79-91.

Norlin, G. " 'That Old Man Eloquent,' " in his Things in the Saddle. Cambridge, Mass.: Harvard University Press, 1940, pp. 208-233.

Proussis, C. "The Orator: Isocrates," in P. Nash, A. M. Kazamias, and H. J. Perkinson, eds., The Educated Man; Studies in the History of Educational Thought. New York: Wiley, 1965, pp. 55-76.

Romilly, J. de. "Eunoia in Isocrates," J Hel S 78 (1958), 92-101.

Schlatter, F. W. "Isocrates, Against the Sophists XVI," AJP 93 (October, 1972), 591-597.

Sheeks, W. "Isocrates, Plato, and Xenophon Against the Sophists," Person 56 (Summer, 1975), 250-259.

Smethurst, S. E. "Cicero and Isocrates," TAPA 84 (1953), 262-320.

Usher, S. "The Style of Isocrates," BICS 20 (1973), 39-67.

Wilcox, S. "Isocrates' Fellow-rhetoricians," AJP 66 (April, 1945), 171-186.

_____. "Isocrates' Genera of Prose," AJP 64 (October, 1943), 427-431.

Wilson, C. H. "Thucydides, Isocrates and the Athenian Empire," G & R 13 (April, 1966), 54-63.

Individual Works

Ad Nicoclem

Jaeger, W. W. "Prince's Education," in Paideia: The Ideals of Greek Culture. Oxford: B. Blackwell, 1944-47. Vol. 3, pp. 84-105.

Areopagiticus

Jaeger, W. W. "Freedom and Authority: The Conflict Within the Radical Democracy," in his Paideia: The Ideals of Greek Culture. Oxford: B. Blackwell, 1944-47. Vol. 3, pp. 106-131.

Panegyricus

Jaeger, W. W. "Political Culture and the Panhellenic Ideal," in his Paideia: The Ideals of Greek Culture. Oxford: B. Blackwell, 1944-47. Vol. 3, pp. 71-83.

Philippus

Markle, M. M. "Support of Athenian Intellectuals for Philip: A Study of Isocrates' Philippus and Speusippus' Letter to Philip," J Hel S 96 (1976), 80-99.

JEROME

General Criticism

Adams, J. du Q. The Populus of Augustine and Jerome; A Study in the Patristic Sense of Community. New Haven, Conn.: Yale University Press, 1971.
Barr, J. "St. Jerome and the Sounds of Hebrew," JSS 12 (Spring, 1967), 1-36.
_____. "St. Jerome's Appreciation of Hebrew," JRLB 49 (Spring, 1967), 281-302.
Bolgar, R. R. "The Background," in his Classical Heritage and Its Beneficiaries. Cambridge: Cambridge University Press, 1954, pp. 13-58.
Case, S. J. "Christian Luminaries in a Darkening Age," in her Makers of Christianity, from Jesus to Charlemagne. New York: Holt, 1934, pp. 147-187.
Cassidy, F. P. "Fathers of the West," in his Molders of the Medieval Mind; The Influence of the Fathers of the Church on the Medieval Schoolmen. Port Washington, N. Y.: Kennikat, 1966, pp. 99-158.
Dunney, J. A. "Saint Jerome: God's Battler," in his Church History in the Light of the Saints. New York: Macmillan, 1944, pp. 59-78.
Gutierrez, L. St. Jerome and Roman Monasticism: A Historical Study on His Spiritual Influence. Manila: University de Santo Tomas, 1975.
Hadas, M. "Writers of Christianity," in his History of the Latin Language. New York: Columbia University Press, 1952, pp. 414-445.
Hagendahl, H. Latin Fathers and the Classics. Stockholm: Almqvist and Wiksell, 1958, pp. 91-328.
Huizinga, L. Hieronymus. Amsterdam: van Kampen, 1946.
Hulley, K. K. "Light Cast by St. Jerome on Certain Palaeographical Points," HSCP 54 (1943), 83-92.
_____. "Principles of Textual Criticism Known to St. Jerome," HSCP 55 (1944), 87-109.
Kelly, J. N. D. Jerome: His Life, Writings, and Controversies. New York: Harper and Row, 1975.
_____. Life and Times as Revealed in the Writings of St. Jerome Exclusive of His Letters. Washington, D. C.: Catholic University of America Press, 1944.
McGiffert, A. C. "From Arnobius to Jerome," in his History of Christian Thought. New York: Scribner's, 1932-33, Vol. 2, pp. 39-70.

Matteo da Ferrara. Life of St. Jerome. Paterson, N.J.: St. Anthony Guild, 1949.
Mierow, C. C. "An Early Christian Scholar," CJ 33 (October, 1937), 3-17.
──────. Saint Jerome, the Sage of Bethlehem. Milwaukee: Bruce, 1959.
Muller, G. F. A Roar from the Cave; A Story of Saint Jerome, by Brother Roberto. Notre Dame, Ind.: Dujarie, 1961.
Murphy, F. X., ed. Monument to Saint Jerome; Essays on Some Aspects of His Life, Works, and Influence. New York: Sheed and Ward, 1952.
Nolan, J. G. Jerome and Jovinian. Washington, D.C.: Catholic University of America Press, 1956.
Oldfather, W. A., ed. Studies in the Text Tradition of St. Jerome's Vitae Patrum. Urbana: University of Illinois Press, 1943.
Pence, M. E. "Satire in St. Jerome," CJ 36 (March, 1941), 322-336.
Quasten, J. "Pythagorean Idea in Jerome," AJP 63 (April, 1942), 207-215.
Semple, W. H. "St. Jerome as a Biblical Translator," JRLB 48 (Autumn, 1965), 227-243.
Steinmann, J. Saint Jerome and His Times. Notre Dame, Ind.: Fides, 1960.
Vernon, A. W. "Saints and Women in the Fourth Century," Chris 10 No. 2 (1945), 163-175.
Wand, J. W. C. "St. Jerome," in his Latin Doctors. London: Faith, 1948, pp. 44-66.
Wiesen, D. S. St. Jerome as a Satirist. Ithaca, N.Y.: Cornell University Press, 1964.

Individual Works

Letters

Diederich, M. D. "The Epitaphium Sanctae Paulae," CJ 49 (May, 1954), 369-372.
Gilliam, J. F. "Pro Caelio in St. Jerome's Letters," HTR 46 (April, 1953), 103-107.
Hritzu, J. N. Style of the Letters of St. Jerome. Washington, D.C.: Catholic University of America Press, 1939.
Levy, H. L. "Claudian's In Rufinum and an Epistle of St. Jerome," AJP 69 (January, 1948), 62-68.
Yarbrough, A. "Christianization in the Fourth Century: The Example of Roman Women," Ch H 45 (June, 1976), 149-165.

Life of St. Hilarion

Cameron, A. "Echoes of Vergil in St. Jerome's Life of St. Hilarion," CP 63 (January, 1968), 55-56.

JUVENAL

General Criticism

Anderson, W. S. Anger in Juvenal and Seneca. Berkeley: University of California Press, 1964.
———. "Juvenal: Evidence on the Years A. D. 117-128," CP 50 (October, 1955), 255-257.
———. "Programs of Juvenal's Later Books," CP 57 (July, 1962), 145-160.
Barish, J. A. "Ovid, Juvenal, and the Silent Woman," PMLA 71 (March, 1956), 213-224.
Boughner, D. C. "Juvenal, Horace and Sejanus," MLN 75 (November, 1960), 545-550.
Bower, E. W. "Notes on Juvenal and Statius," CR (New Series) 8 (March, 1958), 9-11.
Carnochan, W. B. "Satire, Sublimity, and Sentiment: Theory and Practice in Post-Augustan Satire," PMLA 85 (March, 1970), 260-267.
Clack, J. "To Those Who Fell on Agrippina's Pen," CW 69 (September, 1975), 45-53.
Colton, R. E. Juvenal and Martial. Ann Arbor, Mich.: University Microfilms, 1959.
Copley, F. O. "Suetonius and Juvenal," in his Latin Literature from the Beginnings to the Close of the Second Century A. D. Ann Arbor: University of Michigan Press, 1969, pp. 342-349.
Downs, R. B. "Master of Invective: Decimus Junius Juvenalis," in his Famous Books, Ancient and Medieval. New York: Barnes and Noble, 1964, pp. 228-233.
Friedlander, L. Friedlander's Essays on Juvenal, tr. from the German with a Preface by J. R. C. Martyn. Amsterdam: Hakkert, 1970.
Griffith, J. G. "Juvenal, Statius and the Flavian Establishment," G & R 16 (October, 1969), 134-150.
Hadas, M. "Satire," in his History of Latin Literature. New York: Columbia University Press, 1952, pp. 278-301.
Highet, G. "Juvenal: The Making of a Satirist," in his Poets in a Landscape. New York: Knopf, 1957, pp. 196-212.
———. Juvenal the Satirist: A Study. Oxford: Clarendon, 1954.
———. "Juvenal's Bookcase [the Favorite Reading of the Satirist]," AJP 72 (October, 1951), 369-394.
———. "The Life of Juvenal," TAPA 68 (1937), 480-506.
———. "Notes on Juvenal," CR (New Series) 2 (June, 1952), 70-71.
———. "The Philosophy of Juvenal," TAPA 80 (1949), 254-270.
———. "Sound Effects in Juvenal's Poetry," SP 48 (October, 1951), 697-706.
Jefferis, J. D. "Juvenal and Religion," CJ 34 (January, 1939), 229-233.
Mason, H. A. "Is Juvenal a Classic?," Arion 1 (Spring, 1962), 8-44; (Summer, 1962), 39-79.
Musurillo, H. A. "Juvenal: The Critic with a Smirk," in his Symbol and Myth in Ancient Poetry. New York: Fordham University Press, 1961, pp. 165-178.

Phelps, W. G. Three Roman Poets and Their Messages. Shreveport, La.: Centenary College Press, 1938.
Pryor, A. D. "Juvenal's False Consolation," AUMLA No. 18 (November, 1962), 167-180.
Sullivan, J. P. "Propertius and Juvenal," Arion 7 (Autumn, 1968), 477-486.
Ullman, B. L. "Psychological Foreshadowing in the Satires of Horace and Juvenal," AJP 71 (October, 1950), 408-416.

Individual Works (Satires)

General

Anderson, W. S. "Imagery in the Satires of Horace and Juvenal," AJP 81 (July, 1960), 225-260.
―――――. "Studies in Book I of Juvenal," YCS 15, 33-90.
Courtney, E. "Some Thought-Patterns in Juvenal," HA 118 (Winter, 1974), 15-21.
Lindo, L. I. "The Evolution of Juvenal's Later Satires," CP 69 (January, 1974), 17-27.
Thomson, J. O. "Juvenal's Big Fish Satire," G & R 21 (June, 1952), 86-87.
Waters, K. H. "Juvenal and the Reign of Trojan," Antichthon 4 (1970), 62-77.
Watts, W. J. "Race Prejudice in the Satires of Juvenal," AClass 19 (1976), 83-104.

One

Barrett, A. A. "Juvenal: Satire 1; 155-157," CQ (New Series) 27 (1977), 438-440.
Bertman, S. S. "Fire Symbolism in Juvenal's First Satire," CJ 63 (March, 1968), 265-266.
Colton, R. E. "A Client's Day: Echoes of Martial in Juvenal's First Satire," CB 52 (January, 1976), 35-38.
―――――. "Death in the Bath," CJ 65 (April, 1970), 317.
Copley, F. O. "Juvenal, Sat. I, 1. 147-150," AJP 62 (April, 1941), 219-221.
Griffith, J. G. "The Ending of Juvenal's First Satire and Lucilius, Book XXX," Hermes 98 (1970), 56-72.
Harrison, E. "Juvenal i. 81-89," CR 51 (May, 1937), 55.
Helmbold, W. C. The Structure of Juvenal I. Berkeley: University of California Press, 1951.
Kidd, D. A. "Juvenal 1.149 and 10.106-107," CQ (New Series) 14 (1964), 103-108.
MacKay, L. A. "Notes on Juvenal," CP 53 (October, 1958), 236-240.

Two

Colton, R. E. "Juvenal's Second Satire and Martial," CJ 61 (Novem-

ber, 1965), 68-71.
Lelievre, F. J. "Juvenal: Two Possible Examples of Word-play," CP 53 (October, 1958), 241-242.
Martyn, J. R. C. "Juvenal 2. 78-81 and Virgil's Plague," CP 65 (January, 1970), 49-50.

Three

Fredericks, S. C. "Daedalus in Juvenal's Third Satire," CB 49 (1972), 11-13.
_____. "The Function of the Prologue in the Organization of Juvenal's Third Satire," Phoenix 27 (Spring, 1973), 62-67.
Hudson-Williams, A. "Note on Juvenal 3. 198-202," G & R 24 (April, 1977), 29-30.
Moeller, W. O. "Juvenal 3 and Martial De Spectaculis 8," CJ 62 (May, 1967), 369-370.
Motto, A. L., and J. R. Clark. "Per Iter Tenebricosum: The Myth of Juvenal 3," TAPA 96 (1965), 267-276.

Four

Clack, J. "The Structure of Juvenal 4: A Reprise," CB 50 (March, 1974), 77-78.
Helmbold, W. C., and E. N. O'Neil. "Structure of Juvenal IV," AJP 77 (January, 1956), 68-73.
Kidd, D. A. "Juvenal 1. 149 and 10. 106-107," CQ (New Series) 14 (1964), 103-108.
Kilpatrick, R. S. "Juvenal's Patchwork Satires 4 and 7," YCS 23 (1973), 229-241.

Five

Bradshaw, A. T. von S. "Clacie Aspersus Maculis: Juvenal 5. 104," CQ (New Series) 15 (1965), 121-125.
Campbell, A. Y. "Pike and Eel: Juvenal 5, 103-106," CQ 39 (January, 1945), 46-48.
Morford, M. "Juvenal's Fifth Satire," AJP 98 (Fall, 1977), 219-245.
Palmer, L. R. "Juvenal V. 103-106," CR 52 (May, 1938), 56-58.
Sebesta, J. L. "Dine with Us as an Equal," CB 53 (December, 1976), 23-26.

Six

Anderson, W. S. "Juvenal 6: A Problem in Structure," CP 51 (April, 1956), 73-94.
Colton, R. E. "Cruelty and Vanity: Juvenal 6. 490-96, 6. 502-06 and Martial," CB 50 (November, 1973), 5-6.

_____. "Juvenal and Martial on Women Who Ape Greek Ways," CB 50 (January, 1974), 42-44.
Morford, M. "A Note on Juvenal 6.627-61," CP 67 (July, 1972), 198.
Reeve, M. D. "Gladiators in Juvenal's Sixth Satire," CR (New Series) 23 (December, 1973), 124-125.
Singleton, D. "Juvenal VI, 1-20 and Some Ancient Attitudes to the Golden Age," G & R 19 (October, 1972), 151-164.

Seven

Alexander, W. H. "Juvenal 7. 126-128," CP 42 (April, 1947), 123-214.
Clarke, M. L. "Juvenal 7. 242-3," CR (New Series) 23 (March, 1973), 12.
Davey, F. "Juvenal VII, 242ff," CR (New Series) 21 (March, 1971), 11.
Helmbold, W. C., and E. N. O'Neil. "Form and Purpose of Juvenal's Seventh Satire," CP 54 (April, 1959), 100-108.
Kilpatrick, R. S. "Juvenal's Patchwork Satires 4 and 7," YCS 23 (1973), 229-241.
Orentzel, A. E. "Juvenal and Statius," CB 52 (February, 1976), 61-62.
Wiesen, D. S. "Juvenal and the Intellectuals," Hermes 101 (1973), 464-483.

Eight

Fredericks, S. C. "Rhetoric and Morality in Juvenal's 8th Satire," TAPA 102 (1971), 111-132.
Jones, C. P. "Juvenal 8. 220," CR (New Series) 22 (December, 1972), 313.

Ten

Astbury, R. "Juvenal 10, 148-150," Mnemosyne 28 (1975), 40-46.
Colton, R. E. "Martial in Juvenal's Tenth Satire," SP 74 (October, 1977), 341-353.
Eichholz, D. E. "The Art of Juvenal and His Tenth Satire," G & R 3 (March, 1956), 61-68.
Kidd, D. A. "Juvenal 1. 149 and 10. 106-107," CQ (New Series) 14 (1964), 103-108.
LaFleur, R. A. "A Note on Juvenal 10,201f," AJP 93 (October, 1972), 598-600.
Lawall, G. "Exempla and Theme in Juvenal's Tenth Satire," TAPA 89 (1958), 25-31.
Lelievre, F. J. "Juvenal: Two Possible Examples of Word-play," CP 53 (October, 1958), 241-242.
Wiesen, D. "Juvenal 10. 358," CP 64 (April, 1969), 73-80.

136 : Greek and Roman Authors

Eleven

McDevitt, A. S. "The Structure of Juvenal's Eleventh Satire," G & R 15 (October, 1958), 173-179.
Smutny, R. J. "Juvenal 11. 162-175," CP 52 (October, 1957), 248-256.
Weisinger, K. "Irony and Moderation in Juvenal XI," CSCA 5 (1972), 227-240.

Twelve

Helmbold, W. C. "Juvenal's Twelfth Satire," CP 51 (January, 1956), 14-23.

Thirteen

Astbury, R. "Date of Juvenal's Thirteenth Satire," AJP 98 (Winter, 1977), 392-395.
Colton, R. E. "Juvenal's Thirteenth Satire and Martial," CB 52 (November, 1975), 13-15.
Fredericks, S. C. "Calvinus in Juvenal's Thirteenth Satire," Areth 4 (Fall, 1971), 219-231.
Morford, M. P. O. "Juvenal's Thirteenth Satire," AJP 94 (Spring, 1973), 26-36.

Fourteen

Amyx, D. A. "Note on Juvenal XIV. 227-232," CP 36 (July, 1941), 278-279.
Colton, R. E. "Echoes of Martial in Juvenal's Fourteenth Satire," Hermes 105 (1977), 234-246.
O'Neil, E. N. "Structure of Juvenal's Fourteenth Satire," CP 55 (October, 1960), 251-253.
Stein, J. P. "Unity and Scope of Juvenal's Fourteenth Satire," CP 65 (January, 1970), 34-36.

Sixteen

Colton, R. E. "A Note on Juvenal 16 and Martial," CB 51 (March, 1975), 78-79.

LIVY

General Criticism

Allen, A. W. "Livy as Literature," CP 51 (October, 1956), 251-254.

Best, E. E. "Cicero, Livy and Educated Roman Women," CJ 65 (February, 1970), 199-204.
Conway, R. S. Harvard Lectures on the Vergilian Age. New York: Biblo and Tannen, 1967, pp. 113-128.
Copley, F. O. "Augustan Prose: Livy," in his Latin Literature from the Beginnings to the Close of the Second Century A. D. Ann Arbor: University of Michigan Press, 1969, pp. 276-286.
Frank, T. "Republican Historiography and Livy," in his Life and Literature in the Roman Republic. Berkeley: University of California Press, 1957, pp. 169-196.
Grant, M. "From Caesar to Livy," in his Roman Literature. Baltimore: Penguin, 1964, pp. 90-102.
Gries, K. Constancy in Livy's Latinity. Ann Arbor, Mich.: University Microfilms, 1966.
Hadas, M. "Livy and Others," in his History of Latin Literature. New York: Columbia University Press, 1952, pp. 227-242.
_____. "Livy as Scripture," AJP 61 (October, 1940), 445-456.
Laistner, M. L. W. "Livy, the Historian," in his Greater Roman Historians. Berkeley: University of California Press, 1947, pp. 83-102.
_____. "Livy, the Man and the Writer," in his Greater Roman Historians. Berkeley: University of California Press, 1947, pp. 65-82.
Latte, K. "Livy's Patavinitas," CP 35 (January, 1940), 56-60.
Liebschuetz, W. "The Religious Position of Livy's History," JRS 57 (1967), 45-55.
Luce, T. J. Livy: The Composition of His History. Princeton, N. J.: Princeton University Press, 1977.
MacKay, L. A. "On Patavinity," CP 38 (January, 1943), 44-45.
Piper, L. J. "Livy's Portrayal of Early Roman Women," CB 48 (December, 1971), 26-28.
Seager, R. " 'Populares' in Livy and the Livian Tradition," CQ (New Series) 27 (1977), 377-390.
Walsh, P. G. "Livy and Stoicism," AJP 79 (October, 1958), 355-375.
_____. Livy; His Historical Aims and Methods. Cambridge: Cambridge University Press, 1961, pp. 288-292.

Individual Works (History of Rome)

General

Frank, R. I. "The Dangers of Peace," Prudentia 8 (May, 1976), 1-7.
Grant, M. Roman Literature. Baltimore: Penguin, 1964, pp. 98-102.
Gries, K. "Livy's Use of the Dramatic Speech," AJP 70 (April, 1949), 118-141.
Kajanto, I. God and Fate in Livy. Turku, Finland: University of Turku, 1957.
McDonald, A. H. "Style of Livy," JRS 47 (1957), 155-172.

138 : Greek and Roman Authors

Martin, J. M. K. "Livy and Romance," G & R 11 (May, 1942), 124-128.
Smethurst, S. E. "Women in Livy's History," G & R 19 (June, 1950), 80-87.
Syme, R. "Livy and Augustus," HSCP 64 (1959), 27-87.
Walsh, P. G. "The Negligent Historian: 'Howlers' in Livy," G & R 5 (March, 1958), 83-86.
Whatmough, J. " 'Tusca Origo Raetis,' " HSCP 48 (1937), 181-202.

Preface

Walsh, P. G. "Livy's Preface and the Distortion of History," AJP 76 (October, 1955), 369-383.

Books 1-5

Luce, T. J. "Design and Structure in Livy, 5. 32-55," TAPA 102 (1971), 265-302.
Machiavelli, N. "Discourses on the First Decade of Titus Livius," in Machiavelli: The Chief Works and Others, tr. by A. Gilbert. Durham, N.C.: Duke University Press, 1965, Vol. 1, pp. 175-530.
Ogilvie, R. M. A Commentary on Livy, Books 1-5. Oxford: Clarendon, 1965.
_____. "Monastic Corruption," G & R 18 (April, 1971), 32-34.
Rexroth, K. "Livy: Early Rome," in his Classics Revisited. Chicago: Quadrangle, 1968, pp. 90-94.
Robbins, M. A. "Livy's Brutus," SP 69 (January, 1972), 1-20.

Books 1-10

Pinset, J. "Antiquarianism, Fiction and History in the First Decade of Livy," CJ 55 (November, 1959), 81-85.

Book 14

Larsen, J. A. O. "Consilium in Livy xiv. 18. 6-7 and the Macedonian Synedria," CP 44 (April, 1949), 73-90.

Books 21-45

Phillips, J. E. "Form and Language in Livy's Triumph Notices," CP 69 (October, 1974), 265-273.

Book 23

Dunbabin, R. L. "Notes on Livy, Book XXIII," CR 56 (July, 1942), 69-70.

Books 24-29

Springer, L. A. "Livy and the Year 212 B. C.," CJ 47 (April, 1952), 261-264; 298-299.

Book 27

Frant, T. "Livy's Deference to Livia," AJP 59 (April, 1938), 223-224.

Books 31-33

Briscoe, J. A Commentary on Livy, Books 31-33. Oxford: Clarendon, 1973.

LONGINUS

Individual Works

On the Sublime

Atkins, J. W. H. "New Critical Outlook and Methods: 'Longinus,'" in his Literary Criticism in Antiquity; A Sketch of Its Development. Toronto: Macmillan, 1934, Vol. 2, pp. 210-253.
Brody, J. Boileau and Longinus. Ann Arbor, Mich.: University Microfilms, 1957.
Godolphin, F. R. B. "The Basic Critical Doctrine of Longinus' On the Sublime," TAPA 68 (1937), 172-183.
Greene, E. B. Critical Essays. New York: Garland, 1970.
Grube, G. M. A. "Longinus on Great Writing," in his The Greek and Roman Critics. Toronto: University of Toronto Press, 1965, pp. 340-353.
Hall, V. "Longinus," in his A Short History of Literary Criticism. New York: New York University Press, 1963, pp. 16-20.
Henn, J. R. Longinus and English Criticism. Cambridge: Cambridge University Press, 1934.
Hill, J. J. "Aesthetic Principles of the Peri Hupsous," JHI 27 (April, 1966), 265-274.
Menuez, C. B. "Longinus on the Eloquence of the Arts," CJ 36 (March, 1941), 346-353.
Monk, S. H. "Longinus and the Longinian Tradition in England," in his The Sublime; A Study of Critical Theories in XVIII Century England. Ann Arbor: University of Michigan Press, 1960, pp. 10-28.
Olson, E. "Argument of Longinus' 'On the Sublime,'" MP 39 (February, 1942), 225-258.
_____. "Argument of Longinus' 'On the Sublime,'" in R. S. Crane, ed., Critics and Criticism, Ancient and Modern. Chicago: University

of Chicago Press, 1952, pp. 232-259.
Orage, A. R. "Sublime Longinus," in H. Read and D. Saurat, eds., Selected Essays and Critical Writings. London: G. Allen, 1935, pp. 24-27.
Tate, A. "Longinus and the 'New Criticism,'" in his Collected Essays. Denver: Swallow, 1959, pp. 507-527.
——. "Longinus and the New Criticism," in his Essays of Four Decades. Chicago: Swallow, 1968, pp. 471-490.
Wimsatt, W. K., and C. Brooks. "Roman Classicism: Longinus," in their Literary Criticism; A Short History. New York: Knopf, 1957, pp. 97-111.

LONGUS

Individual Works

Daphnis and Chloe

Bonnard, A. "Other Escapisms: Herodas and Realistic Mime, the Novel--Daphnis and Chloe," in his Greek Civilization: From Euripides to Alexandria. New York: Macmillan, 1961, pp. 246-258.
Chalk, H. H. D. "Eros and the Lesbian Pastorals of Longus," J Hel S 80 (1960), 32-51.
Deligiorgis, S. "Longus' Art in Brief Lives," PQ 53 (January, 1974), 1-9.
Haight, E. H. "Lesbian Pastorals of Daphnis and Chloe, by Longus," in her Essays on the Greek Romances. New York: Longmans, 1943, pp. 119-143.
Kestner, J. "Ekphrasis as Frame in Longus' Daphnis and Chloe," C World 67 (December, 1973), 166-171.
McCulloh, W. E. Longus. New York: Twayne, 1970.
Todd, F. A. "Daphnis and Chloe," in his Some Ancient Novels. Freeport, N. Y.: Books for Libraries, 1968, pp. 34-64.

LUCAN

General Criticism

Ahe, F. M. Lucan: An Introduction. Ithaca, N. Y.: Cornell University Press, 1976.
Baca, A. R. "A Mordant Judgement: J. C. Scaliger's Criticism of Lucan," PCP 8 (April, 1973), 5-9.
Blisset, W. "Lucan's Caesar and the Elizabethan Villain," SP 53 (October, 1956), 553-575.
Bonner, S. F. "Lucan and the Declamation Schools," AJP 87 (July, 1966), 257-289.

Bruere, R. T. "Lucan and Claudian: The Invectives," CP 59 (October, 1964), 223-256.
Copley, F. O. "Lucan and Petronius," in his Latin Literature from the Beginnings to the Close of the Second Century A. D. Ann Arbor: University of Michigan Press, 1969, pp. 304-316.
Dick, B. F. "The Technique of Prophecy in Lucan," TAPA 94 (1963), 37-49.
Morford, M. P. O. Poet Lucan: Studies in Rhetorical Epic. New York: Barnes and Noble, 1967.
Pierce, F. "History and Poetry in the Heroic Poem of the Golden Age," HR 20 (October, 1952), 302-312.
Snell, A. "Lucan," G & R 8 (February, 1939), 83-91.
Sullivan, J. P. "Petronius, Seneca, and Lucan: A Neronian Literary Feud," TAPA 99 (1968), 453-468.
Sutherland, D. The Senecan Temper in Lucan. Ann Arbor, Mich.: University Microfilms, 1952.
Thompson, L. "Lucan's Apotheosis of Nero, CP 59 (July, 1964), 147-153.
_____ and T. R. Bruere. "Lucan's Use of Virgilian Reminiscence," CP 63 (January, 1968), 1-21.
Tucker, R. A. "Lucan and the Value of Gold," CB 51 (November, 1974), 10-14.

Individual Works

Civil War, or Bellum Civile, or Pharsalia

Ahl, F. M. "The Pivot of the Pharsalia," Hermes 102 (1974), 305-320.
_____. "The Shadows of a Divine Presence in the Pharsalia," Hermes 102 (1974), 566-590.
Bond, R. W. "Lucan's Pharsalia," G & R 1 (May, 1932), 166-175.
Bruere, R. T. "The Scope of Lucan's Historical Epic," CP 45 (October, 1950), 217-235.
Dick, B. F. "Fatum and Fortuna in Lucan's Bellum Civile," CP 62 (October, 1967), 235-242.
Frank, E. "The Structure and Scope of Lucan's De Bello Civili," CB 46 (February, 1970), 59-61.
Hadas, M. "Silver Epic," in his History of Latin Literature. New York: Columbia University Press, 1952, pp. 260-277.
Highet, G. "Lucan's Civil War: The Epic of a Crime," in his Powers of Poetry. London: Oxford University Press, 1960, pp. 271-277.
Holliday, V. L. Pompey in Cicero's Correspondence and Lucan's Civil War. The Hague: Mouton, 1969.
Jenkinson, J. R. "Sarcasm in Lucan 1. 33-66," CR (New Series) 24 (March, 1974), 8-9.
Lintott, A. W. "Lucan and the History of the Civil War," CQ (New Series) 21 (November, 1971), 488-505.
Lounsbury, R. C. "History and Motive in Book Seven of Lucan's Pharsalia," Hermes 104 (1976), 210-239.

142 : Greek and Roman Authors

Makowski, J. F. "Oracula Mortis in the Pharsalia," CP 72 (July, 1977), 193-202.
Marti, B. M. "Meaning of the Pharsalia," AJP 66 (October, 1945), 352-376.
Martindale, C. A. "Paradox, Hyperbole, and Literary Novelty in Lucan's De Bello Civile," BICS 23 (1976), 45-54.
Thompson, L. Lucan's Bellum Civile and the Tragedies of Seneca. Chicago: Dept. of Photographic Reproduction, University of Chicago Library, 1956.
──── and T. R. Bruere. "The Virgilian Background of Lucan's Fourth Book," CP 65 (July, 1970), 152-172.
Tucker, R. A. "The Banquets of Dido and Cleopatra," CB 52 (December, 1975), 17-20.
────. "The Colors of Lucan: Anti-War Propaganda?," CB 46 (February, 1970), 56-58, 64.
────. "The Speech-Action-Simile Formula in Lucan's Bellum Civile," CJ 64 (May, 1969), 366-370.

LUCIAN

General Criticism

Allinson, F. G. Lucian, Satirist and Artist. New York: Cooper Square, 1963.
Anderson, G. "Lucian and the Authorship of De Saltatione," GRBS 18 (Autumn, 1977), 275-286.
────. Lucian: Theme and Variation in the Second Sophistic. Leiden: Brill, 1976.
────. "Lucian's Classics: Some Short Cuts to Culture," BICS 23 (1976), 59-68.
────. "Some Alleged Relationships in Lucian's Opuscula," AJP 97 (Fall, 1976), 262-275.
────. Studies in Lucian's Comic Fiction. Leiden: Brill, 1976.
Atkins, J. W. H. "Critical Cross-currents: Martial, the Younger Pliny, Plutarch, Dio Chrysostom, and Lucian," in his Literary Criticism in Antiquity; A Sketch of Its Development. Toronto: Macmillan, 1934, Vol. 2, pp. 299-245.
Baldwin, B. "The Authorship and Purpose of Lucian's Demosthenis Encomium," Antichthon 3 (1969), 54-62.
────. "Lucian as Social Satirist," CQ (New Series) 11 (1961), 199-208.
────. "Lucian's Knowledge of Theophrastus," Mnemosyne 30 (1977), 174-176.
────. Studies in Lucian. Toronto: Hakkert, 1973.
Bellinger, A. R. "Lucian's Dramatic Technique," YCS 1, 3-40.
Cast, D. "Aurispa, Petrarch, and Lucian: An Aspect of Renaissance Translation," RQ 27 (Summer, 1974), 157-173.
Downs, R. B. "Master of Satiric Dialogue: Lucian," in his Famous Books, Ancient and Medieval. New York: Barnes and Noble, 1964, pp. 238-242.

Grube, G. M. A. "The Second Sophistic and Its Satirist," in his The Greek and Roman Critics. Toronto: University of Toronto Press, 1965, pp. 333-338.
Householder, F. W. Literary Quotation and Allusion in Lucian. New York: Columbia University Press, 1941.
──────. "The Mock Decrees in Lucian," TAPA 71 (1940), 199-216.
Jones, C. P. "Two Enemies of Lucian," GRBS 13 (1972), 475-487.
McCarthy, B. P. "Lucian and Menippus," YCS 44, 3-55.
Macleod, M. D. "Homeric Parody in Lucian," CR (New Series) 10 (June, 1960), 103.
──────. "Lucian's Knowledge of Theophrastus," Mnemosyne 27 (1974), 75-76.
Read, H. E. "The Dialogue," in his Poetry and Experience. New York: Horizon, 1967, pp. 88-103.

Individual Works

Lucius, or Ass   also   True History

Haight, E. H. "Lucian and His Satiric Romances: The 'True History' and 'Lucius or Ass,'" in her Essays on the Greek Romances. Port Washington, N. Y.: Kennikat, 1965, pp. 144-185.

LUCILIUS

General Criticism

Atkins, J. W. H. "Critical Beginnings at Rome and the Classical Reaction: Terence, Lucilius, and Cicero," in his Literary Criticism in Antiquity; A Sketch of Its Development. Toronto: Macmillan, 1934, Vol. 2, pp. 1-46.
Copley, F. O. "Lucilius," in his Latin Literature from the Beginnings to the Close of the Second Century A.D. Ann Arbor: University of Michigan Press, 1969, pp. 50-55.
Griffith, J. G. "The Ending of Juvenal's First Satire and Lucilius Book XXX," Hermes 98 (1970), 56-72.
Robinson, L. "The Personal Abuse in Lucilius' Satires," CJ 49 (October, 1953), 31-35, 47.
Rozema, B. J. "Complaint of Erotium in Anthologia Palatina 11.88," CP 69 (October, 1974), 284-286.

LUCRETIUS

General Criticism;
and, On the Nature of Things (De Rerum Natura)

Anderson, W. S. "Discontinuity in Lucretian Symbolism," TAPA 91 (1960), 1-29.
Bailey, C. Lucretius. London: Oxford University Press, 1949.
———. "Mind of Lucretius," AJP 61 (July, 1940), 278-291.
Benario, H. W. "Lucretius 2.615," CP 68 (April, 1973), 127-128.
Bergson, H. L. Philosophy of Poetry: The Genius of Lucretius. New York: Philosophical Library, 1959.
Berns, G. "Time and Nature in Lucretius' 'De Rerum Natura,'" Hermes 104 (1976), 477-492.
Betensky, A. "A Lucretian Verse of Pastoral," Ramus 5 (1976), 45-58.
Borthwick, E. K. "Lucretius' Elephant Wall," CQ (New Series) 23 (November, 1973), 291-292.
Bradley, E. M. "Lucretius and the Irrational," CJ 67 (April-May, 1972), 317-322.
Cairns, H., et al. "Lucretius; On the Nature of Things," in their Invitation to Learning. New York: Random House, 1941, pp. 275-290.
Cavendish, A. P. "Lucretius: A Psychological Study," Ratio 5 (June, 1963), 60-81.
Clarke, M. L. "Epicureanism," in his Roman Mind; Studies in the History of Thought from Cicero to Marcus Aurelius. Cambridge, Mass.: Harvard University Press, 1956, pp. 19-31.
———. "Lucretius 3.1-3," CQ (New Series) 27 (1977), 354-355.
Classen, C. J. "Poetry and Rhetoric in Lucretius," TAPA 99 (1968), 77-118.
Clay, D. "De Rerum Natura: Greek Physis and Epicurean Physiologia (Lucretius I.1-148)," TAPA 100 (1969), 31-47.
Commager, H. S. "Lucretius' Interpretation of the Plague," HSCP 62 (1957), 105-118.
Copley, F. O. "Lucretius," in his Latin Literature from the Beginnings to the Close of the Second Century A.D. Ann Arbor: University of Michigan Press, 1969, pp. 87-118.
Cox, A. S. "Lucretius and His Message: A Study in the Prologues of the De Rerum Natura," G & R 18 (April, 1971), 1-16.
Cratwell, P. "Form of Flesh and Blood?," Arion 8 (Spring, 1969), 121-129.
Crawley, L. W. A. The Failure of Lucretius. Auckland: University of Auckland, 1963.
Dalzell, A. "Lucretius' Expostion of the Doctrine of Images," Ha 118 (Winter, 1974), 22-32.
De Lacy, P. "Distant Views: The Imagery of Lucretius 2," CJ 60 (November, 1964), 49-55.
Dinsmore, C. A. "Lucretius: A Materialistic Philosophy Becomes Noble Poetry," in his Great Poets and the Meaning of Life. Boston: Houghton Mifflin, 1937, pp. 87-100.
Downs, R. B. "Poet of Science: Titus Lucretius Carus," in his Famous Books, Ancient and Medieval. New York: Barnes and Noble, 1964, pp. 169-173.
Dudley, D. R., ed. Lucretius. New York: Basic, 1965.
Eden, P. T. "Lucretius 3.444," CP 72 (July, 1977), 248.

Frank, T. "Lucretius and His Readers," in his Life and Literature in the Roman Republic. Berkeley: University of California Press, 1957, 225-250.
Friedlander, P. "The Epicurean Theology in Lucretius' First Prooemium (Lucr. 1.44-49)," TAPA 70 (1939), 368-379.
Furley, D. "Variations on Themes from Empedocles in Lucretius' Proem," BICS 17 (1970), 55-64.
Goar, R. J. "On the End of Lucretius' Fourth Book," CB 47 (March, 1971), 75-77.
Gottschalk, H. B. "Lucretius 1.983," CP 70 (January, 1975), 42-44.
Grant, M. "Poetry of Instruction: Lucretius," in his Roman Literature. Baltimore: Penguin, 1964, pp. 142-147.
Green, W. M. "Dying World of Lucretius," AJP 63 (January, 1942), 51-60.
Hadas, M. "Lucretius and Catullus," in his History of Latin Literature. New York: Columbia University Press, 1952, pp. 69-87.
Hadzsits, G. D. "A Great Roman Rebel," CJ 40 (May, 1945), 449-466.
_____. Lucretius and His Influence. New York: Cooper Square, 1963.
Hall, J. G. "Visualization and Resolution of Tension in Lucretius' De Rerum Natura," HSCP 75 (1971), 207-208.
Hardie, C. G. "Three Roman Poets," in J. P. V. D. Balsdon, ed., The Romans. New York: Basic, 1965, pp. 226-248.
Holland, L. A. Lucretius and the Transpadanes. Princeton, N.J.: Princeton University Press, 1979.
Hose, H. F. "Lucretius," G & R 3 (May, 1934), 161-164.
Hoslett, S. D. Lucretius, His Genius and His Moral Philosophy. Kansas City, Mo.: Midland, 1939.
Howe, H. M. "Amafinius, Lucretius and Cicero," AJP 72 (January, 1951), 57-62.
_____. "The Religion of Lucretius," CJ 52 (April, 1957), 329-333.
Kenney, E. J., ed. De Rerum Natura III. London: Cambridge University Press, 1971, pp. 1-35.
_____. "The Historical Imagination of Lucretius," G & R 19 (April, 1972), 12-24.
_____. "Lucretius," G & RNSC 11 (1977), 3-48.
_____. "Tityos and the Lover," PCPS 16 (1970), 44-47.
Kinsey, T. E. "The Melancholy of Lucretius," Arion 3 (Summer, 1964), 115-130.
Konstan, D. Some Aspects of Epicurean Psychology. Leiden: Brill, 1973.
Lacy, P. H. de. "Lucretius and the History of Epicureanism," TAPA 79 (1948), 12-23.
Lewis, J. "Poet of Materialism--Lucretius," IQR 164 (October, 1939), 491-499.
Lienhard, J. T. "The Prooemia of De Rerum Natura," CJ 64 (May, 1969), 346-353.
Longrigg, J. "Ice of Bronze (Lucretius I. 493)," CR (New Series) 20 (March, 1970), 8-9.

McCrea, N. G. "Humanism, Old and New; Lucretius and Horace," in his Literature and Liberalism, with Other Classical Papers. New York: Columbia University Press, 1936, pp. 43-71.

Mendell, C. W. "Lucretius," in his Latin Poetry: The New Poets and the Augustans. New Haven, Conn.: Yale University Press, 1965, pp. 14-27.

Merlan, P. "Lucretius--Primitivist or Progressivist?," JHI 11 (June, 1950), 364-368.

Michels, A. K. "Death and Two Poets," TAPA 86 (1955), 160-179.

Minadeo, R. "The Formal Design of De Rerum Natura," Arion 4 (Autumn, 1965), 444-461.

_____. The Lyre of Silence. Detroit: Wayne State University Press, 1969.

Montague, W. P. "Epicurus and Lucretius: The Anti-clerical Vision of Free and Happy Mortals in a Godless Society," in his Great Visions of Philosophy. La Salle, Ill.: Open Court, 1950, pp. 162-177.

Mueller, G. E. "Epicur and His Poet Lucretius," in his Philosophy of Literature. New York: Philosophical Library, 1948, pp. 49-60.

Mullett, C. F. "Lucretius in Clio's Chariot," JHI 19 (June, 1958), 307-322.

Murley, C. "Lucretius and the History of Satire," TAPA 70 (1939), 380-395.

_____. "Lucretius, De Rerum Natura, Viewed as Epic," TAPA 78 (1947), 336-346.

Nichols, J. H. Epicurean Political Philosophy: The De Rerum Natura of Lucretius. Ithaca, N.Y.: Cornell University Press, 1976.

Owen, W. H. "Structural Pattern in Lucretius' De Rerum Natura," C World 62 (December, 1968), 121-127; (January, 1969), 166-172.

Packman, Z. M. "Ethics and Allegory in the Proem of the Fifth Book to Lucretius' De Rerum Natura," CJ 71 (February-March, 1976), 206-212.

Pancheri, L. U. "On De Rerum Natura 2.289: A Philosophical Argument for a Textual Point," Aperion 8 (January, 1974), 49-55.

Pope, S. R. "The Imagery of Lucretius," G & R 18 (June, 1949), 70-79.

Powys, L. "Lucretius," in his Rats in the Sacristy. New York: Watts, 1937, pp. 83-89.

Putnam, M. C. J. "Three Philosophical Poets, by George Santayana," Daedalus 103 (Winter, 1974), 131-140.

Rexroth, K. "Lucretius: On the Nature of Things," in his Classics Revisited. Chicago: Quadrangle, 1968, pp. 85-90.

Roller, D. W. "Gaius Memmius, Patron of Lucretius," CP 65 (October, 1970), 246-248.

Santayana, G. "Three Philosophical Poets," in his Essays in Literary Criticism. New York: Scribner's, 1956, pp. 10-30.

Sarton, G. "Philosophy in the Last Two Centuries: Poseidonios, Cicero, and Lucretius," in his History of Science; Hellenistic Science and Culture in the Last Three Centuries, B.C. Cambridge, Mass.: Harvard University Press, 1959, Vol. 2, pp. 250-279.

Saylor, C. F. "Man, Animal, and the Bestial in Lucretius," CJ 67 (April-May, 1972), 306-316.

Schoder, R. V. "Lucretius' Poetic Problem," CJ 45 (December, 1949), 128-135.
_____. "Lucretius' Poetic Problem--Part II," CJ 45 (January, 1950), 177-182.
Segal, C. P. "Lucretius, Epilepsy, and the Hippocratic On Breaths," CP 65 (July, 1970), 180-182.
Shapiro, L. "Lucretian 'Domestic Melancholy' and the Tradition of Vergilian 'Frustration,'" PMLA 53 (December, 1938), 1088-1093.
Shea, J. "Lucretius, Lightning and Lipari," CP 72 (April, 1977), 136-138.
Sikes, E. E. Lucretius, Poet and Philosopher. New York: Russell and Russell, 1971.
Sinker, A. P. Introduction to Lucretius. Cambridge, Mass.: Harvard University Press, 1937.
Smith, J. "On Metaphysical Poetry," in F. R. Leavis, ed., Determinations; Critical Essays. London: Chatto and Windus, 1934, pp. 10-45.
Smith, M. F. "Some Lucretian Thought Processes," Ha 102 (Spring 1966), 73-83.
Snyder, J. M. "Lucretius and the Status of Women," CB 53 (December, 1976), 17-19.
_____. "Lucretius' Empedoclean Sicily," CW 65 (March, 1972), 217-218.
Solmsen, F. "Epicurus on the Growth and Decline of the Cosmos," AJP 74 (January, 1953), 34-51.
Stewart, D. J. "The Silence of Magna Mater," HSCP 74 (1970), 75-84.
Strauss, L. "Notes on Lucretius," in his Liberalism, Ancient and Modern. New York: Basic, 1968, pp. 76-139.
Sullwood, G. J. Lucretius' Imagery: A Poetic Reading of the De Rerum Natura. Ann Arbor, Mich.: University Microfilms, 1958.
Taylor, M. "Progress and Primitivism in Lucretius," AJP 68 (April, 1947), 180-194.
Van Doren, M. "Concerning the Nature of Things," in his Noble Voice; A Study of Ten Great Poems. New York: Holt, 1946, pp. 148-171.
Vertue, H. "Lucretius, the Poet of Our Time," G & R 17 (June, 1948), 49-63.
_____. "Venus and Lucretius," G & R 3 (October, 1956), 140-151.
Wallach, B. P. Lucretius and the Diatribe Against the Fear of Death: De Rerum Natura III 830-1094. Leiden: Brill. 1976.
West, D. A. The Imagery and Poetry of Lucretius. Edinburgh: Edinburgh University Press, 1969.
_____. "Lucretius' Methods of Argument (3.417-614)," CQ 25 (May, 1975), 94-116.
Wigodsky, M. "A Pattern of Argument in Lucretius," PCP 9 (April, 1974), 73-78.
Wiltshire, S. F. "Nunc Age Lucretius as Teacher," CB 50 (January, 1974), 33-37.
Winspear, A. D. Lucretius and Scientific Thought. Montreal: Harvest House, 1963.

Wormell, D. E. W. "Lucretius: The Personality of the Poet," G & R 7 (March, 1960), 54-63.

MARTIAL

General Criticism

Allen, W. "Martial: Knight, Publisher, and Poet," CJ 65 (May, 1970), 345-357.
Anderson, W. S. "Lascivia vs. Ira: Martial and Juvenal," CSCA 3 (1970), 1-34.
Atkins, J. W. H. "Critical Cross-currents: Martial, the Younger Pliny, Plutarch, Dio Chrysostom, and Lucian," in his Literary Criticism in Antiquity; A Sketch of Its Development. Toronto: Macmillan, 1934, Vol. 2, pp. 299-345.
Bailey, D. R. S. "Correction and Explanations of Martial," CP 73 (October, 1978), 273-296.
Best, E. E. "Martial's Readers in the Roman World," CJ 63 (February, 1969), 208-212.
Chaney, V. M. "Women, According to Martial," CB 48 (December, 1971), 21-25.
Colton, R. E. Juvenal and Martial. Ann Arbor, Mich.: University Microfilms, 1969.
_____. "Martial in Juvenal's Tenth Satire," SP 74 (October, 1977), 341-353.
Copley, F. O. "Martial, Statius, and Quintilian," in his Latin Literature from the Beginnings to the Close of the Second Century A.D. Ann Arbor: University of Michigan Press, 1969, pp. 316-326.
Daube, D. "Martial, Father of Three," AJAH 1 (1976), 145-147.
Hadas, M. "Satire," in his History of Latin Literature. New York: Columbia University Press, 1952, pp. 278-301.
Jones, F. L. "Martial, the Client," CJ 30 (March, 1935), 359-361.
Ker, A. "Some Explanations and Emendations of Martial," CQ (New Series) 44 (1950), 12-24.
Sempler, W. H. "The Poet Martial," JRLB 42 (1960), 432-452.
Spaeth, J. W. "Martial and the Roman Crowd," CJ 27 (January, 1932), 244-254.
Steiner, G. "Columella and Martial on Living in the Country," CJ 50 (November, 1954), 85-90.
White, P. "The Presentation and Dedication of the Silvae and the Epigrams," JRS 64 (1974), 40-46.

Individual Works

Apophoreta

Ullman, B. L. "Apophoreta in Petronius and Martial," CP 36 (October, 1941), 346-355.

Epigrams

Carrington, A. G. Aspects of Martial's Epigrams. Sydney: Shakespeare Head, 1960.
Colton, R. E. "Juvenal's Second Satire and Martial," CJ 61 (November, 1965), 68-71.
Donini, G. "Martial, I, 49: Horatius in Martiale," AJP 85 (January, 1964), 56-60.
Downs, R. B. "Creator of the Epigram: Marcus Valerius Martialis," in his Famous Books, Ancient and Medieval. New York: Barnes and Noble, 1964, pp. 217-220.
Hudson-Williams, A. "Some Other Explanations of Martial," CQ (New Series) 2 (1952), 27-31.
Kenney, E. J. "Erotion Again," G & R 11 (March, 1964), 77-81.
Killeen, J. F. "What Was the Linea Dives (Martial, VIII, 78, 7)?" AJP 80 (April, 1959), 185-188.
Lloyd, L. J. "Erotion: A Note on Martial," G & R 22 (February, 1953), 39-41.
Marino, P. A. "Women: Poorly Inferior or Richly Superior," CB 48 (December, 1971), 17-21.
Martin, D. "Similarities Between the Silvae of Statius and the Epigrams of Martial," CJ 34 (May, 1939), 461-470.
Messer, W. S. "Martial IX, 15," CJ 36 (January, 1941), 226-229.
Nixon, P. Martial and the Modern Epigram. New York: Cooper Square, 1963.
Spaeth, J. W. "Martial and the Pisquinade," TAPA 70 (1939), 242-255.

Spectacula

Moeller, W. O. "Juvenal 3 and Martial De Spectaculis 8," CJ 62 (May, 1967), 269-270.

Xenia

Ullman, B. L. "Apophoreta in Petronius and Martial," CP 36 (October, 1941), 346-355.

MENANDER

General Criticism

Arnott, G. "Menander: Discoveries Since the Dyskolos," Areth 3 (Spring, 1970), 49-70.
―――. "Menander, Plautus, Terence," G & RNSC 9 (1975), 5-62.
―――. "Modernity of Menander," G & R 22 (October, 1975), 140-155.

Downs, R. B. "Father of Modern Comedy: Menander," in his Famous Books, Ancient and Medieval. New York: Barnes and Noble, 1964, pp. 135-139.
Feneron, J. S. "Some Elements of Menander's Style," BICS 21 (1974), 81-95.
Gomme, A. W. "Menander," in his Essays in Greek History and Literature. Oxford: Blackwell, 1937, pp. 249-295.
_____, and F. H. Sandbach. Menander: A Commentary. London: Oxford University Press, 1973.
Handley, E. W. Menander and Plautus: A Study in Comparison. London: University College, 1968.
Harsh, P. W. "Menander," in his Handbook of Classical Drama. Stanford, Calif.: Stanford University Press, 1944, pp. 322-327.
Hooker, G. T. W. "The New Menander," G & R 5 (October, 1958), 105-107.
Hourmouziades, N. C. "Menander's Actors," GRBS 14 (Summer, 1973), 179-188.
Lindsay, W. M. Early Latin Verse. London: Oxford University Press, 1968, pp. 11-112.
MacCary, W. T. "Menander's Characters: Their Names, Roles and Masks," TAPA 101 (1970), 277-290.
_____. "Menander's Old Men," TAPA 102 (1971), 303-325.
_____. "Menander's Slaves: Their Names, Roles and Masks," TAPA 100 (1969), 277-294.
_____. "Menander's Soldiers: Their Names, Roles and Masks," AJP 93 (April, 1972), 279-298.
Murray, G. "Ritual Elements in the New Comedy," CQ 37 (January, 1943), 36-54.
Nicoll, A. "From Menander to the Mimes," in his World Drama, from Aeschylus to Anouilh. New York: Harcourt, 1953, pp. 107-137.
Osmun, G. F. Dialogue Technique in Menander. Ann Arbor, Mich.: University Microfilms, 1953.
Perry, H. T. "First Literary Comedy: Aristophanes and Menander," in his Masters of Dramatic Comedy and Their Social Themes. Cambridge, Mass.: Harvard University Press, 1939, pp. 3-48.
Post, L. A. "Aristotle and Menander," TAPA 69 (1938), 1-42.
_____. "Comedy of Menander," in his From Homer to Menander; Forces in Greek Poetic Fiction. Berkeley: University of California Press, 1951, pp. 214-244.
_____. "Menander in Current Criticism," TAPA 65 (1934), 13-34.
_____. "The 'Vis' of Menander," TAPA 62 (1931), 203-234.
_____. "Women's Place in Menander's Athens," TAPA 71 (1940), 420-459.
Turner, E. G. "New Plays of Menander," JRLB 42 (1959), 241-258.
Webster, T. B. L. "The Comedy of Menander," in T. A. Dorey and D. R. Dudley, eds., Roman Drama. New York: Basic, 1965, pp. 1-20.
_____. An Introduction to Menander. Manchester: Manchester University Press, 1974.
_____. "Menander: Plays of Adventure and Satire," JRLB 31 (November, 1948), 180-223.

___. "Menander: Plays of Social Criticism," JRLB 30 (May, 1947), 247-400.
___. "Menander: Production and Imagination," JRLB 45 (September, 1962), 135-172.
___. "Menander's Plays of Reconciliation," JRLB 29 (March, 1946), 369-391.
___. "Restorations in Menander, An Incentive for Restudying Menander Provided by the Papyrus Fragments," JRLB 30 (October, 1946), 115-143.
___. Studies in Menander. Manchester: Manchester University Press, 1960.

Individual Works

Arbitrants, or Epitrepontes

Honigmann, E. The Lost End of Menander's Epitrepontes. Brussels: Palais des Academies, 1950.

Changeling, or Hypobolimaios

Gomme, A. W. "Menander's Hypobolimaios," CQ (New Series) 10 (1960), 103-109.

Curmudgeon, or Dyskolos, or Dyskolus

Anderson, M. Knemon's Hamartia," G & R 17 (October, 1970), 199-217.
Griffith, J. G. "The Distribution of Parts in Menander's Dyskolos," CQ (New Series) 10 (1960), 113-117.
Keuls, E. "Mystery Elements in Menander's Dyskolus," TAPA 100 (1969), 209-220.
Lever, K. "The Dyskolus and Menander's Reputation," CJ 55 (April, 1960), 321-326.
Photiades, P. J. "Pan's Prologue to the Dyskolos of Menander," G & R 5 (October, 1958), 108-122.
Post, L. A. "Some Subtleties in Menander's Dyscolus," AJP 84 (January, 1963), 36-51.
___. "Virtue Promoted in Menander's Dyscolus," TAPA 91 (1960), 152-161.
Reckford, K. J. "Dyskolos of Menander [with Synopsis of Play]," SP 58 (January, 1961), 1-24.

Shield, or Aspis

Konet, R. J. "The Role of Tuche in Menander's Aspis," CB 52 (April, 1976), 90-92.
Lloyd-Jones, H. "Menander's Aspis," GRBS 12 (Summer, 1971), 175-195.

Lombard, D. B. "New Values in Traditional Forms: A Study in Menander's Aspis," AClass 14 (1971), 123-145.
Sherk, R. K. "Daos and Spinther in Menander's Aspis," AJP 91 (July, 1970), 341-343.

Woman of Samos, or Samia

Lloyd-Jones, H. "Menander's Samia in the Light of the New Evidence," YCS 22 (1972), 119-144.

MENIPPUS

General Criticism

McCarthy, B. P. "Lucian and Menippus," YCS 4, 3-55.

MOSCHUS

Individual Works

Megara

Giangrande, G. "On Moschus' Megara," CQ (New Series) 19 (May, 1969), 181-184.

NAEVIUS

General Criticism

Jocelyn, H. D. "The Poet Cr. Naevius, P. Cornelius Scipio and Q. Caecilius Metellus," Antichthon 3 (1969), 32-47.
Stambusky, A. A. "Roman Comedy on Trial in the Republic: The Case of Censorship Against Gnaesus Naevius the Playwright," ETJ 29 (March, 1977), 29-36.

Individual Works

Punic War, or Bellum Punicum

Copley, F. O. "Andronicus, Naevius, and Ennius," in his Latin Literature from the Beginnings to the Close of the Second Century A.D. Ann Arbor: University of Michigan Press, 1969, pp. 9-18.

Hadas, M. "The Beginnings," in his History of Latin Literature. New York: Columbia University Press, 1952, pp. 15-32.
Rowell, H. T. "Original Form of Naevius' Bellum Punicum," AJP 68 (January, 1947), 21-46.

OVID

General Criticism

Avery, M. W. "Ovid's Apologia," CJ 32 (November, 1936), 92-102.
Barsby, J. "Ovid," G & RNSC 12 (1978), 3-49.
Binns, J., ed. Ovid. London: Routledge and K. Paul, 1973.
Bush, D. "Ovid Old and New," in his Mythology and the Renaissance Tradition in English Poetry. New York: Norton, 1963, pp. 69-88.
Copley, F. O. "The Elegists: Tibullus, Propertius, and Ovid," in his Latin Literature from the Beginnings to the Close of the Second Century A. D. Ann Arbor: University of Michigan Press, 1969, 241-275.
Crossland, J. "Ovid's Contribution to the Conception of Love Known as 'l'Amour Courtois,'" MLR 42 (April, 1947), 199-206.
Cunningham, M. P. "Ovid's Poetics," CJ 53 (March, 1958), 253-259.
Currie, H. M. "Ovid's Personality," CJ 59 (January, 1964), 145-155.
DeLacy, P. "Philosophical Doctrine and Poetic Technique in Ovid," CJ 43 (December, 1947), 153-161.
Durling, R. M. "Ovid as Praeceptor Amoris," CJ 53 (January, 1958), 157-167.
Eaton, A. H. Influence of Ovid on Claudian. Washington, D. C.: Catholic University of America Press, 1943.
Ferguson, J. "Catullus and Ovid," AJP 81 (October, 1960), 337-357.
Feuchtwanger, L. "Ovid," in E. Ludwig and H. B. Kranz, eds., Torch of Freedom; Twenty Exiles of History. New York: Rinehart, 1943, pp. 3-16.
Fontenrose, J. E. "Apollo and the Sun-god in Ovid," AJP 61 (October, 1940), 429-444.
Fraenkel, H. Ovid: A Poet Between Two Worlds. Berkeley: University of California Press, 1945.
Fyler, J. M. "Omnia Vincit Amor: Incongruity and the Limitations of Structure in Ovid's Elegiac Poetry," CJ 66 (February, 1971), 196-203.
Gariepy, R. J. "Recent Scholarship on Ovid (1958-1968)," C World 64 (October, 1970), 37-56.
Garlow, L. W. "A Guess as to Why Ovid Was Exiled," CJ 32 (November, 1936), 103-105.
Grant, M. "The New Elegy and the Metamorphoses: Ovid," in his Roman Literature. Baltimore: Penguin, 1964, pp. 207-218.
Hadas, M. "Ovid," in his History of Latin Literature. New York: Columbia University Press, 1952, pp. 201-226.

Henderson, W. J. "What Ovid Tells Us About the Roman Calendar," Akroterion 17, 4 (December, 1972), 9-20.
Highet, G. "Ovid and Romantic Love," in his Classical Tradition; Greek and Roman Influences on Western Literature. New York: Oxford University Press, 1949, pp. 57-62.
―――――. "Ovid: Contrasts," in his Poets in a Landscape. New York: Knopf, 1957, pp. 173-195.
Hoffman, R. L. Ovid and The Canterbury Tales. Philadelphia: University of Pennsylvania Press, 1966.
Jameson, C. Ovid in the Sixteenth Century. London: Routledge and K. Paul, 1973, pp. 210-242.
Johnson, S. "Intimations of Immorality in the Major Lyric and Elegiac Poets of Rome; Ovid," Roy Soc Can Trans (Series 3) 44 Sec. 2 (1950), 85-93.
Johnson, W. R. "The Problem of the Counter-Classical Sensibility and its Critics," CSCA 3 (1970), 123-151.
Mendell, C. W. "Ovid," in his Latin Poetry: The New Poets and the Augustans. New Haven: Yale University Press, 1965, pp. 212-240.
Norwood, F. "Riddle of Ovid's Relegatio," CP 58 (July, 1963), 150-163.
O'Neil, E. N. "Tibullus 2.6: A New Interpretation," CP 62 (July, 1967), 163-168.
Otis, B. Ovid as an Epic Poet. 2nd edition. Cambridge: Cambridge University Press, 1971.
Pemberton, R. E. K. "Literary Criticism in Ovid," CJ 26 (April, 1931), 525-534.
Platnauer, M. Latin Elegiac Verse; A Study of the Metrical Usages of Tibullus, Propertius, and Ovid. Hamden, Conn.: Archon, 1971.
Rand, E, K. Ovid and His Influence. New York: Cooper Square, 1963.
Robathan, D. M. Ovid in the Middle Ages. London: Routledge and K. Paul, 1973, pp. 191-209.
Schevill, R. Ovid and the Renaissance in Spain. Berkeley: University of California Press, 1913.
Scott, K. "Emperor Worship in Ovid," TAPA 61 (1930), 43-69.
Sorley, H. T. Exile; A Study in the Three Books. Ilfracombe, Eng.: Stockwell, 1963.
Syme, R. History in Ovid. New York: Clarendon, 1978.
Thibault, J. C. The Mystery of Ovid's Exile. Berkeley: University of California Press, 1964.
Wain, J. "Ovid in English," in his Preliminary Essays. New York: St. Martin's, 1957, pp. 36-77.
Wheelwright, P. "Rediscovering Ovid [review article]," SR 64 (Spring, 1956), 283-296.
Wilkinson, L. P. Golden Latin Artistry. Cambridge: Cambridge University Press, 1963.
―――――. Ovid Recalled. London: Cambridge University Press, 1955.
―――――. Ovid Surveyed. London: Cambridge University Press, 1962.
Wright, F. A. Three Roman Poets: Plautus, Catullus, Ovid. New York: Dutton, 1938.

Individual Works

Amores

Barsby, J. A. "Desultor Amoris in Amores 1.3," CP 70 (January, 1975), 44-45.
Berman, K. "Some Propertian Imitations in Ovid's Amores," CP 67 (July, 1972), 170-177.
Booth, J., and A. C. F. Verity. "Critical Appreciations IV: Ovid, Amores 2,10," G & R 25 (October, 1978), 125-140.
Cameron, A. "The First Edition of Ovid's Amores," CQ (New Series) 18 (1968), 320-333.
Connor, P. J. "His Dupes and Accomplices: A Study of Ovid the Illusionist in the Amores," Ramus 3 (1974), 18-40.
Curran, L. C. "Desultores Amoris: Ovid Amores 1.3," CP 61 (January, 1966), 47-49.
Dickson, T. W. "Borrowed Themes in Ovid's Amores," CJ 59 (January, 1964), 175-180.
Du Quesnay, I. M. Le M. The Amores. London: Routledge and K. Paul, 1973, pp. 1-48.
Elliot, A. G. "Amores 1.13: Ovid's Art," CJ 69 (December, 1973), 127-132.
Gross, N. P. "Ovid, Amores 3.11A and B: A Literary Melange," CJ 71 (January, 1976), 152-160.
Holleman, A. W. J. "Notes on Ovid Amores 1.3, Horace Carm. 1.14, and Propertius 2.26," CP 65 (July, 1970), 177-180.
Kenney, E. J. "On the Somnium Attributed to Ovid," Agon 3 (1969), 1-14.
_____. "Tradition of Ovid's Amores," CR (New Series) 5 (March, 1955), 13-14; 7 (March, 1957), 16.
Kratins, O. "Pretended Witch: A Reading of Ovid's Amores, 1. viii," PQ 42 (April, 1963), 151-158.
Lateiner, D. "Ovid's Homage to Callimachus and Alexandrian Poetic Theory (AM. 2, I9)," Hermes 106 (1978), 188-196.
Lee, A. G. "'Tenerorum Lusor Amorum,'" in J. P. Sullivan, ed., Critical Essays on Roman Literature: Elegy and Lyric. Cambridge, Mass.: Harvard University Press, 1962, pp. 149-179.
Morgan, K. Ovid's Art of Imitation: Propertius in the Amores. Leiden: Brill, 1977.
Nicoll, W. S. M. "Ovid, Amores I 5," Mnemosyne 30 (1977), 40-48.
Oliver, R. P. "Ovid in His Ring (Amores 2. 15.9-26)," CP 53 (April, 1958), 103-105.
Olstein, K. "Amores 1.3 and Duplicity as a Way of Love," TAPA 105 (1975), 241-257.
Parker, D. "Ovidian Coda," Arion 8 (Spring, 1969), 80-97.
Thomas, E. "Ovid, Amores iii. 9. 35-40," CR (New Series) 15 (June, 1965), 149-151.
_____. "Variations on a Military Theme in Ovid's Amores," G & R 11 (October, 1964), 151-165.
Tracy, V. A. "Ovid and Corinna," CN & V 21 (1977), 86-91.

Watts, W. J. "Ovid, the Law and Roman Society on Abortion," AClass 16 (1973), 89-101.
Yardley, J. C. "Roman Elegists, Sick Girls, and the Soteria," CQ (New Series) 27 (1977), 394-401.

Ars Amatoria

Alexander, W. H. "The Culpa of Ovid," CJ 53 (April, 1958), 319-325.
Blodgett, E. D. "The Well Wrought Void: Reflections on the Ars Amatoria," CJ 68 (April-May, 1973), 322-333.
Buchert, B. T. "The Reasons for Ovid's Banishment," Akroterion 19 (April, 1974), 44-49.
Courtney, E. "Two Cruces in the Ars Amatoria," CR (New Series) 20 (March, 1970), 10-11.
Crossland, J. "Ovid's Contribution to the Conception of Love Known as 'l'Amour Courtois,'" MLR 42 (April, 1947), 199-206.
Edwards, W. M. "Ram and Cerberus (Ovid, A.A. III. 173-178; Met. VII. 408-409)," CR (New Series) 3 (December, 1953), 142-144.
Hollis, A. S. The Ars Amatoria and Remedia Amoris. London: Routledge and K. Paul, 1973, pp. 84-115.
_____. "Ovid, A.A. I. 197-198: The Wrong Phraates?," CR (New Series) 20 (June, 1970), 141-142.
Kenney, E. J. "Ovid, Ars Amatoria i. 147," CR (New Series) 3 (March, 1953), 7-10.
Leach, E. W. "Georgic Imagery in the Ars Amatoria," TAPA 95 (1964), 142-154.
Verstraete, B. C. "Ovid on Homosexuality," CN & V 19 (October, 1975), 79-83.
Wardman, A. E. "The Rape of the Sabines," CQ (New Series) 15 (1965), 101-113.

Epistulae ex Ponto

Broege, V. "Ovid's Autobiographical Use of Mythology in the Tristia and Epistulae ex Ponto," CN & V 16 (April, 1972), 37-42.
Evans, H. B. "Ovid's Apology for Ex Ponto I-3," Hermes 104 (1976), 103-112.

Heroides

Anderson, W. S. The Heroides. London: Routledge and K. Paul, 1973, pp. 49-83.
Baca, A. R. "Ovid's Claim to Originality and Heroides I," TAPA 100 (1969), 1-10.
Bradley, E. M. "Ovid Heroides V: Reality and Illusion," CJ 64 (January, 1969), 158-162.
Cunningham, M. P. "The Novelty of Ovid's Heroides," CP 44 (1949), 100-106.

Jacobson, H. "Ovid's Briseis: A Study of Heroides III," Phoenix 25 (Winter, 1971), 331-356.
_____. Ovid's Heroides. Princeton, N. J.: Princeton University Press, 1974.
Kenney, E. J. "Love and Legalism: Ovid, Heroides 20 and 21," Arion 9 (Winter, 1970), 388-414.
Merchant, W. P. H. "Ovid, Heroides 16. 177," CR (New Series) 17 (December, 1967), 262-263.
Pulbrook, M. A Correction in Ovid, Heroides VII. Dublin: Dublin University Press, 1976.
_____. "The Original Published Form of Ovid's Heroides," Ha 122 (Summer, 1977), 29-45.
Tracy, V. A. "The Authenticity of Heroides 16-21," CJ 66 (April-May, 1971), 328-330.
_____. "Penelope and Medea in the Heroides," CN & V 16 (April, 1972), 43-48.
Vessey, D. W. T. "Humor and Humanity in Ovid's Heroides," Areth 9 (Spring, 1976), 91-110.
_____. "Notes on Ovid, Heroides 9," CQ (New Series) 19 (November, 1969), 349-361.
White, D. G. "Ovid, Heroides 16. 45-46," HSCP 74 (1970), 187-191.

Metamorphoses

Anderson, W. S. "Multiple Change in the Metamorphoses," TAPA 94 (1963), 1-29.
_____. Ovid's Metamorphoses, Books 6-10. Norman: University of Oklahoma Press, 1972, pp. 3-35.
_____. " 'Talaria' and Ovid Met. 10. 591," TAPA 97 (1966), 1-14.
Bass, R. C. "Some Aspects of the Structure of the Phaeton Episode in Ovid's Metamorphoses," CQ (New Series) 27 (1977), 402-408.
Bauer, D. F. "The Function of Pygmalion in the Metamorphoses of Ovid," TAPA 93 (1962), 1-21.
Bowra, C. M. "Orpheus and Eurydice," CQ (New Series) 2 (1952), 113-126.
Brunner, T. F. "The Function of the Simile in Ovid's Metamorphoses," CJ 61 (May, 1966), 354-363.
Clarke, W. M. "Myrrha's Nurse: The Marathon Runner in Ovid?," CP 68 (January, 1973), 55-56.
Coleman, R. "Structure and Intention in the Metamorphoses," CQ (New Series) 21 (November, 1971), 461-477.
Colton, R. E. "Philemon and Baucis in Ovid and La Fontaine," CJ 63 (January, 1968), 166-176.
Curran, L. C. "Transformation and Anti-Augustanism in Ovid's Metamorphoses," Areth 5 (Spring, 1972), 71-91.
Dickie, M. W. "Ovid, Metamorphoses 2. 760-64," AJP 96 (Winter, 1975), 378-390.
Due, O. Changing Forms: Studies in the Metamorphoses of Ovid. Copenhagen: Gyldendal, 1974.
Duke, T. T. "Ovid's Pyramis and Thisbe," CJ 66 (April-May, 1971), 320-327.

Edwards, W. M. "Ram and Cerberus (Ovid, A. A. III. 173-178; Met. VII. 408-409)," CR (New Series) 3 (December, 1953), 142-144.

Ferguson, J. "Some Verbal Effects in Ovid's Metamorphoses," Mus Afr 4 (1975), 17-26.

Galinsky, G. K. "The Cipus Episode in Ovid's Metamorphoses (15. 565-621)," TAPA 98 (1967), 181-192.

―――. Ovid's Metamorphoses: An Introduction to the Basic Aspects. Berkeley: University of California Press, 1975.

Garson, R. W. "The Faces of Love in Ovid's Metamorphoses," Prudentia 8 (May, 1976), 9-18.

Giangrande, L. "Mythic Themes in Ovid Met. 8," CB 50 (December, 1973), 17-21.

Gilbert, C. D. "Ovid, Met. 1. 4," CQ (New Series) 26 (1976), 111-112.

Grant, M. "The New Elegy and the Metamorphoses: Ovid," in his Roman Literature. Baltimore: Penguin, 1964, pp. 207-218.

Griffin, A. H. F. "Ovid's Metamorphoses," G & R 24 (April, 1977), 57-70.

Highet, G. "Ovid's Metamorphoses: The Book of Miracles," in his Powers of Poetry. New York: Oxford University Press, 1960, pp. 264-270.

Jacobson, H. "A Note on Ovid, Met. VI, 115-116," AJP 93 (July, 1972), 459-461.

Kenney, E. J. "In Parenthesis," CR (New Series) 20 (December, 1970), 291.

―――. "Ovidus Prooemians," PCPS (New Series) 22 (1976), 46-53.

―――. The Style of the Metamorphoses. London: Routledge and K. Paul, 1973, pp. 116-153.

Leach, E. W. "Ekphrasis and the Theme of Artistic Failure in Ovid's Metamorphoses," Ramus 3 (1974), 102-142.

Lenz, F. W. Ovid's Metamorphoses; Prolegomena to a Revision of Hugo Magnus' Edition. [Dublin]: Weidmann, 1967.

Little, D. "The Speech of Pythagoras in Metamorphoses 15 and the Structure of the Metamorphoses," Hermes 98 (1970), 340-360.

Littlefield, D. J. "Pomona and Vertumnus: A Fruition of History in Ovid's Metamorphoses," Arion 4 (Autumn, 1965), 465-473.

MacKay, T. S. "Three Poets Observe Picus," AJP 96 (Fall, 1975), 272-275.

Miller, R. P. "Myth of Mar's Hot Minion in Venus and Adonis," ELH 26 (December, 1959), 470-481.

Norwood, F. "Unity in the Diversity of Ovid's Metamorphoses," CJ 59 (January, 1964), 170-174.

Otis, B. Ovid as an Epic Poet. 2nd edition. Cambridge: Cambridge University Press, 1970.

Parry, H. "Ovid's Metamorphoses: Violence in a Pastoral Landscape," TAPA 95 (1964), 268-282.

Richardson, J. "The Function of Formal Imagery in Ovid's Metamorphoses," CJ 59 (January, 1964), 161-169.

Ringler, R. N. "Faunus Episode," MP 63 (August, 1965), 12-19.

Segal, C. "Circean Temptations: Homer, Vergil, Ovid," TAPA 99 (1968), 419-442.

_____. Landscape in Ovid's Metamorphoses: A Study in the Transformations of a Literary Symbol. Wiesbaden: Steiner, 1969.
_____. "Myth and Philosophy in the Metamorphoses: Ovid's Augustanism and the Augustan Conclusion of Book XV," AJP 90 (1969), 257-292.
_____. "Narrative Art in the Metamorphoses," CJ 66 (April-May, 1971), 331-337.
_____. "Ovid's Metamorphoses: Greek Myth in Augustan Rome," SP 68 (October, 1971), 371-394.
_____. "Ovid's Orpheus and Augustan Ideology," TAPA 103 (1972), 473-494.
Smith, J. E. S. "Icarus' Astral Navigation," G & R 21 (April, 1974), 19-20.
Steiner, G. "Ovid's Carmen Perpetuum," TAPA 89 (1958), 218-236.
Stephens, W. C. "Cupid and Venus in Ovid's Metamorphoses," TAPA 89 (1958), 286-300.
_____. "Descent to the Underworld in Ovid's Metamorphoses," CJ 53 (January, 1958), 177-183.
Stirrup, B. E. "Techniques of Rape: Variety of Wit in Ovid's Metamorphoses," G & R 24 (October, 1977), 170-184.
Sullivan, J. P. "Ovid and Epic," OR 4 (1967), 72-80.
Williams, F. "Gods and Gate Crashing," Mnemosyne 30 (1977), 289-291.
Wise, V. M. "Flight Myths in Ovid's Metamorphoses," Ramus 4 (1977), 44-59.

Tristia

Broege, V. "Ovid's Autobiographical Use of Mythology in the Tristia and Epistulae ex Ponto," CN & V 16 (April, 1972), 37-42.
Dickinson, R. J. The Tristia: Poetry in Exile. London: Routledge and K. Paul, 1973, pp. 154-190.
Evans, H. B. "Winter and Warfare in Ovid's Tomis (Tristia 3.10)," CJ 70 (March, 1975), 1-9.
Fredericks, B. R. "Tristia 4.10: Poet's Autobiography and Poetic Autobiography," TAPA 106 (1976), 139-154.
Hauben, F. "Adnuo and Abnuo in Ovid Tristia 5.10, 41-42," AJP 96 (Spring, 1975), 61-63.
Wiedemann, T. "The Political Background to Ovid's Tristia 11," CQ 25 (December, 1975), 264-271.

PAUSANIAS

General Criticism

Diller, A. "The Authors Named Pausanias," TAPA 86 (1955), 268-279.

Glover, T. R. "Prince of Digressors," in his Springs of Hellas, and Other Essays. New York: Macmillan, 1946, pp. 160-181.

PERSIUS

General Criticism

Atkins, J. W. H. "Literary Decline and Contemporary Comments: Tractatus Coislinianus, the Two Senecas, Persius and Petronius," in his Literary Criticism in Antiquity; A Sketch of Its Development. Toronto: Macmillan, 1934, Vol. 2, pp. 137-174.
Hadas, M. "Satire," in his History of Latin Literature. New York: Columbia University Press, 1952, pp. 278-301.
Martin, J. M. K. "Persius--Poet of the Stoics," G & R 8 (May, 1939), 172-182.
Semple, W. H. "The Poet Persius, Literary and Social Critic," JRLB 44 (1961), 157-174.
Sullivan, J. P. "In Defense of Persius," Ramus 1 (1972), 48-62.

Individual Works

Satires

Anderson, W. S. "Part Versus Whole in Persius' Fifth Satire," PQ 39 (January, 1960), 66-81.
Bramble, J. C. Persius and the Programmatic Satire: A Study in Form and Imagery. Cambridge: Cambridge University Press, 1974.
Dessen, C. S. Iunctura Callidus Acri: A Study of Persius' Satires. Urbana: University of Illinois Press, 1968.
Peterson, R. G. "The Unknown Self in the Fourth Satire of Persius," CJ 68 (February-March, 1973), 205-209.
Smith, W. S. "Speakers in the Third Satire of Persius," CJ 64 (April, 1969), 305-308.
Sullivan, J. P. "Ass's Ears and Attises: Persius and Nero," AJP 99 (Summer, 1978), 159-170.

PETRONIUS

General Criticism

Atkins, J. W. H. "Literary Decline and Contemporary Comments: Tractatus Coislinianus, the Two Senecas, Persius and Petronius," in his Literary Criticism in Antiquity: A Sketch of Its Development. Toronto: Macmillan, 1934, Vol. 2, pp. 137-174.

Auerbach, E. "Fortunata," in R. Scholes, ed., Approaches to the Novel; Material for a Poetics. San Francisco: Chandler, 1961, pp. 3-30.
Bagnani, G. Arbiter of Elegance: A Study of the Life and Works of C. Petronius. Toronto: Toronto University Press, 1954.
Best, E. E. "Attitudes Toward Literacy Reflected in Petronius," CJ 61 (November, 1965), 72-76.
Cameron, A. "Petronius and Plato," CQ 19 (November, 1969), 367-370.
Copley, F. O. "Lucan and Petronius," in his Latin Literature from the Beginnings to the Close of the Second Century A.D. Ann Arbor: University of Michigan Press, 1969, pp. 304-316.
Corbett, P. B. "More Petroniana," CP 64 (April, 1969), 111-113.
_____. "Petroniana," CP 62 (October, 1967), 260-261.
_____. Petronius. New York: Twayne, 1970.
George, R. A. "Petroniana," CQ (New Series) 17 (May, 1967), 130-132.
Hadas, M. "Satire," in his History of Latin Literature. New York: Columbia University Press, 1952, pp. 278-301.
Highet, G. "Petronius the Moralist," TAPA 72 (1941), 176-194.
Musurillo, H. A. "Life and Dream; The Poetry of Petronius," in his Symbol and Myth in Ancient Poetry. New York: Fordham University Press, 1961, pp. 159-164.
Paschall, D. M. Vocabulary of Mental Aberration in Roman Comedy and Petronius. Baltimore: Linguistic Society of America, 1939.
Rankin, H. D. Petronius the Artist. The Hague: Nijhoff, 1971.
Rascoe, B. "Petronius," in his Prometheans: Ancient and Modern. New York: Putnam's, 1933, pp. 87-115.
Richardson, T. W. "Problems in the Text-History of Petronius in Antiquity and the Middle Ages," AJP 96 (Fall, 1975), 290-305.
Rose, K. F. C. The Date and Author of the Satyricon. Leiden: Brill, 1971.
_____. "The Petronian Inquisition: An Auto-da-fe," Arion 5 (Autumn, 1966), 275-301.
Schnur, H. C. "Petronius: Sense and Nonsense," CW 66 (1972), 13-20.
Scobie, A. Aspects of the Ancient Romance and Its Heritage; Essays on Apuleius, Petronius, and the Greek Romances. Meisenheim a. Glan: Hain, 1969.
Sullivan, J. P. "Petronius: Artist or Moralist?," Arion 6 (Spring, 1967), 71-88.
_____. "Petronius, Seneca, and Lucian: A Neronian Literary Feud?," TAPA 99 (1968), 453-468.
Walsh, P. G. "Was Petronius a Moralist?," G & R 21 (October, 1974), 181-190.

Individual Works

Capture of Troy, or Halosis Troiae

Walsh, P. G. "Eumolpus, the Halosis Troiae, and the De Bello Civili," CP 63 (July, 1968), 208-212.

162 : Greek and Roman Authors

Poem on the Civil War, or Bellum Civile, or De Bello Civili

George, P. A. "Petronius and Lucan De Bello Civili," CQ 24 (May, 1974), 119-133.
Luck, G. "On Petronius' Bellum Civile," AJP 93 (January, 1972), 133-141.
Sochatoff, A. F. "The Purpose of Petronius' Bellum Civile: A Reexamination," TAPA 93 (1962), 449-458.
Walsh, P. G. "Eumolpus, the Halosis Troiae, and the De Bello Civili," CP 63 (July, 1968), 208-212.

Satyricon

Arrowsmith, W. "Luxury and Death in the Satyricon," Arion 5 (Autumn, 1966), 304-331.
Bacon, H. H. "Sibyl in the Bottle," VQR 34 (Spring, 1958), 262-276.
Bagnani, G. "House of Trimalchio," AJP 75 (January, 1954), 16-39.
Baldwin, B. "Ira Priapi," CP 68 (October, 1973), 294-296.
_____. "A Note on Trimalchio's Zodiac Dish," CQ 20 (November, 1970), 364.
_____. "Trimalchio's Corinthian Plate," CP 68 (January, 1973), 46-47.
Beck, R. "Encolpius at the Cena," Phoenix 29 (1975), 270-283.
_____. "Some Observations on the Narrative Technique of Petronius," Phoenix 27 (1973), 42-61.
Burriss, E. E. "Breaks in Conversation and the Text of Petronius' Satyricon," CP 42 (October, 1947), 244-248.
Cameron, A. "Petronius and Plato," CQ 19 (November, 1969), 267-270.
Cameron, H. D. "The Sibyl in the Satyricon," CJ 65 (May, 1970), 337-379.
Connolly, C. "On Re-reading Petronius," in his Previous Convictions. New York: Harper, 1963, pp. 105-109.
Dupee, F. W. "Libido is a Latin Word," in his 'The King of the Cats' and Other Remarks on Writers and Writing. New York: Farrar, Straus, 1965, pp. 142-148.
George, P. "Style and Character in the Satyricon," Arion 5 (Autumn, 1966), 336-358.
Gill, C. "The Sexual Episodes in the Satyricon," CP 68 (1973), 172-185.
Haight, E. H. "Satire and the Latin Novel," in her Essays on Ancient Fiction. London: Longmans, 1936, pp. 86-120.
Kennedy, G. "Encolpius and Agamemnon in Petronius," AJP 99 (Summer, 1978), 171-178.
Mulroy, D. D. "Petronius 81.3," CP 65 (1970), 254-256.
Pack, R. "Criminal Dossier of Encolpius," CP 55 (January, 1960), 31-32.
Rexroth, K. "Petronius: The Satyricon," in his Classics Revisited. Chicago: Quadrangle, 1968, pp. 99-103.

Rose, K. F. C. "Time and Place in the Satyricon," TAPA 93 (1962), 402-409.
———. "Trimalchio's Accountant," CP 62 (October, 1967), 258-259.
Sandy, G. N. "Petronius and the Tradition of Interpolated Narrative," TAPA 101 (1970), 463-476.
———. "Satire in the Satyricon," AJP 90 (July, 1969), 293-303.
———. "Scaenica Petroniana," TAPA 104 (1974), 329-346.
Schmeling, G. "The Satyricon: Forms in Search of a Genre," CB 47 (February, 1971), 49-52.
Schraidt, N. E. "Literary and Philosophical Elements in the Satyricon of Petronius Arbiter," CJ 35 (December, 1939), 154-161.
Shey, H. J. "Petronius' and Plato's Gorgias," CB 47 (April, 1971), 81-84.
Sochatoff, A. F. "Imagery in the Poems of the Satyricon," CJ 65 (May, 1970), 340-344.
———. "The Satyricon of Petronius: A Book of Satires," in Carnegie Institute of Technology, Dept. of English, Six Satirists. Pittsburgh: The Institute, 1965, pp. 1-15.
Sullivan, J. P. "Interpolations in Petronius," PCPS 22 (1976), 90-122.
———. "Petronius and His Modern Critics," BR 19 (1971), 107-124.
———. Satyricon of Petronius; A Literary Study. Bloomington: Indiana University Press, 1968.
Todd, F. A. "Satiricon," in his Some Ancient Novels. London: Oxford University Press, 1940, pp. 65-101.
Walsh, P. G. The Roman Novel: The Satyricon of Petronius and the Metamorphoses of Apuleius. London: Cambridge University Press, 1970.
Wooten, C. W. "Petronius, the Mime, and Rhetorical Education," Helios (New Series) 3 (1976), 67-74.
Wright, J. "Disintegrated Assurances: The Contemporary American Response to the Satyricon," G & R 23 (April, 1976), 32-39.
Zeitlin, F. I. "Petronius as Paradox: Anarchy and Artistic Integrity," TAPA 102 (1971), 631-684.

PHAEDRUS

General Criticism

Hadas, M. "Satire," in his History of Latin Literature. New York: Columbia University Press, 1952, pp. 278-301.

PINDAR

General Criticism

Barkhuizen, J. H. "Structural Text Analysis and the Problem of Unity in the Odes of Pindar," AClass 19 (1976), 1-19.

Bond, R. W. "Theban Eagle," in his Studia Otiosa; Some Attempts at Criticism. New York: Macmillan, 1938, pp. 133-161.

Borthwick, E. K. "Zoologica Pindarica," CQ (New Series) 26 (1976), 198-205.

Bowra, C. M. Pindar. Oxford: Clarendon, 1964.

Campbell, A. Y. "Pindarica," CR (New Series) 5 (March, 1955), 3-5.

Constantine, D. "Holderlin's Pindar: The Language of Translation," MLR 73 (October, 1978), 825-834.

Downs, R. B. "Theban Eagle: Pindar," in his Famous Books, Ancient and Medieval. New York: Barnes and Noble, 1964, pp. 48-51.

Farnell, L. R. Critical Commentary to the Works of Pindar. Amsterdam: Hakkert, 1967.

Finley, J. H. Pindar and Aeschylus. Cambridge, Mass.: Harvard University Press, 1955.

──────. "Pindar and the Persian Invasion," HSCP 63 (1958), 121-132.

Finley, M. I. "Silver Tongue," NS 69 (April, 9, 1965), 575.

Fogelmark, S. Studies in Pindar with Particular Reference Paean VI and Nemean VII. Lund: Gleerup, 1972.

Freeman, K. "Pindar--The Function and Technique of Poetry," G & R 8 (May, 1939), 144-158.

Grant, M. A. Folktale Motifs in the Odes of Pindar. Lawrence: University of Kansas Press, 1967.

Grimm, R. E. "Pindar and the Beast," CP 57 (January, 1962), 1-9.

Grube, G. M. A. "The Beginnings of Criticism," in his The Greek and Roman Critics. Toronto: University of Toronto Press, 1965, pp. 1-21.

Hamilton, E. "Pindar, the Last Greek Aristocrat," in his Great Age of Greek Literature. New York: Norton, 1942, pp. 85-103.

Hamilton, R. Epinikion: General Form in the Odes of Pindar. The Hague: Mouton, 1974.

Jaegar, W. W. Paideia: The Ideals of Greek Culture. Oxford: B. Blackwell, 1944-47. Vol. 1, pp. 205-222.

Mullen, W. "Pindar and Athens: A Reading in the Aeginetan Odes," Arion (New Series) 1 (1973-1974), 446-495.

Norwood, G. Pindar. Berkeley: University of California Press, 1945.

Parry, H. "Poets and Athletes: Pindar and Some Modern Contrasts," CN & V 15 (April, 1971), 64-70.

Pearson, L. "Catalexis and Anceps in Pindar: A Search for Rhythmical Logic," GRBS 15 (Summer, 1974), 171-191.

Perry, B. E. Babrius and Phaedrus. Cambridge, Mass.: Harvard University Press, 1965, pp. lxxiii-cii.

Rose, H. J. "Pindar and the Tragedians," CR 61 (September, 1947), 43-44.

Simpson, M. "The Chariot and the Bow as Metaphors for Poetry in Pindar's Odes," TAPA 100 (1969), 437-473.

Snell, B. "Pindar's Hymn to Zeus," in his Discovery of the Mind; The Greek Origins of European Thought. Cambridge, Mass.: Harvard University Press, 1953, pp. 71-89.

Stoneman, R. "The 'Theban Eagle,'" CQ (New Series) 26 (1976), 188-1971.

Vivante, P. "On Myth and Action in Pindar," Areth 4 (Fall, 1971), 119-135.

_____. "On Time in Pindar," Areth 5 (Fall, 1972), 107-131.

Individual Works (Odes)

Isthmian

Bundy, E. L. Studia Pindarica, I. Berkeley: University of California Press, 1962.

Bury, J. B. The Isthmian Odes of Pindar. Amsterdam: Hakkert, 1965, pp. xv-xxxviii.

Koehnken, A. "Gods and Descendants of Aiakos in Pindar's Eighth Isthmian Ode," BICS 22 (1975), 25-36.

Lidov, J. B. "The Poems and Performance of Isthmians 3 and 4," CSCA 7 (1974), 175-185.

Slater, W. J. "Two Corrections: Pindar Isthmian 8.70 and Odyssey o469," AJP 98 (Winter, 1977), 348-349.

Willcock, M. M. "On First Reading Pindar: The Fifth Isthmian," G & R 25 (April, 1978), 37-45.

Woodbury, L. "Pindar and the Mercenary Muse: Isthm. 2.1-13," TAPA 99 (1968), 527-542.

Nemean

Bury, J. B. The Nemean Odes of Pindar. Amsterdam: Hakkert, 1965, pp. xi-lxi.

Carey, C. "Pindar's Eighth Nemean Ode," PCPS 22 (1976), 26-42.

Floyd, E. D. "Pindar's Oath to Sogenes (Nemean 7.70-74)," TAPA 96 (1965), 139-152.

Kromer, G. "Homer and Odysseus in Nemean 7,20-27," CW 68 (April-May, 1975), 437-438.

Lee, H. M. "The 'TEPMA' and the Javelin in Pindar, Nemean VII 70-73, and Greek Athletics," J Hel S 96 (1976), 70-79.

Lloyd-Jones, H. "Modern Interpretation of Pindar: The Second Pythian and Seventh Nemean Odes," J Hel S 93 (1973), 109-137.

Pearson, L. "The Dynamics of Pindar's Music: Ninth Nemean and Third Olympian," ICS 2 (1977), 54-69.

Rose, P. W. "The Myth of Pindar's First Nemean: Sportsmen, Poetry, and Paideia," HSCP 78 (1974), 145-175.

Rosenmeyer, T. G. "The Rookie: A Reading of Pindar, Nemean 1," CSCA 2 (1969), 233-246.

Segal, C. "Arrest and Movement: Pindar's Fifth Nemean," Hermes 102 (1974), 397-411.
——. "Pindar's Seventh Nemean," TAPA 98 (1967), 431-480.
Simpson, M. "The Chariot and the Bow as Metaphors for Poetry in Pindar's Odes," TAPA 100 (1969), 437-473.
Stern, J. "The Structure of Pindar's Nemean 5," CP 66 (July, 1971), 169-173.
Young, D. C. "Pindar Nemean 7: Some Preliminary Remarks," TAPA 101 (1970), 633-643.

Olympian

Barrett, W. S. "Pindar's Twelfth Olympian and the Fall of the Deinomenidai," J Hel S 93 (1973), 23-35.
Bundy, E. L. Studia Pindarica, I. Berkeley: University of California Press, 1962.
Carne-Ross, D. S. "Three Preludes for Pindar," Arion (New Series) 2 (1975), 160-193.
——. "Weaving with Points of Gold: Pindar's Sixth Olympian," Arion (New Series) 3 (1976), 5-44.
Demand, N. "Pindar's Olympian 2, Theron's Faith, and Empedocles' Katharmoi," GRBS 16 (Winter, 1975), 347-357.
Farenga, V. "Violent Structure: The Writing of Pindar's Olympian I," Areth 10 (Spring, 1977), 197-218.
Gildersleeve, B. L. Pindar. Olympian and Pythian Odes. Amsterdam: Hakkert, 1965, pp. vii-cxv.
Hamilton, R. "Olympian Five: A Reconsideration," AJP 93 (April, 1972), 324-329.
Kohnken, A. "Pindar as Innovator: Poseidon Hippios and the Relevance of the Pelops Story in Olympian 1," CQ 24 (December, 1974), 199-206.
Kromer, G. "The Value of Time in Pindar's Olympian 10," Hermes 104 (1976), 420-436.
Miller, A. M. "Thalia Erasimolpos: Consolation in Pindar's Fourteenth Olympian," TAPA 107 (1977), 225-234.
Nassen, P. J. "A Literary Study of Pindar's Olympian 10," TAPA 105 (1975), 219-240.
Osmun, C. F. Pindar: Olympian XIV," C World 61 (September, 1967), 6-8.
Ruck, C. A. P. "On the Sacred Names of Iamos and Ion: Ethnobotanical Referents in the Hero's Parentage," CJ 71 (February-March, 1976), 235-252.
Stern, J. "The Myth of Pindar's Olympian 6," AJP 91 (July, 1970), 332-340.
Verdenius, W. J. "Pindar's Seventh Olympian Ode," Mnemosyne 29 (1976), 243-253.
Young, D. C. Three Odes of Pindar. Leiden: Brill, 1968.

Pythian

Barkhuizen, J. H. "A Note on Pindar, Pyth. III, 8-60," AClass 13 (1970), 137-139.

Bowra, C. M. "Pindar, Pythian II," HSCP 48 (1937), 1-28.
Burton, R. W. B. Pindar's Pythian Odes: Essays in Interpretation. London: Oxford University Press, 1962.
Floyd, E. D. "The Premiere of Pindar's Third and Ninth Pythian Odes," TAPA 99 (1968), 181-202.
Gantz, T. N. "Pindar's First Pythian: The Fire Within," Ramus 3 (1974), 143-151.
──────. "Pindar's Second Pythian: The Myth of Ixion," Hermes 106 (1978), 14-26.
Gildersleeve, B. L. Pindar: Olympian and Pythian Odes. Amsterdam: Hakkert, 1965, pp. vii-cxv.
Oates, J. F. "Pindar's Second Pythian Ode," AJP 84 (October, 1963), 377-389.
Robbins, E. "Jason and Cheiron: The Myth of Pindar's Fourth Pythian," Phoenix 29 (Autumn, 1975), 205-213.
Woodbury, L. "Apollo's First Love: Pindar, Pyth, 9.26ff," TAPA 103 (1972), 561-573.
──────. "The Epilogue of Pindar's Second Pythian," TAPA 76 (1945), 11-30.
Young, D. C. Three Odes of Pindar. Leiden: Brill, 1968.

PLATO

General Criticism

Acton, H. B. "The Alleged Fascism of Plato," in R. Bambrough, ed., Plato, Popper and Politics: Some Contributions to a Modern Controversy. New York: Barnes and Noble, 1967, pp. 38-48.
Adam, A. M. K. Plato. Folcroft, Pa.: Folcroft, 1974.
──────. Plato: Moral and Political Ideals. Philadelphia: Inky Press Production, 1977.
Adler, M. J. "Plato," in his Poetry and Politics. New York: Duquesne University Press, 1965, pp. 1-18.
Allen, R. E. ed. Studies in Plato's Metaphysics. New York: Humanities, 1965.
Alpern, H. "Plato," in his March of Philosophy. New York: Dial, 1933, pp. 17-42.
Anderson, F. H. "Notes on Plato's Aesthetic," PR 48 (January, 1939), 65-70.
Anderson, G. "Some Notes on Lucian's Navigium," Mnemosyne 30 (1977), 363-368.
Anderson, W. D. "The Importance of Damonian Theory in Plato's Thought," TAPA 86 (1955), 88-102.
Anton, J. P., and G. L. Kukas, ed. Essays in Ancient Greek Philosophy. Albany: State University of New York Press, 1971.
Armstrong, A. H. "Gods in Plato, Plotinus, Epicurus," CQ 32 (July, 1938), 190-196.
Bambrough, R. "The Disunity of Plato's Thought or: What Plato Did Not Say," Philos 47 (1972), 295-307.
──────, ed. New Essays on Plato and Aristotle. New York: Humanities, 1965.

_____, comp. Plato, Popper and Politics: Some Contributions to a Modern Controversy. New York: Barnes and Noble, 1967.
Barrow, R. Plato and Education. Boston: Routledge & K. Paul, 1976.
_____. Plato, Utilitarianism and Education. London: Routledge & K. Paul, 1975.
Berry, W. E. Studies in Greek Word Order Based Upon the Laws of Plato. Chicago: University of Chicago Press, 1932.
Berti, E. "Ancient Greek Dialectic as Expression of Freedom of Thought and Speech, (tr. by P. P. Wiener), JHI 39 (July, 1978), 347-370.
Bigger, C. P. Participation: A Platonic Inquiry. Baton Rouge: Louisiana State University Press, 1968.
Bluck, R. S. "Plato, Pindar and Metempsychosis," AJP 79 (October, 1958), 405-414.
Boas, G. "Fact and Legend in the Biography of Plato," Ph R 57 (September, 1948), 439-457.
Bolton, R. "Plato's Distinction Between Being and Becoming," RM 29 (September, 1975), 66-95.
Bonnard, A. "The Grand Political Design of Plato," in his Greek Civilization: From Euripides to Alexandria, tr. by R. C. Knight. London: Allen and Unwin, 1961, Vol. 3, pp. 75-87.
_____. "Plato: Beauty and Illusion," in his Greek Civilization: From Euripides to Alexandria, tr. by R. C. Knight. London: Allen and Unwin, 1961, Vol. 3, pp. 88-113.
Brennan, J. G. "Whitehead on Plato's Cosmology," JHP 9 (1971), 67-78.
Brickhouse, T. C. "More on the Paradox of the Philosopher's Rule," Person 59 (July, 1978), 304-306.
Brown, M. M. Plato Weaves the Verbal Veil. Locust Valley, N. Y.: Augustin, 1950.
Brown, P. B. "Soviet Studies on Platonism," IPQ 17 (September, 1977), 293-315.
Brumbaugh, R. S. Plato for the Modern Age. New York: Crowell-Collier, 1962.
_____. Plato's Mathematical Imagination; The Mathematical Passages in the Dialogues and Their Interpretations. Bloomington: Indiana University Press, 1954.
Burge, E. L. "The Irony of Socrates," Antichthon 3 (1969), 5-17.
Burkert, W. Lore and Science in Ancient Pythagoreanism, tr. by E. L. Minar, Jr. Cambridge, Mass.: Harvard University Press, 1972, pp. 15-96.
Burnyeat, M. F. "Examples in Epistemology: Socrates, Theaetetus and G. E. Moore," Philos 52 (October, 1977), 381-398.
_____. "Plato on the Grammar of Perceiving," CQ 26 (1976), 29-51.
Carrol, K. M. "Plato for the Uninitiated," G & R 5 (March, 1958), 144-157.
Cavarnos, C. The Classical Theory of Relations: A Study in the Metaphysics of Plato, Aristotle, and Thomism. Belmont, Mass.: Institute for Byzantine and Modern Greek Studies, 1975.
_____. Plato's Theory of Fine Art. Athens: Astir, 1973.

Plato : 169

──────. Plato's View of Man: Two Bowen Prize Essays Dealing with the Problem of the Destiny of Man and the Individual Life, Together with Selected Passages from Plato's Dialogues on Man and the Human Soul. Belmont, Mass.: Institute for Byzantine and Modern Greek Studies, 1975.
Chance, R. J. F. Until Philosophers Are King; A Study of the Political Theory of Plato and Aristotle in Relation to the Modern State. Port Washington, N. Y.: Kennikat, 1968.
Cherniss, H. "Sources of Evil According to Plato," TAPA 98 (1954), 23-38.
Clark, A. C. The Descent of Manuscripts. Oxford: Clarendon, 1970.
Clay, D. "Platonic Studies and the Study of Plato," Arion (New Series) 2 (1975), 116-132.
Clegg, J. S. "Plato's Vision of Chaos," CQ 26 (1976), 52-61.
──────. The Structure of Plato's Philosophy. Lewisburg, Pa.: Bucknell University Press, 1977.
Coggin, P. A. "Plato," in his Uses of Drama. New York: Braziller, 1956, pp. 6-15.
Collingwood, B. G. "Plato's Philosophy of Art," in his Essays in the Philosophy of Art. Bloomington: Indiana University Press, 1964, pp. 155-183.
Cornford, F. M. Before and After Socrates. Cambridge: Cambridge University Press, 1960.
Coulter, J. A. The Literary Microcosm: Theories in Interpretation of the Later Neoplatonists. Leiden: Brill, 1976.
Crombie, I. M. An Examination of Plato's Doctrines. New York: Humanities, 1962-63, 2 Vols.
Crossnian, R. H. S. Plato Today. 2nd edition. London: Allen and Unwin, 1963.
Cunningham, F. J. "Plato: Archaic or Modern Man?" Thought 50 (December, 1975), 400-417.
Cushman, R. E. Therapeia: Plato's Conception of Philosophy. Westport, Conn.: Greenwood, 1976.
Daiches, D. "Platonic Dilemma," in his Critical Approaches to Literature. New York: Prentice-Hall, 1956, pp. 3-22.
Davies, J. C. "Philosopher and the Cave," G & R 24 (April, 1977), 23-28.
Davison, W. T. Mystics and Poets. Folcroft, Pa.: Folcroft, 1977.
Demand, N. "Plato and the Painters," Phoenix 29 (1975), 1-20.
Demos, R. "Plato's Idea of the Good," Ph R 46 (May, 1937), 245-275.
──────. "Plato's Philosophy of Language." JP 61 (October 29, 1964), 595-613.
Dodds, E. R. "Plato, the Irrational Soul, and the Inherited Conglomerate," in his Greeks and the Irrational. Berkeley: University of California Press, 1951, pp. 207-305.
Dorter, K. "Plato's Image of Immortality," Ph Q 26 (October, 1976), 295-304.
Duncan, T. S. "Plato and Poetry," CJ 40 (May, 1945), 481-494.
Eddy, G. S. "Plato and the Platonist," in his Man Discovers God. New York: Harper, 1942, pp. 15-33.

Edelstein, L. "Function of the Myth in Plato's Philosophy," JHI 10 (October, 1949), 463-481.
──────. "Platonic Anonymity," AJP 83 (January, 1962), 1-22.
──────. Plato's Seventh Letter. Leiden: Brill, 1966.
Eisenberg, P. "Sophrosyne, Self, and State: A Partial Defense of Plato," Apeiron 9 (November, 1975), 31-36.
Faris, J. A. Plato's Theory of Forms and Cantor's Theory of Sets: An Inaugural Lecture Delivered Before the Queen's University of Belfast on 28 February 1968. Belfast: Queen's University, 1968.
Feibleman, J. K. Religious Platonism: The Influence on Plato and the Influence of Plato on Religion. Westport, Conn.: Greenwood, 1971.
Field, G. C. The Philosophy of Plato. London: Oxford University Press, 1969.
──────. Plato and His Contemporaries: A Study in Fourth-Century Life and Thought. New York: Haskell House, 1975.
Findlay, J. N. Plato and Platonism: An Introduction. New York: Times Books, 1978.
──────. Plato: The Written and Unwritten Doctrines. New York: Humanitics, 1974.
Foley, V. The Social Physics of Adam Smith. West Lafayette, Ind.: Purdue University Press, 1976.
Foster, M. B. "Plato," in his Masters of Political Thought. Boston: Houghton Mifflin, 1941, Vol. 1, pp. 17-114.
Fox, A. Plato for Pleasure. Folcroft, Pa.: Folcroft, 1977.
Frank, E. "Fundamental Opposition of Plato and Aristotle," AJP 61 (January, 1940), 34-53.
──────. "Fundamental Opposition of Plato and Aristotle," AJP 61 (April, 1940), 166-185.
Freeman, K. "Plato: The Use of Inspiration," G & R 9 (May, 1940), 137-149.
Freis, R., ed. The Progress of Plato's Progress. Agon 3 (1969), Supp., 1-75.
Friedlander, P. Plato, tr. by H. Meyerhoff. 2nd edition. Princeton, N.J.: Princeton University Press, 1973.
Gauss, H. Plato's Conception of Philosophy. New York: Haskell House, 1974.
Geddes, J. An Essay on the Composition and Manner of Writing of the Ancients, Particularly Plato. New York: Garland, 1970.
Golden, L. "Plato's Concept of Mimesis," BJA 15 (Spring, 1975), 118-131.
Golding, N. H. "Plato as City Planner," Areth 8 (1975), 359-371.
Gosling, J. C. B. Plato. London: Routledge and K. Paul, 1973.
Gould, J. The Development of Plato's Ethics. New York: Russell and Russell, 1972.
──────. "Plato and Aristotle," Arion 7 (Autumn, 1968), 426-434.
──────. "Plato's Hostility to Art," Arion 3 (Spring, 1964), 70-91.
Gregory, M. J. "Myth and Transcendence in Plato," Thought 43 (Summer, 1968), 273-296.
Gross, B. The Great Thinkers on Plato. New York: Putnam's, 1968.
Grote, G. Plato and the Other Companions of Sokrates. New York: Franklin, 1974.

Plato : 171

Grube, G. M. A. Plato's Thought. London: Methuen, 1970.
Guerlac, H. "Amicus Plato and Other Friends," JHI 39 (October, 1978), 627-633.
Gulley, N. "Ethical Analysis in Plato's Earlier Dialogues," CQ 2 (1952), 74-82.
_____. "Plato on Poetry," G & R 24 (October, 1977), 154-169.
_____. Plato's Theory of Knowledge. New York: Barnes and Noble, 1973.
_____. "Plato's Theory of Recollection," CQ 4 (1954), 194-213.
Hackforth, R. "Moral Evil and Ignorance in Plato's Ethics," CQ 40 (July, 1946), 118-120.
Hall, R. W. Plato and the Individual. The Hague: Nijhoff, 1963.
Hardie, W. F. R. A Study in Plato. New York: Oxford University Press, 1936.
Hare, R. M. "Platonism in Moral Education: Two Varieties," Monist 58 (October, 1974), 568-580.
Hart, R. L. "Imagination in Plato," IPQ 5 (September, 1965), 436-461.
Haslam, M. W. "A Note on Plato's Unfinished Dialogues," AJP 97 (Winter, 1976), 336-339.
_____. "Plato, Sophron, and the Dramatic Dialogue," BICS 19 (1972), 17-38.
Havelock, E. A. Preface to Plato. Cambridge, Mass.: Harvard University Press, 1963.
Huby, P. M. Plato and Modern Morality. London: Macmillan, 1972.
Inge, W. R. The Platonic Tradition in English Religious Thought. Folcroft, Pa.: Folcroft, 1977.
Irwin, T. Plato's Moral Theory: The Early and Middle Dialogues. Oxford: Clarendon, 1977.
_____. "Recollection and Plato's Moral Theory," RM 27 (June, 1974), 752-772.
Jaeger, W. W. Paideia: The Ideals of Greek Culture. Oxford: B. Blackwell, 1944-47. Vol. 2, pp. 77-431.
James, E. J. F. Plato's Ideas on Art and Education. York: William Sessions Ltd. for the University of York, 1975.
Kaufmann, W. "Philosophy Versus Poetry," in his From Shakespeare to Existentialism: Studies in Poetry, Religion and Philosophy. Boston: Beacon, 1959, pp. 239-256.
Kerferd, G. B. "Plato's Noble Art of Sophistry," CQ 4 (1954), 84-90.
Keuls, E. Plato and Greek Painting. Leiden: Brill, 1978.
_____. "Plato on Painting," AJP 95 (Summer, 1974), 100-127.
Koyre, A. Discovering Plato. New York: Columbia University Press, 1954.
Kraut, R. "Egoism, Love, and Political Office in Plato," Ph R 82 (1973), 330-334.
Kuhn, H. "True Tragedy: On the Relationship Between Greek Tragedy and Plato," HSCP 52 (1941), 1-40; 53 (1942), 37-88.
Lakin, R. D. "Plato: His Defenders and Detractors," AR 22 (Winter, 1962/63), 496-512.
Lange, S. "Plato and Democracy," CJ 34 (May, 1939), 480-486.

Lesze, W. Logic and Metaphysics in Aristotle; Aristotle's Treatment of Types of Equivocity and its Relevance to His Metaphysical Theories.... Padua: Antenore, 1970.
Levinson, R. B. In Defense of Plato. New York: Russell and Russell, 1970.
Lloyd, A. C. "Plato's Description of Division," CQ 2 (1952), 105-112.
Lodge, R. C. "Mind in Platonism," Ph R 35 (1926), 201-220.
———. "Plato and Progress," Ph R 55 (1956), 651-667.
———. "The Platonic Highest Good" (I), Ph R 36 (1927), 428-449; (II), 535-551.
———. Plato's Theory of Art. New York: Russell and Russell, 1975.
———. Plato's Theory of Education, with an Appendix on the Education of Women According to Plato, by Solomon Frank. New York: Russell and Russell, 1970.
———. "Power in Platonism;" Ph R 36 (1927), 22-43.
———. "Private and Public Spirit in Platonism," Ph R 34 (1925), 1-27.
———. "Reality and the Moral Judgment in Plato," (I) Ph R 29 (1920), 355-373; (II), 453-475.
———. "Soul, Body, Wealth in Plato," (I). Ph R 32 (1923), 470-490; (II). 33 (1924), 30-50.
Luce, J. V. "Plato on Truth and Falsity in Names," CQ 19 (November, 1969), 222-232.
Lycos, K. "Aristotle and Plato on 'Appearing,'" Mind 73 (October, 1964), 496-514.
Meijering, E. Orthodoxy and Platonism in Athanasius; Synthesis or Antithesis? Leiden: Brill, 1969.
More, P. E. Platonism. New York: AMS, 1969.
Mueller, G. E. Plato, the Founder of Philosophy as Dialectic. New York: Philosophical Library, 1965.
———. "Platonism: Philosophy of Tragic Muse," in his Philosophy of Literature. New York: Philosophical Library, 1948, pp. 23-46.
Mulhern, J. J. "Professor Wedberg's Theory of Ideas: Suggestions for Modification," Apeiron 9 (January, 1975), 25-29.
Murdoch, I. The Fire and the Sun: Why Plato Banished the Artists. Oxford: Clarendon, 1977.
Murley, C. "Techniques of Modern Fiction in Plato," CJ 50 (March, 1955), 281-287.
Murray, M. "The Crisis of Greek Poetics: A Re-interpretation," JVI 7 (1973), 173-187.
Nehamas, A. "Confusing Universals and Particulars in Plato's Early Dialogues," RM 29 (1975), 287-306.
Neumann, H. "On the Comedy of Plato's Aristophanes," AJP 87 (October, 1966), 420-426.
North, H. F., ed. Interpretations of Plato: A Swarthmore Symposium. Leiden: Brill, 1977.
Notopoulos, J. A. "Plato's Epitaph," AJP 63 (July, 1942), 272-293.
Novak, D. Suicide and Morality: The Theories of Plato, Aquinas, and Kant and their Relevance for Suicidology. New York: Scholars Studies, 1974.

Oates, W. J. Plato's View of Art. New York: Scribner's 1972.
Ogilvie, J. The Theology of Plato. New York: Olms, 1975.
Okin, S. M. "Philosopher Queens and Private Wives: Plato on Women and the Family," P & PA 6 (Summer, 1977), 345-369.
Oliver, R. P. "Plato and Salutati," TAPA 71 (1940), 315-334.
Olshewsky, T. M. "On the Relations of Soul to Body in Plato and Aristotle," JHP 14 (1976), 391-404.
Partee, M. H. "Inspiration in the Aesthetics of Plato." JAAC 30 (1971), 87-95.
Pater, W. H. Plato and Platonism; A Series of Lectures. New York: Johnson Reprint, 1973.
Patterson, C. H. Plato's Euthyphro, Apology, Crito and Phaedo: Notes. Lincoln, Neb.: Cliffs Notes, 1975.
Patterson, R. L. Plato on Immortality. University Park: Pennsylvania State University, 1965.
Philip, J. A. "The Platonic Corpus," Phoenix 24 (1970), 296-308.
_____. Platonic Diairesis," TAPA 97 (1966), 335-358.
Plass, P. "Philosophical Anonymity and Irony in the Platonic Dialogues," AJP 85 (July, 1964), 254-278.
_____. Plato's Symbolism. Ann Arbor, Mich.: University Microfilms, 1959.
_____. "'Play' and Philosophic Detachment in Plato," TAPA 98 (1967), 343-364.
Quimby, R. W. "The Growth of Plato's Perception of Rhetoric," P & R 7 (1974), 71-79.
Randall, J. H. Plato, Dramatist of the Life of Reason. New York: Columbia University Press, 1970.
_____. "Plato's Treatment of the Theme of the Good Life and His Criticism of the Spartan Ideal," JHI 28 (July, 1967), 307-324.
Raphael, D. D. "The Philosopher as Dramatist--Plato and the Greek Drama," in his The Paradox of Tragedy. Bloomington: Indiana University Press, 1960, pp. 71-89.
Rau, C. Art and Society; A Reinterpretation of Plato. New York: Smith, 1951.
Raven, J. E. Plato's Thought in the Making; A Study of the Development of His Metaphysics. Cambridge: Cambridge University Press, 1965.
Reich, E. Plato as an Introduction to Modern Criticism of Life. Port Washington, N. Y.: Kennikat, 1969.
Reinhold, M. A Simplified Approach to Plato and Aristotle. Great Neck, N. Y.: Barron, 1964.
Rexine, E. Religion in Plato and Cicero. New York: Greenwood, 1959.
Ries, F. W. D. "Plato on the Dance," DS 11 (Spring, 1977), 53-60.
Riginos, A. S. Platonica: The Anecdotes Concerning the Life and Writings of Plato. Leiden: Brill, 1977.
Rist, J. M. Eros and Psyche; Studies in Plato, Plotinus and Origen. Toronto: University of Toronto Press, 1964.
_____. "Plato's Earlier Theory of Forms?" Phoenix 29 (1975), 336-357.
Robinson, R. "Plato's Consciousness of Fallacy," Mind 51 (April, 1942), 97-114.
_____. Plato's Earlier Dialectic. 2nd edition. Oxford: Clarendon, 1953.

Robinson, T. M. Plato's Psychology. Toronto: University of Toronto Press, 1970.
Rogers, A. K. The Socratic Problem. New York: Russell and Russell, 1971.
Rosenmeyer, T. G. Plato and Mass Words," TAPA 88 (1957), 88-102.
Ross, W. D. Plato's Theory of Ideas. Westport, Conn.: Greenwood, 1976.
Rucker, D. "Plato and the Poets," JAAC 25 (1966), 167-170.
Runciman, W. Plato's Later Epistemology. Cambridge: Cambridge University Press, 1962.
Rutenber, C. C. Doctrine of the Imitation of God in Plato. New York: King's Crown, 1946.
Ryan, G. J. "Plato's Ideas in the Light of Early Scholasticism," TAPA 68 (1937), 334-342.
Ryle, G. "Letters and Syllables in Plato," Ph R 69 (October, 1960), 431-451.
──────. Plato's Progress. Cambridge: Cambridge University Press, 1966.
Sahakian, W. S. Plato. Boston: Twayne, 1977.
Sallis, J. Being and Logos: The Way of Platonic Dialogue. Pittsburgh: Duquesne University Press, 1975.
Santas, G. X. Socrates: Philosophy in Plato's Early Dialogues. Boston: Routledge and K. Paul, 1979.
──────. "The Socratic Fallacy," JHP 10 (1972), 127-141.
Saunders, T. J. "Plato's Clockwork Orange," JDU 68 (June, 1976), 113-117.
Sayre, K. M. Plato's Analytic Method. Chicago: University of Chicago Press, 1969.
Schipper, E. W. Forms in Plato's Later Dialogues. The Hague: Nijhoff, 1965.
──────. "Motives and Virtues in the Platonic Ethics," Ratio 13 (1971), 67-75.
Schleiermacher, F. E. D. Schleiermacher's Introductions to the Dialogues of Plato, tr. by W. Dobson. New York: Arno, 1973.
Schuré, E. The Mysteries of Ancient Greece: Orpheus/Plato. Blauvelt, N. Y.: Rudolf Steiner, 1971.
Seligman, P. Being and Not-being: An Introduction to Plato's Sophist. The Hague: Nijhoff, 1974.
Sellars, W. "On Knowing the Better and Doing the Worse," IPQ 10 (1970), 5-19.
Shiner, R. A., and J. King-Farlow. New Essays on Plato and the Pre-Socratics. Guelph: Canadian Association for Publishing in Philosophy, 1976.
Shorey, P. The Unity of Plato's Thought. Hamden, Conn.: Archon, 1968.
Sinaiko, H. L. Love, Knowledge and Discourse in Plato. Chicago: University of Chicago Press, 1965.
Sinnige, T. G. Matter and Infinity in the Presocratic Schools and Plato. Assen: Van Gorcum, 1971.
Skemp, J. B. Plato. Oxford: Clarendon, 1976.
──────. The Theory of Motion in Plato's Later Dialogues. Amsterdam: Hakkert, 1967.

Smith, R. "Mass Terms, Generic Expressions and Plato's Theory of Forms," JHP 16 (April, 1978), 141-153.
Solmsen, F. Plato's Theology. New York: Johnson Reprint, 1967.
Sprague, R. K. Plato's Philosopher-King: A Study of the Theoretical Background. Columbia: University of South Carolina Press, 1976.
―――. Plato's Use of Fallacy. New York: Barnes and Noble, 1962.
Sternfeld, R., and H. Zyskind. Plato's Meno: A Philosophy of Man as Acquisitive. Carbondale: Southern Illinois University Press, 1978.
Stevens, E. B. "Envy and Pity in Greek Philosophy," AJP 69 (April, 1958), 171-189.
Stewart, J. A. Plato's Doctrine of Ideas. Folcroft, Pa.: Folcroft, 1977.
Stormer, G. D. "Plato's Theory of Myth," Person 55 (Summer, 1974), 216-223.
Stroh, G. W. Plato and Aristotle. San Francisco: Boyd and Fraser, 1970, pp. 11-25.
Sweeney, L. "Henry Jackson's Interpretation of Plato," JHP 13 (April, 1975), 189-204.
Swift Riginos, A. Platonica: The Anecdotes Concerning the Life and Writings of Plato. Leiden: Brill, 1976.
Tarrant, D. "Colloquialisms, Semi-proverbs, and Word-play in Plato," CQ 40 (July, 1946), 109-117.
―――. "Plato as Dramatist," J Hel S 75 (1955), 82-89.
―――. "Plato's Use of Extended Oratio Obliqua," CQ (New Series) 5 (1955), 222-224.
―――. "Plato's Use of Quotations and Other Illustrative Material," CQ (New Series) 1 (1951), 59-67.
―――. "Style and Thought in Plato's Dialogues," CQ 42 (January, 1948), 28-34.
Taylor, A. E. Plato. Freeport, N.Y.: Books for Libraries, 1971.
―――. Plato, the Man and His Work. London: Methuen, 1937.
Teloh, H. "Self-Predication or Anaxagorean Causation in Plato," Apeiron 9 (February, 1975), 15-23.
Thayer, H. S. Plato on the Morality of Imagination," RM 30 (June, 1977), 594-618.
―――. Plato's Quarrel with Poetry: Simonides," JHI 36 (1975), 3-26.
Thesleff, H. Studies in the Styles of Plato. Helsinki: Suomalaisen Kirjallisunden Kirjapaino, 1967.
Thorson, T. I., ed. Plato: Totalitarian or Democrat? Englewood Cliffs, N.J.: Prentice-Hall, 1963.
Tigerstedt, E. N. The Decline and Fall of the Neoplatonic Interpretation of Plato: An Outline and Some Observations. Helsinki: Societas Scientarium Fennica, 1974.
―――. Interpreting Plato. Stockholm: Almqvist and Wiksell, 1977.
Tigner, S. S. "Plato's Philosophical Uses of the Dream Metaphor," AJP 91 (April, 1970), 204-212.
Tovar, A. An Introduction to Plato. Chicago: Argonaut, 1969.

Tracy, H. L. "Plato as Satirist," CJ 33 (December, 1937), 153-162.
———. Physiological Theory and the Doctrine of the Mean in Plato and Aristotle. Chicago: Loyola University, 1969, pp. 1-156.
Vass, D. H. Plato's Philosophy of Education. Chicago: University of Chicago Press, 1929.
Verdenius, W. J. Mimesis; Plato's Doctrine of Artistic Imitation and Its Meaning to Us. Leiden: Brill, 1972.
Vlastos, G. Plato: A Collection of Critical Essays. New York: Anchor, 1971.
———. Platonic Studies. Princeton, N. J.: Princeton University 1973.
———. Plato's Universe. Seattle: University of Washington Press, 1975.
———. "Slavery in Plato's Thought," Ph R 50 (May, 1941), 289-304.
Vries, G. J. de. Miscellaneous Notes on Plato. Amsterdam: North-Holland, 1975.
Wa Said, D. Theosophies of Plato, Aristotle and Plotinus. New York: Philosophical Library, 1970.
Warry, J. G. Greek Aesthetic Theory; A Study of Callistic and Aesthetic Concepts in the Works of Plato and Aristotle. New York: Barnes and Noble, 1962.
Weber, P. L. "What Plato Said About War," Person 22 (October, 1941), 376-383.
Weingartner, R. H. The Unity of the Platonic Dialogue: The Cratylus, the Protagoras, the Parmenides. Indianapolis: Bobbs-Merrill, 1973.
Werkmeister, W. H., ed. Facets of Plato's Philosophy. Assen: Van Gorcum, 1976.
White, F. C. "Plato's Middle Dialogues and the Independence of Particulars," Ph Q 27 (July, 1977), 193-213.
White, N. P. Plato on Knowledge and Reality. Indianapolis: Hackett, 1976.
Whittaker, J. God Time Being; Studies in the Transcendental Tradition in Greek Philosophy. Bergen: University of Bergen, 1970.
Wild, J. D. Plato's Modern Enemies and the Theory of Natural Law. Chicago: University of Chicago Press, 1953.
———. Plato's Theory of Men; An Introduction to the Realistic Philosophy of Culture. New York: Octagon, 1974.
Wilkinson, L. P. "Classical Approaches--IV: Homosexuality," Encounter 51 (September, 1978), 20-31.
———. Golden Latin Artistry. Cambridge: Cambridge University Press, 1963.
Wimsatt, W. K., and C. Brooks. "Verbal Medium: Plato and Aristotle," in their Literary Criticism. New York: Knopf, 1957, pp. 57-76.
Winspear, A. D. The Genesis of Plato's Thought. Montreal: Harvest House, 1974.
Wolfson, H. A. "Knowability and Describability of God in Plato and Aristotle," HSCP 56/57 (1947), 233-249.
Wood, E. M. Class Ideology and Ancient Political Theory: Socrates, Plato, and Aristotle in Social Context. Oxford: Blackwell, 1978.

Woodbridge, F. J. E. The Son of Apollo; Themes of Plato. New York: Biblo and Tannen, 1971.
Zakopoulous, A. N. Plato on Man: A Summary and Critique of His Psychology with Special Reference to the Pre-Platonic, Freudian, Behavioristic and Humanistic Psychology. New York: Philosophical Library, 1975.

Individual Works

Apology

Anderson, A. "Was Socrates Unwise to Take the Hemlock?" HTR 65 (1972), 437-452.
Brenk, F. E. "Interesting Bedfellows at the End of the Apology," CB 51 (January, 1975), 44-46.
Calder, W. M., III. "Plato's Apology of Socrates: A Speech for the Defense," BUJ 20 (1972), 42-47.
Guardini, R. The Death of Socrates; An Interpretation of the Platonic Dialogues: Euthyphro, Apology, Crito and Phaedo. Cleveland: World, 1948.
Hathaway, R. F. "Law and the Moral Paradox in Plato's Apology," JHP 8 (1970), 127-142.
Mulgan, R. G. "Socrates and Authority," G & R 19 (1972), 208-212.

Charmides

Schofield, M. "Socrates on Conversing with Doctors," CR 23 (1973), 121-123.
Tuckey, T. G. Plato's Charmides. Amsterdam: Hakkert, 1969.

Cratylus

Anagnostopoulos, G. "Significance of Plato's Cratylus," RM 27 (December, 1973), 318-345.
Gosling, J. C. B. Plato. London: Routledge and K. Paul, 1973.
Kirk, G. S. "Problem of Cratylus," AJP 72 (July, 1951), 225-253.
Kretzmann, N. "Plato on the Correctness of Names," APQ 8 (1971), 126-138.
Levison, R. B. "Language and the Cratylus: Four Questions," RM 11 (1957-58), 28-41.
Lorenz, K., and J. Mittelstrass. "On Rational Philosophy of Language: The Programme in Plato's Cratylus Reconsidered," Mind 76 (January, 1967), 1-20.
Luce, J. V. "Plato on Truth and Falsity in Names," CQ (New Series) 19 (November, 1969), 222-232.
_____. "The Theory of Ideas in the Cratylus," Phronesis 10 (1965), 21-36.
Reed, N. H. "Plato on Flux, Perception, and Language," PCPS 18 (1972), 65-77.

Robinson, R. "Criticism of Plato's Cratylus," Ph R 65 (July, 1956), 324-341.
Slings, S. R. "Plato: Cratylus 417 C," Mnemosyne 29 (1976), 42-51.
Sprague, R. K. "Empedocles, Hera, and Cratylus 404 C," CR 22 (1972), 169.
Weingartner, R. H. The Unity of the Platonic Dialogue: The Cratylus, the Protagorus, the Parmenides. New York: Bobbs-Merrill, 1973.

Crito

Allen, R. E. "Law and Justice in Plato's Crito," JP 69 (1972), 557-567.
Anderson, A. "Was Socrates Unwise to Take the Hemlock?" HTR 65 (1972), 437-452.
Dybikowski, J. "Socrates, Obedience, and the Law: Plato's Crito," Dialogue 13 (1974), 519-535.
Gomme, A. W. "The Structure of Plato's Crito," G & R (New Series) 5 (March, 1958), 45-51.
Guardini, R. The Death of Socrates; An Interpretation of the Platonic Dialogues: Euthyphro, Apology, Crito, and Phaedo. Cleveland: World, 1948.

Epinomis (of doubtful authorship)

Tarán, L. Academica--Plato, Philip of Opus, and the Pseudo-Platonic Epinomis. Philadelphia: American Philosophical Society, 1975.
Taylor, A. E. Plato and the Authorship of "Epinomis." New York: Haskell House, 1975.

Euthyphro

Allen, R. E. Plato's Euthyphro and the Earlier Theory of Forms. London: Routledge and K. Paul, 1970.
Cohen, S. M. "Socrates on the Definition of Piety: Euthyphro 10A-11B," JHP 9 (1971), 1-13.
Guardini, R. The Death of Socrates; An Interpretation of the Platonic Dialogues: Euthyphro, Apology, Crito, and Phaedo. Cleveland: World, 1948.
Hoopes, J. P. "Euthyphro's Case," CB 47 (November, 1970), 1-6.
Lesher, J. H. "Theistic Ethics in the Euthyphro," Apeiron 9 (February, 1975), 24-30.
Moutafakis, N. J. "Plato's Emergence in the Euthyphro," Apeiron 5 (1971), 23-31.
Panagiotou, S. "Plato's Euthyphro and the Attic Code on Homicide," Hermes 102 (1974), 419-437.
Rosen, F. "Piety and Justice: Plato's Euthyphro," Philos 43 (April, 1968), 105-116.

[Various Authors.] "Three Studies on Plato," RM 22 (March, 1969), 433-498.

Euthydemus

Sprague, R. K. Plato's Use of Fallacy. New York: Barnes and Noble, 1962.

Gorgias

Duncan, R. "Philia in the Gorgias," Apeiron 8 (January, 1974), 23-25.
Hall, R. W. "Techne and Morality in the Gorgias," in J. P. Anton and G. L. Kustas, eds., Essays in Ancient Greek Philosophy. Albany: State University of New York Press, 1971, pp. 202-218.
Jaeger, W. W. "Gorgias: The Educator as Statesman," in his Paideia: The Ideals of Greek Culture. Oxford: B. Blackwell, 1944-47. Vol. 2, pp. 126-159.
Kerferd, G. B. "Plato's Treatment of Callicles in the Gorgias," PCPS 20 (1974), 48-52.
Kitto, H. D. F. "Pindar and Plato," in his Poiesis: Structure and Thought. Berkeley: University of California Press, 1966, pp. 243-252.
Linforth, I. M. Soul and Sieve in Plato's Gorgias. Berkeley: University of California Press, 1944.
Spitzer, A. "The Self-Reference of the Gorgias," P & R 8 (1975), 1-22.
Voegelin, E. "Philosophy of Existence: Plato's Gorgias," RP 11 (October, 1949), 477-498.

Hippias Major

Hoerber, R. G. "Plato's Hippias Major," CJ 50 (January, 1955), 183-186.

Ion

Dorter, K. "The Ion: Plato's Characterization of Art," JAAC 32 (1973), 65-78.
Duncan, T. S. "Plato and Poetry," CJ 40 (May, 1945), 481-494.
Moore, J. D. "The Dating of Plato's Ion," GRBS 15 (Winter, 1974), 421-439.
_____. "Limitation and Design in Plato's Ion," PCP 8 (1973), 45-51.
Partee, M. H. "Plato on the Criticism of Poetry," PQ 52 (1973), 629-642.

Laches

Devereux, D. T. "Courage and Wisdom in Plato's Laches," JHP 15 (April, 1977), 129-141.
Hoerber, R. G. "Plato's Laches," CP 63 (April, 1968), 95-105.
Kohak, E. V. "The Road to Wisdom; Lessons on Education from Plato's Laches," CJ 56 (December, 1960), 123-132.
O'Brien, M. J. "The Unity of the Laches," YCS 18 (1963), 131-147.
Umphrey, S. "On the Theme of Plato's Laches," Interpretation 6 (Fall, 1976), 1-10.
───. "Plato's Laches on Courage," Apeiron 19 (February, 1976), 4-22.
[Various Authors.] "Three Studies on Plato," RM 22 (March, 1969), 433-498.

Laws

Caskey, E. G. "Again: Plato's Seventh Letter," CP 69 (1974), 220-227.
Davis, M. "On the Imputed Possibilities of Callipolis and Magnesia," AJP 85 (October, 1964), 394-411.
Hammond, N. G. L. "The Exegetai in Plato's Laws," CQ (New Series) 2 (1952), 4-12.
Jaeger, W. W. "Plato's Laws," in his Paideia: The Ideals of Greek Culture. Oxford: B. Blackwell, 1944-47. Vol. 3, pp. 213-262.
Mohr, R. "Plato's Final Thoughts on Evil: Laws X, 899-905," Mind 87 (October, 1978), 572-575.
Morrow, G. R. "On the Tribal Courts in Plato's Laws," AJP 62 (July, 1941), 314-321.
───. Plato and the Rule of Law," in Plato, Popper and Politics: Some Contributions to a Modern Controversy. New York: Barnes and Noble, 1967, pp. 49-70.
───. Plato's Cretan City: A Historical Interpretation of the Laws. Princeton, N. J.: Princeton University Press, 1960.
───. Plato's Law of Slavery in Its Relation to Greek Law. New York: Arno, 1976.
O'Brien, M. "Plato and the 'Good Conscience': Laws 863E5-864B7," TAPA 88 (1957), 81-87.
Okin, S. M. "Philosopher Queens and Private Wives: Plato on Women and the Family," P & PA 6 (Summer, 1977), 345-369.
Partee, M. H. "Plato's Banishment of Poetry," JAAC 28 (1970), 209-222.
Ries, F. W. D. "Plato on the Dance," DS 11 (Spring, 1977), 53-60.
Saunders, T. J. "The Alleged Double Version in the Sixth Book of Plato's Laws," CP 64 (November, 1970), 230-236.
───. Bibliography on Plato's Laws, 1920-1970. New York: Arno, 1976.
───. Notes on the Laws of Plato. London: University of Classical Studies, 1972.

_____. "Notes on Plato as a City Planner," BICS 23 (1976), 23-26.
_____. "The Penguinification of Plato," G & R 22 (1975), 19-28.
_____. "Penology and Eschatology in Plato's Timaeus and Laws," CQ 23 (1973), 232-244.
_____. "Plato on Killing in Anger: A Reply to Professor Woozley," Ph Q 23 (1973), 350-356.
_____. "Plato's Clockwork Orange," JDU 68 (June, 1976), 113-117.
Strauss, L. The Argument and the Action of Plato's Laws. Chicago: University of Chicago Press, 1975.
Verdenius, W. J. Mimesis; Plato's Doctrine of Artistic Imitation and Its Meaning to Us. Leiden: Brill, 1972.
Woozley, A. D. "Plato on Killing in Anger," PQ 22 (1972), 303-317.

Letters (some of doubtful authorship)

Bluck, R. S. "Notes on Plato's Seventh Letter," CR 60 (April, 1946), 7-8.
Bowra, C. M. "Plato's Epigram on Dion's Death," AJP 59 (October, 1938), 394-404.
Caskey, E. G. "Again: Plato's Seventh Letter," CP 69 (1974), 220-227.
Edelstein, L. Plato's Seventh Letter. Leiden: Brill, 1966.
Mahood, G. H. "Interpersonal Values in the Teaching of Philosophy," PE & W 27 (January, 1977), 23-33.
Von Fretz, K. "The Philosophical Passage in the Seventh Platonic Letter and the Problem of Plato's 'Esoteric' Philosophy," in J. P. Anton and G. L. Kustas, eds., Essays in Ancient Greek Philosophy. Albany: State University of New York Press, 1971, pp. 408-447.

Lysis

Annas, J. "Plato and Aristotle on Friendship and Altruism," Mind 86 (October, 1977), 532-554.
Hoerber, R. G. "Character Portrayal in Plato's Lysis," CJ 41 (March, 1946), 271-273.
Levin, D. N. "Some Observations Concerning Plato's Lysis," in J. P. Anton and G. L. Kustas, eds., Essays in Ancient Greek Philosophy. Albany: State University of New York Press, 1961, pp. 236-258.

Menexenus

Henderson, N. M. "Plato's Menexenus and the Distortion of History," AClass 18 (1975), 25-46.
Kahn, C. H. "Plato's Funeral Oration: The Motive of the Menexenus," CP 58 (October, 1963), 220-234.
Stern, H. S. "Plato's Funeral Oration," The New Scholasticism 48 (1974), 503-508.

Meno

Allen, R. E. "Anamnesis in Plato's Meno and Phaedo," RM 13 (September, 1959), 165-174.
Bluck, R. S., ed. Meno. Edited with introduction and Commentary. Cambridge: Cambridge University Press, 1961.
Cahn, S. M. "A Puzzle Concerning the Meno and the Protagoras," JHP 11 (1973), 535-537.
Calvert, B. "Meno's Paradox Reconsidered," JHP 12 (1974), 143-152.
Ebert, T. "Plato's Theory of Recollection Reconsidered: An Interpretation of Meno 80a-86c," M & Wo 6 (1973), 163-181.
Eckstein, J. The Platonic Method; An Interpretation of the Dramatic --Philosophic Aspects of the Meno. New York: Greenwood, 1968.
Goff, R. "The Language of Self-Transformation in Plato and Augustine," M & Wo 4 (1971), 413-35.
Grimm, L. Definition in Plato's Meno. Oslo: Oslo University Press, 1962.
Hartman, M. "Plato's Philosophy of Education in the Meno," Person 57 (Spring, 1976), 126-131.
Jaeger, W. W. "Meno: The New Knowledge," in his Paideia: The Ideals of Greek Culture. Oxford: B. Blackwell, 1944-47. Vol. 2, pp. 160-173.
Klein, J. A Commentary on Plato's Meno. Chapel Hill: University of North Carolina Press, 1965.
Powers, L. H. "Knowledge by Deduction," PR 87 (July, 1978), 337-371.
Rose, L. E. "Plato's Meno, 86-89," JHP 8 (1970), 1-8.
Simon, H. A. "Polanyi on the Meno Paradox," PC 43 (March, 1976), 147-150.
Sternfeld, R., and H. Zyskind. Plato's Meno: A Philosophy of Man as Acquisitive. Carbondale: Southern Illinois University Press, 1978.

Parmenides

Allen, R. E. "Generation of Numbers in Plato's Parmenides," CP 65 (January, 1970), 30-34.
_____. "Unity and Infinity: Parmenides 142b-145a," RM 27 (June, 1974), 697-725.
Barford, R. "Context of the Third Man Argument in Plato's Parmenides," JHP 16 (January, 1978), 1-11.
Beck, M. "Plato's Problem in the Parmenides: Ideas Are Beyond Quantitative Category," JHI 9 (April, 1947), 232-236.
Block, I. "Plato, Parmenides, Ryle and Exemplification," Mind 73 (July, 1964), 417-422.
Bondeson, W. "Non-Being and the One: Same Connections Between Plato's Sophist and Parmenides," Apeiron 7 (February, 1973), 13-22.
Chen, C. "On the Parmenides of Plato," CQ 38 (July, 1944), 101-114.

Cohen, S. M. "The Logic of the Third Man," PR 80 (1971), 448-475.
Cresswell, M. J. "Is There One or Are There Many One and Many Problems in Plato?" Ph Q 22 (April, 1972), 149-154.
Faj, A. "Platonic Anticipation of Stoic Logic, II," Apeiron 6 (January, 1972), 1-24.
Forrester, J. W. "Plato's Parmenides: The Structure of the First Hypothesis," JHP 10 (1972), 1-14.
Gomperz, H. "Plato's Parmenides," Person 22 (July, 1941), 257-262.
Kaiser, N. "Plato on Knowledge," Apeiron 6 (February, 1972), 36-43.
Knight, T. S. Beyond Parmenides: The Problem of Nonbeing. Ann Arbor, Mich.: University Microfilms, 1956.
Lynch, W. F. Approach to the Metaphysics of Plato Through Parmenides. Washington, D. C.: Georgetown University Press, 1959.
Mourelatos, A. P. D. The Route of Parmenides: A Study of Word, Image, and Argument in the 'Fragments.' London: Yale University Press, 1970.
Mulhern, J. J. "Plato, Parmenides 130d 3-4," Apeiron 5 (1971), 17-22.
Murphy, N. R. "Plato, Parmenides 129 and Republic 475-480," CQ 31 (April, 1937), 71-78.
Panagiotou, S. "A Note on the Translation and Interpretation of Plato Parmenides 132a 1-4," CP 69 (1974), 50-55.
──────. "Relations and Infinite Regress in Plato," Dialogue 13 (1974), 537-542.
Parain, B. A Metaphysics of Language, tr. by M. Mayer. New York: Anchor, 1971.
Peck, A. L. "Plato Versus Parmenides," Ph R 71 (April, 1962), 159-184.
──────. "Plato's Parmenides: Some Suggestions for Its Interpretation," CQ (New Series) 3 (1953), 126-150.
──────. "Plato's Parmenides: Some Suggestions for Its Interpretation II," CQ (New Series) 4 (1954), 31-45.
Peterson, S. "Reasonable Self-Prediction Premise for the Third Man Argument," Ph R 82 (October, 1973), 451-470.
Rist, J. M. "The Neoplatonic One and Plato's Parmenides," TAPA 93 (1962), 389-401.
──────. "Parmenides and Plato's Parmenides," CQ (New Series) 20 (November, 1970), 221-229.
Robinson, R. "Plato's Parmenides," CP 37 (January, 1942), 159-186.
Rochol, H. "The Dialogue Parmenides: An Insoluble Enigma in Platonism?" IPQ 11 (1971), 496-520.
Runciman, W. G. "Plato's Parmenides," HSCP 64 (1959), 89-120.
Ryle, G. "Plato's Parmenides," Mind 48 (April, 1939), 129-151; 48 (July, 1939), 302-325.
Schofield, M. "Antinomies of Plato's Parmenides," CQ 27 (1977), 139-158.
──────. "The Dissection of Unity In Plato's Parmenides," CP 67 (1972), 102-109.

―――――. "A Neglected Regress Argument in the Parmenides," CQ 23 (1973), 29-44.
―――――. "Plato on Unity and Sameness," CQ 24 (1974), 33-45.
Scoon, R. "Parmenides," Mind 51 (April, 1942), 115-133.
Shiner, R. A. "Self-Predication and the Third Man Argument," JHP 8 (1970), 371-386.
Solmsen, F. "Parmenides and the Description of Perfect Beauty in Plato's Symposium," AJP 92 (1971), 62-70.
Stanley, P. "Fantasy on a Theme by Plato," JP 46 (September 29, 1949), 644-651.
Steenburgh, E. W. van. "On Spiking the Imitation Regress," Apeiron 8 (January, 1974), 27-30.
Taylor, A. E. "Parmenides, Zeno, and Socrates," in his Philosophical Studies. New York: Macmillan, 1934, pp. 28-90.
Teloh, H. "Parmenides and Plato's Parmenides 131a-132c," JHP 14 (1976), 125-130.
Vlastos, G. "Third Man Argument in the Parmenides," Ph R 63 (July, 1954), 319-349.
―――――. "Plato's Testimony Concerning Zeno of Elea," J Hel S 95 (1975), 136-162.
Walker, M. G. "One and Many in Plato's Parmenides," Ph R 47 (September, 1938), 488-516.
Weingartner, R. H. The Unity of the Platonic Dialogue: The Cratylus, the Protagoras, the Parmenides. Indianapolis: Bobbs-Merrill, 1973.
Wyller, E. A. "Plato's Parmenides: Another Interpretation," RM 15 (June, 1962), 621-640.

Phaedo

Allen, R. E. "Anamnesis in Plato's Meno and Phaedo," RM 13 (September, 1959), 165-174.
Anderson, G. "Some Notes on Lucian's Navigium," Mnemosyne 30 (1977), 363-368.
Anton, J. P. "The Ultimate Theme of the Phaedo," Areth 1 (1968), 94-99.
Baron, J. R. "On Separating the Socratic from the Platonic in Phaedo 118," CP 70 (1975), 268-269.
Castañeda, H. N. "Plato's Phaedo: Theory of Relations," JP 68 (1971), 617-618.
Cohen, M. "Dying as Supreme Opportunity; A Comparison of Plato's Phaedo and The Tibetan Book of the Dead," PE & W 26 (July, 1976), 317-327.
Cresswell, M. J. "Plato's Theory of Causality: Phaedo 95-106," Australasian Journal of Philosophy 49 (December, 1971), 244-249.
Dorter, K. "Plato's Image of Immortality," Ph Q 26 (1976), 295-304.
―――――. "Reciprocity Argument and the Structure of Plato's Phaedo," JHP 15 (January, 1977), 1-11.
Ferguson, J. "Plato and Phaedo," Mus Afr 1 (1972), 9-17.
Frey, R. G. "Did Socrates Commit Suicide?" Philos 53 (January, 1978), 106-108.

Gill, C. "The Death of Socrates," CQ 23 (1973), 25-28.
―――――. "The Death of Socrates," PCA 69 (1972), 29.
Gooch, P. W. "The Relation Between Wisdom and Virtue in Phaedo 69a 6-c3," JHP 12 (1974), 153-159.
Guardini, R. The Death of Socrates; An Interpretation of the Platonic Dialogues: Euthyphro, Apology, Crito and Phaedo. Cleveland: World, 1948.
Lange, S. "Emotion in Plato's Phaedo," CJ 33 (February, 1938), 296-298.
Lavely, J. H. "The Turning Point in Plato's Life," BUJ 22 (February, 1974), 32-36.
Minadeo, R. "Socrates' Debt to Asclepius," CJ 66 (1971), 294-297.
Nehamas, A. "Plato on the Imperfection of the Sensible World," APQ 12 (April, 1975), 105-117.
O'Brien, D. "The Last Argument of Plato's Phaedo. I," CQ (New Series) 17 (November, 1967), 198-231.
―――――. "The Last Argument of Plato's Phaedo. II," CQ (New Series) 18 (May, 1968), 95-106.
―――――. "A Metaphor in Plato: 'Running Away' and 'Staying Behind' in the Phaedo and the Timaeus," CQ 27 (1977), 297-299.
Olshewsky, J. M. "On the Relations of Soul to Body in Plato and Aristotle," JHP 14 (1976), 391-404.
Russell, B. A. W. R. "Plato's Theory of Immortality," in his History of Western Philosophy. New York: Simon and Schuster, 1945, pp. 132-143.
Schiller, F. S. C. "Plato's Phaedo and the Ancient Hope of Immortality," in his Our Human Truths. New York: Columbia University Press, 1939, pp. 140-154.
Spitzer, A. "Immortality and Virtue in the Phaedo: A Non-ascetic Interpretation," Person 57 (Spring, 1976), 113-125.
Stewart, D. J. "Socrates' Last Bath," JHP 10 (1972), 253-259.
Strachan, J. C. G. "What Did Forbid Suicide at Phaedo-62b?" CQ 20 (1970), 216-220.
Taran, A. L. "Plato. Phaedo, 62," AJP 87 (July, 1966), 326-336.
Tarrant, D. "Metaphors of Death in the Phaedo," CR (New Series) 2 (June, 1952), 64-66.
Taylor, C. C. W. "Forms as Causes in the Phaedo," Mind 78 (January, 1969), 45-59.
Teloh, H. "The Isolation and Correction of the Forms in Plato's Middle Dialogues," Apeiron 10 (January, 1976), 20-23.
Vlastos, G. "Reasons and Causes in the Phaedo," Ph R 78 (July, 1969), 291-325.
White, F. C. "Compresence of Opposites in Phaedo 102," CQ 27 (1977), 303-311.

Phaedrus

Bluck, R. S. "Phaedrus and Reincarnation," AJP 79 (April, 1958), 156-164.
Brown, M. and J. Coulter. "The Middle Speech of Plato's Phaedrus," JHP 9 (1971), 405-423.

Burger, R. Plato's Phaedrus: A Defense of a Philosophic Art of Writing. University: University of Alabama Press, 1979.
Dorter, K. "Imagery and Philosophy in Plato's Phaedrus," JHP 9 (1971), 279-281.
Helmbold, W. C. The Unity of the Phaedrus. Berkeley: University of California Press, 1952.
Herter, H. "The Problematic Mention of Hippocrates in Plato's Phaedrus," ICS (January, 1976), 22-42.
Howland, R. L. "Attack on Isocrates in the Phaedrus," CQ 31 (July, 1937), 151-159.
Jaeger, W. W. "Plato's Phaedrus: Philosophy and Rhetoric," in his Paideia: The Ideals of Greek Culture. Oxford: B. Blackwell, 1944-47. Vol. 3, pp. 182-196.
Kelley, W. G. "Rhetoric as Seduction," P & R 6 (1973), 69-80.
Lebeck, A. "The Central Myth of Plato's Phaedrus," GRBS 13 (1972), 267-290.
Linforth, I. M. Telestic Madness in Plato, Phaedrus 244 DE. Berkeley: University of California Press, 1946.
McGibbon, D. D. "The Fall of the Soul in Plato's Phaedrus," CQ (New Series) 14 (May, 1964), 56-64.
Murley, C. "Plato's Phaedrus and Theocritean Pastoral," TAPA 71 (1940), 281-295.
Murphey, J. J. "The Metarhetorics of Plato, Augustine, and McLuhan; A Pointing Essay," P & R 4 (1971), 201-214.
Oates, W. J. Plato's View of Art. New York: Scribner's, 1972.
Panagiotou, S. "Lysias and the Date of Plato's Phaedrus," Mnemosyne 28 (1975), 388-398.
Partree, M. H. "Plato on the Criticism of Poetry," PQ 52 (1973), 629-642.
Pieper, J. Enthusiasm and Divine Madness. New York: Harcourt, Brace, 1964.
Reed, N. H. "Plato, Phaedrus 245 d-e," CR (New Series) 24 (1974), 5-6.
Robinson, T. M. "The Argument for Immortality in Plato's Phaedrus," in J. P. Anton and C. L. Kustas, eds., Essays in Ancient Greek Philosophy. Albany: State University of New York Press, 1971, pp. 345-353.
Secskin, K. R. "Platonism, Mysticism, and Madness," Monist 59 (October, 1976), 574-586.
Sprague, I. R. K. "Phaedrus 262D," Mnemosyne 31 (1978), 72.
Tejera, V. "Irony and Allegory in the Phaedrus," P & R 8 (1975), 71-87.
Teloh, H. "The Isolation and Connection of the Forms in Plato's Middle Dialogues," Apeiron 10 (Manuary, 1976), 20-23.
Vries, G. J. de. A Commentary on the Phaedrus of Plato. Amsterdam: Hakkert, 1969.
Weaver, R. M. "The Phaedrus and the Nature of Rhetoric," in M. A. Natanson and H. W. Johnstone, eds., Philosophy, Rhetoric and Argumentation. University Park: Pennsylvania State University Press, 1966, pp. 63-79.

Philebus

Cooper, N. "Pleasure and Goodness in Plato's Philebus," PQ 18 (January, 1968), 12-15.
Cresswell, M. J. "Is There One or Are There Many One and Many Problems in Plato?" Ph Q 22 (April, 1972), 149-154.
Dybikowski, J. C. "Mixed and False Pleasures in the Philebus: A Reply," Ph Q 20 (July, 1970), 244-247.
Ficino, M. The Philebus Commentary. Berkeley: University of California Press, 1975.
Fortenbaugh, W. W. "Plato: Temperament and Eugenic Policy," Areth 8 (Fall, 1975), 283-305.
Hackforth, R. "On Some Passages of Plato's Philebus," CQ 33 (January, 1939), 23-29.
⎯⎯⎯, ed. Plato: Philebus. Cambridge: Cambridge University Press, 1972.
Isenberg, M. W. "Unity of Plato's Philebus," CP 35 (April, 1940), 154-179.
Klein, J. About Plato's Philebus. The Hague: Nijhoff, 1972.
McLaughlin, A. "A Note on False Pleasures in the Philebus," PQ 19 (January, 1969), 57-61.
Mueller, G. E. "The Unity of Plato's Philebus," CJ 50 (October, 1954), 21-27.
Murphy, N. R. "Comparison of Lives in Plato's Philebus," CQ 32 (April, 1938), 116-124.
Shiner, R. A. Knowledge and Reality in Plato's Philebus. Assen: Van Gorcum, 1974.

Politicus

Klein, J. Plato's Trilogy. Chicago: University of Chicago Press, 1977.
Robinson, T. M. "Demiurge and World Soul in Plato's Politicus," AJP 88 (January, 1967), 57-66.

Protagorus

Cahn, S. M. "A Puzzle Concerning the Meno and the Protagoras," JHP 11 (October, 1973), 535-537.
Cole, A. T. The Relativism of Protagoras," YCS 22 (1972), 19-45.
Devereux, D. T. "Protagoras on Courage and Knowledge: Protagoras 351 A-B," Apeiron 9 (February, 1975), 37-39.
Drews, R. "Knowledge and Hedonism in Plato's Protagoras," J Hel S 96 (1976), 32-45.
Dyson, M. "Knowledge and Hedonism in Plato's Protagoras," J Hel S 96 (1976), 32-45.
Gagarin, M. "The Purpose of Plato's Protagoras," TAPA 100 (1969), 133-164.
Jaeger, W. W. "Protagoras: Sophistic or Socratic Paideia?" in his Paideia: The Ideals of Greek Culture. Oxford: B. Blackwell, 1944-47. Vol. 2, pp. 107-125.

Santas, G. "Plato's Protagorus and Explanations of Weakness," Ph R 75 (January, 1966), 3-33.
Tiles, J. E. "The Combat of Passion and Reason," Philos 52 (July, 1977), 321-330.
Weingartner, R. H. The Unity of the Platonic Dialogue: The Cratylus, the Protagoras, the Parmenides. Indianapolis: Bobbs-Merrill, 1973.

Republic

Adkins, J. W. H. "Theoria Versus Praxis in the Nicomachean Ethics and the Republic," CP 73 (October, 1978), 297-313.
Allen, V. R. E. "Argument from Opposites in Republic," RM 15 (December, 1961), 325-335.
Anderson, G. "Some Notes on Lucian's Navigium," Mnemosyne 30 (1977), 363-368.
Anderson, T. J. Polis and Psyche: A Motif in Plato's Republic. Stockholm: Almqvist and Wiksell, 1971.
Annas, J. "Plato's Republic and Feminism," Philos 51 (July, 1976), 307-321.
Aronson, S. H. "The Happy Philosopher; A Counterexample to Plato's Proof," JHP 10 (October, 1972), 383-398.
Atkins, J. W. H. "Attack on Poetry: Plato," in his Literary Criticism in Antiquity. Toronto: Macmillan, 1934, Vol. 1, pp. 33-70.
Averroes. Averroes on Plato's Republic, tr. by R. Lerner. Ithaca, N. Y.: Cornell University Press, 1974.
―――――. Commentary on Plato's Republic. Cambridge: Cambridge University Press, 1966.
Bambrough, R., ed. Plato, Popper and Politics: Some Contributions to a Modern Controversy. New York: Barnes and Noble, 1967.
Beatty, J. "Why Should Plato's Philosopher Be Moral and, Hence, Rule?" Person 57 (Spring, 1976), 132-144.
Bloom, A. The Republic of Plato, with Notes and an Interpretive Essay. New York: Basic, 1968.
Boyd, W. An Introduction to the Republic of Plato. London: Allen and Unwin, 1969.
Boyle, A. J. "Plato's Divided Line, Essay I: The Problem of Dianoia," Apeiron 7 (November, 1973), 1-11.
―――――. "Plato's Divided Line, Essay II: Mathematics and Dialectic," Apeiron 8 (May, 1974), 7-18.
―――――. "Plato's Divided Line, Appendix: The Function and Significance of the Line," Apeiron 8 (May, 1974), 19-21.
Brent, A. Philosophical Foundations for the Curriculum. Boston: Allen and Unwin, 1978.
Brumbaugh, R. S. "Colors of the Hemisphere in Plato's Myth of ER (Republic 616 E)," CP 46 (July, 1951), 173-176.
―――――. "New Interpretation of Plato's Republic," JP 64 (October 26, 1967), 661-670.
Calvert, B. "Plato and the Equality of Women," Phoenix 29 (1975), 231-243.

Carter, B. E. "The Function of the Myth of the Earthborn in the Republic," CJ 48 (May, 1953), 297-302.
Cassirer, E. "Plato's Republic," in his Myth of the State. New Haven, Conn. : Yale University Press, 1946, pp. 61-77.
Cooper, J. M. "Psychology of Justice in Plato," APQ 14 (April, 1977), 151-157.
Cross, R. C., and A. D. Woozley. Plato's Republic: A Philosophical Commentary. New York: St. Martin's, 1964.
Cummings, P. W. "Eros as Procreation in Beauty," Apeiron 10 (February, 1976), 23-28.
Davis, M. "On the Imputed Possibilities of Callipolis and Magnesia," AJP 85 (October, 1964), 394-411.
Dorter, K. "Socrates' Refutation of Thrasymachus and Treatment of Virtue," P & R 7 (1974), 25-46.
Dunham, B. "Thrasymachus," in his Man Against Myth. New York: Little, Brown, 1947, pp. 210-214.
Else, G. F. The Structure and Date of Book 10 of Plato's Republic. Heidelberg: Winter, 1972.
Faris, J. A. "Is Plato's Caste State Based on Racial Differences?" CQ 44 (1950), 38-43.
Fireman, P. Justice in Plato's Republic. New York: Philosophical Library, 1957.
Fogelin, R. J. "Three Platonic Analogies," Ph R 80 (July, 1971), 371-382.
Fortenbaugh, W. W. "On Plato's Feminism in Republic V," Apeiron 9 (February, 1975), 1-4.
Foster, M. B. "Mistake of Plato's in the Republic," Mind 46 (July, 1937), 386-393.
_____. "Mistake of Plato's in the Republic: Rejoinder," Mind 47 (April, 1938), 226-232.
Galis, L. "The State-Soul Analogy in Plato's Argument that Justice Pays," JHP 12 (July, 1974), 285-293.
Gallop, D. "Dreaming and Waking in Plato," in J. P. Anton and G. L. Kustas, eds., Essays in Ancient Greek Philosophy. Albany: State University of New York Press, 1971, pp. 187-201.
Garrand, W. J. "Notes on Two Socratic Arguments in Republic I," Apeiron 10 (February, 1976), 11-13.
Gilbert, A. H. "Did Plato Banish the Poets or the Critics?" SP 36 (January, 1939), 1-19.
Golding, N. P. and N. H. "Population Policy in Plato and Aristotle: Some Value Issues," Areth 8 (Fall, 1975), 345-358.
Gulley, N. "Plato on Poetry," G & R 24 (October, 1977), 154-169.
Hall, D. "Philosophers and the Cave," G & R 25 (October, 1978), 169-173.
Hall, R. W. "Egalitarianism and Justice in the Republic," Apeiron 6 (February, 1972), 7-19.
_____. "The Just and Happy Man of the Republic: Fact or Fallacy?" JHP 9 (April, 1971), 147-158.
_____. "Plato's Political Analogy: Fallacy or Analogy?" JHP 12 (1974), 419-435.
Hoare, F. R. "Plato's Republic," in his Eight Decisive Books of Antiquity. New York: Sheed and Ward, 1952, pp. 172-213.

Hourani, G. F. "The Education of the Third Class in Plato's Republic," CQ 43 (January/April, 1949), 58-60.
Jacques, J. H. Plato's 'Republic': A Beginner's Guide. New York: Citadel, 1971.
Jaeger, W. W. "Republic," in his Paideia: The Ideals of Greek Culture. Oxford: B. Blackwell, 1944-47. Vol. 2, pp. 198-431.
James of Rusholme, E. J. F. J., Baron. Plato's Ideas on Art and Education. York: William Sessions Ltd. for the University of York, 1975.
Joseph, H. W. B. "Plato's Republic: The Argument with Polemarchus," in his Essays in Ancient and Modern Philosophy. Oxford: Clarendon, 1935, pp. 1-14.
─────. "Plato's Republic: The Argument with Thrasymachus," in his Essays in Ancient and Modern Philosophy. Oxford: Clarendon, 1935, pp. 15-40.
─────. "Plato's Republic: The Comparison Between the Soul and the State," in his Essays in Ancient and Modern Philosophy. Oxford: Clarendon, 1935, pp. 82-121.
─────. "Plato's Republic: The Nature of the Soul," in his Essays in Ancient and Modern Philosophy. Oxford: Clarendon, 1935, pp. 41-81.
─────. "Plato's Republic: The Proof That the Most Just Man Is the Happiest," in his Essays in Ancient and Modern Philosophy. Oxford: Clarendon, 1935, pp. 122-155.
Kahn, C. H. "The Meaning of Justice and the Theory of Forms," JP 69 (1972), 567-579.
Kenney, A. J. P. "Mental Health in Plato's Republic," PBA 55 (December, 1969), 229-253.
Kraut, R. "Egoism, Love and Political Office in Plato," Ph R 82 (1973), 330-344.
Mabbott, J. D. "Is Plato's Republic Utilitarian?" Mind 46 (October, 1937), 468-474.
McClelland, R. C. The Arts of Music and Poetry in Plato's Republic. Norfolk, Va.: College of William and Mary General Publications Series, 1959.
Maguire, J. P. "The Individual and the Class in Plato's Republic," CJ 60 (January, 1965), 145-150.
Mills, K. W. "Plato's Non-Hypothetical Starting Point," DUJ 31 (June, 1970), 152-159.
Morrison, J. S. "The Origins of Plato's Philosopher-Statesman," CQ (New Series) 8 (1958), 198-218.
Moss, L. "Plato and the Poetics," PQ 50 (1971), 533-542.
Mulhern, J. J. "Population and Plato's Republic," Areth 8 (1975), 265-281.
Murley, C. "Plato's Republic, Totalitarian or Democratic?" CJ 36 (April, 1941), 413-420.
Murphy, N. R. Interpretation of Plato's Republic. Oxford: Clarendon, 1951.
Nettleship, R. L. Lectures on the Republic of Plato. Folcroft, Pa.: Folcroft, 1975.
─────. The Theory of Education in the Republic of Plato. New York: Teachers College Press, 1968.

Neu, J. "Plato's Analogy of State and Individual: The Republic and the Organic Theory of State," Philos 46 (July, 1971), 238-254.
Notopolus, J. A. "Socrates and the Sun," CJ 37 (February, 1942), 260-274.
_____. "Symbolism of the Sun and Light in the Republic of Plato," CP 39 (July, 1944), 163-172; 39 (October, 1944), 223-240.
Okin, S. M. "Philosopher Queens and Private Wives: Plato on Women and the Family," P & PA 6 (Summer, 1977), 345-369.
Ostwald, M. "The Two States in Plato's Republic," in J. P. Anton and G. L. Kustas, eds., Essays in Ancient Greek Philosophy. Albany: State University of New York Press, 1971, pp. 316-327.
Partee, M. H. "Plato on the Criticism of Poetry," PQ 52 (October, 1973), 629-642.
_____. "Plato's Banishment of Poetry," JAAC 28 (1970), 209-222.
Pierce, C. Equality: Republic V. La Salle, Ill.: Open Court, 1973.
Pomeroy, S. B. "Feminism in Book V of Plato's Republic," Apeiron 8 (May, 1974), 33-35.
_____. "Optics and the Line in Plato's Republic," CQ (New Series) 21 (November, 1971), 389-392.
Robertson, J. C. "Plato's Ban upon Poetry," in his Mixed Company. Toronto: Dent, 1939, pp. 80-95.
Rosen, S. "Role of Eros in Plato's Republic," RM 18 (March, 1965), 452-475.
Ross, W. D. Plato's Theory of Ideas. Westport, Conn.: Greenwood, 1976.
Russell, B. A. W. R. "Plato's Utopia," in his History of Western Philosophy. New York: Simon and Schuster, 1945, pp. 108-119.
_____. "Theory of Ideas," in his History of Western Philosophy. New York: Simon and Schuster, 1945, pp. 119-132.
Sachs, D. "Fallacy in Plato's Republic," Ph R 72 (April, 1963), 141-158.
Schiller, F. C. S. "Plato's Republic," in his Our Human Truths. New York: Columbia University Press, 1939, pp. 155-167.
Segal, C. "'The Myth Was Saved': Reflections on Homer and the Mythology of Plato's Republic," Hermes 106 (1978), 315-336.
Sesonske, A., ed. Plato's Republic; Interpretation and Criticism. Belmont, Calif.: Wadsworth, 1966.
Shiner, R. A. "Soul in Republic x, 611," Apeiron 6 (February, 1972), 23-30.
Solmsen, F. "Platonic Values in Aristotle's Science," JHI 39 (January, 1978), 3-23.
Sprague, R. K. Plato's Philosopher-King: A Study of the Theoretical Background. Columbia: University of South Carolina Press, 1976.
Stormer, G. D. "Plato's Theory of Myth," Person 55 (Summer, 1974), 216-223.
Sze, C. P. "Eikasia and Pistis in Plato's Cave Allegory," CQ 27 (1977), 127-138.
Tait, M. D. C. "Spirit, Gentleness and the Philosophic Nature in the Republic," TAPA 80 (1949), 203-211.
Tarrant, D. "Imagery in Plato's Republic," CQ 40 (January, 1946), 27-34.

Taylor, A. E. "Decline and Fall of the State in Republic, VIII," Mind 48 (January, 1939), 23-38.
Teloh, H. "The Isolation and Connection of the Forms in Plato's Middle Dialogues," Apeiron 10 (January, 1976), 20-23.
Thayer, H. S. "Plato on the Morality of Imagination," RM 30 (June, 1977), 594-618.
Tiles, J. E. "The Combat of Passion and Reason," Philos 52 (July, 1977), 321-330.
Verdenius, W. J. Mimesis; Plato's Doctrine of Artistic Imitation and Its Meaning to Us. Leiden: Brill, 1972.
Versenyi, L. G. "Plato and His Liberal Opponents," Philos 46 (1971), 222-237.
Vlastos, G. "Argument in the Republic That Justice Pays," JP 65 (November 7, 1968), 665-674.
──────. "Does Slavery Exist in Plato's Republic?" CP 63 (October, 1968), 291-295.
──────. "Justice and Psychic Harmony in the Republic," JP 66 (August 21, 1969), 505-521.
Waterlou, S. "The Good of Others in Plato's Republic," PAS 73 (1973), 19-36.
Wender, D. "Plato. Misogynist, Paedophile, and Feminist," Areth (Spring, 1973), 75-90.
White, N. P. A Companion to Plato's Republic. Indianapolis: Hackett, 1979.
Wilson, J. R. S. "The Argument of Republic IV," Ph Q 26 (April, 1976), 111-124.
──────. "Basis of Plato's Society," Philos 52 (July, 1977), 313-320.
Young, C. M. "A Note on Republic 335c 9-10 and 335c 12," Ph R 83 (January, 1974), 97-106.

Sophist

Albury, W. R. "Hunting the Sophist," Apeiron 5 (1971), 1-11.
Andic, M., and M. Brown. "False Statement in the Sophist and Theaetetus' Mathematics," Phoenix 27 (Spring, 1973), 26-34.
Bluck, R. S. H. Plato's Sophist: A Commentary, ed. by G. C. Neal. New York: Harper and Row, 1975.
Bondeson, W. "Non-being and the One: Some Connections Between Plato's Sophist and Parmenides," Apeiron 7 (February, 1973), 13-22.
──────. "Plato's Sophist: Falsehoods and Images," Apeiron 6 (February, 1972), 1-6.
──────. "Some Problems About Being and Precation in Plato's Sophist 242-249," JHP 14 (January, 1976), 1-10.
Cobb, W. S. "Anamnesis, Platonic Doctrine or Sophistic Absurdity?" Dialogue 7 (1973), 604-628.
Cornford, F. M., ed. Plato's Theory of Knowledge; The Theaetetus and The Sophist of Plato. New York: Liberal Arts, 1957, pp. 1-13.
Cresswell, M. J. "Is There One or Are There Many One and Many Problems in Plato?" Ph Q 22 (April, 1972), 149-154.

Ferg, S. "Plato on False Statement; Relative Being, a Part of Being, and Not-being in the Sophist," JHP 14 (July, 1976), 336-342.
Gooch, P. W. "Vice Is Ignorance: The Interpretation of Sophist 226A-231B," Phoenix 25 (Summer, 1977), 124-133.
Gosling, J. C. B. Plato. London: Routledge and K. Paul, 1973.
Hackforth, R. "False Statement in Plato's Sophist," CQ 39 (January, 1945), 56-58.
Isenberg, M. W. "Plato's Sophist and the Five Stages of Knowing," CP 46 (October, 1951), 201-211.
Klein, J. Plato's Trilogy. Chicago: University of Chicago Press, 1977.
Lacey, A. R. "Plato's Sophist and the Forms," CQ (New Series) 9 (1959), 43-52.
Lee, E. N. "Plato on Negation and Not-Being in the Sophist," Ph R 81 (July, 1972), 267-304.
Partee, M. H. "Plato's Banishment of Poetry," JAAC 28 (1970), 209-222.
Philip, J. A. "False Statement in the Sophistes," TAPA 99 (1968), 315-328.
Sayre, K. M. "Sophist 263B Revisited," Mind 85 (October, 1976), 581-596.
Schipper, E. W. "Souls, Forms and False Statements in the Sophist," PQ 15 (July, 1965), 240-242.
Seligman, P. Being and Not-Being: An Introduction to Plato's Sophist. The Hague: Nijhoff, 1974.
Sheeks, W. "Isocrates, Plato and Xenophon Against the Sophists," Person 56 (Summer, 1975), 250-259.
Turnbull, R. G. "The Argument of the Sophist," PQ 17 (January, 1964), 23-34.
[Various Authors.] "Three Studies on Plato," RM 22 (March, 1969), 433-498.

Symposium

Cairns, H., et al. "Plato; Symposium," in their Invitation to Learning. New York: Random House, 1941, pp. 35-50.
Cameron, A. "Petronius and Plato," CQ (New Series) 19 (November, 1969), 367-370.
Clay, D. "The Tragic and Comic Poet of the Symposium," Arion (New Series) 2 (1975), 238-261.
Cornford, F. M. "Doctrine of Eros in Plato's Symposium," in his Unwritten Philosophy, and Other Essays. London: Cambridge University Press, 1950, pp. 68-80.
Cummings, P. W. "Eros as Procreation in Beauty," Apeiron 10 (February, 1976), 23-28.
Edelstein, L. "The Role of Eryximachus in Plato's Symposium," TAPA 76 (1945), 85-103.
Jaeger, W. W. "Symposium: Eros," in his Paideia: The Ideals of Greek Culture. Oxford: B. Blackwell, 1944-47. Vol. 2, pp. 174-197.
Kelley, W. G. "Rhetoric as Seduction," P & R 6 (1973), 69-80.

Moore, J. S. "Discourse of Diotima: Interpretative Paraphrase of Portions of the Symposium and Phaedrus of Plato," Person 24 (January, 1943), 57-65.

Moravcsik, J. M. E. "Reason and Eros in the "Ascent" Passage of the Symposium," in J. P. Anton and G. L. Kustas, eds., Essays in Ancient Greek Philosophy. Albany: State University of New York Press, 1971, pp. 285-302.

Morrison, J. S. "Four Notes on Plato's Symposium," CQ 14 (1964), 42-55.

Neumann, H. "Diotima's Concept of Live," AJP 86 (January, 1965), 33-59.

———. "On the Madness of Plato's Apollodorus," TAPA 96 (1965), 283-290.

———. "On the Sophistry of Plato's Pausanias," TAPA 95 (1964), 261-267.

Plochmann, G. K. "Supporting Themes in the Symposium," in J. P. Anton and G. L. Kustas, eds., Essays in Ancient Greek Philosophy. Albany: State University of New York Press, 1971, pp. 328-344.

Reckford, K. J. "Desire with Hope: Aristophanes and the Comic Catharsis," Ramus 3 (1974), 41-69.

Rosen, S. Plato's Symposium. New Haven, Conn.: Yale University Press, 1968.

Spearritt, P. "Love Among the Platonists," DR 92 (October, 1974), 92-101.

Sprague, R. K. "Symposium 211A and Parmenides Frag. 8," CP 66 (October, 1971), 261.

Teloh, H. "The Isolation and Connection of the Forms in Plato's Middle Dialogues," Apeiron 10 (January, 1976), 20-23.

Wolz, H. G. "Philosophy as Drama: An Approach to Plato's Symposium," P & Ph R 30 (March, 1970), 323-353.

Theaetetus

Andic, M., and M. Brown. "False Statement in the Sophist and Theaetetus' Mathematics," Phoenix 27 (Spring, 1973), 26-34.

Barker, A. "The Digression in the Theaetus," JHP 14 (October, 1976), 457-462.

Bierman, A. K. "Socratic Humor: Understanding the Most Important Philosophical Argument," Apeiron 5 (February, 1971), 23-42.

Bluck, R. S. "Knowledge by Acquaintance in Plato's Theaetetus," Mind 72 (April, 1963), 259-263.

Burnyeat, M. F. "Examples in Epistemology: Socrates, Theaetetus and G. E. Moore," Philos 52 (October, 1977), 381-398.

———. "Plato on the Grammar of Perceiving," CQ (New Series) 26 (1976), 29-51.

———. "Protagoras and Self-Refutation in Plato's Theaetetus," Ph R 85 (January, 1976), 172-195.

Cornford, F. M., ed. Plato's Theory of Knowledge; The Theaetetus and The Sophist of Plato. New York: Liberal Arts, 1957, pp. 1-13.

Hackforth, R. "Aviary Theory in the Theaetetus," CQ 32 (January, 1938), 27-29.

Klein, J. Plato's Trilogy. Chicago: University of Chicago Press, 1977.
Lewis, H. D. "Naive Realism and a Passage in the Theaetetus," Mind 47 (July, 1938), 351-356.
Mahood, G. H. "Interpersonal Values in the Teaching of Philosophy," PE & W 27 (January, 1977), 23-33.
Morrow, G. R. "Plato and the Mathematicians: An Interpretation of Socrates' Dream in the Theaetetus (201e-206c)," Ph R 79 (July, 1970), 309-333.
Reed, N. H. "Plato on Flux, Perception, and Language," PCPS 18 (1972), 65-77.
Robinson, R. "Forms and Error in Plato's Theaetetus," Ph R 59 (January, 1950), 3-30.
Rosen, S. "Return to the Origin: Reflections on Plato and Contemporary Philosophy," IPQ 16 (1976), 151-177.
Russell, B. A. W. R. "Knowledge and Perception in Plato," in his History of Western Philosophy. New York: Simon and Schuster, 1945, pp. 149-159.
White, F. C. "The Theory of Flux in the Theaetetus," Apeiron 10 (February, 1976), 1-10.
Williams, C. J. F. "Referential Opacity and False Belief in the Theaetetus," Ph R 22 (October, 1972), 289-302.

Timaeus

Benardete, S. On Plato's Timaeus and Timaeus' Science Fiction. The Hague: Nijhoff, 1971.
Cherniss, H. "Much Misread Passage of the Timaeus (Timaeus 49 c 7-50 B5)," AJP 75 (April, 1954), 113-130.
———. "Relation of the Timaeus to Plato's Later Dialogues," AJP 78 (July, 1957), 225-266.
Clegg, J. S. "Plato's Vision of Chaos," CQ (New Series) 26 (1976), 52-61.
Cornford, F. M., ed. and tr. Plato's Cosmology; The Timaeus of Plato. Indianapolis: Bobbs-Merrill, 1957.
Gulley, N. "Interpretation of Plato, Timaeus 49 D-E," AJP 81 (January, 1960), 53-64.
Hackforth, R. "Notes on Some Passages of Plato's Timeaeus," CQ 38 (January, 1944), 33-40.
———. "Plato's Cosmogony (Timaeus 27 Dff.)," CQ (New Series) 9 (1959), 17-22.
Hall, T. S. "Biology of the Timaeus in Historical Perspective," Arion 4 (Spring, 1965), 109-122.
Hershbell, J. P. "Empedoclean Influences on the Timaeus," Phoenix 28 (Summer, 1974), 145-166.
Holland, A. J. "An Argument in Plato's Theaetetus, 184-186," Ph Q 23 (April, 1973), 97-116.
Keyt, D. "The Mad Craftsman of the Timaeus," Ph R 80 (April, 1971), 230-235.
Krell, D. F. "Female Parts in Timaeus," Arion (New Series) 2 (1975), 400-421.

Lee, E. N. "On Plato's Timaeus, 49 D4-E7," AJP 88 (January, 1967), 1-28.
Miller, H. W. "The Aetiology of Disease in Plato's Timaeus," TAPA 93 (1962), 175-187.
―――――. "The Flux of the Body in Plato's Timaeus," TAPA 88 (1957), 103-114.
Morrow, G. R. "Necessity and Persuasion in Plato's Timaeus," Ph R 59 (April, 1950), 147-163.
O'Brien, D. "Heavy and Light in Democritus and Aristotle: Two Conceptions of Change and Identity," J Hel S 97 (1977), 64-74.
―――――. "A Metaphor in Plato: 'Running Away' and 'Staying Behind' in the Phaedo and Timaeus," CQ (New Series) 27 (1977), 297-299.
Owen, G. E. L. "The Place of the Timaeus in Plato's Dialogues," CQ (New Series) 3 (1953), 79-95.
Pohle, W. "The Mathematical Foundation of Plato's Atomic Physics," I 62 (Spring, 1971), 36-46.
Reed, N. H. "Plato on Flux, Perception, and Language," PCPS 18 (1972), 65-77.
Reiche, H. A. T. "Aristotle on Breathing in the Timaeus," AJP 86 (October, 1965), 404-408.
Rosenmeyer, T. G. "Family of Critias [in Plato's Timaeus]," AJP 70 (October, 1949), 404-410.
Russell, B. A. W. R. "Plato's Cosmogony," in his History of Western Philosophy. New York: Simon and Schuster, 1945, pp. 143-148.
Skemp, J. B. "Plants in Plato's Timaeus," CQ 41 (January, 1947), 53-60.
Solmsen, F. "Platonic Values in Aristotle's Science," JHI 39 (January, 1978), 3-23.
Taran, L. "The Creation Myth in Plato's Timaeus," in J. P. Anton and G. L. Kustas, eds., Essays in Ancient Greek Philosophy. Albany: State University of New York Press, 1971, pp. 372-407.
Tracy, T. J. Physiological Theory and the Doctrine of the Mean in Plato and Aristotle. Chicago: Loyola University Press, 1969, pp. 1-156.
Vlastos, G. "Disorderly Motion in the Timaeus," CQ (April, 1939), 71-83.
Walbank, F. W. "Phalaris' Bull in Timaeus (Diod. Sic. xiii. 90. 4-7)," CR 59 (December, 1945), 39-42.
Welliver, W. Character, Plot and Thought in Plato's Timaeus-Critias. Leiden: Brill, 1977.
West, M. L. "Emendations in Plato, Gorgias and Timaeus," CQ (New Series) 27 (1977), 300-302.
Whittaker, J. "Textual Comments on Timaeus 27c-d," Phoenix 27 (Winter, 1973), 387-391.
Zeyl, D. J. "Plato and Talk of a World in Flux; Timaeus 49a 6-50b 5," HSCP 79 (1975), 125-148.

PLAUTUS

General Criticism

Arnott, G. "Menander, Plautus, Terence," G & RNSC 9 (1975), 5-62.
Balsdon, J. P. V. D. "Humor and Satire," in his The Romans. New York: Basic, 1966, pp. 249-269.
Beede, G. L. "Proverbial Expressions in Plautus," CJ 44 (March, 1949), 357-362.
Callahan, J. F. "Plautus' 'Mirror for a Mirror,'" CP 59 (January, 1964), 1-10.
Chalmers, W. R. "Plautus and His Audience," in T. A. Dorey and D. R. Dudley, eds., Roman Drama. New York: Basic, 1965, pp. 21-50.
Copley, F. O. "Plautus," in his Latin Literature from the Beginnings to the Close of the Second Century A.D. Ann Arbor: University of Michigan Press, 1969, pp. 19-35.
Downs, R. B. "Rome's Greatest Comic Poet: Titus Maccius Plautus," in his Famous Books, Ancient and Medieval. New York: Barnes and Noble, 1964, pp. 147-151.
Duckworth, G. E. The Nature of Roman Comedy: A Study in Popular Entertainment. Princeton, N. J.: Princeton University Press, 1952.
──────. "Unnamed Characters in the Plays of Plautus," CP 33 (July, 1938), 267-282.
Gassner, J. W. "Menander, Plautus, and Terence," in his Masters of the Drama. New York: Random House, 1940, pp. 92-104.
Gratwick, A. S. "Titus Maccius Plautus," CQ (New Series) 23 (May, 1973), 78-84.
Hadas, M. "Comedy and Satire," in his History of Latin Literature. New York: Columbia University Press, 1952, pp. 33-57.
Handley, E. W. Menander and Plautus: A Study in Comparison. London: University College, 1968.
Hanson, J. A. "The Glorious Military," in T. A. Dorey and D. R. Dudley, Eds., Roman Drama. New York: Basic, 1965, pp. 51-85.
──────. "Plautus as a Sourcebook for Roman Religion," TAPA 90 (1959) 48-101.
Harsh, P. W. "Plautus," in his Handbook of Classical Drama. Palo Alto, Calif.: Stanford University Press, 1944, pp. 333-374.
Henderson, M. M. "The Comedy of Plautus," Akroterion 20 (January, 1975), 2-13.
Hough, J. N. "Miscellanea Plautina: Vulgarity, Extradramatic Speeches, Roman Allusions," TAPA 71 (1940), 186-198.
──────. "Plautine Technique in Delayed Exits," CP 35 (January, 1940), 39-48.
──────. "The Reverse Comic Foil in Plautus," TAPA 73 (1942), 108-118.
──────. "Understanding of Intrigue: A Study in Plautine Chronology," AJP 60 (October, 1939), 422-435.

Juniper, W. H. "Character Portrayal in Plautus," CJ 31 (February, 1936), 276-288.
Laidlaw, W. A. Prosody of Terence [and Plautus], a Relational Study. London: Oxford University Press, 1938.
Lindsay, W. M. Early Latin Verse. London: Oxford University Press, 1968, pp. 11-112.
Lloyd, R. B. "Two Prologues: Menander and Plautus," AJP 84 (April, 1963), 146-161.
Marples, M. "Plautus," G & R 8 (October, 1938), 1-7.
Nicoll, A. "From Menander to the Mimes," in his World Drama, from Aeschylus to Anouilh. New York: Harcourt, Brace, 1953, pp. 107-137.
Norwood, G. Plautus and Terence. New York: Cooper Square, 1963, pp. 3-99.
Paterson, C. E. "Heresies in Plautine Hiatus: An Impression," AClass 8 (1970), 1-5.
Perry, H. T. "Roman Imitators: Plautus and Terence," in his Masters of Dramatic Comedy and Their Social Themes. Cambridge, Mass.: Harvard University Press, 1939, pp. 49-78.
Prescott, H. W. "Criteria of Originality in Plautus," TAPA 63 (1932), 103-125.
Rosivach, V. J. "Plautine Stage Settings," TAPA 101 (1970), 445-461.
Segal, E. W. Roman Laughter: The Comedy of Plautus. Cambridge, Mass.: Harvard University Press, 1968.
Stace, C. "The Slaves of Plautus," G & R 15 (April, 1968), 64-77.
Tolliver, H. M. "Plautus and the State Gods of Rome," CJ 48 (November, 1952), 49-57.
Wilkinson, L. P. Golden Latin Artistry. Cambridge: Cambridge University Press, 1963.
Wright, F. A. Three Roman Poets: Plautus, Catullus, Ovid. New York: Dutton, 1938.

Individual Works

Amphitryon, or Amphitruo

Barnes, H. E. "The Case of Sosia Versus Sosia," CJ 53 (October, 1957), 19-24.
Costa, C. D. N. "The Amphitryo Theme," in T. A. Dorey and D. R. Dudley, eds., Roman Drama. New York: Basic, 1965, pp. 85-122.
Galinsky, G. K. "Scipionic Themes in Plautus' Amphitruo," TAPA 97 (1966), 203-236.
Hough, J. N. "Jupiter, Amphitryon, and the Cuckoo," CP 65 (April, 1970), 95-96.
Stewart, Z. "The Amphitruo of Plautus and Euripides' Bacchae," TAPA 89 (1958), 348-373.

Bacchides

Clark, J. R. "Structure and Symmetry in the Bacchides of Plautus,"

TAPA 106 (1976), 85-96.

Braggart Soldier, or Miles Gloriosus

Cleary, V. J. "Se Sectari Simiam: Monkey Business in the Miles Gloriosus," CJ 67 (April-May, 1972), 299-305.

Brothers Menaechmus, or Menaechmi

Fantham, E. "Act IV of the Menaechmi: Plautus and His Original," CP 63 (July, 1968), 175-183.
Leach, E. W. "Meam Quom Formam Noscito: Language and Characterization in the Menaechmi," Areth 2 (Spring, 1969), 30-45.5.
Moorhead, P. G. "The Distribution of Roles in Plautus' Menaechmi," CJ 49 (December, 1953), 123-126.
Woodruff, J. "Mythological Notes in the Menaechmi," CB 51 (November, 1974), 6-10.

Captives, or Captivi

Hough, J. N. "Structure of the Captivi," AJP 63 (January, 1942), 26-37.
Konstan, D. "Plautus' Captivi and the Ideology of the Ancient City-State," Ramus 5 (1976), 76-91.

Casina

Cody, J. M. "The Senex Amator in Plautus' Casina," Hermes 104 (1976), 453-476.
Forehand, W. E. "Plautus' Casina: An Explanation," Areth 6 (Fall, 1973), 233-256.
MacCary, W. T. "The Bacchae in Plautus' Casina," Hermes 103 (1975), 459-463.
_____. "Patterns, of Myth, Ritual, and Comedy in Plautus' Casina," TSLL 15 (1974), 881-889.

Churl, or Truculentus

Dessen, C. S. "Plautus' Satiric Comedy: The Truculentus," PQ 56 (Spring, 1977), 145-168.

Curculio

Fantham, E. "The Curculio of Plautus: An Illustration of Plautine Methods in Adaptation," CQ (New Series) 15 (1965), 84-100.

Epidicus

Keyes, C. W. "Half-sister Marriage in New Comedy and the Epidicus," TAPA 71 (1940), 217-229.

Ghost, or Mostellaria

Barton, I. M. "Tranio's Laconian Key," G & R 19 (April, 1972), 25-31.

Pot of Gold, or Aulularia

Konstan, D. "The Social Themes in Plautus' Aulularia," Areth 10 (Fall, 1977), 307-320.
Kuiper, W. E. J. Greek Aulularia. Leiden: Brill, 1940.
Lange, D. "The Number of Slave Roles in Plautus' Aulularia," CP 68 (January, 1973), 62-63.
Marcovich, M. "Euclio, Cnemon, and the Peripatos," ICS 2 (1977), 197-218.
Minar, E. L. "The Lost Ending of Plautus' Aulularia," CJ 42 (February, 1947), 271-275.

Pseudolous

Wright, J. The Transformation of Pseudolous," TAPA 105 (1975), 403-416.

Rope, or Rudens

Fraenkel, E. "Stars in the Prologue of the Rudens," CQ 36 (January, 1942), 10-14.
Henderson, M. M. "Structural Anomaly in Plautus' Rudens," Akroterion 22 (January, 1977), 8-14.
Highet, G. "Shipwrecked Slaver in Plautus' Rudens," AJP 63 (October, 1942), 462-466.
Leach, E. W. "Plautus' Rudens: Venus Born from a Shell," TSLL 15 (1974), 915-931.

Three Bob, or Trinummus

Fantham, E. "Philemon's Thesauros as a Dramatisation of Perpipathetic Ethics," Hermes 105 (1977), 406-421.

Segal, E. "The Purpose of the Trinummus," AJP 95 (Fall, 1974), 252-264.

PLINY THE ELDER

General Criticism

Bruere, R. T. "Pliny the Elder and Virgil," CP 51 (October, 1956), 228-246.
Burns, M. A. T. "Pliny's Ideal Roman," CJ 59 (March, 1964), 253-258.
Downs, R. B. "The Great Compiler: Pliny the Elder," in his Famous Books, Ancient and Medieval. New York: Barnes and Noble, 1964, pp. 206-210.
Green, P. "Two Gentlemen of Rome; The Elder and the Younger Pliny," HT 6 (April, 1956), 266-273.
Hadas, M. "Learning and Letters in the First Century," in his History of Latin Literature. New York: Columbia University Press, 1952, pp. 302-320.
Scott, K. "The Elder and Younger Pliny on Emperor Worship," TAPA 63 (1932), 156-165.
Stout, S. E. "The Coalescence of the Two Plinys," TAPA 86 (1955), 250-255.
Syme, R. "People in Pliny," JRS 58 (1968), 135-151.
Zirkle, C. "Death of Gaius Plinius Secundus (23-79 A. D.)," I 58 (Winter, 1967), 553-559.

Individual Works

Natural History

Coulson, W. D. E. "The Nature of Pliny's Remarks on Euphranor," CJ 67 (April-May, 1972), 323-326.
―――――. "The Reliability of Pliny's Chapters on Greek and Roman Sculpture," C World 69 (March, 1976), 361-372.
"Good Nature: Pliny's Natural History," NS 20 (August 3, 1940), 108-109.
Lieberman, S. "Who Were Pliny's Blue-eyed Chinese?" CP 52 (July, 1957), 174-177.
Magrath, W. T. "Note on Information in Pliny H. N. 10.33," AJP 97 (Summer, 1976), 138-140.
Newbola, R. F. "Pliny H. N. 2.199," CP 68 (July, 1973), 211-213.
Rees, B. R. "Pliny, N. H. ii. 22," CR (New Series) 8 (December, 1958), 213-215.
Richmond, J. A. "Pliny's Catalogue of Fishes," Hermes 99 (1971), 135-141.
Ridgway, B. S. "Story of Five Amazons," AJA 78 (January, 1974), 1-17.
Schullard, H. H. "Ennius, Cato, and 'Suras' [Carthaginian Elephant in Pliny (N. H. VIII. II)]," CR (New Series) 3 (December, 1953), 140-142.
Schwarz, F. F. "Pliny the Elder on Ceylon," JAH 8 (1974), 21-48.
Stannard, J. "Pliny and Roman Botany," I 56 (Winter, 1965), 420-425.

Starr, C. G. "Roman Emporer and King of Ceylon [N. H. 6. 84-91]," CP 51 (January, 1956), 27-30.
Stuart, M. "Pliny, Historia Naturalis, XXXI, 41; His Statement That the Aqua Marcia Was Once Called Aufeia," AJP 64 (October, 1945), 440-444.
Thompson, D. W. "Pliny, Naturalis Historia, XVIII, 97," AJP 66 (October, 1945), 414-416.
Torrey, C. C. "Magic of Latapes [Proper Name, Appearing in the Elder Pliny's Natural History]," JBL 68 (December, 1949), 325-327.
Traub, H. W. "Pliny's Treatment of History in Epistolary Form," TAPA 86 (1955), 213-232.
Wade-Gery, H. T. "Islands of Peisistratos," AJP 59 (October, 1938), 470-475.
Wethered, H. N. The Mind of the Ancient World: A Consideration of Pliny's Natural History. New York: Longmans, Green, 1937.

PLINY THE YOUNGER

General Criticism

Andrews, A. C. "Pliny the Younger, Conformist," CJ 34 (December, 1938), 143-154.
Atkins, J. W. H. "Critical Cross-currents: Martial, the Younger Pliny, Plutarch, Dio Chrysostom, and Lucian," in his Literary Criticism in Antiquity: A Sketch of Its Development. Toronto: Macmillan, 1934, Vol. 2, pp. 299-345.
Cook, J. M. "Pliny on Icarian Shores," CQ (New Series) 9 (1959), 116-125.
Copley, F. O. "Pliny the Younger and Tacitus," in his Latin Literature from the Beginnings to the Close of the Second Century A. D. Ann Arbor: University of Michigan Press, 1969, pp. 327-341.
Duncan-Jones, R. "The Finances of the Younger Pliny," in Papers of the British School at Rome (New Series) 20 (1965), 177-188.
Dunham, F. S. "The Younger Pliny--Gentleman and Citizen," CJ 40 (April, 1945), 417-426.
Green, P. "Two Gentlemen of Rome; The Elder and the Younger Pliny," HT 6 (April, 1956), 266-273.
Hadas, M. "Learning and Letters in the First Century," in his History of Latin Literature. New York: Columbia University Press, 1952, pp. 302-320.
Sherwin-White, A. N. "Pliny's Praetorship Again," JRS 47 (1957), 126-130.
_____. "Trajan's Replies to Pliny: Authorship and Necessity," JRS 52 (1962), 114-125.
Stout, S. E. "The Coalescence of the Two Plinys," TAPA 86 (1955), 250-255.

Individual Works

Letters

Barrett, D. S. "Pliny, Ep. 6.20 Again," CB 48 (January, 1972), 38-40.

Cameron, A. "The Fate of Pliny's Letters in the Late Empire," CQ (New Series) 15 (1965), 289-298.

Coulter, C. C. "Further Notes on the Ritual of the Bithynian Christians," CP 35 (January, 1940), 60-63.

Forehand, W. E. "Natural Phenomena as Images in Pliny, Ep. 6.20," CB 47 (January, 1971), 33-39.

Grant, R. M. "Pliny and the Christians [Inferences from the Letter to Trajan, Epist. X. 96, in the Year 112]," HTR 41 (October, 1948), 273-274.

Hammond, M. "Pliny the Younger's Views on Government," HSCP 49 (1938), 115-140.

Hough, J. N. "A Few Inefficiencies in Roman Provincial Administration," CJ 35 (October, 1939), 17-26.

McDermott, W. C. "Pliniana," CJ 68 (February-March, 1973), 279-282.

_____. "Pliny the Younger and Inscriptions," CW 65 (November, 1971), 84-94.

Maritz, J. A. "The Eruption of Vesuvius Technicolour and Cinemascope?" Akroterion 19 (March, 1974), 12-15.

Miller, C. L. "The Younger Pliny's Dolphin Story (Epistulae IX 33): An Analysis," C World 60 (September, 1966), 6-8.

Radice, B. "A Fresh Approach to Pliny's Letters," G & R 9 (October, 1962), 160-169.

Saylor, C. F. "The Emperor as Insula: Pliny Epist. 6.31," CP 67 (January, 1972), 47-51.

Sherwin-White, A. N. Letters of Pliny: A Historical and Social Commentary. London: Oxford University Press, 1966.

_____. "Pliny, the Man and His Letters," G & R 16 (April, 1969), 76-90.

Shipp, G. P. "Latin Idiom and Pliny Ep. iv. 2.2," CP 39 (April, 1944), 117-118.

Sullivan, F. A. "Pliny Epistulae 6.16 and 20 and Modern Volcanology," CP 63 (July, 1968), 196-200.

Syme, R. "Friend of Tacitus," JRS 47 (1957), 131-135.

_____. "People in Pliny," JRS 58 (1968), 135-151.

Thompson, G. H. "Pliny's 'What of Humor,'" CJ 37 (January, 1942), 201-209.

Panegyricus

Bruere, R. T. "Tacitus and Pliny's Panegyricus," CP 49 (July, 1954), 161-179.

Hammond, M. "Pliny the Younger's Views on Government," HSCP 49 (1938), 115-140.

Radice, B. "Pliny and the Panegyricus," G & R 15 (October, 1968), 166-172.

Scott, K. "The Elder and Younger Pliny on Emporer Worship," TAPA 63 (1932), 156-165.

PLOTINUS

General Criticism

Armstrong, A. H. The Architecture of the Intelligible Universe in the Philosophy of Plotinus; An Analytical and Historical Study. Cambridge: Cambridge University Press, 1940.
_____. "Elements in the Thought of Plotinus at Variance with Classical Intellectualism," J Hel S 93 (1973), 13-22.
_____. "Gods in Plato, Plotinus, Epicurus," CQ 32 (July, 1968), 190-196.
_____. "Platonic Mysticism," Dub R 216 (April, 1945), 130-143.
_____. "Plotinus," in his The Cambridge History of Later Greek and Early Medieval Philosophy. London: Cambridge University Press, 1967, pp. 193-268.
_____. The Real Meaning of Plotinus' Intelligible World. Oxford: Blackfriars, 1949.
Barnes, T. D. "The Chronology of Plotinus' Life," GRBS 17 (Spring, 1976), 65-70.
Beardsley, M. C. "The Later Classical Philosophers," in his Aesthetics from Classical Greece to the Present; A Short History. New York: Macmillan, 1966, pp. 69-88.
Blumenthal, H. J. "Aristotle in the Service of Platonism," IPQ 12 (September, 1972), 340-364.
_____. Plotinus Psychology: His Doctrines of the Embodies Soul. The Hague: Nijhoff, 1971.
Brehier, E. "Neo-Platonism," in his The Hellenistic and Roman Age. Chicago: University of Chicago Press, 1965, pp. 182-217.
_____. Philosophy of Plotinus. Chicago: University of Chicago Press, 1958.
Burtt, E. A. "Background in Greek Philosophy," in his Types of Religious Philosophy. New York: Harper, 1951, pp. 44-70.
Clark, G. H. "Plotinus' Theory of Sensation," Ph R 51 (July, 1942), 357-382.
Coleridge, S. T. "Decline of Philosophy; Plotinus," in his Philosophical Lectures. New York: Philosophical Library, 1949, pp. 227-246.
Costello, E. B. "Is Plotinus Inconsistent on the Nature of Evil?" IPQ 7 (September, 1967), 483-497.
Deck, J. N. Nature, Contemplation, and the One. Toronto: University of Toronto Press, 1967.
Dodds, E. R. "Tradition and Personal Achievement in the Philosophy of Plotinus," JRS 50 (1960), 1-7.
Duvall, T. G. "Greek's Last Guess--Mysticism," in his Great Thinkers; The Quest of Life for Its Meaning. London: Oxford University Press, 1937, pp. 118-133.

Edman, I. "Logic of Mysticism in Plotinus," in Studies in the History of Ideas. New York: Columbia University Press, 1918-1935, Vol. 2, pp. 49-81.
Fowlie, W. "First Cycle," in his Love in Literature; Studies in Symbolic Expression. Bloomington: Indiana University Press, 1965, pp. 15-36.
Graeser, A. Plotinus and the Stoics: A Preliminary Study. Leiden: Brill, 1972.
Inge, W. R. The Philosophy of Plotinus. Westport, Conn.: Greenwood, 1968.
Jaspers, K. "Plotinus," in his The Great Philosophers, the Original Thinkers. New York: Harcourt, Brace, 1966, Vol. 2, pp. 38-92.
Katz, J. "Plotinus and the Gnostics," JHI 15 (April, 1954), 289-298.
_____. Plotinus' Search for the Good. New York: King's Crown, 1950.
Lodge, R. C. "Plotinus A. D. 204-270," in his Great Thinkers. Boston: Beacon, 1949, pp. 55-82.
Merlan, P. Monopsychism, Mysticism, Metaconsciousness: Problems of the Soul in the Neoaristotelian and Neoplatonic Tradition. The Hague: Nijhoff, 1969.
_____. "Plotinus and Magic," I 44 Pt. 4 (1953), 341-348.
Montague, W. P. "Plotinus and the Neo-Platonic Vision of Descending Spirit," in his Great Visions of Philosophy. La Salle, Ill.: Open Court, 1950, pp. 181-190.
Moore, K. G. "Theory of Imagination in Plotinus," J Psy 22 (July, 1946), 41-51.
Mortley, R. "Negative Theology and Abstraction in Plotinus," AJP 96 (Winter, 1975), 363-377.
O'Daly, G. J. P. Plotinus' Philosophy of the Self. New York: Barnes and Noble, 1973.
Pistorius, P. V. Plotinus and Neoplatonism. Cambridge, Eng.: Bowes and Bowes, 1952.
Randall, J. H. "Intelligible Universe of Plotinus," JHI 30 (January, 1969), 3-16.
Rist, J. M. Eros and Psyche. Toronto: University of Toronto Press, 1964, pp. 56-112; 169-191.
_____. "The One of Plotinus and the God of Aristotle," RM 27 (September, 1973), 75-87.
_____. Plotinus: The Road to Reality. London: Cambridge University Press, 1967.
Russell, B. A. W. R. "Plotinus," in his History of Western Philosophy. New York: Simon and Schuster, 1945, pp. 284-297.
Russell, G. W. "Of Plotinus Again," in his Living Touch. New York: Macmillan, 1938, pp. 286-298.
Santayana, G. "Plotinus and the Nature of Evil," in his Obiter Scripta; Lectures, Essays and Reviews. New York: Scribner's, 1936, pp. 68-87.
Thomas, G. F. "Neo-Platonism: Plotinus," in Religious Philosophies of the West. New York: Scribner's, 1965, pp. 49-69.
Turnbull, G. H. The Essence of Plotinus. Westport, Conn.: Greenwood, 1976.

Wa Said, D. Theosophies of Plato, Aristotle and Plotinus. New York: Philosophical Library, 1970.
Watkin, E. I. "Plotinus: Plato's Inheritance," in his Men and Tendencies. New York: Sheed and Ward, 1937, pp. 168-200.
Watson, R. I. "Plotinus and Augustine: The Patristic Period," in his The Great Psychologists: From Aristotle to Freud. New York: Lippincott, 1963, pp. 82-96.
Whittaker, T. The Neoplatonists. Hildesheim: Ohms, 1961, pp. 26-106.
Wolfson, H. A. "Albinus and Plotinus on Divine Attributes," HTR 45 (April, 1952), 115-130.

Individual Works (Ennead)

I:8

Costello, E. B. "Is Plotinus Inconsistent on the Nature of Evil?" IPQ 7 (September, 1967), 493-496.

II

Clark, G. H. "Plotinus on the Eternity of the World," Ph R 58 (March, 1949), 130-140.

II:4

Rist, J. M. "The Indefinite Dyad and Intelligible Matter in Plotinus," CQ (New Series) 12 (May, 1962), 99-107.

III

Clark, G. H. "Theory of Time in Plotinus," Ph R 53 (July, 1944), 337-358.

III:5

Dillon, J. "Enn. III 5: Plotinus' Exegesis of the Symposium Myth," Agon 3 (1969), 24-44.

IV:3

Warren, E. W. "Imagination in Plotinus," CQ (New Series) 16 (November, 1966), 277-285.
_____. "Memory in Plotinus," CQ (New Series) 15 (November, 1965), 252-260.

IV:4

Warren, E. W. "Memory in Plotinus," CQ (New Series) 15 (November, 1965), 252-260.

IV:7,8

Rist, J. M. "Integration and the Undescended Soul in Plotinus," AJP 88 (October, 1967), 410-422.

IV:7,9

Rist, J. M. "Forms of Individuals in Plotinus," CQ (New Series) 13 (November, 1963), 223-231.

PLUTARCH

General Criticism

Atkins, J. W. H. "Critical Cross-currents: Martial, the Younger Pliny, Plutarch, Dio Chrysostom, and Lucian," in his Literary Criticism in Antiquity: A Sketch of Its Development. Toronto: Macmillan, 1934, Vol. 2, pp. 299-345.

Barrow, R. H. Plutarch and His Times. Bloomington: Indiana University Press, 1967.

Brenk, F. E. " 'A Most Strange Doctrine': Daimon in Plutarch," CJ 69 (October-November, 1973), 1-11.

DeLacy, P. H. "Biography and Tragedy in Plutarch," AJP 73 (April, 1952), 159-171.

_____. "Plutarch and the Academic Sceptics," CJ 49 (November, 1953), 79-85.

Downs, R. B. "Prince of Ancient Biographers: Plutarch," in his Famous Books, Ancient and Medieval. New York: Barnes and Noble, 1964, pp. 221-224.

Gianakaris, C. J. Plutarch. New York: Twayne, 1970.

Gossage, A. J. "Plutarch," in T. A. Dorey, ed., Latin Biography. New York: Basic, 1967, pp. 45-77.

Grube, G. M. A. "After Quintilian," in his The Greek and Roman Critics. Toronto: University of Toronto Press, 1965, pp. 314-318.

Gundry, D. W. "Religion of a Greek Gentleman in the First Century A. D.," JH 44 (July, 1946), 345-352.

Hadas, M. "The Avenue of Survival," in his The Living Tradition. New York: New American Library, 1967, pp. 127-137.

_____. "Religion of Plutarch," SAQ 46 (January, 1947), 84-92.

Hershbell, J. P. "Plutarch and Parmenides," GRBS 13 (Summer, 1972), 193-208.

———. "Plutarch as a Source for Empedocles Re-examined?" AJP 92 (April, 1971), 156-184.
Howard, M. W. The Influence of Plutarch in the Major European Literature of the Eighteenth Century. Chapel Hill: University of North Carolina Press, 1970.
Johnson, V. L. "The Humanism of Plutarch," CJ 66 (October-November, 1970), 26-37.
Jones, C. P. Plutarch and Rome. Oxford: Clarendon, 1971.
———. "Towards a Chronology of Plutarch's Works," JRS 56 (1966), 61-74.
Moellering, H. A. Plutarch on Superstition. North Quincy, Mass.: Christopher, 1963.
Montaigne, M. E. de. "Defence of Seneca and Plutarch," in his Essays of Montaigne, tr. by J. Zeitlin. New York: Knopf, 1935, Vol. 2, pp. 374-380.
Polman, G. H. "Chronological Biography and Akme in Plutarch," CP 69 (1974), 169-177.
Russell, D. A. Plutarch. New York: Scribner's, 1973.
Wardman, A. E. "Description of Personal Appearance in Plutarch and Suetonius: The Use of Statues as Evidence," CQ (New Series) 17 (1967), 414-420.
———. "Plutarch and Alexander," CQ (New Series) 5 (1955), 96-107.
Wilkinson, L. P. Golden Latin Artistry. Cambridge: Cambridge University Press, 1963.

Individual Works

Lives

Carrey, T. F. "Plutarch's Style in the Marius," J Hel S 80 (1960), 24-31.
Ethel, G. "Hell's Marching Music," MLQ 18 (December, 1957), 295-302.
Fornara, C. "Plutarch and the Megarian Decree," YCS 24 (1975), 213-228.
Hamilton, J. R. Plutarch: Alexander, a Commentary. Oxford: Clarendon, 1969.
Herbert, K. "Identity of Plutarch's Lost Scipio," AJP 78 (January, 1957), 83-88.
Lavery, G. B. "Training, Trade and Trickery: Three Lawgivers in Plutarch," CW 67 (April-May, 1974), 369-381.
Martin, H. "The Character of Plutarch's Themistocles," TAPA 92 (1961), 326-339.
———. "Concept of 'Philanthropia' in Plutarch's Lives," AJP 82 (April, 1961), 164-175.
———. "Plutarch's Themistocles, 2 and Nicias, 2, 6," AJP 85 (April, 1964), 192-195.
Means, T. "Plutarch and the Family of Cato Minor," CJ 69 (February-March, 1974), 210-215.
Nicholson, H. "[Plutarch, the Father of Biography]," Spec 189 (November, 21, 1952), 666.

Popantoniou, G. A. "Once or Twice? [Athenian Aid to Sparta]," AJP 72 (April, 1951), 176-181.
Powell, J. E. "The Sources of Plutarch's Alexander," J Hel S 59 (1939), 229-240.
Pye, D. W. "Iambic Rhythm in Plutarch's Life of Marius," J Hel S 82 (1962), 146.
Rexroth, K. "Plutarch: Parallel Lives," in his Classics Revisited. Chicago: Quandrangle, 1968, pp. 108-111.
Russell, D. A. "On Reading Plutarch's Lives," G & R 13 (October, 1966), 139-154.
―――――. "Plutarch's Life of Coriolanus," JRS 53 (1963), 21-28.
Shrimpton, G. S. "Plutarch's Life of Epaminondas," PCP 6 (April, 1971), 55-59.
Smith, R. E. "Cato Censorius of Plutarch," CQ 34 (July, 1940), 105-112.
―――――. "Plutarch's Biographical Sources in the Roman Lives," CQ 34 (January, 1940), 1-10.
Stadter, P. A. "Plutarch's Comparison of Pericles and Fabius Maximus," GRBS 16 (Spring, 1975), 77-85.
Tracy, H. L. "Notes on Plutarch's Biographical Method," CJ 37 (January, 1942), 213-221.
Wade-Gerry, H. T. "Spartan Rhetra in Plutarch's Pycurgus vi," CQ 37 (January, 1943), 62-72; 38 (January, 1944), 1-9; 38 (July, 1944), 115-126.
Wardman, A. Plutarch's Lives. Berkeley: University of California Press, 1974.
―――――. "Plutarch's Methods in the Lives," CQ (New Series) 21 (May, 1971), 254-261.
Williams, M. V. "Plutarch as a Biographer," LQR 165 (April, 1940), 207-212.

Moralia

Aalders, G. J. D. "Political Thought in Plutarch's Convivium Septum Sapientium," Mnemosyne 30 (1977), 28-39.
Berry, E. G. "De Liberis Educandis of Pseudo-Plutarch," HSCP 63 (1958), 387-399.
Bowersock, G. W. "Some Persons in Plutarch's Moralia," CQ (New Series) 15 (1965), 267-270.
Bowra, C. M. "Sophocles on His Own Development; the Passage of Plutarch's Tract De Profectibus in Virtue," AJP 61 (October, 1940), 385-401.
Cherniss, H. "Notes on Plutarch's De Facie in Orbe Lunae," CP 46 (July, 1951), 137-158.
Clement, P. A. "Moralia 614E; the Problem of the Lacuna at the Beginning of Plutarch's Version of Aesop's Fable of the Fox and the Crane," AJP 66 (April, 1945), 192-196.
Dover, K. J. "Anthemocritus and Megarians," AJP 87 (April, 1966), 203-209.
Hamilton, J. R. "Notes on Plutarch (Alex. 47, 70; Brut. 12)," CP 51 (July, 1956), 170-172.

Lowell, J. R. "Plutarch's Morals," in his The Function of the Poet, and Other Essays. Port Washington, N. Y.: Kennikat, 1967, pp. 200-204.
Pearson, L. "Notes on the Text of Plutarch, De Malignitate Herodoti," AJP 80 (July, 1959), 255-275.
Riley, M. "Purpose and Unity of Plutarch's De Genio Socratis," GRBS 18 (Autumn, 1977), 257-273.
Russell, D. A. "On Reading Plutarch's Moralia," G & R 15 (October, 1968), 130-146.
Sandbach, F. H. "Plutarch on the Stoics," CQ 34 (January, 1940), 20-25.
──────. "Rhythm and Authenticity in Plutarch's Moralia," CQ 33 (July, 1939), 194-203.
Stadter, P. A. Plutarch's Historical Methods; An Analysis of the Mulierum Virtues. Cambridge, Mass.: Harvard University Press, 1965.
Whittaker, J. "Ammonius on the Delphic E," CQ (New Series) 19 (May, 1969), 185-192.

PROPERTIUS

General Criticism

Barsby, J. A. "The Composition and Publication of the First Three Books of Propertius," G & R 21 (October, 1974), 128-137.
Connor, P. J. "Propertius' Vein of Humor: In Which Some Discrimination Is Proposed," Ramus 5 (1976), 103-136.
Copley, F. O. "The Elegists: Tibullus, Propertius, and Ovid," in his Latin Literature from the Beginnings to the Close of the Second Century A. D. Ann Arbor: University of Michigan Press, 1969, pp. 241-275.
Edwards, M. W. "Intensification of Meaning in Propertius and Others," TAPA 92 (1961), 128-144.
Fontenrose, J. "Propertius and the Roman Career," in University of California Publications in Classical Philology. Berkeley: University of California, 1949. Vol. 13, No. 11, pp. 371-388.
Grant, M. "Love Lyric and Love Elegy: Catullus and Propertius," in his Roman Literature. Baltimore: Penguin, 1964, pp. 147-162.
Griffin, J. "Propertius and Antony," JRS 67 (1977), 17-26.
Hadas, M. "Tibullus and Propertius," in his History of Latin Literature. New York: Columbia University Press, 1952, pp. 184-200.
Highet, G. "Life Behind the Ivy," HOR 3 (January, 1961), 117-119.
──────. "Propertius: Umbria," in his Poets in a Landscape. New York: Knopf, 1957, pp. 74-105.
Hubbard, N. Propertius. New York: Scribner's, 1975.
Jay, P. "Cynthia: The Dream; Death and Love; Cynthia: A Malediction," Arion (New Series) 1 (1973-1974), 496-498.
Johnson, S. "Intimations of Immortality in the Major Lyric and Elegic Poets of Rome; Propertius," Roy Soc Can Trans (Series 3) 44 Sec. 2 (1950), 78-85.

King, J. K. "Propertius' Programmatic Poetry and the Unity of the Monobiblos," CJ 71 (December-January, 1975-76), 108-124.
Levin, D. N. "Propertius, Catullus, and Three Kinds of Ambiguous Expression," TAPA 100 (1969), 221-235.
McKay, L. A. "Umbrian Rimbaud," G & R 17 (October, 1970), 177-183.
Marcellino, R. "Propertius and Horace," CJ 50 (April, 1955), 34-35.
Mendell, C. W. "Propertius," in his Latin Poetry; The New Poets and the Augustans. New Haven, Conn.: Yale University Press, 1965, pp. 194-211.
Michels, A. K. "Death and Two Poets," TAPA 86 (1955), 160-179.
O'Neil, E. N. "Cynthia and the Moon," CP 53 (January, 1958), 1-8.
Platnauer, M. Latin Elegiac Verse; A Study of the Metrical Usages of Tibullus, Propertius and Ovid. Hamden, Conn.: Archon, 1971.
Potts, A. F. "The Form of Elegy: Anagnorisis," in his The Elegiac Mode; Poetic Form in Wordsworth and Other Elegists. Ithaca, N.Y.: Cornell University Press, 1967, pp. 36-66.
Saylor, C. "Querelae; Propertius' Distinctive Technical Name for His Elegy," Agon 1 (April, 1967), 142-149.
Shackleton Bailey, D. R. Propertiana. London: Cambridge University Press, 1956.
Skutsh, O. "Readings in Propertius," CQ (New Series) 23 (November, 1973), 316-323.
Solmsen, F. "Propertius and Horace," CP 43 (April, 1948), 105-109.
Sullivan, J. P. "Cynthia Prima Fuit: A Causerie," Arion 1 (Autumn, 1962), 34-44.
_____. Propertius: A Critical Introduction. New York: Cambridge University Press, 1976.
_____. "Propertius: A Preliminary Essay," Arion 5 (Spring, 1966), 5-22.
_____. "Propertius and Juvenal," Arion 7 (Autumn, 1968), 477-486.
Townend, G. "Propertius Among the Poets," G & R 8 (March, 1961), 36-49.
Wilkinson, L. P. Golden Latin Artistry. Cambridge: Cambridge University Press, 1963.
Yardley, J. C. "Comic Influences in Propertius," Phoenix 26 (Summer, 1972), 134-139.
_____. "Propertius' Lycinna," TAPA 104 (1974), 429-434.
_____. "Roman Elegists, Sick Girls, and the Soteria," CQ (New Series) 27 (1977), 394-401.

Individual Works (Elegies)

Book 1

Skutsch, O. "Structure of the Propertian Monobiblos," CP 58 (October, 1963), 238-239.

1:1

Allen, A. W. "Elegy and the Classical Attitude Toward Love: Propertius I, 1," YCS 11 (1950), 253-277.

Cairns, F. "Some Observations on Propertius 1.1," CQ (New Series) 24 (May, 1974), 94-110.

Connor, P. J. "Saevitia Amoris: Propertius 1.1," CP 67 (January, 1972), 51-54.

1:2

Curran, L. C. "Nature to Advantage Dressed: Propertius 1.2," Ramus 4 (1975), 1-16.

Gaisser, J. H. "Mythological Exempla in Propertius 1.2 and 1.15," AJP 98 (Winter, 1977), 381-391.

1:3

Harmon, D. P. "Myth and Fantasy in Propertius 1.3," TAPA 104 (1974), 151-165.

Lyne, R. O. A. M. "Propertius and Cynthia: Elegy I.3," PCPS 16 (1970), 60-78.

1:5

Allen, A. "Cynthia's Bedside Manner," Phoenix 27 (Winter, 1973), 381-385.

Lyne, R. O. A. M. "Propertius 15," Mnemosyne 27 (1974), 262-269.

Moritz, L. A. "Well-matched Lovers (Propertius 1.5," CP 62 (April, 1967), 106-108.

1:7

Solmsen, F. "On Propertius, 1.7," AJP 86 (January, 1965), 77-84.

1:8

White, R. E. "Dramatic Unity in Propertius 1.8, 2.29, 2.33," CP 56 (October, 1961), 217-229.

1:10

Khan, H. A. "Irony in Propertius 1.10," CP 63 (April, 1968), 131-134.

1:15

Bennett, A. W. "The Elegiac Lie: Propertius 1. 15," Phoenix 26 (Spring, 1972), 28-29.

Gaisser, J. H. "Mythological Exempla in Propertius 1. 2 and 1. 15," AJP 98 (Winter, 1977), 381-391.

1:18

Cairns, F. "Propertius i. 18 and Callimachus, Acontius and Cydippe," CR (New Series) 19 (June, 1969), 131-134.

1:21

Quinn, K. "Practical Criticism: A Reading of Propertius i. 21 and Catullus 17," G & R 16 (April, 1969), 19-29.

1:21-22

Davis, J. T. "Propertius 1. 21-22," CJ 66 (February, 1971), 209-213.

Book 2

Damon, P. W., and W. C. Helmbold. "The Structure of Propertius, Book 2," in University of California Publications in Classical Philology. Berkeley: University of California, 1952. Vol. 13, No. 6, pp. 214-254.

2:8

Harmon, D. P. "Myth and Proverb in Propertius 2. 8," CW 68 (April-May, 1975), 417-424.

Suits, T. A. "Mythology, Adress, and Structure in Propertius 2,8," TAPA 96 (1965), 427-438.

2:9

Wiggers, N. "Epic Themes in Propertius II. 8," Phoenix 30 (Winter, 1976), 367-374.

2:12

Long, T. "Two Unnoticed Parallels to Propertius 2. 12," CP 73 (April, 1978), 141-142.

2:13

Wilkinson, L. P. "Continuity of Propertius ii. 13," CR (New Series) 16 (June, 1966), 141-144.

2:17

Cairns, F. Further Adventures of a Locked-Out Lover: Propertius 2.17. Liverpool: Liverpool University Press, 1975.

2:19

Wilkinson, L. P. "Propertius II. 19," G & R 22 (April, 1975), 39-41.

2:24a

Felton, K. "Propertius II. 24A," CR (New Series) 33 (March, 1973), 3-5.
MacKay, L. A. "Propertius, II, 24A," AJP 89 (January, 1968), 72-76.

2:28

White, R. E. "The Structure of Propertius 2.28: Dramatic Unity," TAPA 89 (1958), 254-261.

2:29

Cairns, F. "Propertius 2.29A," CQ (New Series) 21 (November, 1971), 455-460.

2:29, 33

White, R. E. "Dramatic Unity in Propertius 1.8, 2.29, 2.33," CP 56 (October, 1961), 217-229.

2:30

Cairns, F. "Propertius, 2.30A and B," CQ (New Series) 21 (May, 1971), 204-213.

Book 3

Courtney, E. "The Structure of Propertius' Book 3," Phoenix 24 (Spring, 1970), 48-53.

Jacobson, H. "Structure and Meaning in Propertius Book 3," ICS 1 (1976), 160-173.

3:1-5

Nethercut, W. R. "The Ironic Priest," AJP 91 (October, 1970), 385-407.

3:7

Morsley, K. "Propertius 3.7," CQ 25 (December, 1975), 315-318.
Robertson, F. "Lament for Paetus: Propertius 3.7," TAPA 100 (1970), 377-386.

3:10

Bramble, J. C. "Critical Appreciations, I: Propertius III, 10," G & R 20 (October, 1973), 155-161.
Cairns, F. "Propertius 3, 10 and Roman Birthdays," Hermes 99 (1971), 149-155.
Lyne, R. O. A. M., and J. H. W. Morwood. "Critical Appreciations, I: Propertius III, 10," G & R 20 (April, 1973), 38-48.

3:11

Nethercut, W. R. "Propertius 3.11," TAPA 102 (1971), 411-443.
Saylor, C. F. "Symbolic Topography in Propertius 1.11," CJ 71 (January, 1976), 126-137.

3:12-14

Nethercut, W. R. "Propertius 3.12-14," CP 65 (April, 1970), 99-102.

3:13

Baker, R. J. "Propertius III 13, 30: Whose Baskets?," Mnemosyne 27 (1974), 53-58.

3:18

Falkner, T. M. "Myth, Setting and Immortality in Propertius 3.18," CJ 73 (October-November, 1977), 11-18.

3:19

Wooten, C. W. "Rhetoric in Propertius III, 19," CW 69 (October, 1975), 118-119.

3:20

Barsby, J. A. "Propertius III 20," Mnemosyne 28 (1975), 30-39.

3:22

Putnam, M. C. J. "Propertius 2.33: Tullus' Return," ICS 2 (1977), 240-254.

3:23

Baker, R. J. "A Literary Burnt Offering," CP 68 (April, 1973), 109-113.

3:24

Bennett, A. W. "Propertius 3.24: A New Approach," CP 64 (January, 1969), 30-35.
Koniaris, G. L. "On Propertius 3.24: A Reply," CP 66 (October, 1971), 253-258.

3:30

Baker, R. J. "Propertius III 13, 30: Whose Baskets?" Mnemosyne 27 (1974), 53-58.

Book 4

Nethercut, W. R. "Notes on the Structure of Propertius, Book IV," AJP 89 (October, 1968), 449-464.

4:2

Dee, J. H. "Propertius 4.2: Callimachus Romanus at Work," AJP 95 (Spring, 1974), 43-45.
Marquis, E. C. "Vertumnus in Propertius 4,2," Hermes 102 (1974), 491-500.
Suits, T. A. "The Vertumnus Elegy of Propertius," TAPA 100 (1969), 475-486.

4:3

Dee, J. H. "Arethusa to Lycotas: Propertius 4.3," TAPA 104 (1974), 81-96.

4:4

Rutledge, H. C. "Propertius' 'Tarpeia': The Poem Itself," CJ 60 (November, 1964), 68-73.
Warden, J. "Another Would-Be Amazon: Propertius 4,4, 71-72," Hermes 106 (1978), 177-187.

4:6

Johnson, W. R. "The Emotions of Patriotism: Propertius 4.6," CSCA 6 (1973), 151-180.
Sweet, F. "Propertius and Political Panegyric," Areth 5 (Fall, 1972), 169-175.

4:7

Lake, A. K. "Interpretation of Propertius IV, 7," CR 51 (May, 1937), 53-55.
Muecke, F. "Nobilis Historia? Incongruity in Propertius 4.7," BICS 21 (1974), 124-132.
Yardley, J. C. "Cynthia's Ghost: Propertius 4.7 Again," BICS 24 (1977), 83-87.

4:8

Evans, S. "Odyssean Echoes in Propertius IV, 8," G & R 18 (April, 1971), 51-53.

4:9

Anderson, W. S. "Hercules Exclusus: Propertius, IV, 9," AJP 85 (January, 1964), 1-12.
McParland, E. H. "Propertius 4.9," TAPA 101 (1970), 349-355.

4:11

Curran, L. C. "Propertius 4:11: Greek Heriones and Death," CP 63 (April, 1968), 134-139.

QUINTILIAN

General Criticism; and, The Education of an Orator (Institutio Oratoria)

Atkins, J. W. H. "Restatement of Classicism: Quintilian;" in his Literary Criticism in Antiquity; A Sketch of Its Development. Toronto: Macmillan, 1934, Vol. 2, pp. 254-298.
Austin, R. G. "Quintilian on Painting and Statuary," CQ 38 (January, 1944), 17-26.
Clarke, M. L. "Quintilian: A Biographical Sketch," G & R 14 (April, 1967), 24-37.
Daube, D. "The Mediocrity of Celsus," CJ 70 (October-November, 1974), 41-42.
Downs, R. B. "Education of the Orator: Marcus Fabius Quintilianus," in his Famous Books, Ancient and Medieval. New York: Barnes and Noble, 1964, pp. 210-214.
Fantham, E. "Imitation and Decline: Rhetorical Theory and Practice in the First Century After Christ," CP 73 (April, 1978), 102-116.
Grube, G. M. A. "Quintilian," in his The Greek and Roman Critics. Toronto: University of Toronto Press, 1965, pp. 284-307.
Gwynn, A. O. Roman Education from Cicero to Quintilian. New York: Russell and Russell, 1964, pp. 180-241.
Hadas, M. "Learning and Letters in the First Century," in his History of Latin Literature. New York: Columbia University Press, 1952, pp. 302-320.
Kennedy, G. "Estimate of Quintilian," AJP 83 (April, 1962), 130-146.
──────. Quintilian. New York: Twayne, 1969.
McDonald, I. R. "The Vir Bonus and Quintilian XI, 3," SP 72 (July, 1975), 237-245.
Mayer, F. "Quintilian," in his The Great Teachers. New York: Citadel, 1967, pp. 97-105.
Ramage, E. S. "Urbanitas: Cicero and Quintilian, a Contrast in Attitudes," AJP 84 (October, 1963), 390-414.
Reinke, E. C. "Quintilian Lighted the Way," CB 51 (March, 1975), 65-71.
Rusk, R. R. "Quintilian," in his The Doctrines of the Great Educators. New York: St. Martin's, 1965, pp. 39-51.
Ulich, R. "Quintilian," in his History of Educational Thought. New York: America Book Co., 1950, pp. 51-60.
Von Fritz, K. "Ancient Instruction in Grammar According to Quintilian," AJP 70 (October, 1949), 337-366.
Winterbottom, M. Problems in Quintilian. London: University of London, Institute of Classical Studies, 1970.
──────. "Quintilian and the Vir Bonus," JRS 54 (1964), 90-97.

SALLUST

General Criticism

Allen, W. "Sallust's Political Career," SP 51 (January, 1954), 1-14.

_____. "The Unity of the Sallustian Corpus," CJ 61 (March, 1966), 268-269.
Earl, D. C. Political Thought of Sallust. Amsterdam: Hakkert, 1966.
Hadas, M. "Caesar, Sallust, and Others," in his History of Latin Literature. New York: Columbia University Press, 1952, pp. 88-107.
Laistner, M. L. W. "Sallust," in his Greater Roman Historians. Berkeley: University of California Press, 1947, pp. 45-64.
Loefstedt, E. "Roman Publicist and Historian," in his Roman Literary Portraits. Oxford: Clarendon, 1958, pp. 93-117.
Mazzolani, L. S. Empire Without End. New York: Harcourt Brace Jovanovich, 1976.
Morel, W. "Notes on Sallust, Statius, and Vegetius," CR 55 (September, 1941), 74-75.
Renehan, R. "A Traditional Pattern of Imitation in Sallust and His Sources," CP 71 (January, 1976), 97-105.
Syme, R. Sallust. Berkeley: University of California Press, 1964.
Usher, S. "Sallust: The Censor of a Decadent Age," HT 13 (August, 1963), 564-572.
Whitehorne, J. E. G. "Sallust and Fausta," CW 68 (April-May, 1975), 425-430.
Wilkinson, L. P. Golden Latin Artistry. Cambridge: Cambridge University Press, 1963.
Wistrand, E. K. H. Sallust on Judicial Murders in Rome. Stockholm: Almqvist and Wiksell, 1968.

Individual Works

Conspiracy of Catiline

Bradley, K. R. "Slaves and the Conspiracy of Catiline," CP 73 (October, 1978), 329-336.
Downs, R. B. "The First Roman Historian: Gaius Sallustius Crispus," in his Famous Books, Ancient and Medieval. New York: Barnes and Noble, 1964, pp. 173-177.
Genovese, E. N. "Cicero and Sallust: Catiline's Ruina," CW 68 (November, 1974), 171-177.
Hands, A. R. "Sallust and Dissimulatio," JRS 49 (1959), 56-60.
Salmon, E. T. "Catilina, Crassus and Caesar," AJP 56 (1935), 302-316.
Stewart, D. J. "Sallust and Fortuna," H & T 7, No. 3 (1968), 298-317.
Syme, R. Sallust. Berkeley: University of California Press, 1964.

Histories

Clausen, W. "Notes on Sallust's Historiae," AJP 68 (July, 1947), 293-301.
Syme, R. Sallust. Berkeley: University of California Press, 1964.

War with Jugurtha

Downs, R. B. "The First Roman Historian: Gaius Sallustius Crispus," in his Famous Books, Ancient and Medieval. New York: Barnes and Noble, 1964, pp. 173-177.
Gilbert, C. D. "Marius and Fortuna," CQ (New Series) 23 (May, 1973), 104-107.
Syme, R. Sallust. Berkeley: University of California Press, 1964.

SAPPHO

General Criticism

Bagg, R. "Love, Ceremony and Daydream in Sappho's Lyrics," Arion 3 (Autumn, 1964), 44-82.
Bonnard, A. "Sappho of Lesbos, Tenth of the Muses," in his Greek Civilization; From the Iliad to the Parthenon. New York: Macmillan, 1957, pp. 86-100.
Cameron, A. "Sappho and Aphrodite Again," HTR 57 (July, 1964), 237-239.
―――. "Sappho's Prayer to Aphrodite," HTR 32 (January, 1939), 1-17.
Devereux, G. "The Nature of Sappho's Seizure in FR 31 LP as Evidence of Her Inversion," CQ (New Series) 20 (May, 1970), 17-31.
Goldsmith, M. L. Sappho of Lesbos; A Psychological Reconstruction of Her Life. London: Rich, 1938.
Moore, V. Distinguished Women Writers. New York: Dutton, 1934, pp. 71-80.
Page, D. L. Sappho and Alcaeus: An Introduction to the Study of Ancient Lesbian Poetry. London: Oxford University Press, 1955.
Rexroth, K. "Sappho: Poems," in his Classics Revisited. Chicago: Quadrangle, 1968, pp. 41-46.
Robinson, D. M. Sappho and Her Influence. New York: Cooper Square, 1963.
Will, F. "Sappho and Poetic Motion," CJ 61 (March, 1966), 259-262.

Individual Works

Book 1, Fragment 1

Castle, W. "Observations on Sappho's Hymn to Aphrodite," TAPA 89 (1958), 66-67.
Putnam, M. C. J. "Throna and Sappho," CJ 56 (November, 1960), 79-83.
Stanley, K. "The Role of Aphrodite in Sappho Fr. 1," GRBS 17 (Winter, 1976), 305-321.
Wyatt, W. F. "Sappho and Aphrodite," CP 69 (July, 1974), 213-214.

Book 1, Fragment 2

McEvilley, T. "Sappho, Fragment 2," Phoenix 26 (Winter, 1972), 323-333.

Book 1, Fragment 31

Lefkowitz, M. R. "Critical Stereotypes and the Poetry of Sappho," GRBS 14 (Summer, 1973), 113-123.
Segal, C. "Eros and Incantation: Sappho and Oral Poetry," Areth 7 (Fall, 1974), 139-160.

Book 4, Fragment 94

McEvilley, T. "Sappho, Fragment Ninety-four," Phoenix 25 (Spring, 1971), 1-11.

SENECA

General Criticism

Alexander, W. H. "The Enquete on Seneca's Treason," CP 47 (January, 1952), 1-6.
―――――. "Julius Caesar in the Pages of Seneca the Philosopher," Roy Soc Can Trans (Series 3) 35 Sec. 2 (1941), 15-28.
―――――. "References to Pompey in Seneca's Prose," Roy Soc Can Trans (Series 3) 42 Sec. 2 (1948), 13-29.
―――――. "Seneca the Philosopher in Account with Roman History," Roy Soc Can Trans (Series 3) 41 (Sec. 2 (1947), 23-46.
Altman, M. "Ruler Cult in Seneca," CP 33 (April, 1938), 198-204.
Anderson, W. S. "Anger in Juvenal and Seneca," in University of California Publications in Classical Philology. Berkeley: University of California, 1964. Vol. 19, No. 3, pp. 127-195.
Boal, S. J. "Seneca's Dialogues," Ha 114 (Winter, 1972), 65-69.
Braden, G. "The Rhetoric and Psychology of Power in the Dramas of Seneca," Arion 9 (Spring, 1970), 5-41.
Brady, J. F. A Study of the Stoicism in Senecan Tragedy. Ann Arbor, Mich.: University Microfilms, 1958.
Calder, W. M. "Seneca, Tragedian of Imperial Rome," CJ 72 (October-November, 1976), 1-11.
Coleman, R. "The Artful Moralist: A Study of Seneca's Epistolary Style," CQ 24 (November, 1974), 276-289.
Copley, F. O. "Augustus to Nero: Seneca the Younger," in his Latin Literature from the Beginnings to the Close of the Second Century A. D. Ann Arbor: University of Michigan Press, 1969, pp. 287-303.
Cornwallis, W. Discourses upon Seneca, the Tragedian. Gainesville, Fla: Scholars' Facsimiles and Reprints, 1952.

Costa, C. D. N., ed. Seneca. Boston: Routledge and K. Paul, 1974.
Downs, R. B. "Moral Essayist and Tragic Dramatist: Lucius Annaeus Seneca," in his Famous Books, Ancient and Medieval. New York: Barnes and Noble, 1964, pp. 199-203.
Dyson, S. L. "The Portrait of Seneca in Tacitus," Areth 3 (Spring, 1970), 71-83.
Evans, E. C. "A Stoic Aspect of Senecan Drama: Portraiture," TAPA 81 (1950), 169-184.
Fantham, E. "Virgil's Dido and Seneca's Tragic Heroines," G & R 22 (April, 1975), 1-10.
Gambet, D. G. "Cicero in the Works of Seneca Philosophus," TAPA 101 (1970), 171-183.
Garton, C. "Background to Character Portrayal in Seneca," CP 54 (January, 1959), 1-9.
Griffin, M. T. Seneca: A Philosopher in Politics. Oxford: Clarendon, 1976.
Gummere, R. M. Seneca, the Philosopher, and His Modern Message. New York: Cooper Square, 1963.
Hadas, M. "Seneca," in his History of Latin Literature. New York: Columbia University Press, 1952, pp. 243-259.
Hall, J. J. "Seneca as a Source for Earlier Thought," CQ (New Series) 27 (1977), 409-436.
Hardeman, T. P. The Philosophy of Lucius Annaeus Seneca. Ann Arbor, Mich.: University Microfilms, 1956.
Harsh, P. W. "Seneca," in his Handbook of Classical Drama. Stanford, Calif.: Stanford University Press, 1944, pp. 401-436.
Henry, D., and B. Walker. "Tacitus and Seneca," G & R 10 (October, 1963), 98-110.
Herington, C. J. "Senecan Tragedy," Arion 5 (Winter, 1966), 422-471.
_____. "Seneca's Tragedies," Arion 7 (Autumn, 1968), 487-490.
Hijmans, B. L. "Drama in Seneca's Stoicism," TAPA 97 (1966), 237-252.
Kamp, H. W. "Concerning Seneca's Exile," CJ 30 (November, 1934), 101-108.
_____. "Seneca's Marriage," CJ 32 (June, 1937), 529-533.
Manning, C. E. "The Consolatory Tradition and Seneca's Attitude to the Emotions," G & R 21 (April, 1974), 71-81.
Marti, B. M. "Prototypes of Seneca's Tragedies," CP 42 (January, 1947), 1-16.
_____. "Seneca's Tragedies: A New Interpretation," TAPA 76 (1945), 216-245.
Mendell, C. W. Our Seneca. Hamden, Conn.: Archon, 1968.
Morford, M. "The Neronian Literary Revolution," CJ 68 (February-March, 1972-1973), 210-215.
Motto, A. L. Guide to the Thought of Lucius Annaeus Seneca, in the Extant Prose Works. Amsterdam: Hakkert, 1970.
_____. Seneca. New York: Twayne, 1973.
_____. "Seneca, Exponent of Humanitarianism," CJ 50 (April, 1955), 315-318; 336.
_____. "Seneca on Death and Immortality," CJ 50 (January, 1955), 186; 187-189.

_____. "Seneca on Trial: The Case of the Opulent Stoic," CJ 61 (March, 1966), 254-258.
_____. "Seneca on Women's Liberation," CW 65 (January, 1972), 155-157.
_____, and J. R. Clark. "Ingenium Facile et Copiosum: Point and Counterpoint in Senecan Style," CB 52 (November, 1974), 1-4.
Nicoll, A. "From Menander to the Mimes," in his World Drama, from Aeschylus to Anouilh. New York: Harcourt, 1953, pp. 107-137.
Noyes, R. "Seneca on Death," JRH 12 (1973), 223-240.
Owen, W. H. "Commonplace and Dramatic Symbol in Seneca's Tragedies," TAPA 99 (1968), 291-314.
Pack, R. A. "On Guilt and Error in Senecan Tragedy," TAPA 71 (1940), 360-371.
Pratt, N. T. Dramatic Suspense in Seneca and in His Greek Precursors. Princeton, N. J.: Princeton University Press, 1939.
_____. "Major Systems of Figurative Language in Senecan Melodrama," TAPA 94 (1963), 199-234.
_____. "The Stoic Base of Senecan Drama," TAPA 79 (1948), 1-11.
_____. "Tragedy and Moralism, Euripides and Seneca," in N. P. Stallknecht and H. Frenz, eds., Comparative Literature: Method and Perspective. Carbondale: Southern Illinois University Press, 1961, pp. 189-203.
Rivenburg, M. J. Fashionable Life in Rome as Portrayed by Seneca. Philadelphia: University of Pennsylvania Press, 1939.
Rozelaar, M. "Seneca: A New Approach to His Personality," Psychiatry 36 (February, 1973), 82-92.
Sevenster, J. N. Paul and Seneca. Leiden: Brill, 1961.
Stewart, Z. "Sejanus, Gaetulicus, and Seneca," AJP 74 (January, 1953), 70-85.
Sullivan, J. P. "Petronius, Seneca, and Lucan: A Neronian Literary Feud?" TAPA 99 (1968), 453-468.
Thompson, L. Lucan's Bellum Civile and the Tragedies of Seneca. Chicago: Dept. of Photographic Reproduction, University of Chicago Library, 1956.
Tobin, R. W. "Tragedy and Catastrophe in Seneca's Theatre," CJ 62 (November, 1966), 64-70.
Watts, W. "Seneca on Slavery," DR 90 (July, 1972), 183-195.
Wetmore, J. H. L. Seneca's Conception of the Stoic Stage as Shown in His Prose Works. Edmonton: University of Alberta Press, 1935.

Individual Works

Ad Helviam Matrem

Ferrill, A. "Seneca's Exile and the Ad Helviam: A Reinterpretation," CP 61 (October, 1966), 253-257.
Motto, A. L. "Seneca on Theology," CJ 50 (January, 1955), 181-182.

Ad Polybium

Alexander, W. H. "Seneca's Ad Polybium de Consolations; A Reappraisal," Roy Soc Can Trans (Series 3) 37 Sec. 2 (1943), 33-55.

Agamemnon

Caider, W. M. "Seneca's Agamemnon," CP 71 (January, 1976), 27-36.
Henry, D., and B. Walker. "Seneca and the Agamemnon: Some Thoughts on Tragic Doom," CP 58 (January, 1963), 1-10.
Shelton, J. A. "The Dramatization of Inner Experience: The Opening Scene of Seneca's Agamemnon," Ramus 6 (1977), 33-43.

Apocolocyntosis

Athanassakis, A. N. "Some Evidence in Defence of the Title Apocolocyntosis for Seneca's Satire," TAPA 104 (1974), 11-21.
Martin, J. M. K. "Seneca the Satirist," G & R 14 (June, 1945), 64-71.
Toynbee, J. M. C. "Nero Artifex: The Apocolocyntosis Reconsidered," CQ 36 (October, 1942), 83-93.

De Consolatione ad Marciam

Boal, S. J. "Doing Battle with Grief: Seneca, Dialogue 6," Ha 116 (Winter, 1973), 44-51.

De Providencia

Theron, L. "Progression of Thought in Seneca's De Providentia c. VI," AClass 13 (1971), 61-72.

Hercules Furens

Haywood, R. M. "Note on Seneca's Hercules Furens," CJ 37 (April, 1942), 421-424.
Shelton, J. A. "Problems of Time in Seneca's Hercules Furens and Thyestes," CSCA 8 (1975), 257-269.

Hercules Oetaeus

King, C. M. "Seneca's Hercules Oetaeus: A Stoic Interpretation of the Greek Myth," G & R 18 (October, 1971), 215-222.

Medea

Bishop, J. D. "The Choral Odes of Seneca's Medea," CJ 60 (April, 1965), 313-316.
Henry, D., and B. Walker. "Loss of Identity: Medea Superest? A Study of Seneca's Medea," CP 62 (July, 1967), 169-181.

Moral Letters, or Epistulae Morales

Manning, C. E. "Seneca's 98th Letter and the Praemeditatio Futuri Mali," Mnemosyne 29 (1976), 301-304.
Motto, A. L., and J. R. Clark. "Decensus Averno in Seneca's Epistle 55," CJ 68 (February-March, 1972-1973), 193-198.
―――――. "Epistle 56: Seneca's Ironic Art," CP 65 (April, 1970), 102-105.
―――――. "Et Terris Iactatus et Alto: The Art of Seneca's Epistle LIII," AJP 92 (April, 1971), 217-225.
Nietmann, W. D. "Seneca on Death: The Courage to Be or Not to Be," IPQ 6 (March, 1966), 81-89.
Wedeck, H. E. "Seneca's Humanitarianism," CJ 50 (April, 1955), 319-320.

Oedipus

Hind, J. "The Death of Agrippina and the Finale of the Oedipus of Seneca," AUMLA 38 (November, 1972), 204-211.
Mastronarde, D. J. "Seneca's Oedipus: The Drama in the Word," TAPA 101 (1970), 291-315.
Motto, A. L., and J. R. Clark. " 'There's Something Wrong With the Sun': Seneca's Oedipus and the Modern Grotesque," CB 54 (1977-1978), 41-44.
―――――. "Violenta Fata: The Tenor of Seneca's Oedipus," CB 50 (April, 1974), 81-87.

On Mercy, or De Clementia

Fears, J. R. "Nero as the Vicegerent of the Gods in Seneca's De Clementia," Hermes 103 (1975), 486-496.
Korfmacher, W. C. "Stoic Apatheia and Seneca's De Clementia," TAPA 77 (1946), 44-52.

Phaedra

Flygt, S. G. "Treatment of Character in Euripides and Seneca: The Hippolytus," CJ 29 (April, 1934), 507-516.
Henry, D., and B. Walker. "Phantasmagoria and Idyll: An Element of Seneca's Phaedra," G & R 13 (October, 1966), 223-239.

Snell, B. "Passion and Reason: Phaedra in Hippolytus I," in his Scenes from Greek Drama. Berkeley: University of California Press, 1964, pp. 23-46.

Thyestes

Poe, J. P. "An Analysis of Seneca's Thyestes," TAPA 100 (1969), 355-376.
Shelton, J. A. "Problems of Time in Seneca's Hercules Furens and Thyestes," CSCA 8 (1975), 257-269.

Trojan Women, or Troades

Calder, W. M. "Originality in Seneca's Troades," CP 65 (April, 1970), 75-82.
Knight, W. F. J. "Magical Motives in Seneca's Troades," TAPA 63 (1932), 20-33.

SOPHOCLES

General Criticism

Adams, S. M. Sophocles the Playwright. Toronto: University of Toronto Press, 1957.
Agius, D. "Mind of Sophocles," Dub R 216 (April, 1945), 143-151.
Bacon, H. H. "Sophocles," in his Barbarians in Greek Tragedy. New Haven, Conn.: Yale University Press, 1961, pp. 64-114.
Bates, W. N. Sophocles. New York: Barnes and Noble, 1961.
Cameron, A. "Maker and the Myth," AR 25 (Spring, 1965), 167-188.
Campbell, L. Tragic Drama in Aeschylus, Sophocles and Shakespeare. New York: Russell and Russell, 1965.
Colchester, L. S. "Justice and Death in Sophocles," CQ 36 (January, 1942), 21-28.
Earp, F. R. The Style of Sophocles. New York: Russell and Russell, 1972.
Easterling, P. E. "Character in Sophocles," G & R 24 (October, 1977), 121-129.
_____. "Repetition in Sophocles," Hermes 101 (1973), 14-34.
Ehrenberg, V. Sophocles and Pericles. Oxford: Blackwell, 1954.
Epps, P. H. "Sophocles: Mere Conservative or True See-r?" SP 42 (July, 1945), 427-439.
Gassner, J. W. "Sophocles, the Serene," in his Masters of the Drama. New York: Random House, 1940, pp. 40-55.
Gellie, G. H. Sophocles: A Reading. Carlton: Melbourne University Press, 1972.
Grene, D. "Introduction: Sophocles," in his Reality and the Heroic Pattern; Last Plays of Ibsen, Shakespeare and Sophocles. Chicago: University of Chicago Press, 1967, pp. 111-117.

Hamilton, E. "Sophocles, Quintessence of the Greek," in her Great Age of Greek Literature. New York: Norton, 1942, pp. 258-270.
Harsh, P. W. "Sophocles," in his Handbook of Classical Drama. Stanford, Calif.: Stanford University Press, 1944, pp. 88-155.
Hester, D. A. "Very Much the Safest Plan or Last Words in Sophocles," Antichthon 7 (1973), 8-13.
Hulton, A. O. "The Prologues of Sophocles," G & R 16 (April, 1969), 49-59.
Jaeger, W. W. "Sophocles and the Tragic Character," in his Paideia: The Ideals of Greek Culture. Oxford: B. Blackwell, 1944-47. Vol. 1, pp. 268-285.
Kamerbeek, J. C. Plays of Sophocles: Commentaries. Leiden: Brill, 1953.
Kirkwood, G. M. A Study of Sophoclean Drama. Ithaca, N.Y.: Cornell University Press, 1958.
Kiso, A. "Sophocles' Phaedra and the Phaedra of the First Hippolytus," BICS 20 (1973), 22-36.
Kitto, H. D. F. "The Idea of God in Aeschylus and Sophocles," in H. J. Rose, ed., La Notion du Divin. Berne: Vandoeuvres-Geneve, 1955, pp. 169-189.
_____. "Sophocles," in his Poiesis: Structure and Thought. Berkeley: University of California Press, 1966, pp. 153-242.
_____. Sophocles: Dramatist and Philosopher. London: Oxford University Press, 1958.
_____. "The Vitality of Sophocles," in W. J. Oates, ed., From Sophocles to Picasso; The Present Day Vitality of the Classical Tradition. Bloomington: Indiana University Press, 1962, pp. 39-64.
Knox, B. M. W. Heroic Temper; Studies in Sophoclean Tragedy. Berkeley: University of California Press, 1964.
Letters, F. J. H. The Life and Works of Sophocles. London: Sheed and Ward, 1953.
Long, A. A. Language and Thought in Sophocles: A Study of Abstract Nouns and Poetic Technique. New York: Oxford University Press, 1968.
Lucas, D. W. "Sophocles," in his Greek Tragic Poets; Their Contribution to Western Life and Thought. Boston: Beacon, 1953, pp. 106-154.
Melchinger, S. Sophocles, tr. by D. A. Scrase. New York: Ungar, 1974.
Muller, H. J. "Sophocles," in his Spirit of Tragedy. New York: Knopf, 1956, pp. 78-102.
Musurillo, H. "Illusion of Prosperity in Sophocles and Gregory of Nyssa," AJP 82 (April, 1961), 182-187.
_____. The Light and the Darkness: Studies in the Dramatic Poetry of Sophocles. Leiden: Brill, 1967.
Nicoll, A. "Glory of the Greek Theatre: Sophocles," in his World Drama, from Aeschylus to Anouilh. New York: Harcourt, 1953, pp. 51-68.
Opstelten, J. C. Sophocles and Greek Pessimism, tr. by J. A. Ross. Amsterdam: North-Holland, 1952.
Pohlsander, H. A. "Lyrical Meters and Chronology in Sophocles," AJP 84 (July, 1963), 280-286.

_____. *Metrical Studies in the Lyrics of Sophocles.* Leiden: Brill, 1964.
Post, L. A. "Sophoclean Tragedy," in his *From Homer to Menander; Forces in Greek Poetic Fiction.* Berkeley: University of California Press, 1951, pp. 88-121.
Reinhardt, K. *Sophocles,* tr. by H. Harvey and D. Harvey. Oxford: Blackwell, 1978.
Rexroth, K. "Sophocles: The Theban Plays," in his *Classics Revisited.* Chicago: Quadrangle, 1968, pp. 51-55.
Saunders, A. N. W. "Plot and Character in Sophocles," *G & R* 4 (October, 1934), 13-23.
Segal, C. P. "Synaesthesia in Sophocles," *ICS* 2 (1977), 88-96.
Sheppard, J. T. *Aeschylus and Sophocles; Their Work and Influence.* New York: Cooper Square, 1963.
_____. *Wisdom of Sophocles.* New York: Macmillan, 1947.
Stinton, T. C. W. "Notes on Greek Tragedy, II," *JHS* 97 (1977), 127-154.
Stone, J. A. *Sophocles and Racine; A Comparative Study in Dramatic Technique.* Geneva: Droz, 1964.
Waldock, A. J. A. *Sophocles the Dramatist.* Cambridge: Cambridge University Press, 1951.
Walter, W. *The Plays of Sophocles.* New York: Simon and Schuster, 1966.
Webster, T. B. L. *An Introduction to Sophocles.* London: Methuen, 1969.
Whitman, C. H. *Sophocles: A Study of Heroic Humanism.* Cambridge, Mass.: Harvard University Press, 1951.
Woodard, T. M., ed. *Sophocles; A Collection of Critical Essays.* Englewood Cliffs, N. J.: Prentice-Hall, 1966.

Individual Works

Ajax

Biggs, P. "Disease Theme in Sophocles' *Ajax, Philoctetes* and *Trachiniae,*" *CP* 61 (October, 1966), 223-235.
Brown, W. E. "Sophocles' Ajax and Homer's Hector," *CJ* 61 (December, 1965), 118-121.
Burian, P. "Supplication and Hero Cult in Sophocles' *Ajax,*" *GRBS* 13 (Summer, 1972), 151-156.
Calder, W. M. "Entrance of Athena in *Ajax,*" *CP* 60 (April, 1965), 114-116.
Cohen, D. "Imagery of Sophocles: A Study of Ajax's Suicide," *G & R* 25 (April, 1978), 24-36.
Davidson, J. F. "The Parodos of Sophocles' *Ajax,*" *BICS* 22 (1975), 163-177.
Grene, D. "Ajax," in his *Reality and the Heroic Pattern; Last Plays of Ibsen, Shakespeare and Sophocles.* Chicago: University of Chicago Press, 1967, pp. 118-136.
Leinieks, V. "Aias and the Day of Wrath," *CJ* 69 (February-March, 1974), 193-201.

Rosivach, V. J. "Sophocles' Ajax," CJ 72 (October-November, 1976), 47-61.
Sicherl, M. "The Tragic Issue in Sophocles' Ajax," YCS 25 (1977), 67-98.
Simpson, M. "Sophocles' Ajax: His Madness and Transformation," Areth 2 (Spring, 1969), 88-103.
Wellein, L. T. Time Past and the Hero: A Suggested Criterion for Sophoclean Tragedy as Exemplified by the Ajax, Trachiniae, and Electra. Ann Arbor, Mich.: University Microfilms, 1959.

Aleadae

Kiso, A. "Sophocles, Aleadae: A Reconstruction," GRBS 17 (Spring, 1976), 5-21.

Antigone

Abel, D. H. "Sophocles--Politikos," CJ 49 (October, 1953), 17-21.
Bradshaw, A. T. von S. "The Watchman Scenes in the Antigone," CQ (New Series) 12 (November, 1962), 200-211.
Coleman, R. "The Role of the Chorus in Sophocles' Antigone," PCPS (New Series) 18 (1972), 4-27.
Daly, E. J. "Three Keys to the Antigone," Thought 42 (Spring, 1967), 85-111.
Else, G. F. The Madness of Antigone. Heidelberg: Winter, 1976.
Fletcher, P. Sophocles: Oedipus Rex, Oedipus at Colonus, Antigone. New York: Barnes and Noble, 1969.
Goheen, R. F. Imagery of Sophocles' Antigone; A Study of Poetic Language and Structure. Princeton, N. J.: Princeton University Press, 1951.
Hoey, T. F. "Inversion in the Antigone: A Note," Arion 9 (Winter, 1970), 337-345.
Hogan, J. C. "The Protagonists of the Antigone," Areth 5 (1972), 93-100.
Kanzer, M. "The Oedipus Trilogy," in L. F. Manheim and E. B. Manheim, eds., Hidden Patterns; Studies in Psychoanalytic Literary Criticism. New York: Macmillan, 1966, pp. 66-78.
Levy, C. S. "Antigone's Motives: A Suggested Interpretation," TAPA 94 (1963), 137-144.
Linforth, I. M. Antigone and Creon. Berkeley: University of California Press, 1961.
McCall, M. "Divine and Human Action in Sophocles: The Two Burials of the Antigone," YCS 22 (1972), 103-117.
McDevitt, A. S. "Sophocles' Praise of Man in the Antigone," Ramus 1 (1972), 152-164.
Macurdy, G. H. "Blood and Tears in Antigone 526-530," CP 41 (July, 1946), 163-164.
Margon, J. S. "The First Burial of Polyneices," CJ 64 (April, 1969), 289-295.
_____. "The Second Burial of Polyneices," CJ 68 (October-November, 1972), 39-49.

Moore, J. A. Sophocles and Arete. Cambridge, Mass.: Harvard University Press, 1939.
Musurillo, H. "Fire-walking in Sophocles' Antigone 618-619," TAPA 94 (1963), 167-175.
Rose, J. L. "The Problem of the Second Burial in Sophocles' Antigone," CJ 47 (March, 1952), 219-221; 251.
Segal, C. P. "Sophocles' Praise of Man and the Conflicts of the Antigone," Arion 3 (Summer, 1964), 67-87.
Summerson, E. J. "The Antigone and Its Epilogue," Pegasus No. 14 (1972), 1-6.
Weissman, P. "Sophocles' Antigone: The Psychology of the Old Maid," in his Creativity in the Theatre; A Psychoanalytic Study. New York: Basic, 1965.
Wiltshire, S. F. "Antigone's Disobedience," Areth 9 (Spring, 1976), 29-36.
Ziobro, W. J. "Where Was Antigone? Antigone, 766-883," AJP 92 (January, 1971), 81-85.

Electra

Kenna, V. E. G. "The Return of Orestes," J Hel S 81 (1961), 99-104.
Kirkwood, G. M. "Two Structural Features of Sophocles' Electra," TAPA 73 (1942), 86-95.
Linforth, I. M. Electra's Day in the Tragedy of Sophocles. Berkeley: University of California Press, 1963.
Schucard, S. C. "Some Developments in Sophocles' Late Plays of Intrigue," CJ 69 (December, 1973), 133-138.
Segal, C. P. "The Electra of Sophocles," TAPA 97 (1966), 473-546.
Stevens, P. T. "Sophocles: Electra, Doom or Triumph?" G & R 25 (October, 1978), 111-120.
Wellein, L. T. Time Past and the Hero: A Suggested Criterion for Sophoclean Tragedy as Exemplified by the Ajax, Trachiniae, and Electra. Ann Arbor, Mich.: University Microfilms, 1959.

Ichneutai

Ussher, R. G. "Sophocles' Ichneutai as a Satyr Play," Ha 118 (Winter, 1974), 130-138.

Oedipus the King, or Oedipus Rex, or Oedipus Tyrannus

Barstow, M. L. "Oedipus Rex: A Typical Greek Tragedy," in L. Cooper, ed., Greek Tragedy and Its Influence. New Haven, Conn.: Yale University Press, 1917, pp. 156-162.
Cameron, A. Identity of Oedipus the King: Five Essays on the Oedipus Tyrannus. New York: New York University Press, 1968.
Champlin, M. W. "Oedipus Tyrannus and the Problem of Knowledge," CJ 64 (April, 1969), 337-345.

Cook, A., ed. Oedipus Rex: A Mirror for Greek Drama. Belmont, Calif.: Wadsworth, 1963.
Devereux, G. "The Self-Blinding of Oidipous in Sophokles' Oidipous Tyrannos," J Hel S 93 (1973), 36-49.
_____. "Why Oedipus Killed Laius," in H. M. Ruitenbeek, ed., Psychoanalysis and Literature. New York: Dutton, 1964, pp. 168-186.
Dimock, G. "Oedipus: The Religious Issue," Hud R 21 (Autumn, 1968), 430-456.
Dodds, E. R. "On Misunderstanding the Oedipus Rex," G & R 13 (April, 1966), 37-49.
Dyson, M. "Oracle, Edict, and Curse in Oedipus Tyrannus," CQ (New Series) 23 (November, 1973), 202-212.
_____. "Where Are You Going To, My Pretty Maids?" CR (New Series) 22 (December, 1972), 311-313.
Fitton, A. D. "Oedipus and the Delegation," CR (New Series) 2 (March, 1952), 2-4.
Fletcher, P. Sophocles: Oedipus Rex, Oedipus at Colonus, Antigone. New York: Barnes and Noble, 1969.
Gould, T. "Innocence of Oedipus: The Philosophers on Oedipus the King," Arion 4 (Autumn-Winter, 1965), 363-386; 582-611; 5 (Winter, 1966), 478-525.
Harshbarger, K. Sophocles' Oedipus. Washington, D.C.: University Press of America, 1979.
Henry, A. S. "Sophocles, Oedipus Tyrannus: The Interpretation of the Opening Scene and the Text of 1.18," CQ (New Series) 17 (1967), 48-51.
Hoey, T. F. "On the Theme of Introversion in Oedipus Rex," CJ 64 (April, 1969), 296-299.
Howe, T. P. "Taboo in the Oedipus Theme," TAPA 93 (1962), 124-143.
Kane, R. L. "Prophecy and Perception in the Oedipus Rex," TAPA 105 (1975), 189-208.
Kanzer, M. "The Oedipus Trilogy," in L. F. Manheim and E. B. Manheim, eds., Hidden Patterns; Studies in Psychoanalytic Literary Criticism. New York: Macmillan, 1966, pp. 66-78.
_____. "The 'Passing of the Oedipus Complex' in Greek Drama," in H. M. Ruitenbeek, ed., Psychoanalysis and Literature. New York: Dutton, 1964, pp. 243-250.
Keddie, J. N. "Justice in Sophocles' Oedipus Tyrannus," Antichthon 10 (1976), 25-34.
Lattimore, S. "Oedipus and Teiresias," CSCA 8 (1975), 105-111.
Leinieks, V. "The Foot of Oidipous," CW 69 (September, 1975), 35-44.
Macurdy, G. H. "References to Thucydides, Son of Melesias, and to Pericles in Sophocles OT 863-910," CP 37 (July, 1942), 307-310.
_____. "Sophoclean Irony in Oedipus Tyrannus 219-221," PQ 21 (April, 1942), 244-247.
Margon, J. S. "Aristotle and the Irrational and Improvable Elements in Oedipus Rex," C World 70 (December, 1976), 249-255.
Mullahy, P. Oedipus: Myth and Complex. New York: Grove, 1955.

Mullens, H. G. "Oedipus and the Tragic Spirit," G & R 7 (May, 1938), 149-155.
Musurillo, H. "Sunken Imagery in Sophocles' Oedipus," AJP 78 (January, 1957), 36-51.
O'Brien, M. J., ed. Twentieth Century Interpretations of Oedipus Rex; A Collection of Critical Essays. Englewood Cliffs, N. J.: Prentice-Hall, 1968.
Rigsby, K. J. "Teiresias as Magus in Oedipus Rex," GRBS 17 (Summer, 1976), 109-114.
Sansone, D. "The Third Stasiman of the Oedipus Tyrannus," CP 70 (April, 1975), 110-117.
Schmiel, R. S. "Texture in the Oedipus Tyrannus," CW 66 (September, 1972), 30-41.
Vellacott, P. H. "The Chorus in Oedipus Tyrannus," G & R 14 (October, 1967), 109-125.
──────. "The Guilt of Oedipus," G & R 11 (October, 1964), 137-148.
──────. "The Guilt of Oedipus," List 71 (March 26, 1964), 515-517.
──────. Sophocles and Oedipus: A Study of Oedipus Tyrannus with a New Translation. Ann Arbor: University of Michigan Press, 1971.
Vernant, J. P. "Ambiguity and Reversal: On the Enigmatic Structure of Oedipus Rex," NLH 9 (Spring, 1978), 475-501.
Versenyi, L. "Oedipus: Tragedy of Self-knowledge," Arion (Autumn, 1962), 20-30.
Winnington-Ingram, R. P. "The Second Stasimon of the Oedipus Tyrannus," J Hel S 91 (1971), 119-135.

Oedipus at Colonus

Burian, P. "Suppliant and Saviour: Oedipus at Colonus," Phoenix 28 (Winter, 1974), 408-429.
Ceadel, E. B. "Division of Parts Among the Actors of Sophocles' Oedipus Coloneus," CQ 35 (July, 1941), 139-147.
Fletcher, P. Sophocles: Oedipus Rex, Oedipus at Colonus, Antigone. New York: Barnes and Noble, 1969.
Forrer, R. "Oedipus at Colonus: A Crisis in the Greek Notion of Deity," Comp D (Winter, 1974-1975), 328-346.
Gratwick, A. "Blood-letting in Polynices' List of Heroes: O. C. 1319-1321," CR (New Series) 15 (December, 1965), 243-246.
Grene, D. "Oedipus at Colonus," in his Reality and the Heroic Pattern; Last Plays of Ibsen, Shakespeare and Sophocles. Chicago: University of Chicago Press, 1967, pp. 154-169.
Howe, T. P. "Taboo in the Oedipus Theme," TAPA 93 (1962), 124-143.
Kanzer, M. "The Oedipus Trilogy," in L. F. Manheim and E. B. Manheim, eds., Hidden Patterns; Studies in Psychoanalytic Literary Criticism. New York: Macmillan, 1966, pp. 66-78.
Linforth, I. M. Religion and Drama in Oedipus at Colonus. Berkeley: University of California Press, 1951.

Stinton, T. C. W. "The Riddle at Colonus," GRBS 17 (Winter, 1976), 323-328.

Philoctetes

Beye, C. R. "Sophocles' Philoctetes and the Homeric Embassy," TAPA 101 (1970), 63-75.
Biggs, P. "Disease Theme in Sophocles' Ajax, Philoctetes and Trachiniae," CP 61 (October, 1966), 223-235.
Calder, W. M., III. "Sophoclean Apologia: Philoctetes," GRBS 12 (Summer, 1971), 153-174.
Cook, A. "The Patterning of Effect in Sophocles' Philoctetes," Areth 1 (Fall, 1968), 82-93.
Fuqua, C. "Studies in the Use of Myth in Sophocles' Philoctetes and the Orestes of Euripides," Traditio 32 (1976), 29-95.
Grene, D. "Philoctetes," in his Reality and the Heroic Pattern; Last Plays of Ibsen, Shakespeare and Sophocles. Chicago: University of Chicago Press, 1967, pp. 136-154.
Hamilton, R. "Neoptolemo's Story in the Philoctetes," AJP 96 (Summer, 1975), 131-137.
Hinds, A. E. "The Prophecy of Helenus in Sophocles' Philoctetes," CQ (New Series) 17 (1967), 169-180.
Kieffer, J. S. "Philoctetes and Arete; Comparison of the Plays of Aeschylus and Euripides with That of Sophocles," CP 37 (January, 1942), 38-50.
Knox, M. W. "Philoctetes," Arion 3 (Spring, 1964), 42-60.
Linforth, I. M. Philoctetes, the Play and the Man. Berkeley: University of California Press, 1956.
Poe, J. P. Heroism and Divine Justice in Sophocles' Philoctetes. Leiden: Brill, 1974.
Pratt, N. T. "Sophoclean Orthodoxy in the Philoctetes," AJP 70 (July, 1949), 273-289.
Robinson, D. B. "Topics in Sophocles' Philoctetes," CQ (New Series) 19 (May, 1969), 34-56.
Schucard, S. C. "Some Developments in Sophocles' Late Plays of Intrigue," CJ 69 (December, 1973), 133-138.
Seale, D. "The Element of Surprise in Sophocles' Philoctetes," BICS 19 (1972), 94-102.
Segal, C. "Philoctetes and the Imperishable Piety," Hermes 105 (1977), 133-158.
Skloot, R. "Philoctetes: Wound and Bow Revisited," Dram S 6 (Spring, 1968), 288-293.
Taplin, O. "Significant Actions in Sophocles' Philoctetes," GRBS 12 (Spring, 1971), 25-44.
Tembeck, R. "Digressions on Philoctetes and Graduate Study in Theatre," Dram S 6 (Spring, 1968), 294-301.
Wilson, E. "Philoctetes: The Wound and the Bow," in his The Wound and the Bow; Seven Studies in Literature. New York: Houghton Mifflin, 1941, pp. 272-295.

Trachiniae

Biggs, P. "Disease Theme in Sophocles' Ajax, Philoctetes and Trachiniae," CP 61 (October, 1966), 223-235.
Earp, F. R. "Trachiniae," CR 53 (September, 1939), 113-115.
Hoey, T. F. "Sun Symbolism in the Parodos of the Trachiniae," Areth 5 (Fall, 1972), 133-154.
──────. "The Trachiniae and Unity of Hero," Areth 3 (Spring, 1970), 1-22.
Kirkwood, G. M. "The Dramatic Unity of Sophocles' Trachiniae," TAPA 72 (1941), 203-211.
Kitto, H. D. F. "Sophocles, Statistics, and the Trachiniae," AJP 60 (April, 1939), 178-193.
Linforth, I. M. The Pyre on Mount Oeta in Sophocles' Trachiniae. Berkeley: University of California Press, 1952.
McCall, M. "The Trachiniae: Structure, Focus, and Herakles," AJP 43 (January, 1972), 142-163.
Musurillo, H. "Fortune's Wheel: The Symbolism of Sophocles' Women of Trachia," TAPA 92 (1961), 372-383.
Segal, C. P. "Sophocles' Trachiniae: Myth, Poetry, and Heroic Values," YCS 25 (1977), 99-158.
Sorem, C. E. "Mosters and the Family: The Exodes of Sophocles' Trachiniae," GRBS 19 (Spring, 1978), 59-73.
Wellein, L. T. Time Past and the Hero: A Suggested Criterion for Sophoclean Tragedy as Exemplified by the Ajax, Trachiniae, and Electra. Ann Arbor, Mich.: University Microfilms, 1959.
Wender, D. "The Will of the Beast: Sexual Imagery in the Trachiniae," Ramus 3 (1974), 1-17.

STATIUS

General Criticism

Bower, E. W. "Notes on Juvenal and Statius," CR (New Series) 8 (March, 1958), 9-11.
Cooke, J. P. "Three Notes on Statius," CP 41 (April, 1946), 102-105.
Copley, F. O. "Martial, Statius, and Quintilian," in his Latin Literature from the Beginnings to the Close of the Second Century A. D. Ann Arbor: University of Michigan Press, 1969, pp. 317-326.
Dilke, O. A. W. "Metrical Treatment of Proper Names in Statius," CR 63 (September, 1949), 50-51.
Gould, G. P. "Transportation in Statius," CR (New Series) 1 (June, 1951), 71-73.
Griffith, J. G. "Juvenal, Statius and the Flavian Establishment," G & R 16 (October, 1967), 134-150.
Hakanson, L. Statius' Silvae: Critical and Exegetical Remarks with Some Notes on the Thebaid. Lund: Gleerup, 1969.
Morel, W. "Notes on Sallust, Statius, and Vegetius," CR 55 (September, 1941), 74-75.
Pavlovskis, Z. "Statius and the Late Latin Epithalamia," CP 60 (July, 1965), 164-177.

Individual Works

Silvae

Bishop, J. H. "Two Notes on Statius, Silvae iv. 1," CR (New Series) 4 (June, 1954), 95-97.
Casson, L. "Maecius Celer's Ship (Statius, Silvae iii. 2.22, 28)," CR (New Series) 18 (December, 1968), 261-262.
Coulter, C. C. "Statius, Silvae, V, 4 and Fiametta's Prayer to Sleep," AJP 80 (October, 1959), 390-395.
Cunningham, J. V. "Classical and Medieval: Statius, On Sleep," in his Tradition and Poetic Structure; Essays in Literary History and Criticism. Denver: Swallow, 1960, pp. 25-39.
Hakanson, L. Statius' Silvae: Critical and Exegetical Remarks with Some Notes on the Thebaid. Lund: Gleerup, 1969.
Holtsmark, E. B. "The Bath of Claudius Etruscus," CJ 68 (February-March, 1972), 216-220.
Martin, D. "Similarities Between the Silvae of Statius and the Epigrams of Martial," CJ 34 (May, 1939), 461-470.
Pavlovskis, Z. "Statius and the Late Latin Epithalamia," CP 60 (July, 1965), 164-177.
Smyth, W. R. "Statius, Silvae, 2.1.130," CR 56 (November, 1942), 112-113.
Vessey, D. W. T. C. "Varia Statiana," CB 46 (February, 1970), 49-55, 64.
Weaver, P. R. C. "The Father of Claudias Etruscus: Statius, Silvae 3.3," CQ (New Series) 15 (1965), 145-154.
White, P. "The Presentation and Dedication of the Silvae and the Epigrams," JRS 64 (1974), 40-61.

Thebaid

Burgess, J. F. "Statius' Altar of Mercy," CQ 22 (November, 1972), 339-349.
Cooke, J. P. "Notes on Statius' Thebaid," CP 41 (July, 1946), 143-149.
Gossage, A. J. "Statius, Thebaid V. 593," CR (New Series) 12 (June, 1962), 114-115.
Hadas, M. "Silver Epic," in his History of Latin Literature. New York: Columbia University Press, 1952, pp. 260-277.
Hakanson, L. Statius' Silvae: Critical and Exegetical Remarks with Some Notes on the Thebaid. Lund: Gleerup, 1969.
Ker, A. "Notes on Statius," CQ (New Series) 3 (1953), 1-10; 175-182.
Moreland, F. L. "The Role of Darkness in Statius: A Reading of Thebaid I," CJ 70 (April, 1975), 20-31.
Pavlovskis, Z. "Statius and the Late Latin Epithalamia," CP 60 (July, 1965), 164-177.
Poyton, J. B. "Statius, Thebaid," CR (New Series) 13 (December, 1963), 259-261.
_____. "Two Notes on the Thebaid of Statius," CR 54 (March, 1940), 13.

Ross, R. C. "Superstitio," CJ 64 (May, 1969), 354-358.
Snijder, H. P. Papinius Statius, Thebaid: A Commentary on Book III. Amsterdam: Hakkert, 1969.
Vessey, D. W. T. C. "Lucan, Statius and the Baroque Epic," CW 63 (March, 1970), 232-234.
_____. "Notes on the Hypsipyle Episode in Statius, Thebaid 4-6," BICS 17 (1970), 44-54.
_____. "Noxia Tela: Some Innovations in Statius' Thebaid 7 and 11," CP 66 (April, 1971), 87-92.
_____. "The Significance of the Myth of Linus and Coroebus in Statius' Thebaid, I, 557-672," AJP 91 (July, 1970), 315-331.
_____. Statius and the Thebaid. London: Cambridge University Press, 1973.

STESICHORUS

General Criticism and Individual Works

Gostoli, A. "Some Aspects of the Theban Myth in the Lille Stesichorus," GRBS 19 (Spring, 1978), 23-27.
Haslam, M. "Versification of the New Stesichorus," GRBS 19 (Spring, 1978), 29-57.
Page, D. L. "Stesichorus: The Sack of Troy and the Wooden Horse," PCPS (New Series) 19 (1973), 47-65.
Robertson, M. "Geryoneis, Stesichorus and the Vase Painters," CQ (New Series) 19 (November, 1969), 207-221.
West, M. L. "Stesichorus," CQ 21 (November, 1971), 302-314.

STRABO

General Criticism and The Geography

Dicks, D. R. "Strabo and the KAIMATA," CQ (New Series) 6 (1956), 243-247.
Downey, G. "Strabo on Antioch: Notes on His Method," TAPA 72 72 (1941), 85-95.
Downs, R. B. "Human Geographer: Strabo," in his Famous Books, Ancient and Medieval. New York: Barnes and Noble, 1964, pp. 188-195.
Richards, G. C. "Strabo," G & R 10 (February, 1941), 79-90.
Sarton, G. "Geography in the Last Two Centuries: Crates and Strabon," in his History of Science; Hellenistic Science and Culture in the Last Three Centuries B. C. Cambridge, Mass.: Harvard University Press, 1959, Vol. 2, pp. 413-433.
Schenkeveld, D. M. "Strabo on Homer," Mnemosyne 29 (1976), 52-64.

SUETONIUS

General Criticism

Baldwin, B. "Suetonius, Birth, Disgrace and Death," AClass 18 (1975), 61-70.
Copley, F. C. "Suetonius and Juvenal," in his Latin Literature from the Beginnings to the Close of the Second Century A.D. Ann Arbor: University of Michigan Press, 1969, pp. 342-349.
Hadas, M. "Tacitus and Suetonius," in his History of Latin Literature. New York: Columbia University Press, 1952, pp. 321-333.
Sanders, H. A. "Suetonius in the Civil Service Under Hadrian," AJP 65 (April, 1944), 113-123.
Townend, G. B. "Suetonius and His Influence," in T. A. Dorey, ed., Latin Biography. New York: Basic, 1967, pp. 79-111.
Wardman, A. E. "Description of Personal Appearance in Plutarch and Suetonius: The Use of Statues as Evidence," CQ (New Series) 17 (1967), 414-420.
Zinn, T. L. "Pun in Suetonius," CR (New Series) 1 (March, 1951), 10.

Individual Works

Lives of the Caesars or De Vita Caesarum

Borthwick, E. K. "Suetonius' Nero and a Pindaric Scholium," CR (New Series) 15 (December, 1965), 252-256.
Bradley, K. R. "The Composition of Suetonius' Caesares Again," JIES 1 (Fall, 1973), 257-263.
─────. "Imperial Virtues in Suetonius' Caesares," JIES 4 (1976), 245-253.
─────. "A Publica Fames in A.D. 68," AJP 93 (July, 1972), 451-458.
Carney, T. F. "How Suetonius' Lives Reflect on Hadrian," PACA 11 (1968), 7-24.
Donald, D. "Suetonius in the Primera Cronica General Through the Speculum Historiale," HR 11 (April, 1943), 95-115.
Downs, R. B. "Biographer of Emperors: Gaius Suetonius Tranquillus," in his Famous Books, Ancient and Medieval. New York: Barnes and Noble, 1964, pp. 233-235.

Of Distinguished Men, or De Viris Illustribus

Enos, R. L. "When Rhetoric Was Outlawed in Rome: A Translation and Commentary of Suetonius' Treatise on Early Roman Rhetoricans," SM 39 (March, 1972), 37-45.
Lewis, R. G. "Pompeius' Freedman Biographer: Suetonius, De Gramm. et Rhet. 27 (3)," CR (New Series) 16 December, 1966), 271-273.
Treggiari, S. "Pompeius' Freedman Biographer Again," CR (New Series) 19 (December, 1969), 264-266.

238 : Greek and Roman Authors

TACITUS

General Criticism

Adams, J. N. "The Vocabulary of the Speeches in Tacitus' Historical Works," BICS 20 (1973), 124-144.
Alexander, W. H. "Tacitean 'Non Liquet' on Seneca," in University of California Publications in Classical Philology. Berkeley: University of California, 1952. Vol. 14, No. 8, pp. 269-386.
_____. "The 'Psychology' of Tacitus," CJ 47 (May, 1952), 326-328.
Atkins, J. W. H. "Critical Revival and Theories of Style: Tacitus and Demetrius," in his Literary Criticism in Antiquity; A Sketch of Its Development. Toronto: Macmillan, 1934, Vol. 2, pp. 175-209.
Baldwin, B. "Women in Tacitus," Prudentia 4 (November, 1972), 83-101.
Benario, H. W. An Introduction to Tacitus. Athena: University of Georgia Press, 1975.
_____. "Tacitus and the Principate," CJ 60 (December, 1964), 97-106.
_____. "Vergil and Tacitus," CJ 63 (October, 1967), 24-27.
Birley, A. R. "Petillius Cerialis and the Conquest of Brigantia," Britannia 4 (1973), 179-190.
Bruere, R. T. "Tacitus and Pliny's Panegyricus," CP 49 (July, 1954), 161-179.
Cairns, H., et al. "Tacitus: History," in their Invitation to Learning. New York: Random House, 1941, pp. 377-391.
Chapman, C. S. "The Artistry of Tacitus," G & R 16 (June, 1947), 85-87.
Clayton, F. W. "Tacitus and Nero's Persecution of the Christians," CQ 41 (July, 1947), 81-85.
Crook, J. A. "Strictum et Aequum: Law in the Time of Nero," IJ 5 (Winter, 1970), 357-368.
Daitz, S. G. "Tacitus' Technique of Character Portrayal," AJP 81 (January, 1960), 30-52.
Dorey, T. A. Tacitus. London: Routledge and K. Paul, 1969.
Dudley, D. R. "Tacitus 1: The Historian," List 72 (August 6, 1964), 193-195.
_____. "Tacitus 2: Man of Letters," List 72 (August 13, 1964), 227-228.
_____. The World of Tacitus. Boston: Little, Brown, 1969.
Easton, S. C. "Freedom and Tyranny in the Ancient World," in K. M. Setton and H. R. Winkler, eds., Great Problems in European Civilization. New York: Prentice-Hall, 1954, pp. 1-46.
Gilmartin, K. "Tacitean Evidence for Tacitean Style," CJ 69 (February-March, 1974), 216-222.
Goodyear, F. R. D. Tacitus. Oxford: Clarendon, 1970.
Grube, G. M. A. "Tacitus," in his The Greek and Roman Critics. Toronto: University of Toronto Press, 1965, pp. 275-283.
Hadas, M. "Tacitus and Suetonius," in his History of Latin Literature. New York: Columbia University Press, 1952, pp. 321-333.

Henry, D., and B. Walker. "Tacitus and Seneca," G & R 10 (October, 1963), 98-110.
Laistner, M. L. W. "Tacitus the Historian," in his Greater Roman Historians. Berkeley: University of California Press, 1947, pp. 123-140.
_____. "Tacitus and His Forerunners," in his Greater Roman Historians. Berkeley: University of California Press, 1947, pp. 103-122.
Leeman, A. D. "Structure and Meaning in the Prologues of Tacitus," YCS 23 (1973), 169-208.
Loefstedt, E. "Style of Tacitus," in his Roman Literary Portraits. Oxford: Clarendon, 1958, pp. 157-180.
_____. "Tacitus as an Historian," in his Roman Literary Portraits. Oxford: Clarendon, 1958, pp. 142-156.
Martin, R. H. "Tacitus and the Death of Augustus," CQ (New Series) 5 (1955), 123-128.
Mendell, C. W. Tacitus, the Man and His Work. Hamden, Conn.: Archon, 1970.
Mierow, C. C. "Tacitus Speaks," SP 38 (October, 1941), 553-570.
_____. "Tacitus the Biographer," CP 34 (January, 1939), 36-44.
Miller, N. P. "Dramatic Speech in Tacitus," AJP 85 (July, 1964), 279-296.
_____. "Tacitus' Narrative Technique," G & R 24 (April, 1977), 13-22.
Reed, N. "Some Neglected Evidence on the Early Career of Tacitus," CQ (New Series) 26 (1976), 309-314.
Roberts, R. L. "Tacitus' Conception of the Function of History," G & R 6 (October, 1936), 9-17.
Ryberg, I. S. "Tacitus' Art of Innuendo," TAPA 73 (1942), 383-404.
Sullivan, D. "Innuendo and the 'Weighted Alternative' in Tacitus," CJ 71 (April-May, 1976), 312-326.
Syme, R. Tacitus. Oxford: Clarendon, 1958.
_____. Ten Studies in Tacitus. Oxford: Clarendon, 1970.
Tanner, R. G. "Tacitus and the Principate," G & R 16 (April, 1969), 95-99.
Trilling, L. "Tacitus Now," in his Liberal Imagination; Essays on Literature and Society. New York: Viking, 1950, pp. 198-204.

Individual Works

Agricola

Austin, R. G. "Epilogue to the Agricola," CR 53 (September, 1939), 116-117.
Liebschuetz, W. "The Theme of Liberty in the Agricola of Tacitus," CQ (New Series) 16 (May, 1966), 126-139.

Annals

Allen, W. "Epic and Etiquette in Tacitus' Annals," SP 58 (October, 1961), 557-572.

Baxter, R. T. S. "Virgil's Influence on Tacitus in Books 1 and 2 of the Annals," CP 67 (October, 1972), 246-269.
Bews, J. "Virgil, Tacitus, Tiberius and Germanicus," PVS 12 (1972-1973), 35-48.
Downs, R. B. "Chronicler of Roman Decadence: Cornelius Tacitus," in his Famous Books, Ancient and Medieval. New York: Barnes and Noble, 1964, pp. 225-228.
Dyson, S. L. "A Portrait of Seneca in Tacitus," Areth 3 (Spring, 1970), 71-83.
Goodyear, F. R. D. "Development of Language and Style in the Annals of Tacitus," JRS 58 (1968), 22-31.
Katzoff, R. "Tacitus Annales I, 74: The Case of Granius Marcellus," AJP 92 (October, 1971), 680-684.
Marshall, A. J. "Tacitus and the Governor's Lady: A Note on Annals III: 33-34," G & R 22 (April, 1975), 11-18.
Mendell, C. W. "Dramatic Construction of Tacitus' Annals," YCS 5, 1-53.
Mierow, C. C. "Tiberius Himself," PQ 22 (October, 1943), 289-307.
Miller, N. P. "An Aspect of Tacitean Style," BICS 17 (1970), 111-119.
──────. "Tiberius Speaks; An Examination of the Utterances Ascribed to Him in the Annals of Tacitus," AJP 89 (January, 1968), 1-19.
Oliver, R. P. "Did Tacitus Finish the Annales?" ICS 2 (1977), 289-314.
Ross, D. O. "The Tacitean Germanicus," YCS 33 (1973), 209-227.
Segal, C. P. "Tacitus and Poetic History: The End of the Annals XIII," Ramus 2 (1973), 107-126.
Shotter, D. C. A. "The Trial of Clutorius Priscus," G & R 16 (April, 1969), 14-18.
Syme, R. "Marcus Lepidus, Capax Imperii," JRS 45 (1955), 22-33.
Vessey, D. W. T. C. "Thoughts on Tacitus' Portrayal of Claudius," AJP 92 (July, 1971), 385-409.
Walker, B. Annals of Tacitus; A Study in the Writing of History. Manchester: Manchester University Press, 1960.
Woodman, A. J. "Remarks on the Structure and Content of Tacitus, Annals 4: 57-67," CQ 22 (May, 1972), 150-158.

Germania

Beare, W. "Tacitus on the Germans," G & R 11 (March, 1964), 64-76.

Histories

Baxter, R. T. S. "Virgil's Influence on Tacitus in Book 3 of the Histories," CP 66 (April, 1971), 93-107.
Benario, H. W. "Priam and Galba," CW 65 (January, 1972), 146-147.

Boyer, B. B. "The Histories of Tacitus," CP 44 (April, 1949), 107-115.
Hainsworth, J. B. "The Starting-point of Tacitus' Historiae: Fear and Favour by Omission," G & R 11 (October, 1964), 128-136.
Miller, N. P. "Tacitus' Narrative Technique," G & R (New Series) 24 (April, 1977), 13-22.
Rexroth, K. "Tacitus: Histories," in his Classics Revisited. Chicago: Quadrangle, 1968, pp. 103-107.
Scott, R. T. Religion and Philosophy in the Histories of Tacitus. Rome: American Academy, 1968.
Walker, B. "A Study in Incoherence: The First Book of Tacitus' Histories," CP 71 (January, 1976), 113-118.
Wellesley, K. "Three Historical Puzzles in Histories 3," CQ (New Series) 6 (1956), 207-214.

TERENCE

General Criticism

Abbott, K. M. "O Dimidiate Menander: An Echo from a Roman Schoolroom?" CJ 57 (March, 1962), 241-251.
Amerasinghe, C. W. "The Part of the Slave in Terence's Drama," G & R 19 (June, 1950), 62-72.
Arnott, G. "Menander, Plautus, Terence," G & RNSC 9 (1975), 5-62.
Atkins, J. W. H. "Critical Beginnings at Rome and the Classical Reaction: Terence, Lucilius, and Cicero," in his Literary Criticism in Antiquity; A Sketch of Its Development. Toronto: Macmillan, 1934, Vol. 2, pp. 1-46.
Clifford, H. R. "Dramatic Technique and the Originality of Terence," CJ 26 (May, 1931), 605-618.
Copley, F. O. "Terence," in his Latin Literature from the Beginnings to the Close of the Second Century A. D. Ann Arbor: University of Michigan Press, 1969, pp. 36-49.
Duckworth, G. E. The Nature of Roman Comedy: A Study in Popular Entertainment. Princeton, N. J.: Princeton University Press, 1952.
Flickinger, R. C. "Terence and Menander," CJ 26 (June, 1931), 676-694.
―――. "Terence and Menander Once More," CJ 28 (April, 1933), 515-522.
Frank, T. "Terence and His Successors," in his Life and Literature in the Roman Republic. Berkeley: University of California Press, 1957, pp. 99-129.
Gassner, J. W. "Menander, Plautus, and Terence," in his Masters of the Drama. New York: Random House, 1940, pp. 92-104.
Gourde, L. "Terence the Philosopher," CJ 42 (April, 1947), 431-433.
Hadas, M. "Comedy and Satire," in his History of Latin Literature. New York: Columbia University Press, 1952, pp. 33-57.

Harsh, P. W. "Terence," in his Handbook of Classical Drama. Stanford University Press, 1944, pp. 375-398.
Kujore, O. "A Note on Contaminatio in Terence," CP 69 (January, 1974), 39-42.
Laidlaw, W. A. Prosody of Terence; A Relational Study. London: Published for St. Andrew's University by H. Milford, Oxford University Press, 1938.
Levin, R. "The Double Plots of Terence," CJ 62 (April, 1967), 301-305.
Lord, C. "Aristotle, Menander, and the Adelphoe of Terence," TAPA 107 (1977), 183-202.
Nicoll, A. "From Menander to the Mimes," in his World Drama from Aeschylus to Anouilh. New York: Harcourt, 1953, pp. 107-137.
Norwood, G. Art of Terence. New York: Russell and Russell, 1923.
──────. Plautus and Terence. New York: Cooper Square, 1963, pp. 100-180.
Perry, H. T. E. "Roman Imitators: Plautus and Terence," in his Masters of Dramatic Comedy and Their Social Themes. Cambridge, Mass.: Harvard University Press, 1939, pp. 49-78.
Robbins, E. W. Dramatic Characterization in Printed Commentaries on Terence, 1473-1600. Urbana: University of Illinois Press, 1951.
Thesleff, H. Yes and No in Plautus and Terence. Helsinki: Finska Vetenskaps-Societeten, 1961.

Individual Works

Adelphoe

Arnott, W. G. "The End of Terence's Adelphoe; A Postscript," G & R 10 (October, 1963), 140-144.
Dorey, T. A. "A Note on the Adelphoe of Terence," G & R 9 (March, 1962), 37-39.
Forehand, W. E. "Syrus' Role in Terence's Adelphoe," CJ 69 (October-November, 1973), 52-56.
Grant, J. N. "The Ending of Terence's Adelphoe and the Menandrian Original," AJP 96 (Spring, 1975), 42-60.
Lloyd-Jones, H. "Terentian Technique in the Adelphi and the Eunuchus," CQ (New Series) 23 (November, 1973), 279-284.
Rosivach, V. J. "Terence, Adelphoe 155-159," CQ (New Series) 23 (May, 1973), 85-87.

Andria

Cairns, F. "Terence, Andria 567-568," CR (New Series) 19 (December, 1969), 263-264.
Levy, H. L. "Terence, Andria, 560-565," AJP 79 (April, 1958), 173-178.

Martin, R. H. "Three Notes on Terence's Andria," CR (New Series) 14 (March, 1964), 3-4.

Eunuchus

Brothers, A. J. "Terence, Eunuchus 189-206," CQ (New Series) 19 (November, 1969), 314-319.
Gilmartin, K. "The Thraso-Gnatho Subplot in Terence's Eunuchus," CW 69 (December, 1975), 263-267.
Lloyd-Jones, H. "Terentian Technique in the Adelphi and the Eunuchus," CQ (New Series) 23 (November, 1973), 279-284.
Pepe, G. M. "The Last Scene of Terence's Eunuchus," CW 65 (January, 1972), 141-145.
Rand, E. K. "The Art of Terence's Eunuchus," TAPA 63 (1932), 54-72.
Saylor, C. F. "The Theme of Planlessness in Terence's Eunuchus," TAPA 105 (1975), 297-311.

Hecyra

Kuiper, W. E. J. Two Comedies by Apollodorus of Carystus; Terence's Hecyra and Phormio. Leiden: Brill, 1938.

Phormio

Arnott, W. G. "Phormio Parasitus: A Study in Dramatic Methods of Characterization," G & R 17 (April, 1970), 32-57.
Bohm, R. K. "Money Matters in Phormio," C World 70 (December, 1976), 267-269.
Kuiper, W. E. J. Two Comedies by Apollodorus of Carystus; Terence's Hecyra and Phormio. Leiden: Brill, 1938.
McCartney, E. S. "The Superstitions of Terence, Phormio 705-710," CJ 32 (June, 1937), 557-560.

TERTULLIAN

General Criticism

Ayers, R. H. "Tertullian's 'Paradox' and 'Contempt for Reason' Reconsidered," ET 87 (July, 1976), 308-311.
Barnes, T. D. Tertullian: A Historical and Literary Study. Oxford: Clarendon, 1971.
⎯⎯⎯⎯. "Tertullian's Scorpiace," JTS 20 (April, 1969), 105-132.
Case, S. J. "Protagonists of a Christian Culture," in his Makers of Christianity, from Jesus to Charlemagne. New York: Holt, 1934, pp. 80-114.

Cassidy, F. P. "Fathers of the West," in his Molders of the Medieval Mind; The Influence of the Fathers of the Church on the Medieval Schoolmen. New York: Herder, 1944, pp. 99-158.
Church, F. F. "Sex and Salvation in Tertullian," HTR 68 (April, 1975), 83-101.
Enslin, M. S. "Puritan of Carthage," JR 27 (July, 1947), 197-212.
Evans, E. "Tertullian's Theological Terminology," CQR 139 (October, 1944), 56-77.
Frend, W. H. C. "A Note on Jews and Christians in Third Century North Africa," JTS (New Series) 21 (April, 1970), 92-96.
⸻. "Their Word to Our Day: Tertullian," ET 81 (February, 1970), 136-141.
Gero, S. "Miles Gloriosus: The Christian and Military Service According to Tertullian," Ch H 39 (September, 1970), 285-298.
Gonzalez, J. L. "Athens and Jerusalem Revisited: Reason and Authority in Tertullian," Ch H 43 (March, 1974), 17-25.
Groh, D. E. "Tertullian's Polemic Against Social Co-optation," Ch H 40 (March, 1971), 7-14.
Hadas, M. "Writers of Christianity," in his History of Latin Literature. New York: Columbia University Press, 1952, pp. 414-445.
Hitchcock, F. R. M. "Tertullian's Views on the Sacrament of the Lord's Supper," CQR 134 (April, 1942), 21-36.
Horbury, W. "Tertullian on the Jews in the Light of De Spectaculis xxx. 5-6," JTS (New Series) 23 (October, 1972), 455-459.
Isichei, E. A. Political Thinking and Social Experience: Some Christian Interpretations of the Roman Empire from Tertullian to Salvian. Christchurch: University of Canterbury Press, 1964.
Lievestro, C. T. "Tertullian and the Sensus Argument," JHI 17 (April, 1956), 264-268.
Lovejoy, A. O. " 'Nature' as Norm in Tertullian," in his Essays in the History of Ideas. Baltimore: Johns Hopkins Press, 1948, pp. 308-338.
McGiffert, A. C. "Tertullian," in his History of Christian Thought. New York: Scribner's 1933, Vol. 2, pp. 3-23.
Macmullen, R. "Tertullian and National Gods," JTS (New Series) 26 (October, 1975), 405-410.
O'Malley, T. P. Tertullian and the Bible: Language, Imagery, Exegesis. Nijmegen, Netherlands: Dekker and Van de Vegt, 1967.
Pelikan, J. "Eschatology of Tertullian," Ch H 21 (June, 1952), 108-122.
⸻. "Montanism and Its Trinitarian Significance (Tertullian's Doctrine)," Ch H 25 (June, 1956), 99-109.
Roberts, R. E. Theology of Tertullian. London: Epworth, 1939.
Sider, R. D. Ancient Rhetoric and the Art of Tertullian. London: Oxford University Press, 1971.
⸻. "On Symmetrical Composition in Tertullian," JTS (New Series) 24 (October, 1973), 405-423.
Stead, G. C. "Divine Substance in Tertullian," JTS 14 (April, 1963), 46-66.
Warfield, B. B. Studies in Tertullian and Augustine. Westport, Conn.: Greenwood, 1970.

Individual Works

De Carne Christi

Schmidt, F. M. The Resurrection of the Body According to Tertullian; An Analysis of De Carne Christi and De Carnis Resurrectione. Washington, D. C.: Catholic University of America Press, 1951.

De Carne Resurrectione

Schmidt, F. M. The Resurrection of the Body According to Tertullian; An Analysis of De Carne Christi and De Carnis Resurrectione. Washington, D. C.: Catholic University of America Press, 1951.

De Spectaculis

Sider, R. D. "Tertullian, On the Shows: An Analysis," JTS 29 (October, 1978), 339-365.

THEOCRITUS

General Criticism

Beatty, F. "Theocritus in Hampstead," CJ 43 (March, 1948), 327-332.
Bonnard, A. "The Paradise of Theocritus," in his Greek Civilization: From Euripides to Alexandria. New York: Macmillan, 1961, pp. 229-245.
Broughton, L. N. The Theocritean Element in the Works of William Wordsworth. Folcroft, Pa.: Folcroft, 1974.
Edquist, H. "Aspects of Theocritean Otium," Ramus 4 (1975), 101-114.
Fabiano, G. "Fluctuation in Theocritus' Style," GRBS 12 (Winter, 1971), 517-537.
Garson, R. W. "Aspect of Theocritean Humor," CP 68 (October, 1973), 296-297.
_____. "Formal Aspects of Theocritean Comparisons," CP 68 (January, 1973), 56-58.
Lawall, G. Theocritus' Coan Pastorals: A Poetry Book. Cambridge, Mass.: Harvard University Press, 1967.
Lindsell, A. "Was Theocritus a Botanist?" G & R 6 (February, 1937), 78-93.
Segal, C. "Landscape into Myth: Theocritus' Bucolic Poetry," Ramus 4 (1975), 115-139.

Sickle, J. V. "Theocritus and the Development of the Conception of Bucolic Genre," Ramus 5 (1976), 18-44.
Thompson, F. "Theocritus," in his Literary Criticism; Newly Discovered and Collected by T. L. Connolly. New York: Dutton, 1948, pp. 517-523.
Van Sickle, J. B. "Is Theocritus a Version of Pastoral?" MLN 84 (December, 1969), 942-946.

Individual Works (Idylls)

1

Williams, F. J. "Theocritus, Idyll i. 81-91," J Hel S 89 (1969), 121-123.

2

Gow, A. S. F. "Theocritus, Id. ii, 59-62," CR 56 (November, 1942), 109-112.
Lawler, L. B. "A Lion Among Ladies (Theocritus II, 66-8)," TAPA 78 (1947), 88-98.
Schmiel, R. "Theocritus ii: The Purblind Poet," CJ 70 (April, 1975), 32-36.

4

Lattimore, S. "Battus in Theocritus' Fourth Idyll," GRBS 14 (Autumn, 1973), 319-324.

5

Giangrande, V. G. "Victory and Defeat in Theocritus' Idyll," Mnemosyne 29 (1976), 143-154.
Pagliaro, A. D. "Amoebaean Song in Ancient Greece," AUMLA 44 (November, 1975), 189-193.

6

Betts, J. H. "Theocritus 6.15-17," CP 66 (October, 1971), 252-253.

7

Gow, A. S. F. "Seventh Idyll of Theocritus," CQ (January, 1940), 47-54; 34 (July, 1940), 117.
McKay, K. J. "Pomp and Pastoraliain Theokritos' Idyll 7," AUMLA 44 (November, 1975), 181-188.

Williams, F. "A Theophany in Theocritus," CQ (New Series) 21 (May, 1971), 137-145.

10

Cairns, F. "Theocritus' Idylls," Hermes 98 (1970), 38-44.
Whitehorne, J. E. G. "The Reapers: Theocritus' Idyll 10," AUMLA 41 (May, 1974), 30-49.

11

Brooke, A. "Theocritus' Idyll 11: A Study in Pastoral," Areth 4 (Spring, 1971), 73-81.
Holtsmark, E. B. "Poetry As Self-enlightenment: Theocritus 11," TAPA 97 (1966), 253-260.

13

Gow, A. S. F. "Thirteenth Idyll of Theocritus," CQ 32 (January, 1938), 10-17.
Mastronarde, D. J. "Theocritus' Idyll 13: Love and the Hero," TAPA 99 (1968), 273-290.

14

Stern, J. "Theocritus' Idyll 14," GRBS 16 (Spring, 1975), 51-58.

15 (Adoniazusae)

Benton, S. "Pet Weasels: Theocritus xv. 28," CR (New Series) 19 (December, 1969), 260-263.
Gow, A. S. F. "The Adoniazusae of Theocritus," J Hel S 58 (1938), 180-204.
Helmbold, W. C. "The Song of the Argive Woman's Daughter," CP 46 (January, 1951), 17-24.
Swigart, R. "Theocritus' Pastoral Response to City Women," BR 21 (Spring, 1973), 145-174.

16

Austin, N. "Idyll 16: Theocritus and Simonides," TAPA 98 (1967), 1-22.

22

Gow, A. S. F. "Twenty-second Idyll of Theocritus," CR 56 (March, 1942), 11-18.

Moulton, C. "Theocritus and the Dioscuri," GRBS 14 (Spring, 1973), 41-47.

24

Gow, A. S. F. "Theocritus, Idyll XXIV--Stars and Doors," CQ 36 (October, 1942), 104-110.
Stern, J. "Theocritus' Idyll 24," AJP 95 (Winter, 1974), 348-361.
White, H. "Doors and Stars in Theocritus, Idyll XXIV," Mnemosyne 30 (1977), 135-140.

25

Gow, A. S. F. "Theocritus Idyll XXV," CQ 37 (July, 1943), 93-100.
Linforth, I. M. "Theocritus XXV," TAPA 78 (1947), 77-87.

28-31

West, M. L. "A Note on Theocritus' Aeolic Poems," CQ (New Series) 17 (1967), 82-84.

THUCYDIDES

General Criticism

Abbot, G. F. Thucydides: A Study in Historical Reality. New York: Russell and Russell, 1970.
Adcock, F. E. Thucydides and His History. Hamden, Conn.: Archon, 1973.
Adkins, J. W. H. "Merit, Responsibility and Thucydides," CQ 25 (December, 1975), 209-220.
Bahr-Volk, M. T. "A Note of the Figurative Use of Works Denoting Posture and Position in Thucydides' Melian Dialogue," CB 52 (February, 1976), 59-60.
Barrett, J. F. "Downfall of Themistocles," GRBS 18 (Winter, 1977), 291-305.
Bluhm, W. T. "Causal Theory in Thucydides' Peloponnesian War," Pol Stud 10 (February, 1962), 15-35.
Bonnard, A. "Thucydides and the War of the City-States," in his Greek Civilization: From Euripides to Alexandria. New York: Macmillan, 1961, pp. 52-63.
Bowersock, W. K. "Personality of Thucydides," AR 25 (Spring, 1965), 135-146.
Broadhead, H. D. "Thucydides: The Philosophic Historian," in in R. S. Allen, ed., Liberty and Learning; Essays in Honor of Sir James Hight. London: Whitcombe and Tombs, 1950, pp. 116-135.

Brunt, P. A. "Thucydides: The Compassionate Scientist," HT 7 (December, 1957), 820-828.
Chambers, M. H. "Thucydides and Pericles," HSCP 62 (1957), 79-92.
Chernick, S. "Historical Manipulation in Thucydides?" CW 65 (December, 1971), 126-130.
Cochrane, C. N. Thucydides and the Science of History. New York: Russell and Russell, 1965.
Connor, W. R. "A Post Modernist Thucydides?" CJ 72 (April-May, 1977), 289-298.
Cornford, F. M. "Mythistoria and the Drama," in Q. Anderson and J. A. Mazzeo, eds., The Proper Study; Essays on Western Classics. New York: St. Martin's, 1962, pp. 121-138.
_____. Thucydides Mythistoricus. New York: Humanities, 1965.
Creed, J. L. "Moral Values in the Age of Thucydides," CQ (New Series) 23 (November, 1973), 213-231.
Deane, P. Thucydides' Dates, 465-431 B.C. Don Mills, Ont.: Longmans, 1972.
Dionysius. "Dionysius of Halicarnassus on Herodotus, Thucydides and Theopompus," in A. J. Toynbee, Greek Historical Thought; From Homer to the Age of Heraclius. Boston: Beacon, 1950, pp. 223-229.
Dover, K. J. Thucydides. Oxford: Clarendon, 1973.
Downs, R. B. "First Scientific Historian: Thucydides," in his Famous Books, Ancient and Medieval. New York: Barnes and Noble, 1964, pp. 72-76.
Duncan, T. S. "Thucydides and the Causes of the Peloponnesian War," Wash Univ St. Lang & Lit (New Series) 14 (1942), 39-53.
Edmunds, L. Chance and Intelligence in Thucydides. Cambridge, Mass.: Harvard University Press, 1975.
Engeman, T. S. Homeric Honor and Thucydidean Necessity. The Hague: Nijhoff, 1974.
Fairchild, W. D. "Evidence of Improvised Speaking in Thucydides," CB 52 (November, 1975), 4-8.
Finley, J. H. "Euripides and Thucydides," HSCP 49 (1938), 23-68.
_____. "Origins of Thucydides' Style," HSCP 50 (1939), 35-84.
_____. Three Essays on Thucydides. Cambridge, Mass.: Harvard University Press, 1967.
_____. "Unity of Thucydides' History," HSCP, Supp. 1 (1940), 255-297.
_____. "Thucydides the Moralist," in his Aspects of Antiquity; Discoveries and Controversies. New York: Viking, 1968, pp. 44-57.
Froberg, B. M. The Dramatic Excursuses in Thucydides' History. Columbus: Ohio State University Press, 1972.
Gomme, A. W. Historical Commentary on Thucydides. Oxford: Clarendon, 1945.
_____. "Thucydides," in Essays in Greek History and Literature. Freeport, N. Y.: Books for Libraries, 1967, pp. 116-189.
_____. "Thucydides," in his Greek Attitude in Poetry and History. Berkeley: University of California Press, 1954, pp. 116-164.
_____, and K. J. Dover. A Historical Commentary on Thucydides. Oxford: Clarendon, 1970.

Grant, J. R. "Toward Knowing Thucydides," Phoenix 28 (Spring, 1974), 81-94.
Grene, D. Man in His Pride; A Study in the Political Philosophy of Thucydides and Plato. Chicago: University of Chicago Press, 1950.
Grube, G. M. A. "Thucydides, Socrates, Isocrates," in his The Greek and Roman Critics. Toronto: University of Toronto Press, 1965, pp. 33-45.
Grundy, G. B. Thucydides and the History of His Age. London: Blackwell, 1948.
Hamilton, E. "Thucydides; The Thing That Hath Been Is That Which Shall Be," in her Great Age of Greek Literature. New York: Norton, 1942, pp. 183-203.
Harding, H. F. The Speeches of Thucydides, with a General Introduction and Introductions for the Main Speeches and Military Harangues. Lawrence, Kan.: Coronado, 1973.
Hooker, E. M. "Buboes in Thucydides?" J Hel S 78 (1958), 78-86.
Hudson-Williams, H. L. "Thucydides, Isocrates, and the Rhetorical Method of Composition," CQ 42 (July, 1948), 76-81.
Hunter, V. J. "Athens Tyrannis: A New Approach to Thucydides," CJ 69 (December, 1973), 120-126.
————. Thucydides: The Artful Reporter. Toronto: Hakkert, 1973.
Immerwahr, H. R. "Ergon: History as a Monument in Herodotus and Thucydides," AJP 81 (July, 1960), 261-290.
Jaeger, W. W. "Thucydides: Political Philosopher," in his Paideia: The Ideals of Greek Culture. Oxford: Blackwell, 1939, pp. 379-408.
Judd, P. H. "Thucydides and the Study of War," in A. M. Cordier, ed., Columbia Essays in International Affairs: The Dean's Papers, 1966. New York: Columbia University Press, 1966, pp. 169-191.
Kagan, D. The Archidamian War. Ithaca, N.Y.: Cornell University Press, 1974.
Kateb, G. "Thucydides' History: A Manual of Statecraft," PSQ 79 (December, 1964), 481-503.
Kitto, H. D. F. "Thucydides," in his Poiesis: Structure and Thought. Berkeley: University of California Press, 1966, pp. 257-354.
Lord, L. E. Thucydides and the World War. New York: Russell and Russell, 1967.
Millar, C. M. "Thucydides for the Amateur," G & R 23 (April, 1976), 5-13.
Montgomery, H. "Thucydides and Geopolitics," CJ 38 (November, 1942), 93-96.
Oost, S. I. "Thucydides and the Irrational: Sundry Passages," CP 70 (July, 1975), 186-196.
Parry, A. "Herodotus and Thucydides," Arion 7 (Autumn, 1968), 409-416.
————. "Thucydides' Historical Perspective," YCS 22 (1972), 47-61.
————. "Thucydides' Use of Abstract Language," YFS 45 (1970), 3-20.
Pearson, L. "Popular Ethics in the World of Thucydides," CP 52 (October, 1957), 228-244.

_____. "Prophasis: A Clarification," TAPA 103 (1972), 381-394.
_____. "Thucydides as Reporter and Critic," TAPA 78 (1947), 37-60.
Percival, J. "Thucydides and the Uses of History," G & R 18 (1971), 199-212.
Rexroth, K. "Thucydides: The Peloponnesian War," in his Classics Revisited. Chicago: Quadrangle, 1968, pp. 65-69.
Romilly, J. De. "Fairness and Kindness in Thucydides," Phoenix 28 (Spring, 1974), 95-100.
_____. Thucydides and Athenian Imperialism. New York: Barnes and Noble, 1963.
Ryder, T. T. B. "Thucydides and Athenian Strategy in the Early 450s: A Consensus of Mistranslations," G & R 25 (October, 1978), 121-124.
Schevill, F. "Thucydides: Political Philosopher and Father of Historical Method," in his Six Historians. Chicago: University of Chicago Press, 1960, pp. 1-31.
Sears, R. D. "Thucydides and the Scientific Approach to International Politics," AJPH 23 (April, 1977), 28-40.
Siewert, P. "Ephebic Oath in Fifth-century Athens," J Hel S 97 (1977), 102-111.
Smith, S. B. "Economic Motive in Thucydides," HSCP 51 (1940), 267-301.
Sobel, R. Review Notes and Study Guide to the Peloponnesian War. New York: Monarch, 1964.
Stadter, P. A., ed. The Speeches in Thucydides: A Collection of Original Studies with a Bibliography. Chapel Hill: University of North Carolina Press, 1973.
Stewart, D. J. "Thucydides, Pausanias, and Alcibiades," CJ 61 (January, 1966), 145-152.
Strauss, L. Preliminary Observations of the Gods in Thucydides' Work. The Hague: Nijhoff, 1974.
Syme, R. "Thucydides," PBA 48 (1962), 39-56.
Tomkins, D. P. "Problem of Power in Thucydides," Arion (New Series) 1 (1973-1974), 401-416.
_____. "Stylistic Characterization in Thucydides: Nicias and Alcibiades," YCS 22 (1972), 181-214.
Wasserman, F. M. "Thucydides and the Disintegration of the Polis," TAPA 85 (1954), 46-54.
_____. "The Voice of Sparta in Thucydides," CJ 59 (April, 1964), 289-297.
Westlake, H. D. "Diplomacy in Thucydides," JRLB 53 (1970), 227-246.
_____. Individuals in Thucydides. London: Cambridge University Press, 1968.
_____. "Nicias in Thucydides," CQ 35 (January, 1941), 58-65.
_____. "Seaborne Raids in Periclean Strategy," CQ 39 (July, 1945), 75-84.
_____. "Sting in the Tail, a Feature of Thucydidean Speeches," GRBS 12 (Winter, 1971), 497-503.
_____. "Thucydides and the Athenian Disaster in Egypt," CP 45 (October, 1950), 209-216.

_____. "Thucydides on Pausanias and Themistocles--A Written Source?" CQ (New Series) 27 (1977), 95-110.
Wilson, C. H. "Thucydides, Isocrates and the Athenian Empire," G & R 13 (April, 1966), 54-63.
Winter, P. E. "Thucydides and History Today," G & R 6 (October, 1959), 168-175.
Woodhead, A. G. Thucydides on the Nature of Power. Cambridge, Mass.: Harvard University Press, 1970.

Individual Works (Peloponnesian War)

Book 1

Adcock, F. E. "Thucydides in Book 1," J Hel S 71 (1951), 2-12.
Alexander, J. A. "Thucydides and the Expedition of Callias Against Potidaea, 432 B.C.," AJP 83 (July, 1962), 265-287.
Andrewes, A. "Thucydides on the Causes of War," CQ (New Series) 9 (1959), 223-239.
Blamire, A. "Pausanias and Persia," GRBS 11 (Winter, 1970), 295-305.
Calder, W. M. "The Corcyraean-Corinthian Speeches in Thucydides," CJ 50 (January, 1955), 179-180.
Cole, J. R. "Cimon's Dismissal, Ephialtes' Revolution and the Peloponnesian Wars," GRBS 15 (Winter, 1974), 369-385.
Dull, C. J. "Thucydides 1.113 and the Leadership of Orchomenus," CP 72 (October, 1977), 305-314.
Eddy, S. K. "Four Hundred Sixty Talents Once More," CP 63 (July, 1968), 184-195.
Hammond, N. G. L. "The Arrangement of the Thought in the Proem and in Other Parts of Thucydides I," CQ (New Series) 2 (1952), 127-141.
Kagan, D. "The Speeches in Thucydides and the Mytilene Debate," YCS 24 (1975), 71-94.
Konishi, H. "Thucydides' Method in the Episodes of Pausanias and Themistocles," AJP 91 (January, 1970), 52-69.
Lang, M. "Kylonian Conspiracy," CP 62 (October, 1967), 243-249.
Libourel, J. M. "The Athenian Disaster in Egypt," AJP 92 (October, 1971), 605-615.
Marshall, M. H. B. "Urban Settlement in the Second Chapter of Thucydides," CQ (New Series) 25 (May, 1975), 26-40.
Prakken, D. W. "Boetian Migration," AJP 64 (October, 1943), 417-423.
Sealey, R. "The Causes of the Peloponnesian War," CP 70 (April, 1975), 89-109.
Siewert, P. "Ephebic Oath in Fifth-century Athens," J Hel S 97 (1977), 102-111.
Stubbs, H. W. "Thucydides 1.2.6," CQ (New Series) 22 (May, 1972), 74-77.
Wassermann, F. M. "The Speeches of King Archidamus in Thucydides," CJ 48 (March, 1953), 193-200.
Westlake, H. D. "Thucydides and the Pentekontaetia," CQ (New Series) 5 (1955), 53-67.

Woodhead, A. G. "The Site of Brea: Thucydides I. 61.4," CQ (New Series) 2 (1952), 57-62.

Book 2

Cawkwell, G. "Thucydides' Judgement of Periclean Strategy," YCS 24 (1975), 53-70.
Cooper, G. L. "Thucydides 2.88.2 and the Sources of the Popularity of Phormio," TAPA 106 (1976), 97-99.
Edmunds, L. "Thucydides II. 40, 2," CR (New Series) 22 (June, 1972), 171-172.
Else, G. F. "Some Implications of Pericle's Funeral Speech," CJ 49 (January, 1954), 153-156.
Grant, J. R. "Thucydides II, 37, 1," Phoenix 25 (Summer, 1971), 104-107.
McKeon, R. P. "Funeral Oration of Pericles," in R. M. MacIver, ed., Great Expressions of Human Rights. New York: Harper, 1950.
Page, D. L. "Thucydides' Description of the Great Plague of Athens," CQ (New Series) 3 (1953), 97-119.
Pearson, L. "Thucydides on the Geographical Tradition," CQ 33 (1939), 48-54.
Shapiro, H. A. "A Note on Pericles' Last Speech," Phoenix 29 (Summer, 1975), 184-186.
Smart, J. D. "Catalogues in Thucydides and Ephorus," GRBS 18 (Spring, 1977), 33-42.
Walcot, P. "The Funeral Speech; A Study of Values," G & R 20 (October, 1973), 111-121.
Wardman, A. E. "Thucydides 2.40.1," CQ (New Series) 9 (1959), 39-42.
Wassermann, F. M. "The Speeches of King Archidamus in Thucydides," CJ 48 (March, 1953), 193-200.

Book 3

Adshead, K. "Thucydides 3.82.8," AUMLA 46 (November, 1976), 234-239.
Edmunds, L. "Thucydides' Ethics as Reflected in the Description of Stasis (3.82-83)," HSCP 79 (1975), 73-92.
Fuks, A. "Thucydides and the Stasis in Corcyra Thuc., III, 82, 3 Versus III, 84," AJP 92 (January, 1971), 48-55.
Harrison, E. L. "The Escape from Plataea: Thucydides 3.23," CQ (New Series) 9 (1959), 30-33.
Hogan, J. C. "Thucydides 3.52-68 and Euripides' Hecuba," Phoenix 26 (Autumn, 1972), 241-257.
Lateiner, D. "The Speech of Teutiaplus," GRBS 16 (Summer, 1975), 175-184.
Macleod, C. W. "Thucydides' Plataean Debate," GRBS 18 (Autumn, 1977), 227-246.
Pearson, L. "Thucydides on the Geographical Tradition," CQ 33 (1939), 48-54.

Book 4

Marshall, M. H. B. "Andocides 1. 8 and Thucydides 4. 63. 1," CQ 24 (May, 1974), 28-32.
Quinn, T. J. "An Additional Note on Thucydides 4. 4. 1," CQ (New Series) 25 (December, 1975), 313-315.
Silhanek, D. K. "Pylos Revisited: Thucydides' Primary Source," CW 64 (September, 1970), 10-13.
Stroud, R. S. "Thucydides and the Battle of Solygeia," CSCA 4 (1971), 227-247.
Westlake, H. D. "Naval Battle at Pylos and its Consequences," CQ 24 (December, 1974), 211-226.
Wilson, J., and T. Beardsworth. "Pylos 425 B. C.: The Spartan Plan to Block the Entrances," CQ (New Series) 20 (May, 1970), 42-52.

Book 5

Anderson, J. K. "Cleon's Orders at Amphipolis," J Hel S 85 (1965), 1-4.
Euben, J. P. "On Political Corruption," AR 36 (Winter, 1978), 103-118.
Hudson-Williams, H. L. "Conventional Forms of Debate and the Melian Dialogue," AJP 71 (April, 1950), 156-169.
Liebeschuetz, W. "The Structure and Function of the Melian Dialogue," J Hel S 88 (1968), 73-77.
Seager, R. "After the Peace of Nicias: Diplomacy and Policy, 421-416 B. C.," CQ (New Series) 26 (1976), 249-269.
West, A. B. "Thucydides, V, 18, 5; V, 18, 6," AJP 58 (April, 1937), 157-173.
Westlake, H. D. "Corinth and the Argive Coalition," AJP 61 (October, 1940), 413-421.
_____. "Thucydides and the Uneasy Peace: A Study in Political Incompetence," CQ (New Series) 21 (November, 1971), 315-325.
_____. "The Two Second Prefaces of Thucydides," Phoenix 26 (Spring, 1972), 12-17.

Book 6

Avery, H. C. "Themes in Thucydides' Account of the Sicilian Expedition," Hermes 101 (1973), 1-13.

Book 7

Adkins, J. W. H. "The Arete of Nicias: Thucydides 7. 86," GRBS 16 (Winter, 1975), 379-392.
Avery, H. C. "Themes in Thucydides' Account of the Sicilian Expedition," Hermes 101 (1973), 1-13.
Dickie, M. W. "Thucydides 7. 42. 3: An Unrecognized Fragment of Philistus," GRBS 17 (Autumn, 1976), 217-221.

_____. "Thucydides, not Philistus," GRBS 17 (Autumn, 1976), 217-219.
Hunter, V. J. "Thucydides and the Historical Fact," CJ 67 (October-November, 1971), 14-19.
Kopff, E. C. "Thucydides 7.42.3: An Unrecognized Fragment of Philistus," GRBS 17 (Spring, 1976), 23-30.
_____. "Philistus Still," GRBS 17 (Autumn, 1976), 220-221.
Rawlings, H. R. "Giving Desertion as a Pretext: Thuc. 7.13.12," CP 73 (April, 1978), 134-136.
Tompkins, D. P. "Stylistic Characterization in Thucydides: Nicias and Alcibiades," YCS 22 (1972), 181-214.

Book 8

Goldstein, M. S. "Athenian-Persian Peace Treaties; Thuc. 8.56.4 and 8.58.2," CSCA 7 (1974), 155-164.
Grayson, C. H. "Two Passages in Thucydides," CQ (New Series) 22 (May, 1972), 62-73.
Kirkwood, G. M. "Thucydides' Judgement of the Constitution of the Five Thousand (VIII, 9, 7, 2)," AJP 93 (January, 1972), 92-103.
Lang, M. "Revolution of the 400: Chronology and Constitutions," AJP 88 (April, 1967), 176-187.
Lateiner, D. "Tessaphernes and the Phoenician Fleet," TAPA 106 (1976), 267-290.
Westlake, H. D. "Phrynichos and Astyochos (Thucydides VIII 50-1)," J Hel S 76 (1956), 99-109.
_____. "The Subjectivity of Thucydides: His Treatment of the Four Hundred at Athens," JRLB 61 (1973), 193-218.

TIBULLUS

General Criticism

Bulloch, A. W. "Tibullus and the Alexandrians," PCPS (New Series) 19 (1973), 71-89.
Copley, F. O. "The Elegists: Tibullus, Propertius, and Ovid," in his Latin Literature from the Beginnings to the Close of the Second Century A. D. Ann Arbor: University of Michigan Press, 1969, pp. 241-275.
Davies, C. "Poetry in the Circle of Messalla," G & R 20 (April, 1973), 25-35.
Elder, J. P. "Tibullus: Tersus Atque Elegans," in J. P. Sullivan, ed., Critical Essays on Roman Literature: Elegy and Lyric. Cambridge, Mass.: Harvard University Press, 1962, pp. 65-105.
Hadas, M. "Tibullus and Propertius," in his History of Latin Literature. New York: Columbia University Press, 1952, pp. 184-200.
Highet, G. "Tibullus: Style," in his Poets in a Landscape. New York: Knopf, 1957, pp. 156-172.

Johnson, S. "Intimations of Immortality in the Major Lyric and Elegiac Poets of Rome; Tibullus," Roy Soc Can Trans (Series 3) 44 Sec. 2 (1950), 75-78.
Mendell, C. W. "Tibullus," in his Latin Poetry. The New Poets and the Augustans. London: Yale University Press, 1965, pp. 181-193.
Musurillo, H. S. J. "The Theme of Time as a Poetic Device in the Elegies of Tibullus," TAPA 98 (1967), 253-268.
Platnauer, M. Latin Elegiac Verse; A Study of the Metrical Usages of Tibullus, Propertius and Ovid. Hamden, Conn. : Archon, 1971.
Powell, B. B. "The Ordering of Tibullus Book 1," CP 69 (1974), 107-112.
Putnam, M. C. J. Tibullus, A Commentary. Norman: University of Oklahoma Press, 1973.
Yardley, J. C. "Roman Elegists, Sick Girls, and the Soteria," CQ (New Series) 27 (1977), 394-401.

Individual Works (Elegies)

Book 1, Poem 3

Bright, D. F. "A Tibullan Odyssey," Areth 4 (Fall, 1971), 197-214.
Campbell, C. "Tibullus: Elegy I. 3," YCS 23 (1973), 147-157.
Cilliers, J. F. "The Tartarus Motif in Tibullus' Elegy 1. 3," AClass 17 (1974), 75-79.
Mills, D. H. "Tibullus and Phaeacia: A Reinterpretation of 1. 3," CJ 69 (February-March, 1974), 226-233.

Book 1, Poem 5

Musurillo, H. "Furtivus Amor: The Structure of Tibullus 1. 5," TAPA 101 (1970), 387-399.

Book 1, Poem 6

Gaisser, J. H. "Structure and Tone in Tibullus I, 6," AJP 92 (1971), 202-216.

Book 1, Poem 7

Gaisser, J. H. "Tibullus I. 7: A Tribute to Messalla," CP 66 (October, 1971), 221-229.
Putnam, M. "Simple Tibullus and the Ruse of Style," YFS 45 (1970), 21-32.

Book 1, Poem 10

Pillinger, H. E. "Tibullus 1. 10 and Lucretius," CJ 66 (February, 1971), 204-208.

Book 2, Poem 5

Ball, R. J. "Tibullus 2.5 and Vergil's Aeneid," Vergilius 21 (1975), 33-50.
Putnam, M. "Simple Tibullus and the Ruse of Style," YFS 45 (1970), 21-32.

Book 2, Poem 6

O'Neil, E. N. "Tibullus 2.6: A New Interpretation," CP 62 (July, 1967), 163-168.

VARRO

General Criticism

Astbury, R. "Varro and Pompey," CQ (New Series) 17 (November, 1967), 403-407.
Hadas, M. "Caesar, Sallust and Others," in his History of Latin Literature. New York: Columbia University Press, 1952, pp. 88-107.
Horsfall, N. "Varro and Caesar: Three Chronological Problems," BICS 19 (1972), 120-128.
Laughton, E. "Observations on the Style of Varro," CQ (New Series) 10 (May, 1960), 1-28.
Taylor, D. J. Declinatio: A Study of the Linguistic Theory of Marcus Terentius Varro. Amsterdam: Benjamins, 1975.

Individual Works

Menippean Satires, or Saturarum Menippearum

Astbury, R. "Petronius, P. Oxy. 3010, and Menippean Satire," CP 72 (January, 1977), 22-31.
McCarthy, B. P. "Form of Varro's Menippean Satires," in R. P. Robinson, ed., Philological Studies in Honor of Walker Miller. Columbia: University of Missouri Press, 1936, pp. 95-107.
Sigsbee, D. L. "The Paradoxa Stoicorum in Varro's Menippeans," CP 71 (July, 1976), 244-248.

On Agriculture, or De Rerum Rusticarum

Rayment, C. S. "Varro Versutus," CJ 40 (March, 1945), 349-357.
Skydsgaard, J. E. Varro the Scholar; Studies in the First Book of Varro's De Rerum Rustica. Hafniae: Munksgaard, 1968.

On the Latin Language, or De Lingua Latina

Taylor, D. J. "Two Notes on Varro," AJP 98 (Summer, 1977), 130-132.
_____. "Varro, De Lingua Latina 10.76," AJP 97 (Summer, 1976), 119-120.

Pseudo-tragedies

Marti, B. M. "Prototypes of Seneca's Tragedies; Varro's Pseudotragoediae," CP 42 (January, 1947), 9-15.

VIRGIL

General Criticism

Allinson, A. C. E. "Virgil and the New Patriotism," in her Selected Essays. New York: Harcourt, 1933, pp. 96-120.
Ashley, A. M. "Poetic Imagery in Homer and Virgil," G & R 2 (October, 1932), 21-28.
Bailey, C. Religion in Virgil. New York: Barnes and Noble, 1969.
Baldwin, B. "Vergilius Graecus," AJP 97 (Winter, 1976), 361-368.
Benario, H. W. "Vergil and Tacitus," CJ 63 (October, 1967), 24-27.
Benario, J. M. "Dido and Cleopatra," Vergilius 16 (1970), 2-6.
Bowra, C. M. "Virgil and the Ideal of Rome," in his From Virgil to Milton. New York: Macmillan, 1945, pp. 33-85.
Claassen, J. N. "The Life and Works of Publius Vergilius Maro," Akroterion 20 (April, 1975), 5-12.
Commager, S., ed. Virgil: A Collection of Critical Essays. Englewood Cliffs, N. J.: Prentice-Hall, 1966.
Conway, R. S. Harvard Lectures on the Vergilian Age. New York: Biblo and Tannen, 1967, pp. 63-72, 94-112.
_____. "Poetry and Government: A Study of the Power of Vergil," in his Makers of Europe. Freeport, N. Y.: Books for Libraries, 1967, pp. 66-83.
Coolidge, J. S. "Great Things and Small: The Virgilian Progression," CL 17 (Winter, 1965), 1-23.
Cowles, F. H. "Vergil's Hatred of War," CJ 29 (February, 1934), 357-374.
Cruttwell, R. W. Virgil's Mind at Work. New York: Cooper Square, 1969.
Dale, F. R. The Stateliest Measure: Form and Color in Virgil. Devon, Eng.: Virgil Society, 1952.
DeWitt, N. W. "Vergil and the Tragic Drama," CJ 26 (October, 1930), 19-27.
Dinsmore, C. A. "Virgil: Who Placed an Ideal Before Imperial Rome," in his Great Poets and the Meaning of Life. Boston: Houghton Mifflin, 1937, pp. 101-124.

Distler, P. F. Vergil and Vergiliana. Chicago: Loyola University Press, 1966.
Doig, G. "Vergil's Art and the Greek Language," CJ 64 (October, 1968), 1-6.
Donlan, W. The Classical World Bibliography of Vergil. New York: Garland, 1978.
Downs, R. B. "Rome's Epic Poet: Publius Vergilius Maro," in his Famous Books, Ancient and Medieval. New York: Barnes and Noble, 1964, pp. 179-182.
Duckworth, G. E. "Variety and Repetition in Vergil's Hexameters," TAPA 95 (1964), 9-65.
_____. Vergil and Classical Hexameter Poetry: A Study in Metrical Variety. Ann Arbor: University of Michigan Press, 1969.
Dudley, D. R., ed. Virgil. London: Routledge and K. Paul, 1969.
Eliot, T. S. "Virgil and the Christian World," in his On Poetry and Poets. New York: Farrar, Straus, 1957, pp. 135-148.
_____. "Vergil and the Christian World," SR 61 (January, 1953), 1-14.
Erskine, J. "Vergil, the Modern Poet," in his Delight of Great Books. Indianapolis: Bobbs-Merrill, 1935, pp. 317-332.
Feder, L. "Vergil's Tragic Theme," CJ 49 (February, 1954), 197-209.
Frank, T. Virgil, A Biography. New York: Russell and Russell, 1965.
_____. "What Do We Know About Vergil?" CJ 26 (October, 1930), 3-11.
Glover, T. R. Virgil. New York: Barnes and Noble, 1969.
_____. "Virgil, An Appreciation," CJ 26 (October, 1930), 28-36.
Graves, R. "The Anti-poet," in his Oxford Addresses on Poetry. New York: Doubleday, 1962, pp. 37-64.
_____. "Virgil Cult," VQR 38 (Winter, 1962), 13-35.
Gregory, T. S. "Vergil, the Countryman," Dub R 217 (July, 1945), 28-38.
Haarhoff, T. J. Vergil, Prophet of Peace. Sanderstead, Eng.: Virgil Society, 1956.
_____. Vergil the Universal. Oxford: Blackwell, 1949.
_____. "Vergil and Cornelius Gallus," CP 55 (April, 1960), 101-108.
_____. Virgil's Garden of Flowers and His Philosophy of Nature," G & R 5 (March, 1958), 67-81.
Hadas, M. "Vergil," in his History of Latin Literature. New York: Columbia University Press, 1952, pp. 140-163.
Hardie, C. G. "Three Roman Poets," in J. P. V. D. Balsdon, ed., The Romans. New York: Basic, 1966, pp. 226-248.
_____. "Virgil on Himself," List 69 (January 24, 1963), 165-168.
Harvey, F. B. "Virgil's Message for To-day," LQR 168 (April, 1943), 103-110.
Highet, G. "Vergil: Landscape," in his Poets in a Landscape. New York: Knopf, 1957, pp. 45-73.
Hill, D. E. "What Sort of Translation of Virgil Do We Need?" G & R 25 (April, 1978), 59-68.
Hornsby, R. A. "The Pastor in the Poetry of Vergil," CJ 63 (January, 1968), 145-152.

_____. "The Vergilian Simile as Means of Judgement," CJ 60 (May, 1965), 337-344.
James, B. S. "Word-painting of Virgil," Dub R 215 (July, 1944), 69-72.
Jocelyn, H. D. "Ancient Scholarship and Virgil's Use of Republican Latin Poetry. I," CQ (New Series) 14 (1964), 280-295.
_____. "Ancient Scholarship and Virgil's Use of Republican Latin Poetry. II," CQ (New Series) 15 (1965), 126-144.
Knight, W. F. J. Poetic Inspiration, An Approach to Virgil. London: Raleigh, 1946.
_____. "Repetitive Style in Virgil," TAPA 72 (1941), 212-225.
_____. Roman Vergil. New York: Barnes and Noble, 1971.
_____. Vergil and Homer. Devon, Eng.: Virgil Society, 1950.
_____. Vergil: Epic and Anthropology. London: Allen and Unwin, 1967.
Leach, E. W. "Parthenian Caverns: Remapping of an Imaginative Topography," JHI 39 (October, 1978), 539-560.
_____. "Sedes Apibus: From the Georgics to the Aeneid," Vergilius 23 (1977), 2-16.
Letters, F. J. H. Virgil. London: Sheed and Ward, 1946.
Lister, R. "Ancients and the Classics," S Romantic 15 (Summer, 1976), 395-404.
McGushin, P. "Virgil and the Spirit of Endurance," AJP 85 (July, 1964), 225-253.
Mack, S. Patterns of Time in Vergil. Hamden, Conn.: Archon, 1978.
MacKail, J. W. Virgil and His Meaning to the World of Today. New York: Cooper Square, 1963.
McKay, A. G. Vergil's Italy. Greenwich, Conn.: New York Graphic Society, 1970.
Martyn, J. R. C., ed. Cicero and Virgil; Studies in Honour of Harold Hunt. Amsterdam: Hakkert, 1972.
Mendell, C. W. "Vergil," in his Latin Poetry; The New Latin Poets and the Augustans. London: Yale University Press, 1965, pp. 67-109.
Ogle, M. B. "The Later Tradition of Vergil," CJ 26 (October, 1930), 63-73.
Otis, B. Virgil, A Study in Civilized Poetry. Oxford: Clarendon, 1964.
Poeschl, V. "The Poetic Achievement of Virgil," CJ 56 (April, 1961), 290-299.
Prescott, H. W. The Development of Virgil's Art. New York: Russell and Russell, 1963.
Rand, E. K. Magical Art of Virgil. Hamden, Conn.: Archon, 1966.
_____. "Virgil, the Magician," CJ 26 (October, 1930), 37-48.
Ryberg, I. S. "Vergil's Golden Age," TAPA 89 (1958), 112-131.
Sargeaunt, J. The Trees, Shrubs, and Plants of Virgil. Freeport, N. Y.: Books for Libraries, 1969.
Segal, C. P. "Achievement of Vergil," Arion 4 (Spring, 1965), 126-149.
_____. "The Song of Iopas in the Aeneid," Hermes (1971), 336-349.
Sellar, W. Y. The Roman Poets of the Augustan Age: Virgil. New York: Biblo and Tannen, 1965.

Silk, M. S. "Virgil and English Poetry: Some Thoughts on Affinities," PVS 11 (1971-1972), 1-25.
Smiley, C. N. "Vergil--His Philosophic Background and His Relation to Christianity," CJ 26 (June, 1931), 660-675.
Spargo, J. W. Virgil the Necromancer. Cambridge, Mass.: Harvard University Press, 1934.
Stark, M. R. "The Golden Bough for the Student of Vergil," CJ 26 (January, 1931), 259-265.
Starr, C. G. "Virgil's Acceptance of Octavian," AJP 76 (January, 1955), 34-46.
Stubbs, H. W. "Virgil and H. G. Wells; Prophets of a New Age," PVS 9 (1969-1970), 34-53.
Sullivan, F. A. "Some Virgilian Beatitudes," AJP 82 (October, 1961), 294-405.
_____. "Virgil and the Latin Epitaphs," CJ 51 (October, 1955), 17-20.
Taylor, M. E. "Primitivism in Virgil," AJP 76 (July, 1955), 261-278.
Thomson, J. O. "Geographica Vergiliana," G & R (New Series) 2 (June, 1955), 50-58.
Townend, G. B. "Changing Views of Vergil's Greatness," CJ 56 (November, 1960), 67-77.
Turnbull, P. "Vergil: Painter with Words," CJ 42 (November, 1946), 97-101.
Vessey, D. W. T. "Silius Italicus: The Shield of Hannibal," AJP 96 (Winter, 1975), 391-405.
Whitfield, B. G. "Virgil and the Bees," G & R 3 (October, 1956), 99-117.
Wiesen, D. S. "Virgil, Minucius Felix and the Bible," Hermes 99 (1971), 70-91.
Wilkinson, L. P. "The Language of Virgil and Horace," CQ (New Series) 9 (1959), 181-192.
Williams, R. D. Virgil. Oxford: Clarendon, 1967.
_____. "Virgil Today," PVS 12 (1972-1973), 25-35.
Woodberry, G. E. "Virgil," in his Literary Essays. Port Washington, N.Y.: Kennikat, 1967.
Young, G. M. "Hesperia," in his Today and Yesterday; Collected Essays and Addresses. Chester Springs, Pa.: Dufour, 1959, pp. 175-193.

Individual Works (Aeneid)

General

Alexander, W. H. Maius Opus (Aeneid 7-12). Berkeley: University of California Press, 1951.
_____. "War in the Aeneid," CJ 40 (February, 1945), 261-273.
Amerasinghe, C. W. "Saturnia Iuno--Its Significance in the Aeneid," G & R 22 (June, 1953), 61-69.
Anderson, W. D. "Venus and Aeneas," CJ 50 (February, 1955), 233-238.
Anderson, W. S. The Art of the Aeneid. Englewood Cliffs, N. J.: Prentice-Hall, 1969.

———. "Juno and Saturn in the Aeneid," SP 55 (October, 1958), 519-532.
———. "Pastor Aeneas: On Pastoral Themes in the Aeneid," TAPA 99 (1968), 1-18.
———. "Vergil's Second Iliad," TAPA 88 (1957), 17-30.
Armstrong, D. "The Other Aeneid," Arion 6 (Summer, 1967), 143-168.
Bassett, E. L. "Regulus and the Serpent in the Punica," CP 50 (January, 1955), 1-20.
Bond, R. P. "Aeneas and the Cardinal Virtues," Prudentia 6 (November, 1974), 67-91.
Bowra, C. M. "Aeneas and the Stoic Idea," G & R 3 (October, 1933), 8-22.
Brinkman, J. A. "The Foundation Legends in Vergil," CJ 54 (October, 1958), 25-33.
Bryce, T. R. "The Dido-Aeneas Relationship: A Re-examination," CW 67 (March, 1974), 257-269.
Burke, P. F. "The Role of Mezentius in the Aeneid," CJ 69 (February-March, 1974), 202-209.
———. "Virgil's Amata," Vergilius 22 (1976), 24-29.
Buxton, C. R. Prophets of Heaven and Hell: Virgil, Dante, Milton, Goethe; an Introductory Essay. New York: Russell and Russell, 1969.
Camps, W. A. An Introduction to Virgil's Aeneid. London: Oxford University Press, 1969.
Cesare, M. A. The Altar and the City: A Reading of Vergil's Aeneid. New York: Columbia University Press, 1974.
Coleiro, E. "Allegory in the Aeneid," PVS 13 (1973-1974), 42-53.
Copley, F. O. "Vergil, the Aeneid," in his Latin Literature from the Beginnings to the Close of the Second Century A. D. Ann Arbor: University of Michigan Press, 1969, pp. 188-240.
Covi, M. C. "Dido in Vergil's Aeneid," CJ 60 (November, 1964), 57-60.
Cowles, F. H. "The Epic Question in Vergil," CJ 36 (December, 1940), 133-142.
Crane, T. "Hunter and Hunted in Aeneid 7-12," CB 50 (December, 1973), 21-25.
Crosby, M. Vergil: The Aeneid. New York: Barnes and Noble, 1968.
Cruttwell, R. W. Virgil's Mind at Work: An Analysis of The Symbolism of the Aeneid. New York: Cooper Square, 1969.
Curne, H. M. "Dido; Pietas and Pudor," CB 51 (January, 1975), 37-39.
Di Cesare, M. A. The Altar and the City; A Reading of Vergil's Aeneid. New York: Columbia University Press, 1974.
Dickinson, A. E. F. "Music for the Aeneid," G & R 6 (October, 1959), 129-147.
Donker, M. "Waste Land and the Aeneid," PMLA 89 (January, 1974), 164-173.
Duckworth, G. E. "The Aeneid as a Trilogy," TAPA 88 (1957), 1-10.
———. "Architecture of the Aeneid," AJP 75 (January, 1954), 1-15.

_____. "Fate and Free Will in Vergil's Aeneid," CJ 51 (May, 1956), 357-364.
_____. Foreshadowing and Suspense in the Epics of Homer, Apollonius, and Vergil. Princeton, N. J.: Princeton University Press, 1933.
_____. "Significance of Nisus and Euryalus for Aeneid IX-XII," AJP 88 (April, 1967), 129-150.
_____. "Vergil, and War in the Aeneid," CJ 41 (December, 1945), 104-107.
Duclos, G. S. "Nemora Inter Cresia," CJ 66 (February-March, 1971), 193-195.
Dudley, D. R. "A Plea for Aeneas," G & R 8 (March, 1961), 52-60.
Dunkle, J. R. "The Hunter and Hunting in the Aeneid," Ramus 2 (1973), 127-142.
Egan, R. B. "Aeneas at Aineia and Vergil's Aeneid," PCP 9 (April, 1974), 37-47.
Eichholz, D. E. "Symbol and Contrast in the Aeneid," G & R 15 (October, 1968), 105-112.
Ellingham, C. J. "Virgil's Pilgram's Progress," G & R 16 (June, 1947), 67-74.
Erskine, J. "Vergil," CJ 36 (April, 1941), 390-400.
Evans, V. B. "A Study of Dido and Aeneas," CJ 33 (November, 1937), 99-104.
Feldman, L. H. "Ascanius and Astyanax: A Comparative Study of Virgil and Homer," CJ 53 (May, 1958), 361-366.
_____. "The Character of Ascanius in Virgil's Aeneid," CJ 48 (May, 1953), 303-313.
Galinsky, G. K. Aeneas, Sicily and Rome. Princeton, N. J.: Princeton University Press, 1969.
Garstang, J. B. "Aeneas and the Sibyls," CJ 59 (December, 1963), 97-101.
_____. "The Crime of Helen and the Concept of Fatum in the Aeneid," CJ 57 (May, 1962), 337-345.
Genovese, E. N. Deaths in the Aeneid. Northridge, Calif.: Philological Association of the Pacific Coast, 1975.
Gosling, A. "The Political Level of the Aeneid," Akroterion 20 (April, 1975), 42-45.
Grandsden, M. W. "Typology, Symbolism and Allegory in the Aeneid," PVS 13 (1973-1974), 14-27.
Grant, M. "Romantic Epic: The Aeneid," in his Roman Literature. Baltimore: Penguin, 1964, pp. 177-190.
Greene, E. B. Critical Essays. New York: Garland, 1970.
Greene, T. M. "Virgil," in his The Descent from Heaven, A Study in Epic Continuity. New Haven, Conn.: Yale University Press, 1963, pp. 74-103.
Grimal, P. Pius Aeneas. London: Virgil Society, 1960.
Gwatkin, W. E. "Dodona, Odysseus, and Aeneas," CJ 57 (December, 1961), 97-102.
Haber, T. B. A Comparative Study of the Beowulf and the Aeneid. New York: Phaeton Press, 1968.
Hadas, M. "Aeneas and the Tradition of the National Hero," AJP 69 (October, 1948), 408-414.

Halperin, D. M. "Man's Fate in the Aeneid," VQR 53 (Winter, 1977), 58-72.
Havelock, E. A. "Aeneid and its Translators," Hud R 27 (Autumn, 1974), 338-370.
Heffner, J. E. "A Bibliographical Handlist on Vergil's Aeneid," C World 60 (May, 1967), 377-388.
Henry, J. Aeneidea, or Critical, Exegetical, and Aesthetical Remarks on the Aeneis. Hildensheim: Olms, 1969.
Henry, R. M. Virgil and the Roman Epic. Manchester: Manchester University Press, 1938.
Highet, G. "The Aeneid: Penetrating a Book," in his Powers of Poetry. London: Oxford University Press, 1960, pp. 244-250.
_____. "Speech and Narrative in the Aeneid," HSCP 78 (1974), 189-229.
_____. The Speeches in Vergil's Aeneid. Princeton, N. J.: Princeton University Press, 1972.
Hornsby, R. A. Patterns of Action in the Aeneid; An Interpretation of Vergil's Epic Similes. Iowa City: University of Iowa Press, 1970.
Horsfall, N. "Dido in the Light of History," PVS 13 (1973-1974), 1-13.
Howe, G. "The Development of the Character of Aeneas," CJ 26 (December, 1930), 182-193.
Hunt, W. J. Forms of Glory: Structure and Sense in Vergil's Aeneid. Carbondale: Southern Illinois University Press, 1973.
Johnson, W. R. "Aeneas and the Ironies of Pietas," CJ 60 (May, 1965), 360-364.
_____. Darkness Visible. Berkeley: University of California Press, 1976.
Johnston, L. "Hic Pietatis Honos?" CB 47 (March, 1971), 73-75.
Keith, A. L. "Nature-imagery in Vergil's Aeneid," CJ 28 (May, 1933), 591-610.
Kelsall, M. M. "What God, What Mortal? The Aeneid and English Mock-heroic," Arion 8 (Autumn, 1969), 359-379.
Kepple, L. R. "Arruns and the Death of Aeneas," AJP 97 (Winter, 1976), 344-360.
Klein, J. The Myth of Virgil's Aeneid. The Hague: Nijhoff, 1971.
Knapp, C. "Some Remarks on the Character of Aeneas," CJ 26 (November, 1930), 99-111.
Knight, W. F. J. Vergil: Epic and Anthropology; Comprising Vergil's Troy, Cumaean Gates and the Holy City of the East. London: Allen and Unwin, 1967.
Lloyd, R. B. "The Character of Anchises in the Aeneid," TAPA 88 (1957), 44-55.
McDevitt, A. S. " 'Hysteron Proteron' in the Aeneid," CQ (New Series) 17 (November, 1967), 316-321.
MacKail, J. W. "The Aeneid as a Work of Art," CJ 26 (October, 1930), 12-18.
MacKay, L. A. "Hero and Theme in the Aeneid," TAPA 94 (1963), 157-166.
Maguinness, J. S. M. "Heroism in Virgil," PVS 10 (1970-1971), 45-56.

Mench, F. "Film Sense in the Aeneid," Arion 8 (Autumn, 1969), 381-397.
Miles, G. "Glorious Peace: The Values and Motivation of Virgil's Aeneas," CSCA 9 (1976), 133-164.
Mohler, S. L. "Sails and Oars in the Aeneid," TAPA 79 (1948), 46-62.
Morris, B. "Virgil and the Heroic Ideal," PVS 9 (1969-1970), 20-34.
Nethercut, W. R. "The Imagery of the Aeneid," CJ 67 (December, 1971-1972), 123-143.
_____. "Invasion in the Aeneid," G & R 15 (April, 1968), 82-95.
_____. "Three Mysteries in the Aeneid," Vergilius 19 (1973), 28-32.
Parry, A. "The Two Voices of Virgil's Aeneid," Arion 2 (Winter, 1963), 66-80.
Pierce, F. "Some Themes and Their Sources in the Heroic Poem of the Golden Age," HR 14 (April, 1946), 95-103.
Poe, J. P. "Success and Failure in the Mission of Aeneas," TAPA 96 (1965), 321-336.
Poeschl, V. Art of Vergil: Image and Symbol in the Aeneid, tr. by Gerda Seligson. Ann Arbor: University of Michigan Press, 1962.
Porter, W. M. "Look at Vergil's Negative Image," Arion (New Series) 3 (1976), 493-506.
Putnam, M. C. J. Poetry of the Aeneid: Four Studies in Imaginative Unity and Design. Cambridge, Mass.: Harvard University Press, 1965.
Quinn, K. "Did Virgil Fail?," in J. R. C. Martyn, ed., Cicero and Virgil; Studies in Honour of Harold Hunt. Amsterdam: Hakkert, 1972, pp. 192-206.
_____. "Some Dying Words: Tragic Insight in the Aeneid and the Question of Virgil's Competence," AUMLA 22 (November, 1964), 178-190.
_____. Virgil's Aeneid: A Critical Description. Ann Arbor: University of Michigan Press, 1968.
Reinhold, M. Barron's Simplified Approach to Vergil: Aeneid, Eclogues, Georgics. Woodbury, N. Y.: Barron, 1966.
Sanderlin, G. "Two Tranfigurations: Gawain and Aeneas," Chaucer R 12 (Spring, 1978), 255-258.
Schlunk, R. R. The Homeric Scholia and the Aeneid: A Study of the Influence of Ancient Homeric Literary Criticism on Virgil. Ann Arbor: University of Michigan Press, 1974.
Segal, C. "Circean Temptations: Homer, Vergil, Ovid," TAPA 99 (1968), 419-442.
_____. "'Like Winds and Winged Dream', A Note on Virgil's Development," CJ 69 (January, 1973), 97-101.
Semple, W. H. "War and Peace in Virgil's Aeneid," JRLS 36 (1953/1954), 211-227.
Simpson, V. "The Annalistic Tradition in Vergil's Aeneid," Vergilius 21 (1975), 22-32.
Smiley, P. O. "In the Steps of Aeneas," G & R 17 (October, 1948), 97-103.
Stachniw, J. "Labor as a Key to the Aeneid," CB 50 (February, 1974), 49-53.

Stewart, D. J. "Morality, Mortality and the Public Life: Aeneas the Politician," AR 32 (1973), 649-664.
Sullivan, F. A. "Mezentius: A Virgilian Creation," CP 64 (October, 1969), 219-225.
──────. "Some Vergilian Seascapes," CJ 57 (April, 1962), 302-309.
──────. "Spiritual Itinerary of Virgil's Aeneas," AJP 80 (April, 1959), 150-161.
──────. "Tendere Manus: Gestures in the Aeneid," CJ 63 (May, 1968), 358-362.
Tanner, R. G. "Some Problems in Aeneid 7-12," IVS 10 (1970-1971), 37-44.
Thompson, D. "Allegory and Typology in the Aeneid," Areth 3 (Fall, 1970), 147-153.
Thorton, A. The Living Universe: Gods and Men in Virgil's Aeneid. Leiden: E. J. Brill, 1977.
Tilly, B. "Virgil's Periplus of Latium," G & R 6 (October, 1959), 194-203.
Tracy, H. L. "Auguria Divom in Vergil's Work," Vergilius 17 (1971), 4-6.
──────. "Fata Deum and the Action of the Aeneid," G & R 11 (October, 1964), 188-195.
──────. "The Gradual Unfolding of Aeneas' Destiny," CJ 48 (May, 1953), 281-284.
Tracy, S. V. "The Marcellus Passage (Aeneid 6.860-886) and Aeneid 9-12," CJ 70 (April, 1975), 37-42.
Van Doren, M. "The Aeneid," in his Noble Voices; A Study of Ten Great Poems. New York: Holt, 1946, pp. 86-121.
Watts, N. "Aeneid and Human Life," in his Vision Splendid. New York: Sheed and Ward, 1946, pp. 128-142.
Weiss, A. H. "The Poem of the Cid and the Aeneid; Two National Epics," CJ 69 (April-May, 1974), 340-347.
West, D. "Cernere Erat: The Shield of Aeneas," PVS 15 (1975-1976), 1-6.
──────. "Multiple-correspondence Similes in the Aeneid," JRS 59 (1969), 40-49.
Weston, A. H. "Three Dreams of Aeneas," CJ 32 (January, 1937), 229-232.
Wilson, J. R. "Action and Emotion in Aeneas," G & R 16 (April, 1969), 67-75.
Woodworth, D. C. "The Function of the Gods in Vergil's Aeneid," CJ 26 (November, 1930), 112-126.

Book 1

Alexander, W. H. "Aeneid, I, 462: A New Approach," AJP 75 (October, 1954), 395-400.
Bews, J. P. "Aeneid I and 618?" Phoenix 24 (Summer, 1970), 130-143.
Clarke, M. L. "Aeneid I 286-296," CR (New Series) 24 (March, 1974), 7-8.

Couch, H. N. "Nausicaa and Dido," CJ 37 (May, 1942), 453-462.
De Grummond, W. W. "Aeneas Despairing," Hermes 105 (1977), 224-234.
Foster, J. "Some Devices of Drama Used in Aeneid 1-4," PVS 13 (1973-1974), 28-41.
Harrison, E. L. "Why Did Venus Wear Boots? Some Reflections on Aeneid I, 314f," PVS 12 (1972-1973), 10-25.
Horsfall, N. "Dido in the Light of History," PVS 13 (1973-1974), 1-13.
_____. "Virgil's Roman Chronography: A Reconsideration," CQ (New Series) 24 (May, 1974), 111-115.
Mullens, H. G. "Tragic Optimism in the Aeneid," G & R 11 (May, 1942), 137-139.
Nethercut, W. R. "Foreshadowing in Aeneid I. 751-752?" Vergilius 22 (1976), 30-33.
Rutledge, H. C. "The Opening of Aeneid 6," CJ 67 (December-January, 1971-1972), 110-115.
Segal, C. "The Song of Iopas in the Aeneid," Hermes 99 (1971), 336-349.
Semple, W. H. "Aeneas at Carthage: A Short Study of Aeneid I and IV," JRLB 34 (1951), 119-136.
Stanley, K. "Irony and Foreshadowing in Aeneid, I, 462," AJP 86 (July, 1965), 267-277.
Williams, R. D. "The Pictures on Dido's Temple," CQ (New Series) 10 (1960), 145-151.

Book 2

Anderson, J. K. "The Trojan Horse Again," CJ 66 (October-November, 1970), 22-25.
Austin, R. G. "Virgil, Aeneid 2. 567-588," CQ (New Series) 11 (1961), 185-198.
_____. "Virgil and the Wooden Horse," JRS 49 (1959), 16-25.
Bullock-Davies, C. "The Image of the Limen in Aeneid II," G & R 17 (October, 1970), 135-141.
Fenik, B. "Parallelism of Theme and Imagery in Aeneid II and IV," AJP 80 (January, 1959), 1-24.
Foster, J. "Some Devices of Drama Used in Aeneid 1-4," PVS 13 (1973-1974), 28-41.
Harrison, E. L. "Divine Action in Aeneid Book Two," Phoenix 24 (Winter, 1970), 320-332.
Jones, J. W. "Trojan Legend: Who Is Sinon?" CJ 61 (December, 1965), 122-128.
Keeson, B. "Petrie's Extracts from Vergil, Aeneid II," Akroterion 20 (April, 1975), 54-63.
Knight, W. F. J. Vergil, Epic and Anthropology, Comprising Vergil's Troy, Cumaean Gates and the Holy City of the East, ed. by J. D. Christie. New York: Barnes and Noble, 1967.
_____. Vergil's Troy; Essays on the Second Book of the Aeneid. Oxford: Blackwell, 1932.
_____. "The Wooden Horse at the Gate of Troy," CJ 28 (January, 1933), 254-262.

Knox, B. M. W. "Serpent and the Flame; the Imagery of the Second Book of the Aeneid," AJP 71 (October, 1950), 379-400.
Lewis, B. "The Rape of Troy; Infantile Perspective in Book II of the Aeneid," Areth 7 (Spring, 1974), 103-113.
McLeod, W. "The Wooden Horse and Charon's Bark; Inconsistency in Vergil's Vivid Particularization," Phoenix 24 (Summer, 1970), 144-149.
Nethercut, W. R. "Snakes in the Aeneid: Two Comments," Vergilius 20 (1974), 20-23.
Schleiner, W. "Aeneas' Flight from Troy," CL 27 (Spring, 1975), 97-112.
Shea, J. "Lucretius, Lightning, and Lipari," CP 72 (1977), 136-138.

Book 3

Duckworth, G. E. "Suspense in Ancient Epic--An Explanation of Aeneid III," TAPA 62 (1931), 124-140.
Dunkle, J. R. "Some Historical Symbolism in Book Three of the Aeneid," C World 62 (January, 1969), 165-166.
Egan, R. B. Aeneas at Aineia and Vergil's Aeneid. PCP 9 (April, 1974), 37-47.
Foster, J. "Some Devices of Drama Used in Aeneid 1-4," PVS 13 (1973-1974), 28-41.
Glenn, J. "The Blinded Cyclops: Lumen Ademptum (Aen. 3 658)," CP 69 (January, 1974), 37-38.
Grimm, R. E. "Aeneas and Andromache in Aeneid III," AJP 88 (April, 1967), 151-162.
Harrison, E. L. "Virgil's Location of Corythus," CQ (New Series) 26 (1976), 293-295.
Horsfall, N. "Corythus: The Return of Aeneas in Virgil and His Sources," JRS 63 (1973), 68-79.
──────. "Mr. Harrison and Corythus: A Reply," CQ (New Series) 26 (1976), 296-297.
Lloyd, R. B. "Aeneid III: A New Approach," AJP 78 (April, 1957), 133-151.
──────. "Aeneid III and the Aeneas Legend," AJP 78 (October, 1957), 382-400.
──────. "On Aeneid, III, 270-280," AJP 75 (July, 1954), 288-299.
Sanderlin, G. "Aeneas as Apprentice: Point of View in the Third Aeneid," CJ 71 (January, 1975), 53-56.
Saylor, C. F. "Toy Troy: The New Perspective of the Backward Glance," Vergilius 16 (1970), 26-28.
Semple, W. H. "A Short Study of Aeneid, Book III," JRLB 38 (1955), 225-240.
Shillington, D. "The Wanderings of Aeneas," Akroterion 20 (April, 1975), 35-41.

Book 4

Austin, R. G. The Fourth Book of the Aeneid. Oxford: Blackwell, 1951.

Barrett, A. A. "Anno's Conduct in Aeneid 4," Vergilius 16 (1970), 21-25.
Bryce, T. R. "The Dido-Aeneas Relationship: A Re-examination," CW 67 (March, 1974), 257-269.
Couch, H. N. "Nausicaa and Dido," CJ 37 (May, 1942), 453-462.
Estevez, V. A. "Queen and City: Three Similes in Aeneid IV," Vergilius 20 (1974), 25-28.
Fantham, E. "Virgil's Dido and Seneca's Tragic Heroines," G & R 22 (April, 1975), 1-10.
Fenik, B. "Parallelism of Theme and Imagery in Aeneid II and IV," AJP 80 (January, 1959), 1-24.
Ferguson, J. "Fire and Wound: The Imagery of Aeneid IV. 1ff," PVS 10 (1970-1971), 57-63.
Foster, J. "Some Devices of Drama Used in Aeneid 1-4," PVS 13 (1973-1974), 28-41.
Gellie, G. H. "Juno and Venus in Aeneid IV," in J. R. C. Martyn, ed., Cicero and Virgil; Studies in Honour of Harold Hunt. Amsterdam: Hakkert, 1972, pp. 138-148.
Hudson-Williams, A. "Lacrimae Illae Inanes," G & R 25 (April, 1978), 16-23.
Khan, H. A. "Dido and the Sword of Aeneas," CP 63 (October, 1968), 283-285.
Newton, F. L. "Recurrent Imagery in Aeneid IV," TAPA 88 (1957), 31-43.
Pearce, T. E. V. "Virgil, Aeneid iv. 440," CR (New Series) 18 (March, 1968), 13-14.
Pearson, J. "Virgil's Divine Vision (Aeneid 4. 238-44 and 6. 724-51)," CP 56 (January, 1961), 33-38.
Phillips, J. E. "Juno in Aeneid 4:693-705," Vergilius 23 (1977), 30-33.
Quinn, K. "The Fourth Book of the Aeneid: A Critical Description," G & R 12 (April, 1965), 16-26.
Raven, D. S. "A Note on Vergil, Aen. IV 9-14," AClass 18 (1975), 147-148.
Sanderlin, G. "Point of View in Virgil's Fourth Aeneid," C World 63 (November, 1969), 81-85.
Semple, W. H. "Aeneas at Carthage: A Short Study of Aeneid I and IV," JRLB 34 (1951), 119-136.
Singer, I. "Erotic Transformations in the Legend of Dido and Aeneas," MLN 90 (December, 1975), 767-783.
Strain, M. "Aeneid 4. 188-194," PVS 14 (1974-1975), 18-21.
Tracy, H. L. "Aeneid IV: Tragedy or Melodrama," CJ 41 (February, 1946), 199-202.

Book 5

Bertram, S. "The Generation Gap and Aeneid 5," Vergilius 17 (1971), 9-12.
Galinsky, G. K. "Aeneid V and the Aeneid," AJP 89 (April, 1968), 157-185.
Pavlovskis, Z. "Aeneid V: The Old and the Young," CJ 71 (February-March, 1976), 193-205.

Putnam, M. C. J. "Unity and Design in Aeneid V," HSCP 66 (1962), 204-239.

Book 6

Bahr-Volk, M. T. "Reality and Non-Reality in Book Six of the Aeneid," PVS 19 (1974-1975), 16-18.
Banham, R. "Up in Sybil's Place," New Soc 4 (September, 1975), 529-530.
Basson, W. P. "Virgil, Roman History, and the Roman's Destiny; Notes on Aen VI, 836-53," Akroterion 20 (April, 1975), 83-92.
Brooks, R. A. "Discolor Aura; Reflections on the Golden Bough," AJP 74 (July, 1953), 260-280.
Harrison, E. L. "Cleverness in Virgilian Imitation," CP 65 (October, 1970), 241-243.
Highbarger, E. L. Gates of Dreams; An Archaelogical Examination of Vergil, Aeneid VI, 893-899. Baltimore: Johns Hopkins Press, 1940.
Knight, W. F. J. "A Prehistoric Ritual Pattern in Aeneid VI," TAPA 66 (1935), 256-273.
_____. Vergil, Epic and Anthropology; Comprising Vergil's Troy, Cumaean Gates and the Holy City of the East, ed. by J. D. Christie. New York: Barnes and Noble, 1967.
Luck, G. "Virgil and the Mystery Religions," AJP 94 (Summer, 1973), 147-166.
MacKay, L. A. "Three Levels of Meaning in Aeneid VI," TAPA 86 (1955), 180-189.
McLeod, W. "The Wooden Horse and Charon's Bark; Inconsistency in Vergil's Vivid Particularization," Phoenix 24 (Summer, 1970), 144-149.
Michels, A. K. "Golden Bough of Plato," AJP 66 (January, 1945), 59-63.
Molyneux, J. H. "Virgil, Aeneid VI, 160-2," CR (New Series) 12 (June, 1962), 120-121.
Murgatroyd, P. "Four Similes from Journey to Hesperia," Akroterion 20 (April, 1976), 72-82.
Norwood, F. "The Tripartite Eschatology of Aeneid 6," CP 49 (January, 1954), 15-26.
Otis, B. "Three Problems of Aeneid 6," TAPA 90 (1959), 165-179.
Paget, R. F. In the Footsteps of Orpheus: The Story of Finding and Identification of the Lost Entrance to Hades, the Oracle of the Dead, the River Styx and the Infernal Regions of the Greeks. London: Hale, 1967.
Pearson, J. "Virgil's Divine Vision (Aeneid 4.238-44 and 6.724-51)," CP 56 (January, 1961), 33-38.
Reed, N. "The Gates of Sleep in Aeneid 6," CQ (New Series) 23 (November, 1973), 311-315.
Rowell, H. T. "Vergil and the Forum of Augustus," AJP 62 (July, 1941), 261-276.
Rutledge, H. C. "The Opening of Aeneid 6," CJ 67 (December-January, 1971-1972), 110-115.

Schoder, R. V. "Vergil's Poetic Use of the Cumae Area," CJ 67 (December-January, 1971-1972), 97-109.
Segal, C. P. "Aeternum Per Saecula Nomen, the Golden Bough and the Tragedy of History," Arion 4 (Winter, 1965), 617-657; 5 (Spring, 1966), 34-72.
Thaniel, G. "Vergil's Leaf and Bird Similes of Ghosts," Phoenix 25 (Autumn, 1971), 237-245.
Tracy, S. V. "Catullan Echoes in Aeneid 6.333-336," AJP 98 (Spring, 1977), 20-23.
Williams, R. D. "The Pageant of Roman Heroes-Aeneid 6.756-853," in J. R. C. Martyn, ed., Cicero and Virgil; Studies in Honour of Harold Hunt. Amsterdam: Hakkert, 1972, pp. 207-217.
──────. "The Sixth Book of the Aeneid," G & R 11 (March, 1964), 48-63.
──────. "Virgil's Underworld: The Opening Scenes," PVS 10 (1970-1971), 1-7.
Zarker, J. W. "Aeneas and Theseus in Aeneid 6," CJ 62 (February, 1967), 220-226.

Book 7

Boas, H. Aeneas' Arrival in Latium; Observations on Legends, History, Religion, Topography and Related Subjects in Vergil, Aeneid VII, 1-135. Amsterdam: North-Holland, 1938.
Highet, G. "A Lacuna in the Aeneid," CP 71 (October, 1976), 337-338.
Horsfall, N. "Corythus: The Return of Aeneas in Virgil and His Sources," JRS 63 (1973), 68-79.
MacKay, T. S. "Three Poets Observe Picus," AJP 96 (Fall, 1975), 272-275.
Putnam, M. C. J. "Aeneid VII and the Aeneid," AJP 91 (October, 1970), 408-430.
Reckford, K. J. "Latent Tragedy in Aeneid VII, 1-285," AJP 82 (July, 1961), 252-269.
Saylor, C. F. "The Magnificent Fifteen: Vergil's Catalogues of the Latin and Etruscan Forces," CP 69 (October, 1974), 249-257.
Small, S. G. P. "The Arms of Turnus: Aeneid 7.783-92," TAPA 90 (1959), 243-252.
Tilly, B. "Some Excursions into Vergil's Sabine Country," Vergilius 19 (1973), 2-19.
Williams, R. D. "The Function and Structure of Virgil's Catalogue in Aeneid 7," CQ (New Series) 11 (1961), 146-153.

Book 8

Bacon, J. R. "Aeneas in Wonderland; A Study of Aeneid VIII," CR 53 (July, 1939), 97-104.
Galinsky, G. K. "Hercules-Cacus Episode in Aeneid VIII," AJP 87 (January, 1966), 18-51.
George, E. V. Aeneid VIII and the Aitia of Callimachus. Leiden: Brill, 1974.

Highet, G. "A Dissertation on Roast Pig," C World 67 (October, 1973), 14-15.

Manton, G. R. "Virgil and the Greek Epic: The Tragedy of Evander," AUMLA 17 (May, 1962), 5-17.

Nethercut, W. R. "Snakes in the Aeneid: Two Comments," Vergilius 20 (1974), 20-23.

Rutledge, H. C. "The Opening of Aeneid 6," CJ 67 (December-January, 1971-1972), 110-115.

Shea, J. "Lucretius, Lightning, and Lipari," CP 72 (1977), 136-138.

Book 9

Fitzgerald, G. J. "Nisus and Euryalus: A Paradigm of Futile Behaviour and the Tragedy of Youth," in J. R. C. Martyn, ed., Cicero and Virgil; Studies in Honour of Harold Hunt. Amsterdam: Hakkert, 1972, pp. 114-137.

Horsfall, N. "Corythus: The Return of Aeneas in Virgil and His Sources," JRS 63 (1973), 68-79.

O'Sullivan, J. N. "Unnoticed Reminiscence of Homer in Virgil," AJP 98 (Spring, 1977), 1-2.

Williams, R. D. "Virgil Aeneid 9.25-32," CP 63 (April, 1968), 148.

Book 10

Benario, H. W. "The Tenth Book of the Aeneid," TAPA 98 (1967), 23-36.

Crane, T. "A Note on Aeneas' Human Sacrifice: Aeneid X, 517-520," C World 67 (December, 1973), 176-177.

Glenn, J. M. "Mezentius and Polyphemus," AJP 92 (April, 1971), 129-155.

_____. "Mezentius, Contempter Divum," Vergilius 17 (1971), 7-8.

Jones, J. W. "Mezentius the Isolated Hero," Vergilius 23 (1977), 50-54.

Leach, E. W. "The Blindness of Mezentius (Aeneid 10.762-768)," Areth 4 (Spring, 1971), 83-89.

Lennox, P. G. "Virgil's Night-Episode Re-Examined (Aeneid IX, 176-449)," Hermes 105 (1977), 331-342.

Nethercut, W. R. "The Characterization of Mezentius: Aeneid 10.843-845," CB 51 (January, 1975), 33-37.

O'Sullivan, J. N. "An Unnoticed Reminiscence of Homer in Vergil," AJP 98 (1977), 1-2.

Book 11

Burke, P. F. "Mezentius and the First Fruits," Vergilius 20 (1974), 28-29.

Kepple, L. R. "Arruns and the Death of Aeneas," AJP 97 (Winter, 1976), 344-360.

Rosenmeyer, T. G. "Virgil and Heroism: Aeneid XI," CJ 55 (January, 1960), 159-164.
Semple, W. H. "The Conclusion of Vergil's Aeneid: A Study of the War in Latium, with Special Reference to Books XI and XII," JRLB 42 (1959), 175-193.
Williams, R. D. "Virgil Aeneid 11.400-409," CP 61 (July, 1966), 184-186.

Book 12

Fontenrose, J. "Gods Invoked in Epic Oaths: Aeneid, XII, 175-215," AJP 89 (January, 1968), 20-38.
Kepple, L. R. "Arruns and the Death of Aeneas," AJP 97 (Winter, 1976), 344-360.
Semple, W. H. "The Conclusion of Vergil's Aeneid: A Study of the War in Latium, with Special Reference to Books XI and XII," JRLB 42 (1959), 175-193.
Thaniel, G. "Turnus' Fatal Stone," CN & V 15 (January, 1971), 20-22.
Thornton, A. H. F. "The Last Scene of the Aeneid," G & R 22 (June, 1953), 82-84.
West, D. "The Deaths of Hector and Turnus," G & R 21 (April, 1974), 21-31.
Williams, R. D., and C. J. Carter. "Critical Appreciations, II: Virgil, Aeneid XII. 843-86," G & R 21 (October, 1974), 165-177.
Zeitlin, F. I. "Analysis of Aeneid, XII, 176-211; the Differences Between Oaths of Aeneas and Latinus," AJP 86 (October, 1965), 337-362.

Other Individual Works

Catalepton, or Trifles

Clarke, M. L. "Three Notes on Virgil," PVS 12 (1972-1973), 48-50.
Courtney, E. "Catalepton 3.9-10," CR (New Series) 19 (March, 1969), 15.
Frank, T. "Subject of Catalepton VI and XII," AJP 59 (April, 1938), 227-228.
Khan, H. A. "Humor of Catullus, Carm. 4, and the Theme of Virgil, Catalepton 10," AJP 88 (April, 1967), 163-172.

Eclogues

Berg, W. "Daphnis and Prometheus," TAPA 96 (1965), 11-24.
―――. Early Virgil. London: Athlone, 1974.
Berkowitz, L. "Pollio and the Date of the Fourth Eclogue," CSCA 5 (1972), 21-38.
Bowersock, G. W. "A Date in the Eighth Eclogue," HSCP 75 (1971), 73-80.

Boyle, A. J. "A Reading of Virgil's Eclogues," Ramus 4 (1975), 187-203.
Clarke, M. L. "Three Notes on Virgil," PVS 12 (1972-1973), 48-50.
Clausen, W. "Cynthius," AJP 97 (Fall, 1976), 245-247.
Coleman, R. "Vergil's Pastoral Modes," Ramus 4 (1975), 140-162.
Copley, F. O. "Vergil, Eclogues and Georgics," in his Latin Literature from the Beginnings to the Close of the Second Century A.D. Ann Arbor: University of Michigan Press, 1969, pp. 172-187.
Currie, H. M. "Third Eclogue and the Roman Comic Spirit," Mnemosyne 29 (1976), 411-420.
Dick, B. F. "Ancient Pastoral and the Patnetic Fallacy," CL 20 (Winter, 1968), 27-44.
_____. "Vergil's Pastoral Poetic: A Reading of the First Eclogue," AJP 91 (July, 1970), 277-293.
Dyer, R. R. "Vergil Eclogue 10.73-74 and the Suckering Habit of the White Alder," CP 64 (October, 1969), 233-234.
Fantazzi, C. "Virgilian Pastoral and Roman Love Poetry," AJP 87 (April, 1966), 171-191.
Flintoff, T. E. S. "Characterization of Virgil's Eclogues," PVS 15 (1975-1976), 16-26.
Garson, R. W. "Theocritean Elements in Virgil's Eclogues," CQ (New Series) 21 (May, 1971), 188-203.
Grant, M. "Pastoral Poetry: The Eclogues," in his Roman Literature. Baltimore: Penguin, 1964, pp. 163-170.
Hahn, E. A. "Body and Soul in Vergil," TAPA 92 (1961), 193-219.
_____. "The Character of the Eclogues," TAPA 75 (1944), 196-241.
Highbarger, E. L. "Notes on Vergil's Bucolics," CP 40 (January, 1945), 43-45.
Highet, G. "Performances of Vergil's Bucolics," Vergilius 20 (1974), 24-25.
Hubbard, M. "The Capture of Silenus," PCPS (New Series) 21 (1975), 53-62.
Kelly, S. T. "The Gallus Quotation in Vergil's Tenth Eclogue," Vergilius 23 (1977), 17-20.
Kollmann, E. D. "A Study of Proper Names in Virgil's Eclogues," CQ 69 (September, 1975), 97-112.
Leach, E. W. "Eclogue IV: Symbolism and Sources," Areth 4 (Fall, 1971), 167-184.
_____. "Nature and Art in Vergil's Second Eclogue," AJP 87 (October, 1966), 427-445.
_____. Vergil's Eclogues: Landscapes of Experience. Ithaca, N.Y.: Cornell University Press, 1974.
Lewis, B. "Time and Tense: The Central Problem in Virgil's First Eclogue," CB 50 (February, 1974), 59-63.
MacKay, K. J. "Frustration of Anticipation in Vergil Ecl. VI?" Antichthon 6 (1972), 53-59.
MacKay, L. A. "Meliboeus Exul," Vergilius 18 (1971), 2-3.
Mountford, J. F., and A. Y. Campbell. "Virgil, Eclogue IV, 23," CR 52 (May, 1938), 54-56.

Virgil : 275

Muecke, F. "Virgil and the Genre of Pastoral," AUMLA 44 (November, 1975), 169-180.
Nethercut, W. R. "Menalca's Answer: The Hyacinth in Bucolic 3. 106-107," CJ 65 (March, 1970), 248-254.
―――――. "Vergil and Horace in Bucolic 7," C World 62 (November, 1968), 93-98.
Pavlovskis, Z. "Man in a Poetic Landscape: Humanization of Nature in Virgil's Eclogues," CP 66 (July, 1971), 151-168.
Powell, B. I. "Thrust and Counter-Thrust in Eclogue 3," ICS 1 (1976), 113-121.
Putnam, M. C. J. "Virgil's First Eclogue: Poetics of Enclosure," Ramus 4 (1975), 163-186.
―――――. Virgil's Pastoral Art. Princeton, N. J.: Princeton University Press, 1970.
Reinhold, M. Barron's Simplified Approach to Vergil: Aeneid, Eclogues, Georgics. Woodbury, N. Y.: Barron, 1966.
Richmond, J. A. "Symbolism in Vergil: Skeleton Key or Will-o'-the-Wisp?" G & R 23 (October, 1976), 142-158.
Robertson, F. "Virgil and Theocritus," PVS 10 (1970-1971), 8-23.
Rose, H. J. Eclogues of Vergil. Berkeley: University of California Press, 1942.
Savage, J. J. H. "The Art of the Second Eclogue of Vergil," TAPA 91 (1960), 353-375.
―――――. "The Art of the Third Eclogue of Vergil (55-111)," TAPA 89 (1958), 142-158.
―――――. "The Art of the Seventh Eclogue of Vergil," TAPA 94 (1963), 248-267.
Segal, C. "Tamen Cantabitis, Arcades--Exile and Arcadia in Eclogues One and Nine," Arion 4 (Summer, 1965), 237-266.
―――――. "Two Fauns and a Naiad?" AJP 92 (January, 1971), 56-61.
―――――. "Vergil's Caelatum Opus: An Interpretation of the Third Eclogue," AJP 88 (July, 1967), 279-308.
―――――. "Vergil's Sixth Eclogue and the Problem of Evil," TAPA 100 (1969), 407-435.
Skutsch, O. "The Original Form of the Second Eclogue," HSCP 74 (1970), 95-99.
Smith, P. L. "Vergil's Avenda and the Pipes of Pastoral Poetry," TAPA 101 (1970), 497-510.
Stewart, Z. "The Song of Silenus," HSCP 64 (1959), 179-205.
Van Sickle, K. B. "The Unity of the Eclogues: Arcadian Forest, Theocritean Trees," TAPA 98 (1967), 491-508.
Williams, R. D. "Virgil Eclogues 4. 60-63," CP 71 (January, 1976), 119-121.
Winterbottom, M. "Virgil and the Confiscations," G & R 23 (April, 1976), 55-59.
Wormell, D. E. W. "The Riddles in Virgil's Third Eclogue," CQ (New Series) 10 (1960), 29-36.

Georgics

Abbe, E. M. Plants of Virgil's Georgics; Commentary and Woodcuts.

Ithaca, N. Y.: Cornell University Press, 1965.
Addison, J. "An Essay on Virgil's Georgics," in S. Elledge, ed., Eighteenth Century Critical Essays. Ithaca, N. Y.: Cornell University Press, 1961, Vol. 1, pp. 1-8.
Bovie, S. P. Dominant Themes in Virgil's Georgics. Ann Arbor, Mich.: University Microfilms, 1955.
──────. "Imagery of Ascent-descent in Vergil's Georgics," AJP 77 (October, 1956), 337-358.
Bowra, C. M. "Orpheus and Euydice," CQ (New Series) 2 (1952), 113-126.
Bradley, A. "Augustan Culture and a Radical Alternative: Vergil's Georgics," Arion 8 (Autumn, 1969), 347-358.
Chalker, J. The English Georgic; A Study in the Development of a Form. Baltimore: Johns Hopkins Press, 1969.
Clausen, W. "Cynthius," AJP 97 (Fall, 1976), 245-247.
Coleman, R. "Gallus, the Bucolics, and the Ending of the Fourth Georgic," AJP 83 (January, 1962), 55-71.
Copley, F. O. "Vergil, Eclogues and Georgics," in his Latin Literature from the Beginnings to the Close of the Second Century A. D. Ann Arbor: University of Michigan Press, 1969, pp. 172-187.
Crabbe, A. M. "Ignoscenda Quidem: Catullus 64 and the Fourth Georgic," CQ (New Series) 27 (1977), 342-351.
Doig, G. "Vergil, Georgics, I, 491-2," AJP 86 (January, 1965), 85-88.
Duckworth, G. E. "Vergil's Georgics and the Laudes Galli," AJP 80 (July, 1959), 225-237.
German, A. "On Georgics I," CJ 65 (March, 1970), 263-266.
Getty, R. J. "Some Astronomical Cruces in the Georgics," TAPA 79 (1948), 24-45.
Grant, M. "The Land of Italy: The Georgics," in his Roman Literature. Baltimore: Penguin, 1964, pp. 170-177.
Hahn, E. A. "Body and Soul in Vergil," TAPA 92 (1961), 193-219.
Jermyn, L. A. S. "Virgil's Agricultural Lore," G & R 18 (June, 1949), 49-68.
Kenny, M. "Those Surprising Georgics," CJ 28 (January, 1933), 243-253.
Kingsbury, A. "The Hero Is a Bee," CJ 51 (May, 1956), 396-401.
Liebeschuetz, W. "Beast and Man in the Third Book of Virgil's Georgics," G & R 12 (April, 1965), 64-77.
Lilly, M. L. The Georgic; A Contribution to the Study of Vergilian Type of Didactic Poetry. Baltimore: Johns Hopkins Press, 1919.
McDonald, M. "Acies: Virgil Georgics I, 395," CP 68 (July, 1973), 203-205.
McKay, A. G. "Vergil's Glorification of Italy," in J. R. C. Martyn, ed., Cicero and Virgil; Studies in Honour of Harold Hunt. Amsterdam: Hakkert, 1972, pp. 149-168.
Martyn, J. R. C., ed. "Virgilius Satiricus," in his Cicero and Virgil; Studies in Honour of Harold Hunt. Amsterdam: Hakkert, 1972, pp. 169-191.
Mattingly, H. "Notes on Virgil: Caesar in the First Georgic, Diana-Bellona," CR 56 (March, 1942), 18-20.
Miles, G. B. "Georgics 3.209-294, Amor and Civilization," CSCA 8 (1975), 177-197.

Otis, B. "Virgilian Narrative in the Light of its Precursors and Successors," SP 73 (January, 1976), 1-28.
Putnam, M. C. J. Virgil's Poem of the Earth: Studies in the Georgics. Princeton, N. J.: Princeton University Press, 1979.
Reinhold, M. Barron's Simplified Approach to Vergil: Aeneid, Eclogues, Georgics. Woodbury, N. Y.: Barron, 1966.
Royds, T. F. The Beasts, Birds, and Bees of Virgil; A Naturalist's Handbook to the Georgics. Oxford: Blackwell, 1914.
Schechter, S. "The Aition and Virgil's Georgics," TAPA 105 (1975), 347-391.
Segal, C. " 'Like Winds and Winged Dream'; A Note on Virgil's Development," CJ 69 (January, 1973), 97-101.
_____. "Orpheus and the Fourth Georgic: Vergil on Nature and Civilization," AJP 87 (July, 1966), 307-325.
Stehle, E. M. "Virgil's Georgics: The Threat of Sloth," TAPA 104 (1974), 347-369.
Sullican, F. A. "Some Vergilian Seascapes," CJ 57 (April, 1962), 302-309.
Tanner, R. G. "The Georgics and Mark Anthony," PVS 9 (1969-1970), 86-106.
Wilkinson, L. P. The Georgics of Virgil: A Critical Survey. London: Cambridge University Press, 1969.
_____. "The Intention of Virgil's Georgics," G & R 19 (January, 1950), 19-28.
_____. "Virgil's Theodicy," CQ (New Series) 13 (1963), 75-84.
Williams, R. D. "Virgil's Fourth Eclogue: A Literary Analysis," PVS 14 (1974-1975), 1-6.

XENOPHANES

General Criticism

Bowra, C. M. "Xenophanes and the Olympic Games," AJP 59 (July, 1938), 257-279.
Guthrie, W. K. C. "Xenophanes," in his A History of Greek Philosophy. London: Cambridge University Press, 1962, Vol. 1, pp. 360-402.
Heidel, W. A. "Hecataeus and Xenophanes," AJP 64 (July, 1943), 257-277.
Jaeger, W. W. "Philosophical Speculation: The Discovery of the World-order," in his Paideia: The Ideals of Greek Culture. Oxford: Blackwell, 1939, Vol. 1, pp. 148-183.
_____. "Xenophanes' Doctrine of God," in his The Theology of the Early Greek Philosophers. London: Oxford University Press, 1968.
Snell, B. "Human Knowledge and Divine Knowledge among the Greeks," in his Discovery of the Mind; the Greek Origins of European Thought. Cambridge, Mass.: Harvard University Press, 1953, pp. 136-152.

Individual Works (Fragments)

Bowra, C. M. "Xenophanes, Fragment 1," CP 33 (October, 1938), 353-367.

──────. "Xenophanes, Fragment 3," CQ 35 (July, 1941), 119-126.

XENOPHON

General Criticism

Anderson, J. K. Military Theory and Practice in the Age of Xenophon. Berkeley: University of California Press, 1970.
──────. Xenophon. New York: Scribner's, 1974.
Hamilton, E. "Xenophon, the Ordinary Athenian Gentlemen," in her Great Age of Greek Literature. New York: Norton, 1942, pp. 204-226.
Jacks, L. V. Xenophon, Soldier of Fortune. New York: Scribner's 1930.
Jaeger, W. W. "Xenophon: The Ideal Squire and Soldier," in his Paideia: The Ideals of Greek Culture. Oxford: Blackwell, 1944. Vol. 3, pp. 156-181.
Morrison, J. S. "Socrates and Antiphon," CR (New Series) 5 (March, 1955), 8-12.
Saintsbury, G. E. B. "Xenophon," in his Last Vintage; Essays and Papers. London: Methuen, 1950, pp. 66-71.
Sarton, G. "Xenophon," in his History of Science; Ancient Science Through the Golden Age of Greece. Cambridge, Mass.: Harvard University Press, 1952, Vol. 1, pp. 454-466.
Sheeks, W. "Isocrates, Plato, and Xenophon Against the Sophists," Person 56 (Summer, 1975), 250-259.
Stadter, P. A. "Xenophon in Arrian's Cynegeticus," GRBS 17 (Summer, 1976), 157-167.
Strauss, L. Xenophon's Socrates. Ithaca, N. Y.: Cornell University Press, 1972.
Usher, S. "Xenophon and His Times," HT 12 (July, 1962), 496-505.
Weathers, W. "Xenophon's Political Idealism," CJ 49 (April, 1954), 317-321, 330.
"Xenophon's Prophetic Dreams," in R. L. Woods, ed., World of Dreams; An Anthology. New York: Random House, 1947, pp. 357-359.

Individual Works

Anabasis

Barnett, R. D. "Xenophon and the Wall of Media," J Hel S 83 (1963), 1-26.

Downs, R. B. "Incredible Retreat: Xenophon," in his Famous Books, Ancient and Medieval. New York: Barnes and Noble, 1964, pp. 81-85.
MacLaren, M. "Xenophon and Themistogenes," TAPA 65 (1934), 240-247.
Nussbaum, G. B. The Ten Thousand: A Study in Social Organization and Action in Xenophon's Anabasis. Leiden: Brill, 1967.
Scott, J. A. "The Withered Palm Trees in the Anabasis," CJ 32 (December, 1936), 172-173.

Apology

Chroust, A. H. Socrates, Man and Myth; The Two Socratic Apologies of Xenophon. London: Routledge and K. Paul, 1957.
Strauss, L. Xenophon's Socrates. Ithaca, N. Y.: Cornell University Press, 1972.

Cyropaedia

McCarthy, J. M. "Xenophon's Cyropaedia, a Neglected Education Tract," Cithara 10 (1970), 70-75.

Hellenica

Dorjahn, A. P., and W. D. Fairchild. "On Xenophon, Hellenica 2.3.24-49," CB 61 (February, 1975), 60-62.
Ehrhardt, C. "Xenophon and Diodorus on Aegospotami," Phoenix 24 (Autumn, 1970), 225-228.
Henry, W. P. Greek Historical Writing. Chicago: Argonaut, 1967.
Rahn, P. J. "Xenophon's Developing Historiography," TAPA 102 (1971), 497-508.
Usher, S. "Xenophon, Critias and Theramenes," J Hel S 88 (1968), 128-135.
Westlake, H. D. "Individuals in Xenophon, Hellenica," JRLB 49 (Autumn, 1966), 246-269.
_____. "Xenophon and Epaminodas," GRBS 16 (Spring, 1975), 23-40.

Hieron

Lichtheim, G. "Tyrants Ancient and Modern," in his The Concept of Ideology, and Other Essays. New York: Random House, 1967, pp. 156-165.
Strauss, L. On Tyranny, An Interpretation of Xenophon's Hiero. New York: Free Press, 1963.

Hipparchicus

Wycherley, R. E. "Xenophon, Hipparchicus, 3.6-7: Cavalry at the

Lyceum," CR (New Series) 13 (March, 1963), 14-15.

Memorabilia

Berns, L. "Socratic and Non-Socratic Philosophy: A Note on Xenophon's Memorabilia, 1.1.13 and 14," RM 28 (September, 1974), 85-88.

Chroust, A. H. Socrates, Man and Myth; The Two Socratic Apologies of Xenophon. London: Routledge and K. Paul, 1957.

Morrison, J. S. "Xenophon, Memorabilia I.6: The Encounters of Socrates and Antiphon," CR (New Series) 3 (March, 1953), 3-6.

Oeconomicus

Strauss, L. Xenophon's Socratic Discourse: An Interpretation of the Oeconomicus. Ithaca, N.Y.: Cornell University Press, 1970.

Wellman, R. R. "Socratic Method in Xenophon," JHI 37 (April-June, 1976), 307-318.

Polity

Atkinson, K. M. T. The Respublica Lacedaemoniorum Ascribed to Xenophon; Its Manuscript Tradition and General Significance. Manchester: Manchester University Press, 1948.